GROUP COMMUNICATION IN CONTEXT

STUDIES OF BONA FIDE GROUPS

LEA'S COMMUNICATION SERIES
Jennings Bryant/Dolf Zillmann, General Editors

Selected titles in Small Group Communication
(Dennis Gouran, Advisory Editor) and related areas include:

Harris • Applied Organizational Communication: Principles and
Pragmatics for Future Practice, Second Edition

Hummert/Nussbaum • Aging, Communication, and Health: Linking
Research and Practice for Successful Aging

Ray • Communication and Disenfranchisement: Social Health Issues
and Implications

Socha/Diggs • Communication, Race, and Family: Exploring
Communication in Black, White, and Biracial Families

Whaley • Explaining Illness: Research, Theory, and Strategies

Williams/Nussbaum • Intergenerational Communication Across
the Life Span

For a complete list of titles in LEA's Communication Series,
please contact Lawrence Erlbaum Associates, Publishers at
www.erlbaum.com

GROUP COMMUNICATION IN CONTEXT

STUDIES OF BONA FIDE GROUPS

SECOND EDITION

Edited by

Lawrence R. Frey
University of Colorado at Boulder

LEA
2003

LAWRENCE ERLBAUM ASSOCIATES, PUBLISHERS
Mahwah, New Jersey   London

Lawrence Erlbaum Associates, Inc., Publishers
10 Industrial Avenue
Mahwah, NJ 07430

Cover design by Kathryn Houghtaling Lacey

Library of Congress Cataloging-in-Publication Data

Group communication in context : studies of bona fide groups /
    edited by Lawrence R. Frey.
        p. cm.
        Includes bibliographical references and index.
    ISBN 0-8058-3149-5 (cloth : alk. paper)
    ISBN 0-8058-3150-9 (pbk. : alk. paper)
    1. Communication in small groups. I. Frey, Lawrence R.
    P95.535 .G76 2002
    302.3'4—dc21   2002067197
                                                        CIP

Books published by Lawrence Erlbaum Associates are printed on acid-
free paper, and their bindings are chosen for strength and durability.

Printed in the United States of America
10 9 8 7 6 5 4 3 2 1

CONTENTS

Introduction

Epilogue

GROUP COMMUNICATION IN CONTEXT: STUDYING BONA FIDE GROUPS

Lawrence R. Frey
University of Colorado at Boulder

The study of group communication has never been healthier. Recent texts—most notably, *The Handbook of Group Communication Theory & Research* (Frey, Gouran, & Poole, 1999) and *New Directions in Group Communication* (Frey, 2002)—document, respectively, the depth and breadth of current knowledge about and the wealth of new and innovative directions for group communication theory, research methods, research topics, pedagogy, facilitation, and other applications and practices. And the creation of a Group Communication Division (requiring 300 members) in the National Communication Association demonstrates that there is a thriving research community devoted to its study.

Given its current status, it is hard to believe that only a few short years ago scholars were lamenting the state of the field (see, e.g., Frey, 1994a; Poole, 1990) and dialoguing in a special journal issue about how to "revitalize the study of group communication" (Frey, 1994e). Although there are many reasons for its revitalization, the resurgence of group communication scholarship is due, in no small measure, to researchers moving from the laboratory to the field—that is, to studying groups in context.

STUDYING GROUPS IN CONTEXT

Studying groups in their natural environment is certainly not new; in fact, some of the most influential and widely cited research has been conducted with, on, or about natural groups. Lewin and associates' classic work on the superiority of a democratic style of group leadership over authoritarian and laissez-faire styles, for instance, was based, in large measure, on a landmark study of four groups of 10-year-old boys who met in five-member clubs after school to engage in hobby activities (see White & Lippitt, 1968). Sherif and Sherif's (1953) field experiment that involved first creating hostility between two groups formed on the basis of selected activities at a boys' summer camp, and then attempting to establish harmony and integration between the groups, demonstrated how a common goal requiring collaborative effort can lead to positive intergroup relations. Janis's (1972, 1982) investigations of real-world group policy decisions and fiascoes—such as the group meetings that led to the Bay of Pigs invasion, Cuban missile crisis, and Watergate cover-up—resulted in the formulation of the popular concept of *groupthink* to describe the type of faulty decision making that can occur when groups are too cohesive. And in the communication field, studies by Gouran, Hirokawa, and Martz (1986) and Hirokawa, Gouran, and Martz (1988) of the critical factors affecting the group decision making that led to the launching of the ill-fated *Challenger* space shuttle played a significant role in the development of the functional perspective of group communication and decision making.

It was during the 1990s, however, that the study of natural groups flourished and reached a critical mass, especially in the communication discipline. The decade started with the publication of Hackman's (1990) edited text featuring 27 studies of real-world groups comprising 7 distinct types of work groups (top management teams, task forces, professional support teams, performing groups, human service teams, customer service teams, and production teams) that sought to understand why some work groups succeed whereas others fail. Miller and McKinney's (1993) edited text highlighted case studies of communication in government commissions, including the Warren Commission's investigation of the assassination of President John F. Kennedy (McKinney, 1993) and the 1970 (Soenksen, 1993) and 1985 (Gouran, 1993) U.S. government commissions on pornography. The first edition of *Group Communication in Context: Studies of Natural Groups* (Frey, 1994c), featuring 12 such studies, was quickly followed by Frey's (1995) edited volume of studies explaining how facilitation techniques had been used to address important real-life problems faced by natural groups, such as how interactive management (a method for solving complex problem situations) was employed by Comanche Native Americans to create an action plan to promote greater participation in the governance of the tribe (Broome, 1995); how the System for the Multiple Level Observation of Groups (SYMLOG; a theory and method for studying groups, developed by Bales and Cohen, 1979) was used as a self-analytical facilitation technique to ease tensions within a functional work group composed of physicians, medical residents, and nursing staff

(Keyton, 1995); and how a group decision support system (an electronic meeting system that combines communication and computer technologies with decision support technologies) aided in an ongoing quality enhancement effort at a large service organization (Poole, DeSanctis, Kirsch, & Jackson, 1995).

These and other investigations of natural groups had a significant effect on the study of group communication. Indeed, Gouran (1999), in his historical overview of group communication scholarship, was so impressed with the sheer volume of such studies that he labeled the decade of the 1990s as being concerned with "diversification, application, and a growing concern with context" (p. 18). Along with such studies came important discussions of the ways in which natural groups ought to be conceived and studied. Frey (1994b), for instance, identified some salient methodological challenges faced by researchers who study natural groups and demonstrated ways of responding to such challenges based on the experiences of those who contributed studies to the first edition of this text. Frey (1994d) also articulated how the naturalistic paradigm (as explained by Lincoln & Guba, 1985)—a central tenet of which is a commitment to studying phenomena, in this case, groups, in situ—could serve as an alternative to the positivist paradigm that had dominated the study of groups and that privileged laboratory research, and he provided an illustration from his own research on communication and community building in a residential facility for people living with AIDS (Adelman & Frey, 1994; see also Adelman & Frey, 1997). Probably the most powerful conceptual/theoretical perspective offered, however, was that of the bona fide group perspective.

THE BONA FIDE GROUP PERSPECTIVE

First articulated by L. L. Putnam and Stohl in 1990, and later expanded on by L. L. Putnam (1994), Stohl and Putnam (1994), and L. L. Putnam and Stohl (1996) (for recent reviews of this and other perspectives on group communication, see Gouran, 1999; Poole, 1999; Waldeck, Shepard, Teitelbaum, Farrar, & Seibold, 2002), the bona fide group perspective offers an alternative to a traditional "container model" of groups. In the container model, at least as operationalized in research studies, a group is considered to be a relatively closed entity with fixed boundaries and borders that define who is and is not a member, and the focus of study is on internal processes as groups attempt to solve problems, make decisions, provide members with social support, and so forth; in the few cases in which the environment or context within which a group is embedded is acknowledged, it is treated "as an external input that resides in the background" (L. L. Putnam & Stohl, 1996, p. 149). The bona fide group perspective challenges this conception of a group by proposing that *bona fide groups* demonstrate two important and interrelated characteristics: stable yet permeable group boundaries and interdependence with their relevant contexts.

The first characteristic, *stable yet permeable group boundaries*, acknowledges that the boundaries and borders of a group are simultaneously defined and firm—for there can be no group without some constructed boundaries differentiating it from other entities and recurring patterns of group interaction create and reinforce that differentiation—yet dynamic and fluid—in that boundaries are continuously negotiated, redefined, and changed through group members' interaction. The permeability of group boundaries occurs, according to L. L. Putnam and Stohl (1996), because of at least four features that characterize bona fide groups: "(a) multiple group memberships and conflicting role identities, (b) representative roles, (c) fluctuations in group membership, and (d) group identity formation" (p. 150). The first feature references the fact that people are simultaneously members of many different groups (e.g., family, friendship, and work groups) and that these multiple memberships potentially influence the roles group members enact or are expected to enact (e.g., a leader of one group may be expected by members of another group to assume a leadership role in that group) and may produce conflict between role identities (e.g., a leader of one group may not wish to be a leader of another group). The second feature implies that because people are members of multiple groups, they are boundary spanners and often serve or are expected to serve in one group as official or unofficial representatives to or for another group (e.g., the only African American jury member may be expected by the other jurors to represent an "African American point of view" in a racial hate crime case). The third feature explicitly states that the membership of bona fide groups often changes, with some members leaving and new members joining the group, and that these changes can significantly affect internal group dynamics (e.g., a new star pitcher who joins a baseball team can significantly change the team's pitching rotation and other pitchers' roles). The fourth feature acknowledges that people vary in the degree to which they demonstrate a sense of belonging, loyalty, or commitment to the various groups in which they are members and that the identity of any particular group for members and for the group as a whole is affected by these multiple group allegiances (e.g., a faculty member who belongs to two committees may be far more committed to one of them and, consequently, identify more with that committee and put more effort into it).

The recognition that group boundaries are stable yet permeable has the potential to offer valuable new insights into group processes. Consider, for instance, the case of *socialization,* the processes by which new group members are integrated into and become part of the pattern of activities of a group. Traditional research has focused on the phases—"qualitatively different subperiods within a total continuous period of interaction" (Bales & Strodtbeck, 1951, p. 485)—that characterize socialization processes, such as Van Maanen's (1976) three-phase model of organizational newcomer socialization: (a) anticipatory (the formation of a newcomer's expectations), (b) encounter (the newcomer's learning that occurs from daily experiences), and (c) metamorphosis (the newcomer's acceptance of the organization's culture). Virtually all of this work, however, has assumed that the group (or organization) to which a newcomer is being socialized is a stable, bounded entity and has focused on the internal group processes by which that newcomer is socialized. Anderson, Riddle, and Martin (1999) recently offered a different conceptualization of group socialization that rests on the premise that "socialization processes influence and affect individuals and groups not only in solo but also in multiple group experiences, because individuals hold membership in more than one group at any given time and past group experiences influence future group experiences" (p. 145). They, too, construct a phase model that describes five phases of individuals' socialization into a group (antecedent, anticipatory, encounter, assimilation, and exit phases), but they illustrate those phases visually using multiple, overlapping wheels to signify the multiple groups to which individual members simultaneously belong and to make clear that "individuals are located in time and space in different phases of socialization in the multiple phases of socialization in the multiple groups to which they belong" (p. 146). They also construct a corollary model to explicate the nature and effects of socialization at the group level and they explicitly acknowledge when explaining the model that "groups have permeable boundaries that permit outside influences to affect the socialization process" (p. 155).

The second characteristic of bona fide groups, *interdependence of a group with its relevant contexts*, references the reciprocal relationship that exists between a group and the environments within which it is embedded; those contexts influence what occurs within a group and what occurs within a group influences those contexts. Relevant contexts include, among many others, the historical context within which a group is created and develops, the geophysical context within which it is located, the economic context within which it is funded, and the cultural context that establishes appropriate norms and values for how it should operate. According to L. L. Putnam and Stohl (1996), the interdependence of a group with its relevant contexts is a result of "(a) intergroup communication, (b) coordinated actions among groups, (c) negotiation of jurisdiction or autonomy, and (d) interpretations or frames for making sense of intergroup relationships" (p. 153). The first feature acknowledges that individual members and groups as a unit frequently interact, both formally and informally, with other groups and their members (e.g., a team from the marketing division of a company obtaining information from other divisions of that company before finalizing its marketing plan). The second feature recognizes that some problems and tasks, especially complex ones, demand that groups coordinate their actions together (e.g., groups of physicians and nurses working together in an operating room). The third feature points to group interaction as a means for negotiating the boundary conditions of a group's purview (e.g., university faculty senators debating whether policies regarding university expenditures are part of the group's jurisdiction). The fourth feature speaks to the issue of how group members make sense individually and collectively of the intergroup relationships that exist (e.g., one sports team viewing another sports team sometimes as an ally, such as when it defeats a third team, and sometimes as a threat, such as when they play against each other).

As an example of how the recognition of the interdependence of a group with its relevant contexts might transform the study of groups, consider the case of the *functional perspective,* which seeks to explain "the role of communication in determining the extent to which particular task requirements are fulfilled and how their satisfaction, in turn, contributes to the appropriateness of choices groups make" (Gouran, Hirokawa, Julian, & Leatham, 1993, pp. 537–574). Researchers working from this perspective have discovered such important task functions as the establishment of operating procedures, analysis of the problem, generation of alternative solutions, establishment of evaluation criteria, and evaluation of operating procedures (for reviews of this research, see, e.g., Gouran & Hirokawa, 1996; Hirokawa & Salazar, 1999). Researchers, however, have concentrated almost exclusively on the communication processes internal to problem-solving and decision-making groups, leading Hirokawa, Erbert, and Hurst (1996) to claim that a "reason why previous research has failed to provide us with a better understanding of the relationship between group communication and group decision-making performance is because those investigations have not been particularly sensitive to contextual influences" (p. 287). Stohl and Holmes (1993), recognizing that "communication also functions to situate the group temporally and spatially and to shape the group's decision as a coherent part of that situation" (p. 610), proposed two additional classes of functions: "one set that accomplishes the embedding of a decision in ongoing group life (historical functions), and one that accomplishes the embedding of a decision in a permeable context (institutional functions)" (p. 610). Among other things, historical functions demand the sequencing of "group action in relation to actions of other interdependent actors or groups"; institutional functions demand "the group's need to identify the actors in the larger system who are stakeholders in the current decision" (p. 611). Both functions emerge from the realization that group activities cannot be divorced from the relevant contexts within which a group is embedded.

The bona fide group perspective, thus, stands in stark contrast to a traditional container model of groups. It does not privilege external environments over internal group processes; rather, it argues that external environments and internal group processes are intrinsically and intricately related and, thereby, "presents an orientation that necessitates moving back and forth continually between them. Neither arena can be understood fully without incorporating the dynamics of the other. Both arenas work in tandem, reflecting and reverberating one within the other" (Stohl & Putnam, 1994, p. 287). The explicit linking of the internal and external avoids the "social psychological error" (Farris, 1981) that has plagued most previous studies of groups: the tendency to explain groups from observations independent of their contexts. As Poole (1999) explained, researchers have paid

> so much attention to what happens within a group that they neglect the real and very interesting problems posed by a group's interaction with its environment[s] and the contextual constraints that impinge on and affect groups. The Bona Fide Group Perspective places this environmental interaction firmly in the foreground. (p. 59)

The bona fide group perspective also suggests that simply moving the locus of research from the laboratory to the field is not sufficient in and of itself, for doing so "without careful consideration of how we study group communication ... does not necessarily capture the key characteristics of actual groups ... [and] reap the dividends of real-world significance" we seek (L. L. Putnam & Stohl, 1990, pp. 248, 251, 248). In that regard, "a bona fide group perspective advocates a more fundamental break with past literature, one that extends beyond simply focusing on groups in natural contexts" (L. L. Putnam, 1994, p. 109).

The bona fide group perspective offers an exciting new direction for thinking about and studying groups and group communication. As L. L. Putnam and Stohl (1990) concluded:

> Reliance on the criteria of stable yet permeable boundaries and interdependence with immediate context[s] can help to remove the static container metaphor that underlies small group research, can add ecological validity to our studies, can reframe traditional group concepts, and can revitalize research through the addition of new puzzles that inspire the imagination of small group researchers. (p. 262)

Unfortunately, the perspective has largely been conceptual in nature with virtually no empirical research devoted to studying communication in bona fide groups (for an important exception, see Lammers & Krikorian, 1997). Thus, was born the need for this text.

OVERVIEW OF THE TEXT

The purpose of this text is to showcase original research studies conducted on and about communication in bona fide groups. The fundamental mission of the text is to demonstrate the conceptual promise of the bona fide group perspective as realized in research practice. The text is divided into the following seven sections and chapters, followed by an epilogue.

Part I. Tales From the Home and Hood: Managing Group Boundaries and Borders

For most people, their first group experiences occur in a family and in the neighborhood in which they live (see Socha, 1997). Given the ubiquitousness of these groups and the significant role they potentially play in shaping people's later experiences in groups (see, e.g., Keyton, 1994; Socha & Socha, 1994), it is surprising that group communication scholars have virtually ignored them (see Socha, 1999). The two chapters in this section attempt to rectify that situation by focusing, respectively, on families and neighborhoods, showing how, from a bona fide group perspective, what appear to be physically defined, stable group boundaries and borders (e.g., based on blood ties or spatial markers) are also permeable and ambiguous and, consequently, must be managed on an ongoing basis.

Sandra Petronio, Susanne Jones, and Mary Claire Morr begin the text in chapter 1 by applying the bona fide group perspective and communication privacy management theory to the ways in which families regulate boundaries to manage privacy dilemmas. Using a survey research design, they asked people to identify family privacy dilemmas they had experienced and how they attempted to manage those dilemmas. Their findings reveal the types of privacy dilemmas families experience, how family members become implicated in those dilemmas, the decision choices they make to cope with them, and the consequences they experience as they attempt to manage them. The study, thus, shows how members of bona fide groups— family members, specifically—manage their individual and collective boundaries regarding, in this case, privacy.

In chapter 2, Rona Buchalter presents a case study of how the physical, spatial context plays a critical role in the development of a Philadelphia neighborhood. Using the bona fide group perspective, as well as dialectical theory and the literature on space and place, Buchalter uses material acquired from in-depth interviews with residents to closely examine various aspects of the relationship between the Queen Village neighborhood and the Southwark public housing project located within the neighborhood's formal boundaries. By showing how the borders of this neighborhood shift and turn, seeming both permeable and impermeable simultaneously, Buchalter emphasizes the importance of thinking of groups as fluid, rather than static, entities. She concludes that tension can be a vital aspect of group life in helping groups to manage the inconsistencies and dissonance created by the necessity of shared space.

Part II. Community Groups: Engaging in Group Decision Making, Deliberation, and Development

If, as many have claimed, groups are the fundamental unit by which a society organizes itself, community groups are the building blocks of a civic society. Although known for its ideology of individualism, the United States demonstrates a deep history of volunteerism in community groups; even "de Tocqueville, himself, was astounded that, in the face of such individualism, the United States was a county of joiners, where social connections abounded in voluntary associations" (Adelman & Frey, 1997, p. 2). Despite recent claims about U.S. citizens' inability to conceive of the public good (Bellah, Madsen, Sullivan, Swidler, & Tipton, 1991) and people "bowling alone" rather than participating in civic group life (R. D. Putnam, 2000), there is still a profound commitment to community group participation (see, e.g., Pitts, 1999). The two chapters in this section explore two such community groups—a youth group and a school board—showing how factors such as their history, membership changes, and constituencies affect their decision making, deliberations, and, ultimately, their development.

In chapter 3, Sharon Howell, Bernard Brock, and Eric Hauser explore Detroit Summer, a group of inner-city adult and youth volunteers who came together in response to the twin concerns of youth violence and urban decay. Like many other naturally emerging groups, this group faced the challenge of attracting and maintaining members within an ever-changing environment. To understand the evolution of this group, Howell et al. examine how ideologies, structures, and strategies emerged as the group responded to and attempted to alter its social context. Their analysis draws on three bodies of literature: (a) the bona fide group perspective to examine the permeability of the group's boundaries and the impact of relevant contexts on the group's identity and experience; (b) Bormann's (1972, 1985) theory of rhetorical vision to examine the group's ideology; and (c) Poole, Seibold, and McPhee's (1985) work on structuration to discuss the group's structures and decision-making strategies. Through these perspectives, Howell et al. share the story of how this community group, despite multiple changes, has successfully sustained itself for more than a decade.

Chapter 4, by Karen Tracy and Christina Standerfer, presents a case study of the deliberations that occurred in one district's school board meetings about the process to put in place to select its next superintendent. On the basis of a close analysis of the meeting talk, Tracy and Standerfer argue why it would be useful for group communication scholars to reframe the typical focus of attention from "decision making" to "deliberation." After reviewing and critiquing the bona fide group perspective, they describe the school board and its meetings, relevant group history, and how the board's focal decision was initially framed on the agenda. They then show how using the concept of decision making takes attention away from how the discourse functioned to create information for future decisions, to speak to influential constituencies beyond the seven-person board, and to reframe what the group even should be deciding. Their analysis also shows how members constructed "the group" and its boundaries differently at different junctures in the deliberative process. Conceptualizing what bona fide groups usually do as deliberation rather than decision making, Tracy and Standerfer argue, will make visible and lead to inquiries about how decisions are, in fact, activities that are embedded in other group activities.

PART III. Groups Confronting Crisis: Contextual Effects on Group Communication

Unfortunately, as is the case for individuals, crisis is sometimes part of group life. In some cases, such as an expedition team being trapped on a mountain because of bad weather, a group suddenly finds itself in the midst of a crisis; in other cases, such as support groups for those living with AIDS, groups are created to help people cope with a crisis they already are experiencing. In both cases, the crisis plays a major role in shaping the communication processes that characterize the group (see, e.g., Gladstein & Reilly, 1985). The two chapters in this section explore the contextual effects of crisis on group communication.

In chapter 5, Renée Houston examines the fateful case of the ascent of Mt. Everest in May 1996, which cost the lives of 12 individuals. Using structuration theory and the bona fide group perspective, Houston explores the intergroup and intragroup communication processes that occurred in the context of this, the tallest mountain in the world, where the air is so thin that the higher functions of the brain (e.g., perception, memory, and judgment) routinely fail. Her analysis reveals two central implications for the bona fide group perspective and for the structuring of groups. First, the negotiation of intergroup boundaries shifts dramatically in crisis situations. In this particular case, expedition group identity initially was organized primarily around the leader of the group, creating a loosely coupled system, but these borders crumbled in crisis because the climbers needed to rely on the links between groups to coordinate survival and rescue operations. This reorganization of groups into a tightly coupled system demonstrated the strong degree of loyalty to all those operating within the context, as participants recognized their interdependence as climbers rather than as members of a particular expedition group. The second implication concerns the lack of structured norms or rules that characterized these expedition groups; operating under circumstances in which there existed no predetermined guidelines, the expedition group members behaved in ways in which their actions created unintended consequences for both themselves and for other climbers on the mountain. Ultimately, as Houston shows, it was the permeability of the group boundaries that sustained these climbers and that may serve as a lesson for other groups in crisis.

Gust Yep, Sachiko T. Reece, and Emma L. Negrón begin chapter 6 by pointing out that as we enter the third decade of the HIV and AIDS epidemics, more and more "Asian Americans" are living with HIV and/or AIDS and, consequently, seeking help by participating, for instance, in support groups. Using the bona fide group perspective, Yep et al. examine how culture and stigma affected group boundaries and the context of group life in a "closed" support group consisting of eight "Asian Americans" living with HIV infection. The findings indicate that culture and stigma affected the internal communication of the support group: Culture influenced group members such that their discourse was consistent with "Asian American" cultural values; stigma affected internal group communication in that much of the interactions that occurred in the group attempted to counteract social and cultural influences. Yep et al.'s study shows that no matter how closed a group may appear or consider itself to be, it is always embedded within and influenced by its relevant contexts.

PART IV. Cooperatives and Collaborations: Communicating Amidst Multiple Identities, Boundaries, and Constituents

The late 20th century witnessed a radical change in how organizations were structured, with many organizations moving from a hierarchical, top-down model to a more lateral, flattened system. To a large degree, these flattened organizations are defined by the importance they place on organizational members working in groups. Whether one talks about work units, self-directed teams, team-directed workforces, worker cells, or any of the myriad number of names used to describe autonomous and semi-autonomous groups (see, e.g., Seibold, 1995), "the work group has become the primary means by which the business of organizations is accomplished" (Frey, 1999, p. xiv). The chapters in this section examine how groups are used in contemporary organizations. The first chapter explores how employing teams in a *cooperative*—a collectively owned organization in which members share in the benefits—created multiple identities for members that had important consequences; the remaining two chapters focus on how activities such as boundary spanning and constituent/intergroup communication affected communication within a *collaboration*—a temporarily formed group of stakeholders from many organizations who share in the decision making and coordinated joint actions needed to address a common goal.

In chapter 7, John G. Oetzel and Jean Robbins analyze the Natural Food Cooperative Supermarket (NFC; a pseudonym), a member-owned cooperative that is organized into teams. Twenty-two employees were interviewed and questionnaires were collected from 49 employees. The findings show that NFC employees construct three predominate identities: (a) an organizational identity that emphasizes the values of NFC and cooperatives in general, (b) a strong or weak ingroup identity depending on the team, and (c) an organizational position identity derived from the individual's position in the hierarchy. The organizational hierarchy, strong ingroup identity of some departments, and lack of "living up" to the cooperative principles resulted in relatively autonomous units at NFC that essentially attempted to treat themselves as separate "containers." The strong-identity teams, in particular, avoided direct confrontation with external team members and demonstrated an insular concern for their team; upper management and the Board of Directors also demonstrated a similar insular concern and did not engage in direct communication with employees. Oetzel and Robbins use the bona fide group perspective to explain the construction and consequences of these three identities. They suggest that the NFC case has important implications for theorizing about bona fide groups that struggle to live up to the values on which they are founded and grounded.

In chapter 8, Jonathan I. Lange tells the story of the Applegate Partnership, a renowned environmental collaboration, within the context of constituency communication processes. Focusing on both communication between Partnership representatives and constituents and on communication within constituency groups, Lange uncovers a set of critical forces that affect environmental collaborations and potentially many other types of bona fide groups: extraordinary complexity, inherent paradoxes, shifting alliances, power disparity, and intraconstituency conflict. A radical critique of environmental collaborations and the identification of extensive practical difficulties they involve notwithstanding, Lange shows how environmental collaborations offer important opportunities for community building and transformational conflict management.

In chapter 9, Joann Keyton and Virginia Stallworth present a case study of the Drug Dealer Eviction Program in Memphis, Tennessee. The emergent process of a collaboration is described with respect to four essential elements (shared goal, member interdependence, equal input of participants, and shared decision making) that are products of the reflexive relationship between the communication of collaboration members and the development of a collaboration's culture and operating procedures. Keyton and Stallwoth evaluate this particular case against the theoretical ideal of the collaborative process described in the chapter and use the bona fide group perspective to illuminate the challenges presented by the collaboration's permeable and fluid boundaries, shifting borders, and multilayered environments. They conclude the chapter by addressing the implications of the findings for collaborations and for other bona fide groups.

PART V. Global Groups: Interfacing the Macro and the Micro

The term *global village* typically describes how the media link together people from all over the world (see McLuhan & Powers, 1989), but it also aptly describes how groups in different nations now influence one another and the growing number of groups that transcend national and other geographical boundaries and borders. The interdependence and interaction of groups at the global level offers opportunities to understand how macro-level contexts influence micro-level group practices and products. The two chapters in this section investigate that relationship by focusing, in the first case, on how the consulting practices of international business teams were carried over from country to country and, in the second case, on how the historical past of a nation influenced present-day interactions in a group struggling to enact the group practices used in another nation.

In chapter 10, John C. Sherblom uses the bona fide group perspective to analyze the recommendations made by international business consulting teams. After describing the 15 teams and their projects, and the general influences of permeable boundaries and interdependence with contexts on those teams, Sherblom provides a detailed analysis of the implications of those influences on two of the teams. The analysis of the recommendations made by one team for a prospective joint international business venture focuses on the effects of permeable and fluid boundaries; the analysis of the strengths and weaknesses identified for a corporation created through a merger of three companies with branches in eight countries focuses on the influences of contextual interdependence on the recommendations made by a second team. Sherblom's overall conclusion is that, in addition to explicit, recognized influences on their decision-making and recommendation-generating processes, specific implicit boundary and context influences—such as implicit company boundaries; the immediate information-gathering context; the timing, frequency, and degree of novelty exhibited when an idea was mentioned during the information-gathering process; and the endorsement of an idea by a particular subgroup—affected how information was imported, managed, and used by these groups in their recommendation-generating process and that similar influences may well be at work for other bona fide groups called on to make recommendations.

John Parrish-Sprowl begins chapter 11 by pointing out how difficult the process of enacting successful macro-level societal change and transformation can be. Developing an understanding of that process, he argues, necessitates, in part, a focus on the groups that, through their collective efforts, enact the new order. As Parrish-Sprowl shows, the dramatic events in Poland provide a historically unique opportunity to understand how changes at the macro level influence and, in turn, are influenced by changes at the micro level—in this case, in the groups that are helping to forge those changes. As the analysis of these events reveals, the bona fide group perspective is particularly illuminating in revealing the critical role groups play in the process of systemic change and transformation. As such, this study highlights the importance of understanding groups not only within the contexts in which they operate but also as the embodiment of and genesis for those contexts.

PART VI. Mediated Groups: Negotiating Communication and Relationships Electronically

The communications revolution has certainly affected group life; audioconferencing, videoconferencing, group decision support systems, electronic mail, and the Internet are merely some of the new electronic communication technologies used to create groups and facilitate their interaction (see, e.g., McLeod, 1996; Scott, 1999). These technologies offer exciting opportunities for studying group communication, but unfortunately, as Scott (1999) pointed out:

> Despite the fact that these systems supporting groups are primarily *communication* technologies ... and that many of the "1,001 research questions" that remain in this area ... seem well suited to examination from a communication perspective, relatively little scholarship on these systems has emerged from the Communication field. (p. 433)

The three chapters in this section seek to understand how, from a bona fide group perspective, communication and relationships are negotiated in three types of mediated groups: Internet support groups, online newsgroups, and groups meeting via videoconferencing.

In chapter 12, Stewart C. Alexander, Jennifer L. Peterson, and Andrea B. Hollingshead present a comparative case analysis of four Internet support groups that address a wide range of health-related issues: cancer, attention-deficit disorder, depression, and alcoholism. Examining these groups from a bona fide group perspective, the authors focus on (a) membership and group boundaries, in terms of how membership is defined in these Internet support groups; (b) intragroup communication, with respect to how social support is provided in these groups; and (c) intergroup communication, representing the interdependence of these groups with their mediated context. Using participant observation and self-reports, Alexander et al. analyzed a total of 2,197 Internet messages produced during a 3-week period of time, as well as responses to questionnaires from some of the Internet support group participants. The examination of these messages through the tenets of the bona fide group perspective indicate that although all four Internet support groups focused on health issues, the groups functioned quite differently and served different purposes for their members. Alexander et al. conclude that the bona fide group perspective offers researchers an important theoretical lens for understanding the internal and external communication processes that characterize computer-mediated groups.

In chapter 13, Dean Krikorian and Toru Kiyomiya apply the bona fide group perspective to Internet newsgroups. Qualitative data analyses are used to describe the communication activities and barriers of a sample of 26 alternative (alt.) newsgroups. The authors employ self-organizing systems theory as a theoretical framework for understanding how bona fide groups are characterized by both internal (endogenous) and external (exogenous) factors that systematically affect group processes and outcomes. They then develop a self-organizing model that predicts Internet newsgroup development and decline on the basis of the message constructs of message participation, threads, crossposts, and spams. Krikorian and Kiyomiya conclude the chapter by examining the theoretical implications of this model for further understanding bona fide groups and by identifying practical applications for its potential use.

Christoph Meier, in chapter 14, concludes this section of the text by pointing out that although videoconferencing technology has been around for some time, little is known, as yet, about the implications of this technology for the achievement of "groupness" in bona fide groups. Meier's main argument is that efforts to establish groupness in telecooperation have to be appreciated in light of the specific properties of the situation in which members find themselves; these specific situational properties derive, to a significant extent, from the features and properties of the telecooperation technology employed. Meier demonstrates this claim by engaging in a detailed analysis of a short episode recorded during an authentic business meeting conducted via videoconferencing technology. Such technical features as time lag, unpredictable sound systems, and limited resolution of television screens are implicated in the interactional dynamics observed: fragile foci of joint attention, reduced participation opportunities, action coordination across the video link occasionally being thrown off, and communicative actions provided "here" being less than fully transparent for participants "there." Meier concludes the chapter by explaining how the findings provide starting points for offering advice to members of bona fide groups participating in videoconferences and how those findings suggest that similar processes may be involved when using other types of telecooperation technologies, such as groupware, to support collaboration in distributed teams and organizations.

Epilogue

The text concludes with an epilogue by Cynthia Stohl and Linda L. Putnam, the initial proponents of the bona fide group perspective, that places these texts in context. As they explain, the chapters in this text help to empirically flesh out the conceptual tenets of the bona fide group perspective, demonstrating the promise of the perspective in practice and suggesting important directions for future research.

CONCLUSION

The study of group communication has never been more critical. The tragic events of September 11, 2001 at the World Trade Center in New York City, the subsequent actions that have followed, and the uncertain future that lies ahead point to the fragility of group life. That fragility became apparent when what we thought were stable and secure boundaries and borders suddenly became permeable and the realization that our communication with some other groups in the world was not as effective as we hoped it had been.

The bona fide group perspective offers much hope for improving group communication, for it recognizes that any group—whether it be a family, neighborhood, community group, expedition team, social support group, organizational work group, interorganizational collaboration, international team, or any of the many other forms groups take—regardless of how it meets—whether face-to-face, via videoconferencing, or in the supposedly disembodied depths of cyberspace—is not a container that can be understood apart from the multiple contexts in which it is deeply embedded and enmeshed and that significantly affect who is considered to be part of the group and what occurs within that group and between that group and other groups. As the chapters in this text show, such a realization has the power to transform our thinking about groups and group communication and, in time, the practices in which groups and group members engage. The text, thus, demonstrates that the bona fide group perspective is, indeed, bona fide.

ACKNOWLEDGMENTS

As with the first edition of this text, whoever created all those jokes about groups (e.g., "A group meeting is a cul-de-sac down which promising ideas are lured and quietly strangled") certainly didn't have the pleasure of working with this group of scholars. I want to thank them for the contribution they made to this text and to the study of group communication. I also want to thank Linda Bathgate, Communication Editor at Lawrence Erlbaum Associates (LEA), for her support of this text and for our friendship; she is a valuable professional ally to the field of group communication, but even more important, she is a valued personal friend. I also want to thank Sara Scudder, Senior Book Production Editor at LEA, for her help with the production of the text. Finally, I want to thank the members of my family group, friendship groups (especially those in Denver, Chicago, and Memphis), and professional task groups for teaching me about group communication.

REFERENCES

Adelman, M. B., & Frey, L. R. (1994). The pilgrim must embark: Creating and sustaining community in a residential facility for people with AIDS. In L. R. Frey (Ed.), *Group communication in context: Studies of natural groups* (pp. 3–22). Hillsdale, NJ: Lawrence Erlbaum Associates.

Adelman, M. B., & Frey, L. R. (1997). *The fragile community: Living together with AIDS*. Mahwah, NJ: Lawrence Erlbaum Associates.

Anderson, C. M., Riddle, B. L., & Martin, M. M. (1999). Socialization processes in groups. In L. R. Frey (Ed.), D. S. Gouran, & M. S. Poole (Assoc. Eds.), *The handbook of group communication theory & research* (pp. 139–163). Thousand Oaks, CA: Sage.

Bales, R. F., & Cohen, S. P. (with Williamson, S. A.). (1979). *SYMLOG: A system for the multiple level observation of groups*. New York: Free Press.

Bales, R. F., & Strodtbeck, F. L. (1951). Phases in group problem solving. *Journal of Abnormal and Social Psychology, 46*, 485–495.

Bellah, R. N., Madsen, R., Sullivan, W. M., Swidler, A., & Tipton, S. M. (1991). *The good society*. New York: Knopf.

Bormann, E. G. (1972). Fantasy and rhetorical vision: The rhetorical criticism of social reality. *Quarterly Journal of Speech, 58*, 396–407.

Bormann, E. G. (1985). Symbolic convergence theory: A communication formulation. *Journal of Communication, 35*(4), 128–138.

Broome, B. J. (1995). The role of facilitated group process in community-based planning and design: Promoting greater participation in Comanche tribal governance. In L. R. Frey (Ed.), *Innovations in group facilitation: Applications in natural settings* (pp. 27–52). Cresskill, NJ: Hampton Press.

Farris, G. F. (1981). Groups and the informal organization. In R. Payne & C. L. Cooper (Eds.), *Groups at work* (pp. 95–117). Chichester, England: Wiley.

Frey, L. R. (1994a), The call of the field: Studying communication in natural groups. In L. R. Frey (Ed.), *Group communication in context: Studies of natural groups* (pp. ix–xiv). Hillsdale, NJ: Lawrence Erlbaum Associates.

Frey, L. R. (1994b). Call and response: The challenge of conducting research on communication in natural groups. In L. R. Frey (Ed.), *Group communication in context: Studies of natural groups* (pp. 293–304). Hillsdale, NJ: Lawrence Erlbaum Associates.

Frey, L. R. (Ed.). (1994c). *Group communication in context: Studies of natural groups*. Hillsdale, NJ: Lawrence Erlbaum Associates.

Frey, L. R. (1994d). The naturalistic paradigm: Studying small groups in the postmodern era. *Small Group Research, 25*, 551–577.

Frey, L. R. (Ed.). (1994e). Revitalizing the study of small group communication [Special issue]. *Communication Studies, 45*(1).

Frey, L. R. (Ed.). (1995). *Innovations in group facilitation: Applications in natural settings*. Cresskill, NJ: Hampton Press.

Frey, L. R. (1999). Introduction. In L. R. Frey (Ed.), D. S. Gouran, & M. S. Poole (Assoc. Eds.), *The handbook of group communication theory & research* (pp. ix–xxi). Thousand Oaks, CA: Sage.

Frey, L. R. (Ed.). (2002). *New directions in group communication*. Thousand Oaks, CA: Sage.

Frey, L. R. (Ed.), Gouran, D. S., & Poole, M. S. (Assoc. Eds.). (1999). *The handbook of group communication theory & research*. Thousand Oaks, CA: Sage.

Gladstein, D. L., & Reilly, N. P. (1985). Group decision making under threat: The tycoon game. *Academy of Management Journal, 28*, 613–627.

Gouran, D. S. (1993). Factors affecting the decision-making process in the Attorney General's Commission on Pornography: A case study of unwarranted collective judgment. In C. M. Miller & B. C. McKinney (Eds.), *Government commission communication* (pp. 123–144). Westport, CT: Praeger.

Gouran, D. S. (1999). Communication in groups: The emergence and evolution of a field of study. In L. R. Frey (Ed.), D. S. Gouran, & M. S. Poole (Assoc. Eds.), *The handbook of group communication theory & research* (pp. 3–36). Thousand Oaks, CA: Sage.

Gouran, D. S., & Hirokawa, R. Y. (1996). Functional theory and communication in decision-making and problem-solving groups: An expanded view. In R. Y. Hirokawa & M. S. Poole (Eds.), *Communication and group decision making* (2nd ed., pp. 55–80). Thousand Oaks, CA: Sage.

Gouran, D. S., Hirokawa, R. Y., Julian, K. M., & Leatham, G. B. (1993). The evolution and current status of the functional perspective on communication in decision-making and problem-solving groups. In S. A. Deetz (Ed.), *Communication yearbook* (Vol. 16, pp. 573–600). Newbury Park, CA: Sage.

Gouran, D. S., Hirokawa, R. Y., & Martz, A. E. (1986). A critical analysis of factors related to decisional processes involved in the *Challenger* disaster. *Central States Speech Journal, 37*, 119–135.

Hackman, J. R. (Ed.). (1990). *Groups that work (and those that don't): Creating conditions for effective teamwork*. San Francisco: Jossey-Bass.

Hirokawa, R. Y., Erbert, L., & Hurst, A. (1996). Communication and group decision-making effectiveness. In R. Y. Hirokawa & M. S. Poole (Eds.), *Communication and group decision making* (2nd ed., pp. 269–300). Thousand Oaks, CA: Sage.

Hirokawa, R. Y., Gouran, D. S., & Martz, A. E. (1988). Understanding the sources of faulty group decision-making: A lesson from the *Challenger* disaster. *Small Group Behavior, 19,* 411–433.

Hirokawa, R. Y., & Salazar, A. J. (1999). Task-group communication and decision-making performance. In L. R. Frey (Ed.), D. S. Gouran, & M. S. Poole (Assoc. Eds.), *The handbook of group communication theory & research* (pp. 167–191). Thousand Oaks, CA: Sage.

Janis, I. L. (1972). *Victims of groupthink: A psychological study of foreign-policy decisions and fiascos.* Boston: Houghton Mifflin.

Janis, I. L. (1982). *Groupthink: Psychological studies of policy decisions and fiascos* (2nd ed.). Boston: Houghton Mifflin.

Keyton, J. (1994). Going forward in group communication research may mean going back: Studying the groups of children. *Communication Studies, 45,* 40–51.

Keyton, J. (1995). Using SYMLOG as a self-analytical group facilitation technique. In L. R. Frey (Ed.), *Innovations in group facilitation: Applications in natural settings* (pp. 148–176). Cresskill, NJ: Hampton Press.

Lammers, J. C., & Krikorian, D. H. (1997). Theoretical extension and operationalization of the bona fide group construct with an application to surgical teams. *Journal of Applied Communication Research, 25,* 17–38.

Lincoln, Y. S., & Guba, E. G. (1985). *Naturalistic inquiry.* Beverly Hills, CA: Sage.

McKinney, B. C. (1993). The Warren Commission. In C. M. Miller & B. C. McKinney (Eds.), *Government commission communication* (pp. 75–101). Westport, CT: Praeger.

McLeod, P. L. (1996). New communication technologies for group decision making: Toward an integrative framework. In R. Y. Hirokawa & M. S. Poole (Eds.), *Communication and group decision making* (2nd ed., pp. 426–461). Thousand Oaks, CA: Sage.

McLuhan, M., & Powers, B. R. (1989). *The global village: Transformations in world life and media in the 21st century.* New York: Oxford University Press.

Miller, C. M., & McKinney, B. C. (Eds.). (1993). *Government commission communication.* Westport, CT: Praeger.

Pitts, E. T. (1999). *People and programs that make a difference in a multicultural society: Volunteerism in America.* Lewiston, NY: E. Mellen Press.

Poole, M. S. (1990). Do we have any theories of group communication? *Communication Studies, 41,* 237–247.

Poole, M. S. (1999). Group communication theory. In L. R. Frey (Ed.), D. S. Gouran, & M. S. Poole (Assoc. Eds.), *The handbook of group communication theory & research* (pp. 37–70). Thousand Oaks, CA: Sage.

Poole, M. S., DeSanctis, G., Kirsch, L., & Jackson, M. (1995). Group decision support systems as facilitators of quality team efforts. In L. R. Frey (Ed.), *Innovations in group facilitation: Applications in natural settings* (pp. 299–321). Cresskill, NJ: Hampton Press.

Poole, M. S., Seibold, D. R., & McPhee, R. D. (1985). Group decision-making as a structurational process. *Quarterly Journal of Speech, 71,* 74–102.

Putnam, L. L. (1994). Revitalizing small group communication: Lessons learned from a bona fide group perspective. *Communication Studies, 45*, 97–102.

Putnam, L. L., & Stohl, C. (1990). Bona fide groups: A reconceptualization of groups in context. *Communication Studies, 41*, 248–265.

Putnam, L. L., & Stohl, C. (1996). Bona fide groups: An alternative perspective for communication and small group decision making. In R. Y. Hirokawa & M. S. Poole (Eds.), *Communication and group decision making* (2nd ed., pp. 147–178). Thousand Oaks, CA: Sage.

Putnam, R. D. (2000). *Bowling alone: The collapse and revival of American community*. New York: Simon & Schuster.

Scott, C. R. (1999). Communication technology and group communication. In L. R. Frey (Ed.), D. S. Gouran, & M. S. Poole (Assoc. Eds.), *The handbook of group communication theory & research* (pp. 371–394). Thousand Oaks, CA: Sage.

Seibold, D. R. (1995). Developing the "team" in a team-managed organization: Group facilitation in a new-design plan. In L. R. Frey (Ed.), *Innovations in group facilitation: Applications in natural settings* (pp. 282–298). Cresskill, NJ: Hampton Press.

Sherif, M., & Sherif, C. W. (1953). *Groups in harmony and tension: An integration of studies on intergroup relations*. New York: Harper & Row.

Socha, T. J. (1997). Group communication across the life span. In L. R. Frey & J. K. Barge (Eds.), *Managing group life: Communicating in decision-making groups* (pp. 3–28). Boston: Houghton Mifflin.

Socha, T. J. (1999). Communication in family units: Studying the first "group." In L. R. Frey (Ed.), D. S. Gouran, & M. S. Poole (Assoc. Eds.), *The handbook of group communication theory & research* (pp. 475–492). Thousand Oaks, CA: Sage.

Socha, T. J., & Socha, D. M. (1994). Children's task-group communication: Did we learn it all in kindergarten? In L. R. Frey (Ed.), *Group communication in context: Studies of natural groups* (pp. 270–246). Hillsdale, NJ: Lawrence Erlbaum Associates.

Soenksen, R. A. (1993). The 1970 Commission on Obscenity and Pornography. In C. M. Miller & B. C. McKinney (Eds.), *Government commission communication* (pp. 103–122). Westport, CT: Praeger.

Stohl, C., & Holmes, M. E. (1993). A functional perspective for bona fide groups. In S. A. Deetz (Ed.), *Communication yearbook* (Vol. 16, pp. 601–614). Newbury Park, CA: Sage.

Stohl, C., & Putnam, L. L. (1994). Group communication in context: Implications for the study of bona fide groups. In L. R. Frey (Ed.), *Group communication in context: Studies of natural groups* (pp. 284–292). Hillsdale, NJ: Lawrence Erlbaum Associates.

Van Maanen, J. (1976). Breaking in: Socializing to work. In R. Dubin (Ed.), *Handbook of work, organization, and society* (pp. 67130). Chicago: Rand McNally.

Waldeck, J. H., Shepard, C. A., Teitelbaum, J., Farrar, W. J., & Seibold, D. R. (2002). New directions for functional, symbolic convergence, structuration, and bona fide group perspectives of group communication. In L. R. Frey (Ed.), *New directions in group communication* (pp. 3–24). Thousand Oaks, CA: Sage.

White, R., & Lippitt, R. (1968). Leader behavior and member reaction in three "social climates." In D. Cartwright & A. Zander (Eds.), *Group dynamics: Research and theory* (3rd ed., pp. 318–335). New York: Harper & Row.

TALES FROM THE HOME AND HOOD: MANAGING GROUP BOUNDARIES AND BORDERS

1

FAMILY PRIVACY DILEMMAS: MANAGING COMMUNICATION BOUNDARIES WITHIN FAMILY GROUPS

Sandra Petronio
Wayne State University

Susanne Jones
University of Wisconsin-Milwaukee

Mary Claire Morr
University of Denver

People frequently struggle with privacy issues everyday (Altman, Vinsel, & Brown, 1981, Alderman & Kennedy, 1995; Petronio, 2000a, 2002). However, making choices about managing private information is often not an individual's lone plight; instead, decisions about revealing or concealing frequently take place within a group context. Perhaps the most important group to which people belong may be their family. Privacy within the family is critical to the functioning of its group members (Berardo, 1974), although there may be times when the comfort found in maintaining privacy is altered and, instead, becomes a source of discomfort.

Family privacy dilemmas represent situations that compromise the capacity to maintain control over private information within family groups. Families facing privacy dilemmas are compelled to reexamine the choices made about privacy rules they established as a group. Consequently, this reexamination often means that a family group can no longer depend on the agreed-on coordinated rules used to control family privacy among members. These dilemmas force a condition of boundary turbulence that challenges the unified state of boundary coordination the family group routinely and effectively uses to manage its privacy.

In this chapter, we focus on how families, as bona fide groups, contend with privacy dilemmas that threaten group members' management and coordination of privacy boundaries. When bona fide groups function effectively, they are typified by:

> *permeable and fluid boundaries* and *interdependence with context*. The idea of "groupness" itself and the social processes that form and sustain a group rest on a continual negotiation of borders, boundaries, and arenas. Boundaries then are not reified structures that separate groups from their environments or from other groups. Rather, boundaries are socially constructed through interactions that shape group identity, create connections with internal and external environments, and reflexively define group processes. (Putnam & Stohl, 1996, p. 149)

Family privacy dilemmas call into question the way boundaries are usually regulated by members both within the family and to outsiders. Studying family privacy dilemmas, thus, provides a way to understand how members cope with the fluidity of boundary management when obstacles are presented and routine rules for regulation no longer apply (Petronio, 2002).

In general, the focus on families offers a unique example of group interaction that allows for a life-span perspective and that considers the interface of contexts and social processes (Socha, 1999). By examining privacy dilemmas within families, we extend the exploration of group interaction to consider how members cope with problematic situations where they must find a solution. Because the stakes are high for family group members due to their ongoing relationships, contending with dilemmas is both frustrating and necessary. As a result, we seek to offer insight into the way groups manage dilemmas and the impact they have on the entire family.

Family privacy dilemmas and the interplay between individually held secrets and family borders of privacy are understood through the lens of Petronio's (1991, 2000a, 2000b, 2002) communication privacy management theory (CPM). The theory examines the regulation of private information across and within individual and collective levels. Some of the basic assumptions dovetail with the bona fide group perspective (Putnam & Stohl, 1990, 1996). As a result, each position contributes to the other, offering an integration that plays a part in the overall understanding of how family groups cope with boundary management when confronted with privacy dilemmas.

SETTING THE STAGE

To set the stage for explaining the concept of family privacy dilemma, the decisions enacted, and the consequences that families face, consider the following narrative offered by a 19-year-old college sophomore:

> My mother asked me to clean the garage while she went to the store. I was working away when I moved a table and letters fell to the ground. They looked special; they had a ribbon tied around them. I noticed that they were addressed to my mother—just last year. The handwriting did not look like my dad's. I wondered what they were, who they were from. I was afraid to open them, yet intrigued. My curiosity got the best of me. I opened just one to see. My world took a dive. There before me was a love letter to my mom— just this last year. They were from some man I never heard of. What could she be thinking? I was mad at her. I read on, even though it made me sick to my stomach. What nerve she had to hurt us like this. After I read them all, I panicked. What do I do now? I know something that is a secret of my mom's and she doesn't know I have proof. I told myself to calm down. I put the letters back where I found them—hidden out of view. "Now what?" I asked myself. "Who do I tell?" I can't live with knowing this by myself. But if I told my dad, he would go crazy. I didn't want to be the messenger. If I told my sister, she would be a wreck. My little brother was out of the question; he could not keep a secret. "Should I tell my mom?" I wondered. "How do I solve this dilemma?" I asked myself.

As this narrative illustrates, these events led to a family privacy dilemma. The son happened to discover information that was private to his mother, but once known, the son became an unwilling coconspirator. To reduce his burden, he considered others he should tell. As with many privacy dilemmas, the recipient (in this case, the son) of private information is a reluctant confidant (Petronio, 2000b).

Because the son is a family member, his obligation to the group makes his choices about relieving this informational burden problematic. The ramifications of his options are considerable for both him and his family as a group. The rub of this situation is the improbability of finding a solution that has some benefit for one or more of the family members. The greater likelihood is an outcome resulting in disruption and conflict for the group. Consequently, understanding family privacy dilemmas rests more with comprehending the process of privacy management than with focusing on outcomes or solutions for the family group.

To investigate family privacy dilemmas, we first discuss the theoretical frame of communication privacy management theory used to decipher the parameters of this phenomenon. We then present data that explore the types of dilemmas found in family groups and consider the decision-making processes used to manage the privacy dilemmas family members encounter.

COMMUNICATION PRIVACY MANAGEMENT

Communication privacy management (CPM) represents a practical theory that is used to understand the ways people regulate their privacy. In general, the theory is based on several premises (Petronio, 2002). First, people believe that they own their private information and, therefore, have the right to control the flow to others. The desire to control private information stems from both the need to protect privacy rights and the need to protect potential vulnerability (Petronio, Ellemers, Giles, & Gallois, 1998).

Second, a boundary metaphor is used in CPM theory to illustrate that people mark ownership lines, making a distinction between the private information they own and information that other people own. In addition, CPM theory argues that people manage both personal and collective boundaries around private information. For example, individuals have personally private boundaries, dyadically private boundaries, family group private boundaries, other group private boundaries, and organizationally private boundaries.

Third, the way in which people control their privacy boundaries is through a rule-management system. People develop rules to regulate linking others into their privacy boundaries, establish rules regulating co-ownership, and manage the degree of permeability determining when, where, with whom, and how much of their private information they reveal or conceal from others.

In addition, because people manage collective privacy boundaries, they have to coordinate the rules used to control the flow of information. One of the more complex coordination processes is seen within family groups. Through the construction, management, and changing of boundaries, families identify ownership of information for those residing inside and those outside the family system (Karpel, 1980; Petronio, 1991; Vangelisti & Caughlin, 1997). Families have both interior privacy boundaries that reflect dyadic and triadic (or more) group privacy boundaries and one unified exterior boundary that protects private information belonging to all family members (Petronio, 2002). Understanding the exterior and interior structure of these boundaries further helps to define the nature of privacy for families.

Family Privacy Boundaries

Within the unified exterior boundary, members have a protective environment that gives them a backstage to talk about private matters and to test out ideas in a safety zone. Family members, consequently, are able to learn needed lessons and have the flexibility to explore the ways in which they can meet outside demands. For example, airing controversial views on a topic inside the family may help a family member to understand other people's reaction before he or she talks about those views in public. Maintaining a sense of privacy is one way in which to develop a group identity and sense of solidarity because the members all share in the maintenance of the information (Berardo, 1974).

The information shared within the family becomes owned collectively by the group. To manage the permeability of the collectively owned information, the members either negotiate boundary rules or learn them from their parents (Petronio, 2002). When they negotiate rules, there is an explicit set of conditions (rules) under which the boundary can become permeable and the degree of porousness allowed to people outside the family (Petronio, 2002). In some cases, there are preexisting privacy rules that have already been adopted by the family as a group. Where necessary, they are taught to children so that they can manage revealing and concealing according to the expected rules for the family group.

In these ways, members are jointly responsible for regulating the permeability of information according to coordinated and mutually agreed-on rules for information privy to only the family members. Vangelisti and Caughlin (1997) called these "whole family secrets" because the information is known and co-owned by all members. Consequently, there is a need for unified boundary coordination of the way rules are used for concealing and revealing to third parties.

Families, however, also have interior privacy boundaries that reflect cells within the unified external privacy boundary. Linkages may be established between some family members so that dyadic and triadic (and additional) boundaries form around private information within the unified exterior boundary. For example, there may be times when children tell their mother—but not their father—private information. Siblings might tell each other private information but not disclose it to their parents, creating another boundary cell within the family.

Linkages may be coupled when there is a need to regulate certain private information and uncoupled when the need no longer exists. For each boundary cell developed within the family, the same type of rule-management processes (negotiations and socialization) are used to regulate the permeability of collective private information.

Development of Privacy Rules

Rules formulated to regulate and maintain privacy needs for family group members help them to understand the limits of who owns the information and how it should be controlled (Petronio, 1991, 2000a). Both individually and as a group, family members are expected to honor those boundary limits and the coordinated rules used to manage permeability. For example, feeling humiliated by an incident at work, a husband tells his wife about the episode. Not wanting his children or anyone else to know, he asks his wife not to talk about the incident. In this way, the husband sets the boundary limits so that only his wife has access and, thereby, creates an interior boundary cell within the family around this private information.

For both the unified exterior boundary and interior family privacy boundaries, rules are developed through a set of criteria. According to CPM theory, at least five criteria facilitate the formulation of rules managing privacy (Petronio, 2002). First, rules derive from the type of cultural expectations about privacy. For example, living in a culture that has a high demand for privacy is likely to lead a person to engage in fewer disclosures, infringe infrequently on others' territory and space, and not use others' possessions without their permission. Second, differential gender expectations affect privacy rules; for instance, men and women may define privacy needs differently and their rules reflect the disparity in desired privacy. Third, privacy rules depend on different individual motivations for revealing and concealing. Fourth, the group or individual making the rules evaluates the level of risk–benefit ratio involved in disclosing or remaining private. Fifth, the context affects the types of privacy rules people develop. Thus, with exigent circumstances, a person who typically does not disclose private information may have a high need to talk; for instance, divorce is one such situation that often changes the established rules to meet immediate needs. Together, these criteria lay the foundation for rule production.

Privacy rule production is complicated in families because members manage both individual and collective boundaries (Greene & Serovich, 1996; Karpel, 1980; Petronio, 1991, 2000a, 2002; Petronio & Kovach, 1997). On the individual level, each family member believes himself or herself to have ownership rights to the information and to set his or her own rules to manage boundary permeability and linkage. However, as members change boundary lines to include or exclude others from the information, they modify the expectation for ownership. In other words, beyond the individual level, family members often expect a degree of co-ownership for private information when someone is linked into a boundary. Knowing private information, then, is accompanied by an obligation by the recipients to contribute to boundary maintenance by adhering to privacy rules.

Co-ownership calls for the family group or dyads and triads (and larger coalitions) within the family to coordinate rules and collectively negotiate the regulation of the mutually controlled boundary lines. Thus, coordination of rules manages the level of access to private information or the permeability of the boundary and further linkages with others. When coordination functions effectively, family members inside the boundary lines act cooperatively, forming and enacting rules that are acceptable to all involved parties. Putnam and Stohl's (1990) proposal that boundary stability with concomitant permeability is at the core of understanding "membership and survival of the group within the intergroup system" (p. 257) is analogous to this point. When family members are clear about boundary parameters and agree with the rule expectations, family functioning is more successful (Minuchin, 1974); consequently, achieving a level of coordination positively affects the family. However, there are times when the coordination process does not work. CPM theory suggests that family privacy dilemmas are an example of boundary turbulence (Petronio, 2002).

Boundary Turbulence

Not all instances of privacy boundary coordination between family group members produce smooth transactions. Sometimes families have to cope with situations where there may be too much permeability, a lack of clarity, or uncertainty about appropriate rules for regulating private information. Any one of these situations may generate family privacy dilemmas. Such dilemmas stem from knowing private information that, if kept confidential, causes family problems, and if told, causes conflict for both the family and individual members. Therefore, managing privacy boundaries at times is plagued by the disruptive effect of these predicaments. The boundary lines become unclear, the privacy rules no longer function, and the choices for how to manage the disruption trigger consequences for family members. Thus, family privacy dilemmas cause turbulence because the coordination process becomes asynchronous. Repairing the process depends on finding paths that give family members ways to successfully manage the dilemmas and return to a synchronous coordination of privacy boundaries.

PERSONAL AND GROUP DILEMMAS

Although studied in a wide range of disciplines and contexts, the concept of dilemma is still difficult to discern. At the most basic level, a *dilemma* is "any situation involving a choice between two unpleasant alternatives" (Neufeldt, 1990, p. 168). More specifically, scholars differentiate between dilemmas and issues. *Issues* involve a straightforward choice between right and wrong, whereas dilemmas, in contrast, are more complicated; they reflect situations in which there are conflicts between multiple values and interests in which actors are uncertain about appropriate courses of action to take (Snell, 1996). Scholars also distinguish several types and functions of dilemmas, two of which—social and accommodative dilemmas—are salient to developing a definition of family privacy dilemmas.

Social dilemmas focus on choices between personal and common gain that are in conflict (see e.g., Baron, 1997; Kerr & Kaufman-Gilliland, 1997). In the context of family privacy dilemmas, this choice seems a likely consideration. In such social dilemmas, choosing a collective good, social actors sacrifice personal benefits by opting for a decision that advantages the group. For example, in managing a family privacy dilemma involving a sister confiding in her sibling that she stole money from their parents, the confidant-sibling might opt to tell her parents, reasoning that it would benefit the whole family. If this happened, however, her sister would be angry with her because she did not keep her confidence.

The personal gain option, in contrast, privileges individual concerns over group concerns and offers increased personal benefits through actions that are undesirable for the group. When personal gains are privileged, the group may become upset with an individual family member for sacrificing a positive outcome for the group. The outcomes for the group are, thus, often worse when people choose personal over collective gains (see Van Lange, Van Vugt, Meertens, & Ruiter, 1998). Consequently, although the choice of personal gain might seem beneficial initially, the group's reaction to the choice becomes an important source in evaluating the decision. These issues underscore the significance of the consequences that may not be realized until an action is taken in hopes of finding a solution.

As a related concept, accommodative dilemmas stress group concerns that are central to defining family privacy dilemmas. *Accommodative dilemmas* are situations in which members behave in ways that are potentially harmful or destructive to the group. Consequently, other group members are positioned in a dilemma because they must decide whether to respond in kind (destructively) or to accommodate the negative behavior (Arriaga & Rusbult, 1998). The dilemma ensues because "although individuals often feel inclined to reciprocate destructive acts, doing so is likely to be detrimental to broader ... functioning" (p. 928).

CONCEPTUALIZING FAMILY PRIVACY DILEMMAS

Although the nature of family privacy dilemmas is relatively unclear, the characteristics of social and accommodative dilemmas help to isolate aspects that are important to understanding this group phenomenon. At a basic level, *family privacy dilemmas* are privacy predicaments managed by family members making decisions collectively or individually that result in consequences (costs and benefits) for one or more family group members where there is no satisfying solution.

Family Privacy Dilemmas as Predicaments

Family privacy dilemmas are predicaments that reflect within-family tensions arising out of being privy to confidential information that can cause conflict between family members. However, the ways in which family members come to be involved in these predicaments has yet to be determined. One possibility is becoming a confidant, with one family member revealing private information to another member in an attempt to alleviate a burden; in so doing, the confidant may be thrust into a dilemma.

Dilemma cases such as these may explain research findings that demonstrate being a confidant is, at times, unsettling (Pennebaker, 1990; Petronio, 2000a). Hearing accounts of traumatic events, for instance, particularly when they involve family members that a confidant cares about, may complicate the confidant's ability to cope with the information. The discloser often expects the confidant to become a co-owner of the private information; as such, the confidant is then jointly responsible for making choices about how the information is managed.

CPM theory argues that this process represents efforts to synchronize boundary coordination (development and execution of boundary rules for access and protection) between co-owners of private information shared to a group (Petronio, 2002). Synchronization, however, is not always a clear outcome for family members, especially when they are unwillingly propelled into dilemmas. As a result, coordination is diminished. Members often find themselves in boundary turbulence where there is asynchronization at play and no clear solution for managing the private information they have been told. Hence, being a confidant means people become embroiled in a dilemma with individuals who are significant to them.

Playing a confidant role is only one means by which family members may become involved in family privacy dilemmas; undoubtedly, there are other ways as well. To date, however, it is not clear in what other ways family members become part of these privacy dilemmas. Thus, the first research question asks:

> **RQ1:** How do family members become involved in family privacy dilemmas?

Decisions Managing Dilemmas

Decisions that manage family privacy dilemmas are a core feature of these predicaments. As is the case for group decision making, from a functional perspective (see, e.g., Gouran & Hirokawa, 1996; Hirokawa & Salazar, 1999), determining a way to handle family privacy dilemmas likely depends on developing a set of alternatives to tackle the dilemma, establishing criteria for evaluating the merits of those alternatives, and assessing their potential consequences. With family privacy dilemmas, decisions used to manage them, by definition, compromise the coordination of a boundary system for privacy among family members.

Family privacy dilemmas take place because they undermine how families attempt to maintain synchronized patterns of privacy rules that cause boundary turbulence (for a more extensive discussion of boundary turbulence, see Petronio, 2002). For example, routinely two sisters may pledge to keep each other's confidences. However, if one sister tells the other about

her illegal drug habit, following their rule of keeping confidences may cause
harm to the sister with the drug problem because she might not get the medical help she needs. Telling someone for the purpose of helping her sister
puts the sister who was privy to the information in a bind because she would
have to breach the expected privacy rule she and her sister typically follow.
Consequently, the boundary rules customarily used between the sisters may
no longer function in a way that meets the needs of all parties involved with
the private information. New rules might need to be devised and old ones
breached if the dilemma makes the usual rules ineffective.

CPM theory argues that boundary turbulence, such as the case with family privacy dilemmas, destabilizes the coordination of three interrelated
processes used in boundary maintenance (Petronio, 2002). First, because
coordinating privacy boundaries in families depends on boundary permeability, or how much is revealed to and concealed from family members,
managing family privacy dilemmas often produces further complications if
too much or not enough information is told to someone else in the family
(Petronio, 2002; Putnam & Stohl, 1996). As a result, there may be times
when family members are told more information than they are prepared to
hear or for which they have the ability to cope. They may also be told too
little information, causing an overabundance of ambiguity and anxiety.
Knowing some information, but not being sufficiently informed, can be as
problematic as knowing too much information. When families are able to
coordinate effectively, rules are developed to adjust the privacy needs of
family members to attain a functional level of permeability or information
flow among members within the family system. When decisions are made
about how to cope with dilemmas that involve varying degrees of permeability (too much or not enough), the outcome can complicate finding a
way out of the dilemma.

Second, boundary linkages are critical because they define who knows
what private information within the family. Decisions that determine who
should be drawn into the boundary surrounding the dilemma and who
should be excluded once a dilemma occurs are often difficult because the
privacy rules may not be clear. Given that families are bona fide groups
with relational histories and expectations regarding information flow,
there are logical possibilities about who is more likely to learn the type of
private information that triggered the dilemmas (Derlega, Metts, Petronio,
& Margulis, 1993; Vangelisti & Caughlin, 1997). Some members may expect to be recipients of private information from other members, whereas
others do not. For example, marital partners often expect each other to
share confidences about financial information; their boundary rules are
geared to regulate the flow of information according to these expectations.
However, parents may not necessarily share such information with their
children. When rules are synchronized, coordination is achieved. However, decisions to breach commonly expected privacy rules within the fam-

ily throw the boundary coordination process into turbulence, making it difficult to cope with managing the dilemmas.

Third, boundary ownership or co-ownership regulates rights and responsibilities for the private information. Whomever is given the private information, as co-owner, is responsible for coordinating collectively held rules or abiding by rules established by the original owner of the private information. These rules set the parameters for third-party disclosures. Managing dilemmas may become complicated because there are times when the ownership markers are not clear and family members do not endorse collectively held rules, are uncertain about the rules, or make mistakes and do not follow the rules (Petronio, 2002).

When boundary coordination runs smoothly, these three dimensions function in conjunction with each other in a synchronized fashion; however, by definition, family privacy dilemmas characterize situations where coordination becomes turbulent and out of harmony. Decisions made about how to manage family privacy dilemmas often further complicate the situation.

Some of the issues that present obstacles with family privacy dilemmas revolve around the management decisions that further disrupt boundary rule coordination for family members. Consequently, no clear solutions exist, only choices that may alleviate one aspect of the situation and confound other concerns. The lack of coordinated actions that follow expected privacy rules tends to interfere with anticipated and predictable patterns of boundary permeability, linkages, and co-ownership of private information within the family system. Not only do these decisions cause disruption in coordination, they also force the recipient into a predicament where no clear privacy rules used in the family can easily apply.

Family privacy dilemmas, because they are turbulent, disturb the operating boundary rules and lead members to cast about for alternative rules to deal with the demands initiated by the dilemma. Therefore, determining boundary permeability (how much is known), membership or boundary linkages of those drawn into the boundary (who knows), and revising existing ownership rules regulating third-party revealing and concealing are likely part of the management package that people in family privacy dilemmas address.

To better understand how family members manage decisions about family privacy dilemmas, the following research question is posed:

> RQ2: What decisions do family members make to manage family privacy dilemmas?

Consequences of Decision Choices

As the literature on dilemmas, in general, suggests, attempting to find a way to cope with a dilemma is often considered in relation to anticipated or actual consequences (Arriaga & Rusbult, 1998; Gifford & Hine, 1998;

Kerr & Kaufman-Gilliland, 1997). Family members may anticipate the consequential effects of a potential decision choice, although in many cases, such effects may be inaccurately understood or not be known until a course of action has been undertaken. Family members' perceptions may fluctuate from believing that their actions would have little impact to not being able to predict how they might deal with the burden (Kerr & Kaufman-Gilliland, 1997).

Coping with family privacy dilemmas is tricky because people tend to think that being a recipient of confidential information is affirming, both from the discloser's and the confidant's perspective (Pennebaker, 1990). Family members often turn to each other as confidants, which may seem flattering, but after they know the disclosed information, it places a family member in a predicament; being privy may be more a burden than an affirmation (Petronio, 2002). Learning the details of a painful memory, health problems, or difficulties with relational partners, for instance, may make a confidant feel out of control (LaGaipa, 1990). The recipient may also be unable to provide the emotional support needed by the person disclosing. If too much information is revealed, with high expectations for support, the confidant may feel overwhelmed (Pennebaker, 1990). The discloser may also choose a bad time to talk about such problems, not taking into account the confidant's needs (Eckenrode & Wethington, 1990). The impact of disclosing on the recipient may not be clearly understood by the discloser; likewise, confidants may not recognize the potential burden because they may not be able to anticipate the type of dilemma situation they could experience.

The burden created by the choices for coping with family privacy dilemmas is significant because the outcome has the potential to alter patterns of interaction within the family structure, cause conflict between members, or result in personal problems (Arriaga & Rusbult, 1998; Minuchin, 1974; Swanson, 1993). Family members, therefore, likely weigh rewards and costs associated with various ways of managing these predicaments. For instance, a sister may struggle with revealed knowledge of her sibling's health problems. If she alters the boundaries by sharing that information with her parents, her sibling may be angry or humiliated and the sisters' relationship may be seriously damaged. If her parents are told, however, that may increase the sibling's chances of getting help and shares the burden of responsibility. Keeping the boundaries intact by not revealing the information to any other family member may meet the sibling's needs and strengthen the sisters' relationship but may increase the sister's (recipient) feelings of guilt and responsibility and reduce the chances that the sibling gets needed help.

The dialectical tension between keeping confidences and making them known can have important consequences for family members. Because there is often no good solution, the family member as confidant is faced with finding the best possible path to manage being privy to an informational "hot potato." Management of these dilemmas may be hampered by boundaries prescribing differential access for certain family members, and, possibly, for those outside the family.

There is, therefore, no clear way to resolve such dilemmas. Moreover, certain paths have consequences that accentuate tensions between loyalties that different members may have with each other within the family. For instance, parents may feel tension between their commitment to let each other know about private information that their children have shared with them and their desire to foster a trusting relationship with their children. Likewise, siblings may feel tension between keeping each other's information private versus telling their parents.

Coming to grips with these dilemmas ultimately means taking into account risks and benefits for the individual(s) managing the dilemma, the other family members, and the family as a group. One way to think about concomitant risks and benefits is to frame them in terms of consequences that pit personal gain against common good (Dijk & Wilke, 1997). For example, the costs for choosing a personal good by ignoring the problem may result in feelings of guilt or criticism by other members (Kerr & Kaufman-Gilliland, 1997); the reward, however, might be self-preservation.

Although there are a number of choices available to manage family privacy dilemmas, the ways in which such consequences are experienced by members seems unclear. Thus, the third research question asks:

> **RQ3:** What consequences do family members experience from attempts to manage family privacy dilemmas?

METHOD

Participants

Participants were recruited from introductory and upper level communication classes at a large southwestern U.S. university. Data were collected from this convenient sample at two points in time. One hundred twenty-one students participated in the study. Demographic data showed that the mean age was 22 years (range = 18 to 47); 74 were men and 47 were women; and 8 students were married, 110 students were single, and 3 students were divorced.

Procedure

Because this is a preliminary investigation, we relied on open-ended responses to questions about family privacy dilemmas to answer the three research questions. Respondents were given the example appearing earlier in this chapter of a son discovering his mother's love letters in the garage.

They then were given the following statement and asked the accompanying question:

> Living in a family often means that we are told about problems or issues faced by members because they think that we can help them. Sometimes hearing about these problems puts us into a dilemma. We might feel that we should talk about the information with someone else. Yet, doing so might cause more difficulties not only for the person who told, but for us as well. Could you describe below any situation or situations like this that you might have experienced at some time with your family?

Respondents then were asked what they did to deal with or solve similar dilemmas they had faced. The purpose of this procedure was to identify the communication dynamics of family privacy dilemmas.

Data Analysis

The data were analyzed using a thematic analytic technique proposed by Owen (1984). Owen argued that the identification of themes within a written text demands that three criteria be met: (a) recurrence, (b) repetition, and (c) forcefulness. *Recurrence* is defined as observing at least two reports that have the same thread of meaning. *Repetition* represents the duplication of key words and phrases. *Forcefulness* refers to a verbal dimension (and written documents representing verbalizations of conversations) encompassing vocal inflections or dramatic pauses that

> stress or subordinate some utterances from other locutions in oral reports; it also refers to the underlining of words and phrases, the increased size of print or use of colored marks circling or otherwise focusing on passages in the written reports. (p. 276)

These criteria were used to identify the themes that could answer the research questions.

FINDINGS AND INTERPRETATION

The data were interpreted using CPM theory, which is especially appropriate to understanding family privacy dilemmas within a context that extends the bona fide group perspective, for the theory is notably pertinent to the concepts of boundary permeability and fluidity (Petronio, 2002; Putnam & Stohl, 1996). For example, as will be shown, when there is boundary turbulence, families are forced to shift and change who is and who is not linked into a privacy boundary. This shifts, in turn, modifies a larger family system of group membership by excluding those who might likely be privileged to know private information under different circumstances.

Situations where a person assumes membership within a particular privacy boundary—that is, a co-owned dyad or subgroup within the family (e.g., a brother identifies his affiliation with a sibling subgroup regulating private information for just his sister and himself)—may hinder the relationship because that member may be temporarily barred from knowing a problem within that co-owned dyad or subgroup. Alternatively, being drawn into a family privacy boundary unwillingly means accepting a responsibility that may not be desired. Through observing family privacy dilemmas, these findings show that there is a level of coordination members in a group enact to manage borderlines even though they may not actively seek linkage into the boundary. Illustrating how boundary fluctuation impacts group members gives insights into the processes that bona fide groups use to continually regulate boundaries that define the ebb and flow of membership.

The findings also demonstrate ways that family members caught in dilemmas negotiate "jurisdiction and autonomy" (Putnam & Stohl, 1996, p. 153). Putnam and Stohl argued that interactions in bona fide groups often revolve around responsibility and accountability. Internal and external communication set the stage for "interpreting group goals, seeking approval for actions, negotiating and legitimizing authority, deciding on ownership, and accountability for decisions" (p. 154). CPM theory suggests that this kind of decision making takes place as part of negotiating rules for privacy boundary coordination. From the data, we find that family privacy dilemmas call on members to make decisions that shift the level of ownership for private information. In addition, the kind of responsibility changes to fit the demands of the situation, especially when the consequences of the choices are taken into account.

The application of CPM theory to study family privacy dilemmas, as the findings suggest, also extends some of the principles articulated about bona fide groups in a more general way. For example, we learn that although boundary permeability does occur between members of the family and those outside as they regulate an external privacy boundary, family members also manage internal privacy boundaries where they form co-ownership groups. Although the same principles of fluidity and permeability apply, however, the rules for managing private information change given the groups' needs.

The findings also highlight the way family members, who have permanent relationships with each other, handle situations that rupture boundary control and pose a threat to family relationships for the members as a group. In the following sections, we examine the specific answers to the three research questions guiding this study.

Implicated in Family Privacy Dilemmas

The first research question centers on the ways in which family members become involved in family privacy dilemmas. From the analysis, three themes emerged: confidant, accidental, and illicit dilemmas. Interestingly, the decision making used to manage these dilemmas and the consequences of those decisions are woven together as an integrated package rather than perceived by respondents as being conceptually different. Simply receiving or discovering private information, for example, does not inherently cause a dilemma; instead, these data show that dilemmas arise out of the combination of perceived options that can be used to cope with the dilemma and their associated consequences. For the purposes of explication, the type of dilemma is used to organize the discussion of the ways these situations become predicaments for family members.

Confidant privacy dilemmas are those that occur when a family member reveals a circumstance to another family member that demands an action difficult to enact. This situation creates a dilemma because each option available to manage the predicament has consequences that result in uncomfortable outcomes. The following account from a young man (respondent #43) illustrates the confidant privacy dilemma:[1]

> One specific situation I experienced with my family was with my uncle's recent drug problem. In confidentiality, he told me about his problem and about how he was still using drugs. This put me in an awkward situation. I either had to tell someone who could help him or I could keep it a secret like he asked me to. By keeping his problem private, I could not get him any help. By breaking my word and not protecting his privacy, I could offer him some help.... This situation is very stressful and difficult for me.

Accidental privacy dilemmas refer to predicaments where a family member inadvertently learns private, problematic information about another family member and must determine what to do with the discovery. This is a dilemma because there is no good option to handle the accidentally gained private information. Because it was accidental, the family member was not prepared to know the information; given that there are no apparent mutually beneficial choices to resolve the dilemma, the predicament and its related consequences put that family member in a bind that is unexpected and unwelcome. For example, respondent #124 stated:

> I have an aunt who is an alcoholic. One of the first times I knew she was getting out of control [was] when my sister and I happened to be at her house. My aunt was so drunk that she was being really mean to her kids. Finally, she hit my cousin who is around 3 years old. We took the kids and left. We knew we had to tell my mom about it but we were scared.

Illicit privacy dilemmas refer to situations where a family member intentionally pries, "snoops, " or spies on another family member and dis-

---

[1]Each excerpt is corrected for syntactical and grammatical errors but is otherwise presented in its original form.

covers private information that creates a dilemma for the snoop and potentially for those implicated by the private information. For example, respondent #072 stated, "I was in my younger sister's room, she is 14, and I found a pack of cigarettes. I was shocked because I thought she was too young to smoke. My parents would kill her if they found out." This respondent acknowledged that she was snooping in her sister's room when she made the discovery.

Although there were explicit reports of snooping by the respondents, they talked more about predicaments that were caused by other family members spying on them. This tendency may be due to a social desirability bias in that respondents may have been more inclined to report situations where a family member snooped on them than to reveal that they had breached a social expectation of respecting another family member's privacy.

These three types of family privacy dilemmas extend the characteristics of social and accommodative dilemmas examined earlier. The three family privacy dilemma types distinctively focus on ways in which family members are lured or thrust into such predicaments. In addition, the dilemmas underscore the interdependence of these bona fide group members as the actions of one person touch on each member in ways that have significance for the family group.

Managing Dilemmas and Consequences

The data also show that part of negotiating jurisdiction and autonomy for family groups depends on boundary coordination of the privacy rules used to determine ways to manage the dilemmas. Whether proactively seeking private information or being the recipient of another's proactive behavior, family members are faced with the need to consider choices for ways to handle information that turns out to be a liability.

Considering these dilemmas helps us to understand the ways in which bona fide groups such as families make decisions about communication strategies to control informational boundaries among members when there is turbulence. Thus, dilemmas focus our attention on situations when boundary maintenance does not go smoothly (Petronio, 2002). Examining family privacy dilemmas, in particular, draws attention to the liabilities members face with co-ownership of private information. As these data indicate, the choices members considered to cope with the dilemmas were ones that recognized the fragility of liaisons developed in the family. Because they cared about the impact the information might have on others and on themselves, they were careful to weigh the risks and benefits of possible options and consequences.

The second and third research questions target the ways in which respondents managed family privacy dilemmas and the associated consequences. In general, the findings suggest that the most consistent way family members managed these dilemmas was to consider including or excluding others in the privacy boundary containing the dilemma information. Thus, these results focus attention on the ways families that experience privacy dilemmas regulate boundary linkages, ownership issues, and permeability regarding private information.

We found that although the initial circumstance producing the dilemma may have concerned only two family members, managing the predicament often forced those two members to consider whether to expand the boundary and explicitly link more members. When the decision to link other family members was made, the boundary around the privacy dilemma became permeable to the target members. Once others were told, they became co-owners and privacy rules for regulating the information were considered. Even when someone was excluded, it was not without consideration of how that decision would influence the larger family group. Consequently, the "bona fide family group" as a whole was never far from any decision made to manage the privacy dilemma.

Using CPM theory, we analyzed the data for privacy rules respondents used to judge whether to include or exclude other family members; this analysis resulted in the several themes. Inclusion or involvement in the privacy boundary was predicated on decision rules representing boundary permeability, boundary linkages, and boundary ownership. Thus, privacy rules were discovered for whom to tell, how much to tell, the circumstances of telling, and the timing of telling the dilemma information. The inclusion rules linked others into the privacy boundary by making the boundary permeable to some degree and, at times, temporarily shifting the membership and making them co-owners of the private information. As co-owners, they were given responsibility for knowing some level of information that implicated them in the dilemma.

Exclusion from the privacy boundary, or not being linked, depended on decision rules that took into account whether the person was a family member, was in good standing, and needed protection, as well as the desire on the part of the decision maker(s) to avoid embarrassment or humiliation. These exclusion rules restricted access to the privacy dilemma information and controlled who was involved.

Through rules for inclusion and exclusion, the family members entangled in a dilemma coordinated their actions to manage the private information. This decision-making process aided members in developing an "interpretive frame" (Putnam & Stohl, 1996, p. 154) for the situation; in turn, the interpretive frame was instrumental in affecting members' judgments about the consequences for those involved in the dilemma. The consequences were defined in terms of whether the choice for inclusion or exclusion led to risks or benefits for those in the privacy dilemma or others in the family.

The data indicate that the themes for consequences, whether antici-pated or unanticipated, perceived or actual, revolved around calculated risks and benefits associated with the inclusion or exclusion of others. These risks and benefits often focused on trade-offs between personal ver-sus collective good. Respondents defined consequences as decisions that benefited or hurt the person(s) caught in the dilemma or implicated the whole family. For example, some of the consequence themes focused on the peril or gain concerning further boundary permeability and linkage for the person triggering the predicament (e.g., telling other family members about a brother taking drugs). Besides considering consequences for the person who initiated the dilemma, respondents also estimated the stakes for including or excluding other family members.

To provide a better understanding of family privacy dilemma manage-ment and the ways in which consequences were handled, an analysis of the data is presented taking into account the context of each type of family pri-vacy predicament identified in the first research question. In this way, we can see the options respondents selected and the consequences they en-countered within each type of dilemma.

Boundary Management and Consequences of Confidant Family Privacy Dilemmas

The data suggest two themes that reflect the overall decision management of privacy boundaries for confidant dilemmas and their related conse-quences. The first reoccurring theme involved situations where respon-dents managed these family dilemmas through using personal boundary rules instead of developing collective privacy rules to handle boundaries surrounding information about confidant privacy dilemmas in the family. The second reoccurring theme reflected situations where family members functioned as privacy spanners, resulting in risky decisions about ways to cope with the privacy dilemma. This second theme reflected situations where the family lost control over the dilemma information.

Dependence on Personal Boundary Rules. As stated previously, con-fidant privacy dilemmas occur when problematic information belonging to one family member is shared with another family member and, thereby, links the recipient into a dilemma boundary. These dilemmas are often caused by implicit assumptions about the way confidants should treat the shared knowledge that may not be jointly understood by the discloser and recipient (Petronio, 2002). Thus, rules for coordination of privacy bound-aries regarding inclusion (e.g., who, how much, timing, and circumstance) or exclusion are not explicitly discussed.

Management of confidant privacy dilemmas often becomes more com-plicated when family members do not define the sharing process as changing the boundary borders surrounding the private information from personally held boundaries to ones that are regulated dyadically or by the family group. In other words, although a family member discloses to one or more confidants in the family, he or she may still define the information as his or hers alone; doing so often means that the discloser does not use boundary coordination to set the privacy rules for permeability and ownership of the shared information. Confusion over ownership not only happens for the discloser but also occurs for confidants. Thus, confidants can assume that once the private information is told to them, it is theirs to make decisions about, just as disclosers in these dilemmas define shared information as continuing to be under their personal control. Nevertheless, the private information is shared. Because the discloser may disregard the fact that others have been told private information and because confidants treat disclosed private information as personally under their sole control, these dilemmas become more confounded. In turn, the consequences are also based on personal rather than collective concerns and, thereby, further complicate the situation.

For confidant privacy dilemmas, the following example (respondent #86) illustrates a recipient using personal privacy rules to regulate privacy boundaries for dilemma information instead of developing collective rules:

> When I was 13, my older brother told me that he was going to steal my neighbor's bike. I didn't like my neighbor but his younger sister was very pretty and I wanted to get with her. So having given in to her beauty, I ratted on my brother. In turn, she told her brother and the two of them ended up fighting. I apologized to my brother for telling and realized how evil pretty women can be.

In this confidant privacy dilemma, the younger brother used a personal privacy rule to manage the situation. He did not confer with his brother to coordinate boundary rules or to determine whether his choice to tell about his older brother's plans was the best way to cope with the predicament created by the older brother. Because the younger brother's actions did not involve a collective decision about how to handle the information, the consequences negatively affected the older brother and risked the relationship between the siblings.

Research suggests that social responsibility is evoked only when group members consider solutions to dilemmas in terms of the consequences of their behavior for others (Dijk & Wilke, 1997). The younger brother, in this example, focused on the consequence of personal gain rather than taking into account the feelings of his brother. As a result, the older brother and neighbor had a physical fight about the bike theft once it was revealed by the neighbor's younger sister. When the older brother linked his younger sibling into the predicament by disclosing his plans to him, the younger

1. FAMILY PRIVACY DILEMMAS

brother was faced with the responsibility of co-owning that information. However, it is clear from the example that the younger brother did not recognize that the information was actually co-owned, belonging to both he and his brother and, thereby, mutually restricting available actions that could be taken on it. Hence, this serves as a good example of a case where divergent interpretive frames led to a negative outcome for members of the family group (see Putnam & Stohl, 1996).

The decision to tell the neighbor's sister was apparently contrary to the wishes of the older brother and the boundary rules that reflected the interpretive frame he set for disclosing this information (although this is only implied in the narrative). The younger brother who "ratted" chose to define the situation as one in which he was in control rather than acknowledge co-ownership with his brother. In addition, the younger brother's use of the term *ratted* suggests that he knew he was mishandling the information. After the younger brother discovered the consequences of his action, he felt compelled to redeem himself in the eyes of his brother in explaining his actions to the researcher. The interpretive frame the younger brother used as a justification for his actions focused on uncontrollable feelings of attraction for the neighbor's sister and how the information his brother told him in confidence enabled him to engage her in conversation. In this case, the rationale underscored a need to justify making a choice for privacy management that ended up benefitting the individual who breached a confidence.

This respondent found it necessary to go beyond a rationalization. Because of his brother's reactions, he recognized that he had violated the boundaries surrounding the private information. To balance the consequences of his actions, the younger brother pointed out that his actions taught him a lesson about "pretty women, " as well as the consequences of opting for personal gain and using personal boundary rules rather than taking the needs of his brother into account.

As this example illustrates, being a confidant, especially in family privacy dilemmas, makes the responsibility for private information complicated. Family members have long-term relationships that depend on following certain rules. The expectations for the way brothers should have treated each other was embedded in the consequences for decisions on how these dilemmas were managed. Choosing personal gain may have short-term positive outcomes for one family member but long-term negative consequences for another member of the family or the family as a group.

Privacy Spanning in a Confidant Privacy Dilemma.   Receiving private information from another family member that creates a dilemma is problematic. To ease the tensions of knowing, many people opt to tell a third party, often a nonfamily member, and, thereby, become privacy spanners (adopted from the notion of boundary spanners; see Huber & Daft, 1987). Although using a third party as a confidant may help, the data from this study show that privacy spanning often puts the spanner at risk. The two examples that follow illustrate the manner in which family members may misjudge a third-party's commitment to keeping confidences and the difficulties with privacy spanning.

The first example shows some of the difficulties that family members faced with privacy spanning. As respondent #28 explained:

> My sister told me a problem that she was having with her boyfriend and I told my friend who [was] a friend [of] the boyfriend. Things ended up getting back to everyone. It would have been best if I had kept things to myself. I apologized to my sister and ever since, I think about the consequences of the things that I [say].

As this example shows, controlling private information once it has been revealed is potentially troublesome, especially when the target is not a family member although the person may be close to other family members. Research suggests that individuals often pass on other people's private matters, even if they are told they should not tell anyone (Petronio & Bantz, 1991). Private information can "leak" through the boundary from one person to another because, on balance, people may have more to gain from telling someone else than they have from keeping information confidential. Confidants are selected on the basis of their level of trustworthiness and ability to handle the responsibility of co-ownership (Berg & Derlega, 1987; Petronio, 2002). Inappropriately revealing, either because a person selects an untrustworthy target or because someone may be chosen who has little obligation to the family, can easily result in negative outcomes for the privacy spanner and directly implicate the family as a whole (Petronio, 2002).

The next example highlights what happens when third-party targets have little personal obligation to family members. Having little personal obligation to family members increases the difficulty of controlling the subsequent flow of information (Bergmann, 1993; Petronio, 2002). As the strength of ties and linkages between people grows weak, controlling information flow is burdensome because the good of the family is no longer a compelling reason for keeping the information confidential. If the third or fourth recipient of the private information is not linked to any other family members, self-interest on the part of the confidant may prevail more strongly than common interest. For example, respondent #14 offered the following illustration of this point:

> Last fall, my mom decided that she didn't love her husband anymore. She wanted to get a divorce. This was a big deal because it would involve my sister and me, the house and land they owned, as well as a flower business my

mom owned. My mom told us because she thought it was important [that] my sister and I know. This was really upsetting for me because it was her second divorce. I told my friend and my friend told her mom. Her mom was a real-estate agent and found out about the flower business. It was a big mess and my mom got mad. [She was mad because the person owning the real-estate business (and friend's mom) found out before the respondent's mother was able to tell her husband she wanted a divorce. The friend's mom, the real-estate broker, acted on this information by telling prospective buyers the flower business would soon be coming on the market before the husband knew.] The only thing I could do was talk to my mom. I explained to her that I had to vent my feelings and [my friend] was there to listen to me. She was too busy with everything else that I couldn't talk to her.

This example shows the difficulty of trying to control the flow of private information once a "trusted" friend has been told and that person feels the need to tell someone else. In this case, the mother of the friend (real-estate broker) had a stake in the information but not in protecting the mother who was divorcing her husband. Although privacy spanners can play a very useful role in linking groups into privacy boundaries and bringing needed information to others, in this case, a dilemma resulted because the consequences of telling led to a person with weak ties to the original owner of the private information. Privacy spanning to people outside of the family may, thus, result in breaching confidences in ways that have significant consequences for the members because the confidants have less to lose by breaching the information because there is little expectation of loyalty to the family members.

Although the daughter in the example was given the responsibility for this risky information and she selected a confidant whom she believed was reliable, the third-party disclosure of this information compromised the girl's mother. The daughter offered a rationale for breaching her mother's confidences, hoping to explain away the consequences that ensued because of this decision. As both of these examples demonstrate, there are implicit and explicit expectations for the confidant's role found in family privacy dilemmas. Spanning to someone outside the family is potentially risky because the recipient's loyalties to the family members may not be a factor in decisions that he or she subsequently makes regarding how to manage the confidential information.

Boundary Management and Consequences
for Accidental Family Privacy Dilemmas

Accidental privacy dilemmas, as explained earlier, involve predicaments where family members inadvertently discover something that is supposed to remain private; the surprise and unexpected nature of the discovery makes this dilemma especially problematic. The data from this study revealed two themes that explain how family members cope with accidental privacy dilemmas and the kind of consequences that emerge. First, the lack of preparedness or surprise element of the dilemma affects how members define boundary management and subsequent consequences. Second, an initial discovery often leads to subsequent discoveries, making the management of the dilemma difficult and consequences convoluted.

Preparedness in Accidental Family Privacy Dilemmas. When family members unwittingly discovered a situation that thrust them into an uncomfortable predicament, the outcome often was stressful because they were unprepared to accept the responsibility for the information they unearthed. The element of surprise meant that the ways to manage the privacy boundaries and to cope with the consequences were ambiguous. As respondent #49 noted:

> My mother lives with her boyfriend of 8 years. I love him and he is the only dad I have. He is a wonderful father of two boys and has accepted me graciously into his life. We have a good relationship that is a friendship. He has never tried to be a parent to me when I didn't ask. Unfortunately, I found out that he hit my mom on some occasions. I strongly believe in anti-violence and have volunteered many hours in domestic violence shelters. This information shocked and upset me. My mother is a very strong-willed woman; I, at times, have problems dealing with her. I know what it's like to try and communicate with her and how she doesn't listen to anyone. I understand his frustrations but I *do not* agree with his actions. I am afraid to pry. My mother and I have a very hands-off approach to one another and she has taught me to take care of my own problems. Therefore, I don't feel I have a place to do or say anything. I am very torn by this. I have ignored it since it doesn't happen often. He has never hurt her but, of course, there is the potential of danger. I have talked with her and explained that therapy for both [of them] could only be helpful. I don't push the issue but [will] feel awful when it happens again.

Learning an unexpected truth about family members that disrupts the family system brings into question the nature of the shared realities that families construct (Broderick, 1993). Through communication, family members co-construct meanings about one another and the family as a group. When those meanings are violated, family members must adjust their perceptions and expectations of one another and their relationships. In the example just given, accidentally discovering private information was a catalyst for the daughter to reevaluate the accepted definition of the relationship between her mother and the mother's boyfriend.

Knowing that her mother's boyfriend hit her mother was difficult enough, but part of the dilemma stemmed from the daughter's commitment, in voice and action, to fighting against domestic abuse. Interestingly, she offered a rationale for why the boyfriend might hit her mother, stating that her mother was a difficult person with whom to live. The daughter, however, also emphatically pointed out that regardless of her mother's personality, she could not condone the boyfriend's actions.

This respondent took a relatively cautious path to managing the privacy boundary by trying to ignore the fact that her mother was being physically abused and ultimately suggesting therapy to her mother. The consequences of these actions for the respondent appears to be having felt discomfort and guilt in knowing about this situation and not seeing a clear way to manage the dilemma (Petronio, Reeder, Hecht, & Mon't Ros-Mendoza, 1996). This daughter's reaction to this particular kind of family privacy dilemma involving domestic violence is not unusual because shame often functions as a "secret-keeper" (Kaufman, 1993, p. 196).

In this example, becoming a privacy spanner had potential benefits for the mother but it had risks as well. Although bringing information about abuse outside the family boundaries has certain advantages, family members often find it difficult to span the family's privacy boundaries with this kind of information because telling outsiders may bring shame to the family or worse, more violence to the victim (Ray, 1996). Consequently, family privacy rules for disclosing abuse tend to be very restrictive and, thereby, preserve the secret and positive group image of the family to outsiders.

In this example, the daughter followed the established boundary rules that were used by her family to collectively manage the flow of private information. Even so, her choice seems at odds with how she felt, yet she could not bring herself to change the collectively held rules for revealing this problem. Consequently, this daughter's dilemma was twofold. First, she did not want to bring shame on herself or her mother by telling others, despite being an advocate for other women through her volunteer work. Second, she did not wish to risk losing the only "dad" she has known; hence, she did not talk to her mother's boyfriend about the abuse. Her solution, although still problematic in its consequences, let her and her mother keep the co-constructed reality of her family life intact.

Multiple Discoveries of Accidental Privacy Dilemmas.   Sometimes accidental privacy dilemmas lead to embedded layers of discoveries, as observed in the following account provided by respondent #108:

> This situation is an ongoing situation and has yet to be resolved. Up until the age of 13, I believed my family to be mine. One day one of my sisters (who are younger) found my baby book and noticed that I had a different name than the one we have. When I couldn't think of why, we brought the book to my mother and asked about it. Her only reply was that I had a different father and was asked never to mention it again. And that was what happened until last year. In the fall semester, I had a 3-hour gap between classes, so I usually

would hang out in the computer commons and play on the computer. Well, one day, I found a "people finder" search on the [World Wide] Web and started putting in names of people that I lost track of. Then I decided to try to find my father. All I had to go on was what I thought his name was and where he lived at one point in time. So I put all the information I knew into the computer and four responses came back. I wrote down all numbers and waited for 2 weeks until I could call. Then the first number I called turned out to be him. I met him for the first time last November and have had contact with him ever since. The only problem is that no one in the family knows about this. For one problem, my sisters don't know I have a different father. I don't know how to bring this up to my mother or father since they have held this information from me for so long. The only way I have dealt with this situation is to keep it to myself.

The accidental discovery of private information pertaining to personal identity placed this respondent in a dilemma. His account showed several ways he considered managing this dilemma and how, with each new level of discovery, he weighed options and consequences. First, after the accidental discovery, he and his sisters believed that their mother was the best source of information for deciphering the puzzling discovery, although it is not clear from the account whether the children worked through any consequences of selecting the mother. The mother gave an explanation that offered minimal, but important, information. She controlled the amount disclosed and, thereby, tightly restricted the privacy boundaries around the information about her son.

This seemed to satisfy the children for a number of years until a second discovery took place sometime later. Obviously, the initial management of the dilemma did not completely convince the son; he must have been bothered by the information because he searched, as an adult, for his birth father. Once he found his father, a second related, but more complicated, dilemma emerged: He was not sure how to reveal his knowledge about his birth father to his parents. From their past behavior, he assumed that his parents did not want him to know much about his birth father. The son subsequently made a decision to be cautious about disclosing that he had met his birth father. Although this decision was made from an individual point of view, his understanding of the ramifications demonstrated the interconnectedness of the family as a group. Hence, in this situation, the private information did not belong only to the son, although it was about him, or only to the parents; the private information was co-owned by the family members and, therefore, had significance for them all, especially the parents and son. The consequences of the son's actions to manage these dilemmas were both long term and short term for him and his family.

The son and his parents, thus, were managing parallel boundaries around private information that were kept separate on some dimensions and interconnected on others. For example, the son drew a private boundary that excluded his parents from knowing about his meetings with his birth father. The parents believed that their son was unaware of his birth father, thinking that the rigidly held borders around the boundary protecting information about their son's parentage was still unbroken. The parents formed what they hoped were impermeable boundaries around private information about the son's identity and birth father.

When certain kinds of private information, such as that found in this example, have the potential to harm family members, boundaries often are tightly drawn to protect unwanted breaches (Petronio, 2002). Sometimes families form internal networks that create cells of interlinking privacy boundaries within the family; for instance, husbands and wives form one boundary cell, whereas siblings form another. In some situations, there is coordination between privacy boundary cells; in other situations, linkages may not exist, making coordination impossible and resulting in boundary turbulence that keeps some members unaware of private information about other family members (see Karpel, 1980; Vangelisti, 1994; Vangelisti & Caughlin, 1997). When internal family boundaries shift without warning, some family members may be caught thinking they know private information about others when, in fact, they have been shut out of the network. For the parents in this example, boundary turbulence took place when they learned about their son's discovery. The parents thought they were keeping their son out of the boundary by protecting his birth identity; ironically, the parents were the ones who did not know about the son's discovery. The lack of coordination of internal family privacy boundaries makes the consequences of revealing private information for members unclear. Anticipating what will happen under such circumstances may be difficult because the problem is complex and some family members lack critical information to judge outcomes.

Interestingly, it may be that lacking a clear idea about the consequences impinges on a decision about how to manage the dilemma. For the son in this example, both his decision to keep the knowledge of his birth father secret and his parent's decision to restrict information about his parentage had consequences for the family as a group. Holding secrets such as these undoubtedly is a burden and can seriously affect communication between family members.

Boundary Management and Consequences of Illicit Family Privacy Dilemmas

As explained, snooping, spying, or prying by one or more family members into the affairs of another family member has the potential to generate a family privacy dilemma. Engaging in such behaviors is invasive and can compromise a family member's right to privacy. As the data from this study show, this type of dilemma appears to be the most difficult to manage and has the most negative consequences for family members (see also Burgoon et al., 1989; Petronio, 1994). The most significant theme that emerged from an examination of respondents' narratives about the ways they managed decisions and related consequences was framed in terms of a *chain reaction* to the invasion. As respondent #68 stated:

> When I was in high school and my parents were still married, I used to keep a journal for my English class. In one of my entries, I wrote about a conversation my mom and I had about how she no longer loved my father. Everyone in the house knew this was my journal and I trustingly left it on the table one day. My dad picked it up and read the one particular journal about the private conversation my mother and I had. He had no idea my mom felt this way and he was mad at me!! He invaded my privacy and my parents are now divorced. Luckily, I was old enough to realize that the divorce wasn't my fault and my dad and I have a closer relationship [now].

Research indicates that there is often a relationship between the type of privacy violation and the use of particular strategies to restore control over the information (Burgoon et al., 1989; Hosman & Siltanen, 1995). In this case, the father knowingly invaded his daughter's privacy. He reacted by focusing his anger on his daughter for writing about the conversation with her mother. The daughter felt violated by her father's actions and suffered additional humiliation when her father became angry at her. For the father, although his decision to uncover information without considering his daughter's privacy put him at risk, he clearly did not consider available alternatives to the actions he took. His actions perhaps gave him short-term benefits, such as a release of anger, but the long-term consequences for his relationship with his daughter and wife were, no doubt, great. For the daughter, losing control over information that had significant implications for the whole family made her loss more potent. In the end, however, she did not place the blame for the divorce squarely on herself.

In this particular case, the daughter co-owned the information about her mother's feelings toward her husband. The daughter obviously felt it was safe to write about those feelings in her diary because she mentioned that "everyone knew this was my journal, " implying that their family rule was that "no one should pry" into one another member's private journal. Privacy violations of this type can lead to negative consequences for family relationships (Kelley, 1988), particularly for parent–child relationships, that may be difficult to overcome (Petronio, 1994). In this case, however, the father and daughter were able to mend the trust that was breached during this dilemma.

CONCLUSION

In this chapter, we have attempted to answer the challenge of studying natural groups posed by Frey (1994a, 1994b) within the framework of the bona fide group perspective articulated by Putnam (1994) and Putnam and Stohl (1990, 1996) by offering an examination of how families manage boundaries when confronted with privacy dilemmas using CPM theory. Stohl and Putnam (1994) argued that looking at the ways in which group boundaries shift and change in bona fide groups can help scholars and practitioners alike to "capture the emotional intensity, temporal fluctuations, and historical influences of group processes" (Putnam & Stohl, 1996, p. 148). Our research blends the bona fide group perspective and communication privacy management theory to illustrate ways in which group members—in this case, family members—manage their individual and collective boundaries regarding private information.

The results from this study show that families experience different types of family privacy dilemmas. We now know that families encounter dilemmas that stem from being confidants within the family, from accidentally discovering problematical information, and from snooping on other family members. Beyond isolating the types of family privacy dilemmas, we also learned that the management of these predicaments hinges on the decisions made to handle them and the consequences these decisions have for individual family members and for the family as a group. There are no easy ways to contend with confidant, accidental, and illicit privacy dilemmas; sometimes the decisions that members make to manage these predicaments result in additional dilemmas. Underpinning all of these dilemmas is the responsibility for private information. Keeping secrets, especially from family members, is not an easy task (Lane & Wegner, 1995); trying to do so is likely to temporarily or permanently change the group's dynamics. There is, however, often a need to keep information private because of the fear of a real or an imagined backlash that disclosing the information can engender. However, for family members who must interact with each other on a regular basis, the distress they feel may be compounded when they inadvertently become confidants, accidentally discover private information, or have others spy on their personal matters. In each case, family members must devote effort to finding ways to manage the dilemmas and to cope with the consequences of their choices or someone else's options.

In general, the conundrum surrounds the contradictory expectation that, on the one hand, family members are supposed to be privy to intimate family information, yet, on the other hand, family members may wish to maintain some level of separateness and autonomy if the consequence of a decision to manage the dilemma has the potential to hurt themselves or other family members. This paradox underscores the joint position of being both a *group member* and, simultaneously, an *individual member of a group*.

As the results from this study show, the duality of membership frames the actions family members take when confronted with privacy dilemmas. In such cases, privacy management decisions tend to revolve around inclusion and exclusion choices and, to some extent, decisions about consequences that privilege personal gain or the collective good. The focus on the risks and who benefits often depends on the ways the individuals in the know handle their responsibilities to the family as a group.

Although being the recipient of disclosure has been considered an admirable position, when there is boundary turbulence resulting in privacy dilemmas, being a confidant is not always a privilege; in fact, knowing is often a burden that may need to be subsequently shared with other family group members (Derlega et. al., 1993). As the private information is revealed, responsibility for that information increases and, consequently, the boundaries grow, becoming more interconnected. Members, accordingly, may become linked to a problem in ways they might prefer to avoid. However, because the problem involves one or more of their family members, they have less choice than if it involved nonfamily members.

This study of family privacy dilemmas provides a glimpse into an important phenomenon of family group life that has probably been experienced at one time or another by every family member. Learning about family privacy dilemmas offers insights into the ways internal group boundaries are formed and maintained by establishing temporary or permanent networks among group members. Through ascertaining the choices that family members make for including or excluding each other in internal family privacy boundaries, we gain a working understanding of the way boundaries shift and change for members. Members are linked into boundaries for many reasons; this research highlights the ways managing privacy dilemmas influence those choices. The investigation of such dilemmas promises to contribute to a better understanding of many internal group interactional issues, in addition to isolating the dynamics of privacy management within the family. Moreover, as illustrated in this study, extending the notion of boundary found in the bona fide group perspective by using communication privacy management theory sets the groundwork for a more detailed examination of the ways in which bona fide groups regulate privacy.

REFERENCES

Alderman, E., & Kennedy, C. (1995). *The right to privacy*. New York: Knopf.
Altman, I., Vinsel, A., & Brown, B. (1981). Dialectic conceptions in social psychology: An application to social penetration and privacy regulation. In L. Berkowitz (Ed.), *Advancement in experimental social psychology* (Vol. 14, pp. 107–160). New York: Academic Press.
Arriaga, X. B., & Rusbult, C. E. (1998). Standing in my partner's shoes: Partner perspective taking and reactions to accommodative dilemmas. *Personality and Social Psychology Bulletin, 24*, 927–948.
Baron, J. (1997). The illusion of morality as self-interest: A reason to cooperate in social dilemmas. *Psychological Science, 8*, 330–335.

Berardo, F. M. (1974). Family invisibility and family privacy. In S. Margulis (Ed.), *Privacy* (pp. 55–71). Stony Brook, NY: Environmental Design Research Association.

Berg, J. H., & Derlega, V. J. (1987). Themes in the study of self-disclosure. In V. J. Derlega & J. H. Berg (Eds.), *Self-disclosure: Theory, research, and therapy* (pp. 1–8). New York: Plenum Press.

Bergmann, J. R. (1993). *Discreet indiscretions: The social organization of gossip.* New York: Aldine de Gruyter.

Broderick, C. B. (1993). *Understanding family process: Basics of family systems theory.* Newbury Park, CA: Sage.

Burgoon, J., Parrott, R., LePoire, B. A., Kelley, D., Walther, J. B., & Perry, D. (1989). Maintaining and restoring privacy through communication in different types of relationships. *Journal of Social and Personal Relationships, 6,* 131–158.

Derlega, V. J., Metts, S., Petronio, S., & Margulis, S. T. (1993). *Self-disclosure.* Newbury Park, CA: Sage.

Dijk, E., & Wilke, H. (1997). Is it mine or is it ours? Framing property rights and decision making in social dilemmas. *Organizational Behavior and Human Decision Processes, 71,* 195–209.

Eckenrode, J., & Wethington, E. (1990). The process and outcome of mobilizing social support. In S. Duck (Ed.), *Personal relationships and social support* (pp. 122–139). Newbury Park, CA: Sage.

Frey, L. R. (1994a). Call and response: The challenge of conducting research on communication in natural groups. In L. R. Frey (Ed.), *Group communication in context: Studies of natural groups* (pp. 293–304). Hillsdale, NJ: Lawrence Erlbaum Associates.

Frey, L. R. (1994b). The naturalistic paradigm: Studying small groups in the postmodern era. *Small Group Research, 25,* 551–577.

Gifford, R., & Hine, D. W. (1998). "I'm cooperative, but you're greedy": Some cognitive tendencies in a commons dilemma. *Canadian Journal of Behavioural Science, 29,* 257–265.

Gouran, D. S., & Hirokawa, R. Y. (1996). Functional theory and communication in decision-making and problem-solving groups. In R. Y. Hirokawa & M. S. Poole (Eds.), *Communication and group decision making* (2nd ed., pp. 55–80). Thousand Oaks, CA: Sage.

Greene, K., & Serovich, J. M. (1996). Appropriateness of disclosure of HIV-testing information: The perspective of PLWAs. *Journal of Applied Communication Research, 24,* 50–65.

Hirokawa, R. Y., & Salazar, A. J. (1999). Task-group communication and decision-making performance. In L. R. Frey (Ed.), D. S. Gouran, & M. S. Poole (Assoc. Eds.), *The handbook of group communication theory & research* (pp. 167–191). Thousand Oaks, CA: Sage.

Hosman, L. A., & Siltanen, S. A. (1995). Relationship intimacy, need for privacy, and privacy restoration behaviors. *Communication Quarterly, 43,* 64–74.

Huber, G. P., & Daft, R. L. (1987). Information environments of organizations. In F. M. Jablin, L. L. Putnam, K. H. Roberts, & L. W. Porter (Eds.), *Handbook of organizational communication: An interdisciplinary perspective* (pp. 130–164). Newbury Park, CA: Sage.

Karpel, M. A. (1980). Family secrets: Implications for research and therapy. *Family Process, 19,* 295–306.

Kaufman, G. (1993). The mysterious disappearance of battered women in family therapists' offices: Male privilege colluding with male violence. In E. Imber-Black (Ed.), *Secrets in families and family therapy* (pp. 196–214). New York: W. W. Norton.

Kelley, D. L. (1988). Privacy in marital relationships. *Southern Speech Communication Journal, 53*, 441–456.

Kerr, N. L., & Kaufman-Gilliland, M. (1997). "… and besides, I probably couldn't have made a difference anyway": Justification of social dilemma defection via perceived self-inefficacy. *Journal of Experimental Social Psychology, 33*, 211–230.

LaGaipa, J. J. (1990). The negative effects of informal support systems. In S. Duck (Ed.), *Personal relationships and social support* (pp. 122–139). Newbury Park, CA: Sage.

Lane, J. D., & Wegner, D. M. (1995). The cognitive consequences of secrecy. *Journal of Personality and Social Psychology, 69*, 237–253.

Minuchin, S. (1974). *Families & family therapy*. Cambridge, MA: Harvard University Press.

Neufeldt, V. (Ed.). (1990). *Webster's new world dictionary*. New York: Pocket Books.

Owen, W. F. (1984). Interpretive themes in relational communication. *Quarterly Journal of Speech, 70*, 274–287.

Pennebaker, J. W. (1990). *Opening up: The healing power of confiding in others*. New York: Avon Books.

Petronio, S. (1991). Communication privacy management: A theoretical model of managing disclosure of private information between marital couples. *Communication Theory, 1*, 311–335.

Petronio, S. (1994). Privacy binds in family interactions: The case of parental privacy invasion. In W. R. Cupach & B. H. Spitzberg (Eds.), *The dark side of interpersonal communication* (pp. 241–258). Hillsdale, NJ: Lawrence Erlbaum Associates.

Petronio, S. (2000a). The boundaries of privacy: Praxis of everyday life. In S. Petronio (Ed.), *Balancing the secrets of private disclosures* (pp. 37–50). Mahwah, NJ: Lawrence Erlbaum Associates.

Petronio, S. (2000b). The reluctant confidant: Problems of hearing private disclosures. In A. C. Richards & T. Schumrum (Eds.), *Invitations to dialogue: The legacy of Sidney Jourard* (pp. 113–132). Dubuque, IA: Kendall/Hunt.

Petronio, S. (2002). *The boundaries of privacy: Dialectics of disclosure*. Albany: State University of New York Press.

Petronio, S., & Bantz, C. (1991). Controlling the ramifications of disclosure: "Don't tell anybody but …." *Journal of Language and Social Psychology, 10*, 263–269.

Petronio, S., & Kovach, S. (1997). Managing privacy boundaries: Health providers' perceptions of resident care in Scottish nursing homes. *Journal of Applied Communication Research, 25*, 115–131.

Petronio, S., Ellemers, N., Giles, H., & Gallois, C. (1998). (Mis)communicating across boundaries: Interpersonal and intergroup considerations. *Communication Research, 25*, 571–595.

Petronio, S., Reeder, H. M., Hecht, M., & Mon't Ros-Mendoza, T. (1996). Disclosure of sexual abuse by children and adolescents. *Journal of Applied Communication Research, 24*, 181–199.

Putnam, L. L. (1994). Revitalizing small group communication: Lessons learned from a bona fide group perspective. *Communication Studies, 45*, 97–102.

Putnam, L. L., & Stohl, C. (1990). Bona fide groups: A reconceptualization of group in context. *Communication Studies, 41*, 248–265.

Putnam, L. L., & Stohl, C. (1996). Bona fide groups: An alternative perspective for communication and small group decision making. In R. Y. Hirokawa & M. S. Poole (Eds.), *Communication and group decision making* (2nd ed., pp. 147–178). Thousand Oaks, CA: Sage.

Ray, E. B. (1996). Challenging the stigmatizing messages: The emerging voices of adult survivors of incest (pp. 273–292). In E. B. Ray (Ed.), *Communication and disenfranchisement: Social health issues and implications* (pp. 273–292). Mahwah, NJ: Lawrence Erlbaum Associates.

Snell, R. S. (1996). Complementing Kohlberg: Mapping the ethical reasoning used by managers for their own dilemma cases. *Human Relations, 49*, 23–49.

Socha, T. (1999). Communication in family units: Studying the first "group." In L. R. Frey (Ed.), D. S. Gouran & M. S. Poole (Assoc. Eds.), *The handbook of group communication theory & research* (pp. 475–492). Thousand Oaks, CA: Sage.

Stohl, C., & Putnam, L. L. (1994). Group communication in context: Implications for the study of bona fide groups. In L. R. Frey (Ed.), *Group communication in context: Studies of natural groups* (pp. 285–292). Hillsdale, NJ: Lawrence Erlbaum Associates.

Swanson, G. E. (1993). The structure of family decision-making: Personal and societal sources and some consequences for children. In P. A. Cowan, D. Field, D. A. Hansen, A. Skolnick, & G. Swanson (Eds.), *Family, self, and society: Toward a new agenda for family research* (pp. 235–263). Hillsdale, NJ: Lawrence Erlbaum Associates.

Vangelisti, A. L. (1994). Family secrets: Forms, functions and correlates. *Journal of Social and Personal Relationships, 11*, 113–135.

Vangelisti, A. L., & Caughlin, J. P. (1997). Revealing family secrets: The influence of topic, function, and relationships. *Journal of Social and Personal Relationships, 14*, 679–705.

Van Lange, P. A. M., Van Vugt, M., Meertens, R. E., & Ruiter, R. A. C. (1998). A social dilemma analysis of commuting preferences: The roles of social value orientation and trust. *Journal of Applied Social Psychology, 28*, 796–820.

2

NEGOTIATING (IM)PERMEABLE NEIGHBORHOOD BORDERS

Rona Buchalter
University of Pennsylvania

By and large, scholars (and, in a slightly different way, practitioners) are apt to conceptualize community in an idealized fashion: They tend to see it as a positive, voluntary, static, cohesive, and clearly identifiable and definable entity. Despite repeated efforts by academics, researchers, and planners to draw concrete group borders and then proceed as if those reified borders are real and stable, real-life groups are remarkably uncooperative in such ventures. So-called group members stubbornly refuse to comply with group definitions and borders that are laid out for them.

Recognizing this fact, and the significance of people's emotions and attitudes toward the places they live, some scholars have focused on understanding the nature of community attachment (e.g., Brown, 1990; Fischer, 1984; Ginsberg, 1985; Hunter, 1974). Seeking to identify criteria for strong affective connection to communities, these scholars generally conclude that people who are more involved in community activities and who socialize with their neighbors feel more attached to the place they live (Gerson, Stueve, & Fischer, 1977; Kasarda & Janowitz, 1982). Similarly, R. D. Putnam (1995) and Bellah, Madsen, Sullivan, Swidler, and Tipton (1986) found that people's sense of group belonging is enhanced by participation in civic and community groups. Although this body of scholarship implicitly acknowledges the multiplicity of people's experiences, community is still conceptualized as a singular and static entity to which one is either attached or isolated.

Such approaches obscure rather than reveal the nuanced and complex reality of group life and, thereby, minimize and homogenize its beauty and richness. A typical definition commonly offered by such scholars or practitioners says that *community* is "a group of people who share common symbol systems, ideologies and structures of meaning." This notion of community rings hollow when transferred into real-world settings, however, because it calcifies relationships between people and places that are best understood as primarily fluid and ambivalent.

The social and organizational boundaries of natural groups are rarely stable in everyday practice—indeed, they are more typically fuzzy and imprecise, with both interpersonal and organizational allegiances and alliances shifting to suit whatever situation is at hand. The same is true of the physical borders of spatially constituted groups, which also shift and change situationally. Neighborhoods are particularly interesting in this regard, in that they are a spatially constituted bona fide group in which social, organizational, and physical boundaries interact to create vibrant and complex group dynamics.

How, then, do we approach the natural, real-world community setting, with its dizzying array of shifting allegiances and alliances, in a way that appreciates and reflects its richness and complexity? Rather than focusing on the question of whether and why a collection of individuals forms a cohesive community, the questions to be asked regarding diverse natural groups concern the nature of the interactions and negotiations that occur along the edges of these groups. The really interesting task for scholars of group communication, therefore, is to understand and articulate the ways in which community is a continuously negotiated social agreement (Durkheim, 1984, 1995) rather than a static entity.

The bona fide group perspective (L. L. Putnam & Stohl, 1990, 1996; Stohl & Putnam, 1994) provides conceptual grounding for examining the nature of such active group borders. This perspective sees the boundaries and borders of bona fide groups as fluid and shifting rather than static and concrete. This ambiguity allows groups to change shape and form in response to environmental and contextual shifts. By focusing on the interdependence of and movement between internal and external factors, the bona fide group perspective focuses attention on the existence and everyday practice of situated group life by highlighting the importance of fluid border-defining practices.

Scholarship that addresses the notion of space and place is also useful for understanding the nature of complex natural groups, such as diverse urban neighborhoods, in that it focuses attention on the intersection of people and their environments (Altman & Lowe, 1992). This perspective draws attention to the ways in which place can be distinguished from space by the presence of a human boundary (Tuan, 1977). Scholars working from this perspective have demonstrated how physical space is transformed into something called *place* by people's experiences there—experiences that give meaning and contour to the space. Thus, different groups sharing the same space might create different meanings for and interpretations of that space, such that a single space might contain multiple "places" (see, e.g., Agnew & Duncan, 1989; Harper, 1988; Hufford, 1986; Massey, 1994; Ryden, 1993). This "place-making" process is not neutral, however; as Hayden (1990, 1995) emphasized, the process of defining a place-based community is always charged with political and economic power.

Although the romanticized model of a stable and secure community composed of like-minded individuals might exist in some capacity somewhere, this body of scholarship reminds us that a vibrant and dynamic neighborhood is not likely to meet such stringent criteria. There are too many systems of meaning and too many histories vying with one another for a single definition of place to survive. The literature on space and place is, thus, useful for the ways in which it situates and contextualizes the relationship between communication and community: Although neighbors live together and share common spaces, they typically lack truly unified systems of meaning. Within such a context, communication, or, more specifically, the management and negotiation of difference, is what makes this "living together" possible. As Carey (1992) noted, "Communication produces the social bonds that tie men together and make associated life possible" (p. 22).

Scholars (e.g., Krase, 1982; Lofland, 1973; Suttles, 1968, 1972) have implicitly addressed the relationship between communication and community by examining the symbolic construction of place. Their work shows ways in which group identity and group borders can be represented, interpreted, and negotiated within a physical neighborhood space. I seek to extend this work by explicitly showing how community—or, more specifically, neighborhood identity—is, in practice, a continuously negotiated social agreement.

The following case study closely examines the construction and operation of a contested group border, demonstrating the nature of the social agreement that helps diverse neighbors to manage the tensions of shared daily life. In particular, I consider the interstices of group life to show how the definition of a neighborhood is challenged and negotiated. In addition, I demonstrate that this negotiation occurs in the everyday practices that take place within the framework of a spatial relationship. Thus, I consider how group borders and boundaries shift, interacting and interpenetrating in ways that, at times, profoundly influence the shape of residents' shared lives.

STUDYING THE QUEEN VILLAGE STORY

This case study examines the dynamics of one of Philadelphia's oldest neighborhoods, known today as Queen Village. The recent story of this neighborhood is a familiar one in the history of urban neighborhoods in the United States. Settled by Swedes in the 17th century, this area along the Delaware River has been home to successive waves of immigrants. By the middle of the 20th century, residents were predominantly working-class Irish, Polish, Jewish, and African American. Over the past 40 years, however, the neighborhood has changed dramatically. By the early 1960s, the area had become run down, with dilapidated houses occupied by either old-time immigrant families or hippie squatters and renters. The urban renewal projects of that era, which included several highway projects and a superblock-style, high-rise public housing complex, dramatically altered the neighborhood landscape. Sensing the need for political organization in the face of these changes, neighbors "incorporated" themselves with the city in 1964, created the name Queen Village, and defined explicit, geographic borders for themselves. In the 1970s, Queen Village experienced an enormous amount of development and rehabilitation, and in the 1980s, downtown professionals furthered the gentrification of the neighborhood.

Today, Queen Village is something of a transitional neighborhood that bridges the gap between the cosmopolitan climate of Philadelphia's downtown and the more parochial attitude of its South Philly neighborhoods. Once an eclectic neighborhood of homes, factories, schools, shops, and churches and synagogues, Queen Village is now primarily a residential neighborhood. Most of the old industrial and religious buildings have been converted into apartments or condominiums, and the shopping that remains is largely confined to two commercial streets. The majority of the rowhouses in Queen Village have been renovated and upgraded, and many (although certainly not all) neighborhood residents work in professional careers. Queen Village houses a diverse mix of high- and middle-income homeowners and renters, with many "old-timer," multigenerational residents still living there. Mike,[1] a middle-aged White homeowner, described the neighborhood to me as follows:

> Queen Village represents the best example of urban American life. It has diversity. It has everything going on. It has arts. It's got blue collar, white collar. It's got gay, it's got straight. It's got Black, it's got White, it's got Spanish. It has an entertainment area. It's got charming old—it's the best representation, the best still-existing example of 18th century, lower income housing. These are the houses of sail-makers and so the architecture was wonderful. And the feeling of neighborhood, you really feel in a neighborhood. Every-

---

[1]Names of residents have been changed.

body on this block knows one another and they come from all kinds of backgrounds. It's stevedores and college professors. It's Polish and Jewish. It's young upwardly mobile and older retired folks. There are dog lovers and cat lovers and really interesting people; we all know one another. It's really truly the urban experience here. It's got a housing project, so it's got poor folks. It's got both well-to-do, middle-class, lower income Black and White. It's really got everything that makes a city. It's what I need in a city life.

As these comments suggest, this neighborhood (like most groups to varying degrees) has multiple dimensions, each of which represents a different way one might draw appropriate and meaningful group boundaries to define just what and who constitute this particular neighborhood. Possible dimensions include, but are not limited to, history, politics, race, economics, architecture, ethnicity, profession, social networks, and organizational structure.

To understand what it means, if anything, for this diverse "group" of urban residents to share the neighborhood name of Queen Village, I conducted in-depth interviews with 48 individuals in and across this neighborhood over the course of 18 months. In doing so, I quickly encountered the kinds of methodological questions that often thwart the study of bona fide natural groups: Who is a part of the neighborhood and who is apart from it? Which of the previously identified dimensions should be used to define and bound the neighborhood? Is there even anything here that might usefully be called a *group* and what would it mean to say there is? Are there particular voices that represent the sentiments of the group or is the collectivity merely the additive accumulation of those who comprise it? Must individuals feel a strong identification with the group before a researcher can consider their voices as speaking the sentiment of the group? Is there such a thing as a group sentiment or opinion?

To begin to address these thorny questions, I initially accepted the geographic borders of the neighborhood as delineated in the Queen Village Neighbors Association documents. Given the lack of a universally accepted definition of the neighborhood, these spatial borders provided a rational starting point for an examination of the process of contextualized group identification and boundary negotiation. From there, the focus of the research shifted to look at what role those spatial borders play in the negotiation of group identity. Given this focus, the views of any individual who lived within that space were considered equally important and valid, regardless of whether the individual felt strong identification with the neighborhood entity. This approach fit well with the goal of examining how multiple subgroups interact under an umbrella of a larger group identification.

To reach as broad a range of residents living within the neighborhood's geographic borders as possible, purposive sampling was used to select interviewees. The criteria for selecting people changed over the course of the research as different questions became salient and different people were sought who could speak to these new issues; criteria included age, race, ethnicity, and occupation, as well as geographic location, tenure, and activism in the neighborhood.

Interviews were normally arranged in advance, typically by written letter first and then with a follow-up telephone call. Introductory letters simply stated that I was interested in learning about residents' understandings of their neighborhood. Consent forms were signed and most interviews were audiotaped and transcribed.[2] Interviews ranged from 2 to 4 hours and generally followed oral history and ethnographic in-depth interview techniques. Among other things, I asked residents how they viewed their neighborhood, what issues they felt were important, what they knew about the history of the neighborhood, what their experiences there had been like, and what they cared about most in their neighborhood.

These interviews revealed that multiple factors interact and interpenetrate in Queen Village to create complex group dynamics within what might, at times, appear to be a single, relatively stable group. Although any number of potential subgroups might be considered independently as bona fide groups and examined for their own interesting and fluid group identity, I focus here on the struggles and negotiations between Queen Village itself and Southwark Plaza (known simply as Southwark), a public housing project located within the neighborhood's formal, geographical boundaries.[3] The struggle between residents of both Queen Village and Southwark to understand the peculiar nature of their relationship effectively illuminates ways in which a physical setting can influence the character of bona fide group life.

LOCATING AND UNDERSTANDING NEIGHBORHOOD BORDERS

The Queen Village neighborhood officially extends from Front Street west to 6th Street and from Lombard Street south to Washington Avenue (see Fig. 2.1). The Southwark public housing project was built within the southern section of this area, and extends from 3rd to 5th Streets and from Christian Street to Washington Avenue. Although Queen Village residents often reminded me that Southwark lies squarely within the boundaries of Queen Village, none seem to live under the illusion that they form one seamless neighborhood group.

Traveling from the surrounding neighborhood of Queen Village into the housing project embedded within it, it is unmistakably clear where

---

[2]Interview materials are archived with Temple University's Urban Archives in Philadelphia.

[3]Although I use the terms *Queen Village* and *Southwark,* it is important to keep in mind that these are not monolithic entities. Both Queen Village and Southwark have many internal divisions and crosscurrents, any of which might be mobilized to reveal other important divisions under other circumstances.

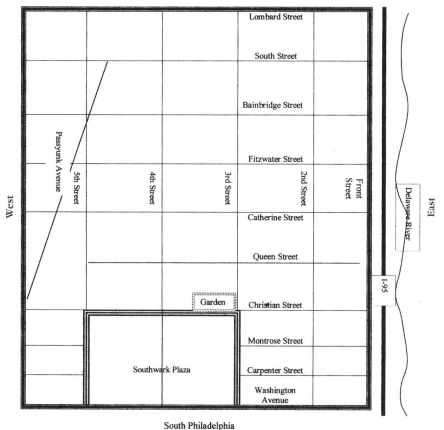

FIG. 2.1.   Map of the Queen Village neighborhood of Philadelphia.

Queen Village ends and Southwark begins. The disjunction is dramatic. The built environment of Queen Village, characterized by three- and four-story rowhouses of various architectural vintages mixed in with occasional industrial and commercial buildings, was partially demolished to create the public housing project. In its place, three high-rise towers were constructed, ringed by courtyards of homogenous two-story homes; no commercial activity was integrated into the development. Over time, as Queen Village became gentrified, renovated, cleaner, and better maintained, Southwark became deteriorated, run down, boarded up, litter-strewn, and overgrown. Due to ongoing renovation negotiations between representatives of Southwark, Queen Village, the City of Philadelphia, and the federal Department of Housing and Urban Development, two of the three high-rise towers now sit vacant and the low-rise buildings and grounds have never been properly maintained. As the population of the rest of Queen Village became more diverse in race and income, Southwark became less so. Despite the fact that Southwark began as a mixed-race and mixed-income development in the 1960s, its tenants became nearly completely African American and poor.

These distinctions are echoed in the area's organizational structures. Specifically, the Southwark Tenant Council remains a separate entity from the Queen Village Neighbors Association (QVNA), although QVNA receives some federal funding to provide assistance and services to Southwark residents. To demonstrate the extent to which this organizational boundary has been defended over the years, one resident told of an attempt some time ago to create a simple letterhead containing the imprint of both organizations. The proposal met with fierce resistance from some residents of both Queen Village and Southwark and ultimately failed.

Beyond these physical, demographic, and organizational distinctions, the different kinds of place-based concerns typically faced by Queen Village and Southwark residents point to the very different types of lives that residents of these two areas lead. When Queen Village residents mobilize over neighborhood concerns, they are likely to be bemoaning the dearth of on-street parking, lobbying for more stringent zoning restrictions for area businesses, or managing the conflict between dog owners and children in neighborhood parks. In stark contrast, Southwark residents talked about how, over the years, they have had to confront street-corner gambling and drug dealing and have been unable to get basic home repairs made, such as blocking out the cold winter air that blows in through the shoddy brickwork or stopping the feces that periodically backs up in their sinks.

Even given such clear material differences, group borders are ultimately articulated in everyday social practice. Accordingly, much of the everyday behavior of Queen Village and Southwark residents affirms a distinction between the two areas. Southwark residents regularly mentioned that they feel uncomfortable and even fearful in certain Queen Village shops or on certain Queen Village blocks and, thus, try to avoid them. Similarly, many Queen Village residents described how they, too, fear confrontation or even violence and, therefore, avoid walking on certain blocks around the housing project. Young Queen Village residents interviewed in a group setting discussed the lengths to which they go to avoid contact with Southwark:

> Toni: When we run down to Penn's Landing, we like to run down
>   Delaware Avenue. We don't run down Christian Street [along
>   the edge of Southwark]. We'll go over to Queen [Street] and

	down and around. When we walk home, we'll walk up 7th. We won't walk up Passyunk and Christian.
Becky:	You avoid [Southwark], you block it out.
Jeff:	The only way that [Southwark] affects me, or that I perceive that it affects me, is that when you have people come in from out of town, you gotta throw a footnote in—"They're not that bad. No, really."
David:	I have a very specific set of directions that I have printed up. I have people picking up and dropping off things all the time [for my job]. "Okay, [from Front Street], you make a left on Washington, go all the way to 7th," we live at 3rd, "make a right onto 7th and then follow that all the way to Bainbridge, make a right onto Bainbridge, and follow that all the way back to 3rd."
Becky:	I send people up Front [Street].
David:	To where? To Catherine and then around?
Becky:	To do that little "dit dadit dit" [a serious of short turns].
David:	See, I prefer to take them all the way around; that's very intentional.
Becky:	You could either go to Front and cut across or all the way to 7th and cut across.
Interviewer:	So you wouldn't send them up 3rd Street?
Becky:	No.
David:	No.

Many residents of both areas, thus, go through convoluted maneuvers, such as those described here by Queen Villagers, to avoid contact with one another. These everyday behaviors reify a semifixed boundary between the two areas.

The bona fide group perspective (L. L. Putnam & Stohl, 1990, 1996), however, emphasizes that group boundaries can be simultaneously stable and unstable, permeable and impermeable. Consequently, although group borders might exert powerful influence, they can still be ambiguous and shifting. Indeed, the border between Queen Village and Southwark is not as stable and easily identifiable as it sometimes appears to be. Despite many dimensions of distinction, Queen Village and Southwark interpenetrate each other in so many ways that it is impossible to see a clear and methodical distinction between them. This is apparent in the way residents affirmed the disjunction between the two areas but then, often in the same breath, struggled to express the complex nature of the relationship. Shelly, a long-time Queen Village resident, explained her difficulty in understanding the relationship:

It's really confusing, even to me. I mean we are [one neighborhood], but we're not. It's like we care about [Southwark] in a way, and we know it's important, but then again, sometimes it's like, do we really have to do this? I know that sounds terrible, but do you know what I mean? We are clearly together, one neighborhood, but then just as clearly, we're not. Like I said, it's confusing.

Similarly, Robert, a fairly new Queen Village resident, tried to articulate the slippery nature of the divide that he sensed in his new neighborhood: "Something should be done to increase the understanding between two pretty distinct communities that share real close physical space. [They are] in fact, one community, but really they are two distinct communities." Residents, even long-time ones, have good reason to be confused by the nature of the relationship between Queen Village and Southwark.

Unifying Interactions in Neighborhood Spaces

Although distinct in so many ways, drawing a firm boundary between Queen Village and Southwark is problematic, for their borders are not as clear-cut, stable, impermeable, or easily identifiable as they seem. As the literature on space and place (e.g., Altman & Lowe 1992) affirms, multiple definitions of a place can exist side by side, with some everyday practices affirming the impenetrable border and others affirming the connections. In the context of a neighborhood, geographic space is constructed as many different neighborhood places simultaneously. Thus, although some residents make a clear distinction between entities called Queen Village and Southwark, there are also many everyday practices that create and sustain other understandings of the space, conceptualizations that enhance connection rather than division across this particular border.

In actual practice, there are many ways in which everyday behaviors minimize the significance of the boundary between Queen Village and Southwark residents. Significantly, residents of each area sometimes interact with one another in daily life. These interactions are, in some instances, the spontaneous and unplanned result of living in shared space; at other times, connections and relationships form as the result of intentional, self-aware efforts to overcome a perceived border. In either case, interactions between residents of Queen Village and Southwark create and sustain an alternative to the definition of the neighborhood described previously, an alternative in which racial and economic boundaries are minimized. With regard to spontaneous interactions, Eric, a young Queen Village renter, described how he has found himself interacting with residents of Southwark, despite the differences between them:

> I talk to the [Southwark] kids sometimes in the street. They play football in front of my house. Sometimes I talk to them, goof around with them, steal the football, and throw it back to them. I've skateboarded through [Southwark]

a couple of times. There's a beer distributor on Washington [Avenue], so I take my skateboard down there sometimes, through the middle of it. You know, sometimes people would say things, y'know, "Hello," or "Yo, White boy," or whatever. [It doesn't make me uncomfortable, though.] Most people, if you say hello to them, they'll say hello back, maybe talk about the weather.

Another Queen Villager, Robert, described a similar kind of spontaneous, unifying interaction, this one occurring in a commercial enterprise rather than on the street:

The laundromat's really cool, at 4th and Queen. I really like that. I see the same people as anal as I am who do their laundry at the same day and time every week. Because of the proximity to the projects, it's mostly all Black. It's a really good time, hanging out with people for a few hours.

These remarks, both from young, White, male renters, indicate ways in which shared spaces—the streets and shops of Queen Village—can create opportunities for people to interact and get to know each other a bit. These spontaneous, unplanned everyday interactions penetrate the borders and boundaries and, thereby, minimize their strength and impermeability (although, as will be discussed, this penetration typically occurs in one direction only).

At other times, interaction is the result of an intentional effort on the part of individuals to identify areas of commonality and breach an acknowledged divide between Queen Village and Southwark residents. Ruth, a young African American Southwark resident, described one such effort she had been involved with in the 1980s. As part of an academically based project, Queen Village and Southwark residents were brought together and asked to come up with common goals and suggest actions to achieve them. As Ruth described:

[That started] by us trying to communicate with one another and get along as a whole community instead of split, like Queen Village here and Southwark here. We kept meeting with one another to break down the attitude barrier on both sides, and that's how that came about. We wrote out things, in both communities, that we wanted to work on and then they would pick so many people from Southwark and so many people from Queen Village. Like, say, the recycling thing; it'll be a group working on that. Then it'll be a group working on something else—maybe planting flowers or something. [There were] different things in the area. We started off with a bang, and then somewhere down the line, everybody sort of dwindled; but we noticed it, so I think somewhere we be getting them groups back together.

It is notable that the common goals articulated by neighbors during this project all revolved around a desire to improve the condition of the physical space they share; in this instance, the goals were to plant flowers and implement a recycling program. This focus on shared physical concerns remains true today; when Queen Village and Southwark residents work together most effectively, it seems to be over tangible, environmental issues, such as improving street lighting, assuring regular trash pick-up, or planting street trees. The shared physical spaces seem to provide opportunities to deconstruct the borders and, thereby, create a kind of (limited) shared identity for the residents of Queen Village and Southwark.

As another example of how neighborhood residents can purposefully abrogate the border, numerous residents cited the effectiveness of a community garden in drawing people together. The garden is one of the rare places in the neighborhood where residents have worked together on a more-or-less equal footing. As Mary, a long-time Queen Village resident, described it:

> If you could see the people working there, you know how wonderful it is to see people working next to each other on, like, their "victory garden," they used to call it. Squash this big [outstretched arms] and turnips and cucumbers. And the tomatoes are, like, better than you could get in Jersey. And here's something that they're all proud of, and they all worked side-by-side together. That's what I'm talking about—community. That's how you get around that "you and them." That's how you get over it, you really do. It really is the truth.... Who would have thought that bringing people together for a vegetable garden would have turned into something so wonderful? I mean, it was something I would have never thought of.... There are gay people over there, there are Blacks, and there are Spanish, and there are Polish. Everybody's got their spot. And it's "My tomatoes are bigger than yours." "Yeah? Show me a basket." Here they are, all working together.

The garden was intentionally designed to serve this community-building purpose, from its name, "The Queen Village-Southwark Community Garden," to its location, right at the junction of the housing project and the surrounding neighborhood. The intention of the garden's founders was for it to create linkages and connections between residents of Southwark and Queen Village, and it has, by and large, achieved that goal. As Mary noted earlier, the garden, more than anything else in the neighborhood, has provided an alternative to the divisiveness that has permeated the area in the past.

This garden, like a few other spaces in the neighborhood, provides a site for Queen Village and Southwark residents to come together and set aside the perceived differences between them. At times, Southwark and Queen Village residents come together (either spontaneously, such as in laundromats, or in planned activities, such as gardening or community meetings). In the very next moment, however, they might divide even more strongly than before. It is not that a conscious choice is ever made between these two alternatives; it is more like ever-evolving and changing motion. A limitless range of definitions of community coexists side by side in this neighborhood, from the most expansive and inclusive to the most constrictive and narrow. In this way, boundaries and borders can be reified in the everyday behavior of individuals and, slippery things that they are, simultaneously deconstructed. The neighborhood identity that is formed in this environment is, thus, by necessity, a fluid one: The areas remain simultaneously one neighborhood and not one neighborhood. It is precisely this kind of fluidity and ambiguity that defines the complex nature of bona fide groups.

(Im)Balanced, (Im)Permeable Borders

The story becomes even more complex, however, as the border between Southwark and Queen Village is examined more closely. Boundaries and borders of bona fide groups can be simultaneously permeable and impermeable, permeable for some individuals but not for others, and sometimes permeable only in one direction and at other times permeable in both directions. The border between Queen Village and Southwark seems permeable only sometimes, in some directions, to some people.

Because Southwark was built to be exclusively residential, residents have to use the commercial and recreational resources of the surrounding neighborhoods. For necessities such as hardware stores, grocery stores, and laundromats, as well as for amenities like restaurants, salons, playgrounds, and music stores, Southwark residents have no choice but to use the surrounding neighborhood resources to meet their daily commercial and recreational needs.

Some Southwark residents described feeling unwelcome in certain parts of Queen Village, however, being harassed, and even sensing hatred on certain blocks or in certain stores. Elizabeth, a long-time African American Southwark resident, described meeting Queen Village residents at a neighborhood playground to which she took her children, and how she found this common neighborhood space to be rather inhospitable:

> I used to take my children when they was young up to that park up there. I used to sit there and look at them with their children, and look at my children, and look at their children, and say [to myself], "Now mine's just as light[-skinned] as theirs," or "Their hair's just as pretty," or whatever. Why would they—? They somehow keep their kids over there. Mine would ask to play or whatever, and they wouldn't let them, they wouldn't let theirs play. I said [to myself], "Well I wonder why? Mine looks just as good as theirs. The kids don't know no difference. I would let mine play with them." No, no. Then I looked, they moved somewhere else; they'd get up and go somewhere else. I used to wonder about that.

Miriam, a Polish woman who grew up in Queen Village and raised her family there, confirmed Elizabeth's perception of the inhospitality of some of Queen Village's shared spaces:

> I think what killed the area was the [Southwark housing] project that we have, that project at 3rd and Christian.... I think the Wawa [a convenience store located a block away] being open 24 hours a day is also a very dangerous thing. Now, in the winter, it's quieter 'cause windows are closed. But in the summertime, 2:00, 3:00 in the morning, [Southwark residents] come out of the project, cursing all the way up Christian Street, right to Wawa. How many times, in the summer, [my daughter] says, "They woke me out of a dead sleep, they're out there screaming, carrying on"? You hear gunshots, this and that. Now here, we don't have that. That's only half a block away. See, they come out of the project, they come up to Wawa. If they could close this Wawa at midnight, even if they opened at 4:30, 5:00 in the morning, that would be 4 hours of good sleep you could get. Personally, I'm afraid to go out after 9:00. I think that's what wrong. They can go to Wawa, 24 hours a day, and we can't 'cause we're afraid. I think that's the problem.

In addition to expressing the way some Queen Village residents resist, even resent, the presence of Southwark residents on what they consider to be their streets, Miriam also expressed discomfort over a perceived imbalance in how neighborhood spaces get used and shared: Queen Village is largely penetrable by Southwark residents but Southwark is felt to be impenetrable to Queen Villagers. In part, this is because (given the lack of commercial activity or recreational space in Southwark) there is little if any reason for Queen Villagers to enter Southwark. Porous borders are reinforced over impenetrable ones, and vice versa, in these very ordinary, everyday situations and practices.

Moreover, because many Queen Villagers perceive Southwark to be a dangerous place, by and large they do not cross the border. Indeed, many outsiders believe the place to be utterly impenetrable. It is, thus, significant that the examples of unplanned, spontaneous interactions cited previously occurred only in Queen Village spaces. It is extremely unusual to find Queen Villagers passing through Southwark on their daily business and, consequently, having opportunities to interact with Southwark residents there.

It is interesting to note, in this light, that even the Queen Village–Southwark Community Garden discussed previously, with its self-conscious placement at the juncture of the two areas, was placed clearly on the Queen Village side of Christian street. Had it been located on the other side of the street, Queen Village gardeners would have a reason to penetrate at least the edge of the housing project. As it is, there is really nothing that draws them, or other Queen Village residents, across the border. Hence, it remains the case that Queen Village is seen, by and large, as being open and permeable to Southwark residents, whereas Southwark is seen, by and large, as being closed and inaccessible to Queen Village residents. The border is porous in one direction, impenetrable in the other.

It seems evident that variably permeable boundaries and borders such as these can affect bona fide groups in varying ways. In this case, at least, having group borders that are not uniformly permeable in all directions has led to situations with quite serious implications for the group. Stories circulate, in both Southwark and Queen Village, about the deleterious effect this one-way border has on criminal activity in the area. Residents told of times when criminals from other areas of the city had gotten away by hiding out in Southwark; of people who were robbed but were afraid to (or warned not to) give chase into Southwark; of how the police themselves were afraid to enter Southwark and, consequently, had let criminals escape without making arrests; or of how Southwark residents had been mistakenly blamed for crimes that had occurred in Queen Village. Marlyn, a long-time Southwark resident, addressing this latter issue, said:

> Southwark has a very ill-deserved reputation. We are not in prison here, and because there are no fences around here, anybody—Black, White, blue, green with polka dots and all that other stuff—can come in here. [They could] have done some damage out there to somebody and the first thing you hear, with no proof whatsoever, "Oh, they live in Southwark and we couldn't find them." That's a bunch of crap. There is no way you can—they say this is public ground, right? Anybody can walk in here, commit whatever crime they've committed out there, and immediately, without any proper investigation, [people say,] "It's a Southwark resident." Please, give me a break.

Interestingly, Marlyn's argument rests on refuting the perception that Southwark is impenetrable to outsiders. Her comments, however, seem to implicitly acknowledge that Southwark might actually be more permeable to criminals than it is to police or other law-abiding citizens.

Variations of these stories were repeatedly recounted by Queen Village and Southwark residents, both by long-time residents who remember when these incidents occurred and by newer residents who have been told about them. In each of these cases, residents emphasized the problems created by a border that is perceived to be permeable in one direction only. In each case, the imbalanced situation had a strong negative effect on all elements of the neighborhood. Because Queen Village and Southwark coexist in physical space, however, the variable and unequal permeability of the border leads to more than the simple isolation of these two groups from one another: It produces a peculiar kind of engagement, one in which residents of both areas exert an odd sort of influence on the other.

INTERDEPENDENCE IN CONTEXT

In addition to highlighting the flexibility of group boundaries and borders, the bona fide group perspective focuses attention on the importance of context, emphasizing its significance in the way that groups are created and sustained (L. L. Putnam & Stohl, 1990, 1996). In this instance of a dense urban neighborhood, the physical setting of Queen Village and Southwark, their relation to one another in space, is an essential element of the context in which these entities exist. The physical context in which these group processes play out affords opportunities for, perhaps even necessitates, that border-crossings occur with some regularity, whether by accident or in an intentional, planned manner. This results in a kind of interweaving of the two areas, a type of mutual monitoring, that ties together their existences and marries their fates, at least in certain limited, interdependent ways.

A residential neighborhood is, above all else, a physically defined entity; it exists in the streets, houses, trees, and bodies that comprise it and in the spatial relationships between those elements. Because Southwark is physically embedded within Queen Village, residents share streets by necessity rather than by choice. Neighbors interact with one another because they have to, interactions that, for better or for worse, are part and parcel of living in close proximity. *Copresence*, the sense of being in each other's faces and lives, is, thus, a defining characteristic of life in this neighborhood.

Walking outside of one's home always carries the possibility of confronting (or avoiding) one another. Public spaces provide opportunities for people to meet, interact, form and express common interests, and create linkages in daily life. Alternatively, or even simultaneously, public spaces can be sites where people disassociate from and avoid one another. Even the route a resident chooses to walk from point A to point B can become an act of unification or division—one that affirms or problematizes an (im)permeable border, as the previous comments from Queen Villagers attest.

Copresence pervades the texture of everyday neighborhood life, creating both exigencies and opportunities for the negotiation of neighborhood experiences. The availability of neighbors to one another in daily life, however, can both enhance and detract from their ability to confront and overcome problems. Much of the interaction between residents of Queen Village and Southwark over the years has, in fact, been anything but positive. In the 30-some years since Southwark was first built, relations between those residents and Queen Village residents have vacillated between open hostility, determined indifference, and occasional attempts at unity. This range of feeling results from the fact that residents of Queen Village and Southwark share common physical spaces and, therefore, must, for their own self-interest, attempt to continue to address and manage their differences rather than ignore them.

Shiela, a Southwark resident, describing an instance in which an acknowledgment of shared space led to an increased sense of interdependence between the two groups, said of the relationship between Queen Village and Southwark:

> [It] is not near as bad as it used to be. It was all blame this on that, ... that's how it was. Queen Village was Queen Village and Southwark was Southwark. And when we would go to meetings, it was always like, "You guys," like the drugs was just coming from here. And we had to let them know, "Hey, some of y'all come down here and buy them drugs." We see them all the time.

Physical proximity created a situation in which Queen Village residents came to Southwark to buy drugs, and the ensuing concerns about these interactions impelled a sense of common interest. By acknowledging that drug deals at times involve both Queen Village and Southwark residents and by recognizing that such activity threatens the stability of both areas, residents identified a common interest in trying to address the problem together. Queen Village and Southwark, thus, were tied together by their spatial relationship, which forced residents to take account of and even integrate the desires, motivations, and actions of the other into their own.

It is important to recognize that shared public space does not necessarily lead to an idealized or positive relationship, nor does it necessarily produce tangible benefits for group members. It does, however, create the necessity for some kind of engagement, or at least some kind of interaction, between those who live there. Such interactions can be a mixed blessing, at times easing tensions among residents, at other times exacerbating them. From the perspective of group relations, even hostility and conflict are forms of engagement that indicate porous boundaries.

Perhaps the most dramatic instance in which shared space compelled a reluctant joint effort involved ongoing discussions over planned renovations of Southwark. For nearly 15 years, residents of both areas, along with the Philadelphia Housing Authority and the U.S. Department of Housing and Urban Development, have engaged in negotiations over the shape and form of these much-needed renovations. Rumors abound over the development's final form; some possibilities considered include converting the upper units of the high-rises into high-income penthouses with low-income units below, demolishing two of the high-rises and converting the remaining one into exclusive senior citizen housing, or wresting ownership and control away from the city's Housing Authority and turning it over to a private developer who would run the development in some kind of shared ownership arrangement with the tenants.

These renovation discussions have been the flash point for residents' fears about their futures. Many area residents, whether they live in Southwark or Queen Village itself, fear for the future stability of their homes and their personal safety, and each group of residents seems to perceive the other as the primary threat to its own security and well-being. For Southwark residents, one of the most salient questions has been whether they will be permitted to remain in their homes. Some Southwark residents see the gentrification of Queen Village as a threat to their own existence, fearing that they will be pushed out in the desire to more fully gentrify the area. Marlyn, a long-time Southwark resident, explained her perspective on this question:

> For whatever reason, like I say, I believe somebody wants this development. I believe that because here you have access to every avenue of travel that you could want. You could go anywhere in the world right from here. And I don't think that they want Blacks living here. But guess what? They better get their shovel and start digging in 'cause I ain't going nowhere unless the good Lord takes me away from here. I'll go when I get ready, not when they get ready.

As Marlyn pointed out, the property would be valuable on the open market, given admittedly strong development pressure in the area; hence, Southwark residents do have reason to fear for the continued existence of their homes.

Some Queen Village residents do, indeed, feel threatened by Southwark, fearing for the long-term vitality and value of their neighborhood, as well as for their own safety and security. Some confessed that, if it were possible, they would, in fact, like to ensure their own security, both physical and financial, by eliminating Southwark and more fully gentrifying the neighborhood. They worry that if Southwark continues to decline, if, perhaps, it were to return to its darkest days of active drug dealing and periodic shootings, real estate values would plummet for everyone in the surrounding neighborhood.

These fears, or at least perhaps a sense of "enlightened self-interest," have pushed residents of both areas to work together closely, if not always smoothly, to develop a satisfactory plan to renovate the housing project and improve living conditions there. Many residents of both Southwark and Queen Village seem to be aware, at some level, of the strong connection between their respective fates, even if the nature of that shared fate remains fuzzy. Stohl and Putnam (1994) asserted that "it is possible to see groups as pitted against one another while at the same time interfused and amorphous" (p. 291), and this is, indeed, the case with Queen Village and Southwark.

David, a leader of the Queen Village Neighbors Association, explained his view of the situation:

> Some people say, "Southwark is dying; rip it down and maybe those people will just go away." But there are people in Queen Village, including myself,

who know that if "we" continue to look at "them" that way, then all of us—"we" and "them"—got nothing. And there are people in Queen Village, including myself, who know that there are plenty of people in Southwark who just want to live in dignity and become part of the larger Queen Village community.... It's time to recognize we have a shared fate.

David noted that the tendency to draw strong lines of division between "we" and "them" does a disservice to the whole area, for it obscures all the ways in which each part of the neighborhood affects the other parts. He recognized that there is a level at which Southwark and Queen Village are interdependent, for the long-term health and stability of Queen Village depend, to some extent, on the health and stability of Southwark.

One Queen Villager described Southwark as a cancer, a disease that spreads blight and destruction around it into the "healthy tissue" of Queen Village. He went on to explain, however, that when one has cancer, the body, both its healthy and afflicted parts, must work together to heal the whole or the whole dies. With this physical description, this resident articulated how, in Stohl and Putnam's (1994) terms, Queen Village and Southwark are simultaneously "pitted against one another" and "interfused."

Long-time Queen Villager Marty articulated a similar view in very practical terms, noting that the mere existence of Southwark benefits Queen Village by keeping real estate taxes down:

Some people would like to get rid of [Southwark], but what they don't understand, and I'm always explaining, is that it keeps their real estate taxes down, artificially suppressed. You're still living in Queen Village, within walking distance of Market Street [downtown], within walking distance effectively of City Hall, and you're paying Kensington or whatever level of real estate taxes [very low]. "Oh. Well. Oh," [they say]. They get very quiet.

As Marty's comments make clear, the mere presence of a public housing project in Queen Village means that taxes and real estate values remain somewhat suppressed, which allows a certain diversity of income to continue to exist in Queen Village. Thus, at some level, it is in the interest of Queen Villagers, who claim to highly value the diversity of their neighborhood, to sustain the presence of Southwark in their neighborhood, for that presence ensures that Queen Village remains an interesting and eclectic neighborhood—and one with low taxes.

Marty's comments also reveal that the dynamics of the Queen Village–Southwark relationship are embedded not only in an immediate physical context but also within a larger structural context. These areas are interdependent not only in terms of residents' everyday experiences but also in the view of the city and federal governments. Federal and local agencies, tax rates, real estate values, and other structural and economic elements all play a role in the desire and ability of residents to develop and alter their neighborhood in satisfactory ways. For its part, Southwark needs the participation and support of Queen Village, not to mention the political leverage and power of its residents, to negotiate the complexities of public housing bureaucracies and to assure that renovations do, in fact, finally get completed.

Queen Village and Southwark, thus, coexist in a symbiotic relationship: Although residents of each area fear one another, they also need each other. This paradoxical relationship produces simultaneous competing desires on the part of group members toward agglomeration and acceptance on the one hand and toward fractionalization and distinction on the other.

Ruth, a Southwark resident, explained what she thought was getting in the way of a better relationship between Southwark and Queen Village:

> I don't think there's nothing stopping it now. Well, being informed, I think. We get our wires crossed there a lot. Sometimes they're not informed about things and then sometimes we are not informed about things. And I don't think it's done intentionally; it's just that you be moving and striving for your goals, just like I said. Sometime you just get lost somewhere.

Because these competing movements are played out within close physical proximity, they never fully rupture and they are never fully resolved. Total disengagement is not a real possibility for these two groups because they share the same physical space and, consequently, have a powerful effect on one another. When "wires get crossed," as they frequently do, or when group members "get lost somewhere," these two groups are impelled back together because of their inescapable physical relationship.

Accordingly, the relationship between these two groups is perpetually in flux, simultaneously moving toward unity and toward disjunction. This perpetual motion creates tensions that must be dealt with, managed, in some way.

MANAGING TENSIONS

May, a leader of the Southwark Tenant Council, recounted an incident that encapsulates the complexity of the relationship between Queen Village and Southwark:

> [Some years ago, a QVNA member] asked me what was going on. I said, "You know, y'all got it lily-White over there, but you talking about Black poor people. And we need each other. I need to come down and sign for y'all to get your [grant money]. We need y'all to help us get things in. So it ain't one-

sided; it's togetherness." And this is what I did, and I talked. And so he went back and he told them the same thing. They called him a bunch of nigger-lovers, called him names, and he got out of there.

The view of this neighborhood leader is fascinating for it points to the duality that exists in the neighborhood. Although May expressed a strong sense of shared fate between Queen Village and Southwark, she also acknowledged that the relationship is characterized by a high degree of tension and animosity. The tension and animosity are a product of residents' struggle to balance their fear of one another with the recognition that their destinies depend on each other. As May observed, the sense of shared destiny goes hand in hand with the tension and animosity it produces.

As suggested by dialectical theory, tensions between simultaneous conflicting desires are part and parcel of group life (see Barge & Frey, 1997; Johnson & Long, 2002; Smith & Berg, 1987). At each point where group borders meet and intersect, sources of tension are likely to arise. These tensions are the natural result of human variation, of the juxtaposition of different interests, desires, and goals. These implicit, largely unstated, tensions form the foundation on which intergroup relationships play out.

Given the dramatic economic and racial differences between their populations, there are significant sources of tension that exist at the intersection of Queen Village and Southwark. Primarily, these tensions revolve around the relationships between race, poverty, and crime. Given the sharp differences in racial composition of the two areas, there is fear that criticism of one another is likely to be read as racially motivated. Indeed, during interviews, nearly every negative comment about Southwark made by a Queen Village resident was prefaced with the comment, "Not that I'm racist, but ...." Queen Village residents are afraid that directly addressing concerns about race, poverty, and crime will result in them being labeled racist (somewhat correctly, as it turns out). Similarly, Southwark residents feel that they have to defend themselves against such cultural stereotypes in all circumstances to avoid inflicting further insult and injury on their much-maligned community and to avoid provoking the wrath of their fellow residents (also somewhat correctly, as it turns out).

These tensions must, of course, be managed, although they are seldom resolved, resulting in a situation in which group members exist in a sustained state of dissonance. For the group comprised of Queen Village and Southwark residents, with members' diverse backgrounds, needs, and identities, to continue its very existence, the conflicts and tensions must be managed on an ongoing, daily basis. Queen Village and Southwark residents try to manage these tensions by avoiding direct confrontation of the underlying issues of race, poverty, and crime. In so doing, residents sustain the tense relationship that allows them to continue to develop and grow, share neighborhood streets and shops, and live together. This is precisely the situation Adelman and Frey (1997) envisioned when they claimed that "community life is like a tightrope, held taught by the sustained tensions of daily living" (p. 17). By sustaining a delicate balance between confrontation and denial, residents derive practical benefits from the ongoing conceptual and pragmatic muddiness inherent in their real-life situation.

When tensions are managed smoothly, there is nothing problematic for an outside observer to see; hence, the tensions, and their ability to be managed, are witnessed most clearly when management fails. When the tightrope falters, "community life" fractures. In this particular case, when the border between Southwark and Queen Village is confronted directly, the tentative, operational stability of the group is threatened. James, a young, African American Queen Village resident, described a QVNA meeting he attended that was largely taken up by heated discussions about proposed details of the Southwark renovations:

> [Southwark] stirs up much controversy, and for many legitimate reasons—security and basically a blight in Queen Village. And so it is a major controversy and a major issue that has faced the Queen Village neighbors. So at this meeting, this was the—I guess they were introducing a lot of ideas and concepts as to what they were going to do with Southwark, and people were absolutely in arms. Some people were so vocal and so extreme in their behavior as to be intolerable. And I was shocked, because I was amazed by the amount of emotion that was actually at this meeting. The level of tension was very high.

The threat to group stability might be manifested simply as strong emotion, as it was here, or it might be more potent than that. The QVNA member mentioned by May in the narrative that began this section made the mistake of confronting the border head on rather than finessing his way around it. The response was that he was alienated and excluded from participation in the neighborhood association. Similarly, a Southwark resident told me of a former resident, a young woman, who tried to reach out and work directly with Queen Village on the issue of neighborhood crime. Southwark residents themselves closed ranks against her for this breach and, in the words of the resident, "made that girl's life a living hell." These strong, visceral reactions indicate just how deeply important these concerns are to area residents.

Bernadette, a Queen Village resident, has also been hurt by her neighbors' efforts to sustain the tensions inherent to the neighborhood rather than try to address them directly. She raised the ire of many of her neighbors by speaking openly about her concern for neighborhood security. By doing so, she (intentionally) made it uncomfortable for people to "manage" the tensions by avoiding and evading them and challenged her neighbors to address the underlying issues head on and work to resolve them. Bernadette spoke to me of her overriding concern about the shared future of the two areas, expressing frustration at her inability to get the support and backing of the whole neighborhood for her efforts:

> The [rest of the neighborhood] may be just as concerned [as I am about crime and safety issues], although I find that most people are not concerned unless they are personally affected. I got a call from one of our neighbors a few weeks ago. They had been on vacation, their house was burglarized, and she wanted me to get some information from the [police] captain. I ended my conversation because she said people on her street where the burglary occurred met and they didn't want any of this information to get out, even though they knew there had been another burglary a couple of blocks away. It could have been the same perp[etrator], I don't know. [They didn't want the information to get out] because they did not want to destroy the ambiance of the street. I remember saying, "Well, I'm not concerned about the ambiance of the street, and I'm not concerned about the fact that it wasn't my house that was burglarized. I am concerned about the fact that this is going on in the community at all." There was another incident two blocks away, and everybody's clamming up. It's not a community concern because all of a sudden [they think], "Oh, we live on this very pretty tree-lined street. We don't want anybody to get the idea that this is something that's happening all over the neighborhood," when, in fact, it could very well be. I personally do not ask for full reports from the police anymore because I emotionally cannot deal with the same things happening over and over again, knowing what you have to do to address the problem and knowing that that is not going to happen here. The community support is simply not there. After 10 years of trying to make it happen, I have finally come to the realization that it's not.

In this situation, the relational tensions came to a head. The kind of paradoxical response that Bernadette experienced from her neighbors allowed them to maintain their perception of personal security, even within the context of their respective fears. Her bold claims about crime, along with the tacit implications about Southwark being the source of that crime, however, made it difficult, if not impossible, for Queen Villagers to continue to effectively deny the issues of danger and criminality in their neighborhood. For doing this, she was roundly vilified by both Queen Village and Southwark residents as a racist and viewed as being extremely detrimental to the fragile relationship that exists between these two groups. The latter claim is undoubtedly true, for she made it nearly impossible for residents to not notice the thin, tense line that sustains their largely peaceful neighborhood. The end result was that the neighborhood was unable to deal with the challenge that Bernadette represented; feeling isolated and attacked by the very neighbors she believed she was trying to protect, she and her husband moved out of the area.

In Queen Village and Southwark Plaza, residents continue to struggle to define and understand themselves, their relationship to one another, and their relationship to their environment. They constantly deal with new challenges that arise in ways that allow for the continued existence of this complex group. The strategy of sustaining ambiguity and dissonance allows this diverse and eclectic urban neighborhood to function more or less on a day-to-day basis. In so doing, however, residents have unfortunately obscured and neglected one of the most pressing and urgent problems they face: They have been unable to honestly and adequately address the very much-needed renovations to Southwark Plaza. Moreover, Queen Village and Southwark have both alienated individual residents who have come forward to try to directly confront the unspeakable. The result is that the development has continued to deteriorate and has damaged both the lives and properties of nearly everyone in and near to it. This "schizophrenic" behavior, although providing some benefit for the neighborhood in the short run, is ultimately counterproductive in that it assures that the concrete, material problems faced by residents of Southwark and the surrounding Queen Village neighborhood are never adequately addressed or dealt with, nor are the confoundingly difficult underlying issues of poverty, racism, and crime. With the crucial redevelopment of Southwark hanging in the balance, the very dynamics that sustain this group threaten to destroy it.

CONCLUSION

In this case study, I have closely examined the complex nature of the borders of a bona fide group. I have argued that the physical context for group life and, consequently, the ensuing physical availability of group members to one another, is more than incidental to the construction and maintenance of borders. By both enabling and constraining opportunities for everyday interaction and influence between and among group members, spatial relationships play a dramatic role in the way in which populations connect with and differentiate themselves from one another. As borders shift and turn and alliances are created and then fade away, group tensions are at once exacerbated and managed. The management of these tensions is a normal part of everyday group life. Together, these forces of attraction and repulsion, of unity and distinction, make for a continual dance of group definition. This ongoing, fluid negotiation process may affect a group's long-term vitality as the concrete existence of people's lives is held in the balance.

REFERENCES

Adelman, M. B., & Frey, L. R. (1997). *The fragile community: Living together with AIDS*. Mahwah, NJ: Lawrence Erlbaum Associates.

Agnew, J. A., & Duncan, J. S. (1989). *The power of place: Bringing together geographical and sociological imaginations*. Boston: Unwin Hyman.

Altman, I., & Lowe, S. M. (Eds.). (1992). *Place attachment*. New York: Plenum Press.

Barge, J. K., & Frey, L. R. (1997). Life in a task group. In L. R. Frey & J. K. Barge (Eds.), *Managing group life: Communicating in decision-making groups* (pp. 29–51). Boston: Houghton Mifflin.

Bellah, R. N., Madsen, R., Sullivan, W. M., Swidler, A., & Tipton, S. M. (1986). *Habits of the heart: Individualism and commitment in American life* (2nd ed.). New York: Harpers & Row.

Brown, S. R. (1990). *Community attachment in a racially integrated neighborhood*. Unpublished doctoral dissertation, University of Pennsylvania, Philadelphia.

Carey, J. (1992). *Communication as culture: Essays on media and society* (2nd ed.). New York: Routledge.

Durkheim, E. (1984). *Division of labor in society* (W. D. Halls, Trans.). New York: Free Press.

Durkheim, E. (1995). *Elementary forms of religious life* (K. E. Fields, Trans.). New York: Free Press.

Fischer, C. S. (1984). *The urban experience*. San Diego, CA: Harcourt Brace Jovanovich.

Gerson, K., Stueve, C. A., & Fischer, C. S. (1977). Attachment to place. In C. S. Fischer, R. Jackson, C. A. Stueve, K. Gerson, & L. Jones (Eds.), *Networks and places: Social relations in the urban setting* (pp. 139–162). New York: Free Press.

Ginsberg, Y. (1985). Attachment to a neighborhood: The women's responses in an Israeli new town. *Ekistics, 310*, 45–50.

Harper, S. (1988). Rural reference groups and images of place. In D. C. D. Pocock (Ed.), *Humanistic approaches in geography* (pp. 32–49). Durham, NC: University of Durham, Department of Geography.

Hayden, D. (1990). Using ethnic history to understand urban landscapes. *Places, 7*, 11–17.

Hayden, D. (1995). *The power of place: Urban landscapes as public history*. Cambridge, MA: MIT Press.

Hufford, M. (1986). *One space, many places: Folklife and land use in New Jersey's Pinelands National Reserve: Report and recommendation to the New Jersey Pinelands Commission for cultural conservation in the Pinelands National Reserve*. Washington, DC: American Folklife Center.

Hunter, A. (1974). *Symbolic communities: The persistence and change of Chicago's local communities*. Chicago: University of Chicago Press.

Johnson, S. D., & Long, L. (2002). "Being a part and being apart": Dialectics and group communication. In L. R. Frey (Ed.), *New directions in group communication* (pp. 25–41). Thousand Oaks, CA: Sage.

Kasarda, J., & Janowitz, M. (1982). Community attachment in mass society. *American Sociological Review, 39*, 28–39.

Krase, J. (1982). *Self and community in the city*. Washington, DC: University Press of America.

Lofland, L. H. (1973). *A world of strangers: Order and action in urban public space*. New York: Basic Books.

Massey, D. (1994). *Space, place and gender*. Minneapolis: University of Minnesota Press.

Putnam, L. L., & Stohl, C. (1990). Bona fide groups: A reconceptualization of groups in context. *Communication Studies, 41*, 248–265.

Putnam, L. L., & Stohl, C. (1996). Bona fide groups: An alternative perspective for communication and small group decision making. In R. Y. Hirokawa & M. S. Poole (Eds.), *Communication and group decision making* (2nd ed., pp. 147–178). Thousand Oaks, CA: Sage.

Putnam, R. D. (1995). Bowling alone: America's declining social capital. *Journal of Democracy, 6*, 65–78.

Ryden, K. C. (1993). *Mapping the invisible landscape: Folklore, writing and the sense of place*. Iowa City: University of Iowa Press.

Smith, K. K., & Berg, D. N. (1987). *Paradoxes of group life: Understanding conflict, paralysis, and movement in group dynamics*. San Francisco: Jossey-Bass.

Stohl, C., & Putnam, L. L. (1994). Group communication in context: Implications for the study of bona fide groups. In L. R. Frey (Ed.), *Group communication in context: Studies of natural groups* (pp. 285–292). Hillsdale, NJ: Lawrence Erlbaum Associates.

Suttles, G. D. (1968). *The social order of the slum: Ethnicity and territory in the inner city*. Chicago: University of Chicago Press.

Suttles, G. D. (1972). *The social construction of communities*. Chicago: University of Chicago Press.

Tuan, Y-F. (1977). *Space and place: The perspective of experience*. Minneapolis: University of Minnesota Press.

II

COMMUNITY GROUPS: ENGAGING IN GROUP DECISION MAKING, DELIBERATION, AND DEVELOPMENT

3

A MULTICULTURAL, INTERGENERATIONAL YOUTH PROGRAM: CREATING AND SUSTAINING A YOUTH COMMUNITY GROUP

Sharon Howell
Oakland University

Bernard Brock
Eric Hauser
Wayne State University

Voluntary activist groups play an important role in building a strong community, but like many other naturally emerging groups, they face the challenge of attracting and maintaining members within an ever-changing environment. These challenges are significantly magnified for inner-city activist groups, as lack of resources, pressures from family, and competition with other necessary activities, to name a few, are all greater in the pressure cooker of the inner city. Perhaps because of these very challenges, the need for constructive community groups is also greater.

This study explores a group of inner-city adult and youth volunteers who came together in response to the twin concerns of youth violence and urban decay. To understand the evolution of this group, we examine how ideology, structure, and strategies emerged as the group responded to and attempted to alter its social context. We draw primarily on Putnam and Stohl's (1990, 1996; Stohl & Putnam, 1994) treatment of the bona fide group perspective, especially their concepts of the permeability of group boundaries and the impact of the context on group identity and experience. We also draw on Bormann's (1972, 1985) theory of rhetorical vision in examining ideology, and Poole, Seibold, and McPhee's (1985) work when discussing structure and decision-making strategies.

Two of the authors have been involved in this group from its inception. We had been working as members of a community group protesting casino gambling, participating in anticrack house marches, and hosting town meetings and public discussions of development issues. In the course of these activities, the idea of *Detroit Summer* was formed. Howell served as cochairperson of the group, and Brock attended many of the events and discussions.

Detroit Summer is a multicultural youth movement engaged in redeveloping the city of Detroit. Since 1992, youth volunteers from Detroit and around the country have come together for 4 weeks during the summer to work in small groups on collaborative projects such as turning vacant lots into playgrounds, creating murals and other public art, planting urban gardens, and rehabilitating homes. Through these projects, young people challenge themselves, learn about each other, and join with adults to explore questions of personal identity, urban development, and the creation of meaningful lives and livelihoods. In this chapter, we share the story of Detroit Summer.

IDEOLOGY: COMMITMENT TO BUILDING COMMUNITY

Detroit Summer was created by a small group of volunteer community activists who—coming from differing backgrounds, ethnicities, and life experiences—shared an ideology rooted in the belief that community redevelopment was essential to secure a more human, compassionate, and productive future. These volunteers created a loosely structured organization that has grown from a hopeful idea to a sustained program that both develops youth leaders and contributes to the revitalization of Detroit.

Detroit Summer emerged as a natural political group in relation to a larger social context and had an ideology of communitarianism as its motivating force. It began in response to growing concern in the community about the future of children. In the late 1980s, youth violence was at an all-time high in Detroit. City newspapers reported almost daily on shootings in schools and neighborhoods, which were often the result of one young person trying to steal another's shoes, jacket, or jewelry. Crack houses were a common sight and attracted young people as users, dealers, and runners. As unemployment soared, many youth perceived there to be value in a short but lucrative career in the drug business.

At the same time, across the city, citizen initiatives to reclaim streets and restore and protect parks and libraries abandoned by a cash-strapped budget sprung up. The failure of downtown development to spark often-promised renewal and the abandonment of the city by industrial job providers resulted in many neighborhoods having to organize themselves, taking over what had formerly been the province of municipal government. Most often elders and younger women, who were determined to overcome the growing violence and steady decay that marked their local community, led these initiatives. The two questions with which these community members were most concerned were how to rebuild the city and what to do about the young people. This type of sensitivity to the social context is one of the primary characteristics of bona fide groups (see Putnam & Stohl, 1990, 1996) and captures the evolution of Detroit Summer as a group that strives to understand and respond to the shifting forces influencing urban life. These forces helped to weave the "tapestry of group experiences" (Stohl & Putnam, 1994, p. 288) that became Detroit Summer.

The social context framing these issues was captured by Grace Boggs (1998), one of the founders of Detroit Summer and a community activist for more than 50 years, who said in an account of the beginnings of the group:

> Since the invasion of crack in 1985, thousands of young people have become part of the "drug economy," bringing a tremendous increase in violence. But out of the depths of a city in crisis, a new spirit of struggle and solidarity is stirring at the grass-roots. The turning point was in 1986–87. In 1986, 43 children were killed and 365 children were shot in street violence. As a result, wherever people got together informally in the black community the discussion eventually got around to the question, "what is happening to our young people?" (p. 50)

Boggs was part of a small group of activists who were organizing a number of community-building efforts during that time. Some of those activists worked to stop efforts to bring casino gambling into Detroit; some worked against child violence; some worked on artistic and cultural projects designed to engage people in thinking about the future; some marched in neighborhoods to protest crack houses; and some joined the newly emerging U.S. Green party. All shared a belief that cities could no longer look to big business or big government to solve their problems; community members had to develop their own solutions. Many of these activists joined together in a loose coalition to develop a People's Festival to be held in November of 1991 that would highlight the community-building initiatives of ordinary people and promote alternative courses of development within Detroit based on neighborhood revitalization.

Although few would have articulated it at the time, the members of this coalition shared an ideology of communitarianism that grew out of their desire and experience of placing the needs of neighborhood life ahead of the demands by business interests for downtown development. The slogan of the People's Festival highlighted key shared values: building a city of compassion, peace, productivity, cooperation, and joy. Self-reliance, social responsibility, respect of difference, and the need for imaginative thinking to solve problems of the city were recurring themes of the festival. The common ground provided by group members' experiences as activists and the problems they faced fostered identification with this ideology (see Cheney, 1983).

At the festival, James Boggs, an internationally known writer and speaker with deep roots in the labor and Black power movements, gave a keynote speech that emphasized the idea of *active citizenship*. He issued a challenge to the young people of the 1990s to respond to the plight of cities such as Detroit in the same way that their counterparts in the civil rights struggle during the 1960s had responded to the call for Freedom Summer.

This speech articulated the outline of what became the core "rhetorical vision" (Bormann, 1972) uniting the ideology, organizational structure, and strategies of Detroit Summer. According to Bormann (1985):

> A rhetorical vision is a unified putting-together of the various scripts that gives the participants a broader view of things. Rhetorical visions are often integrated by the sharing of a dramatizing message that contains a master analogy, which pulls the various elements together into a more or less elegant and meaningful whole. (p. 133)

As we show in the following section, a "group consciousness" began to take shape among the members of Detroit Summer that revolved around the value of rebuilding community, a process that Bormann (1985) called *symbolic convergence*.

Rebuilding Community

Following the People's Festival, a small group of five activists, who had a history of working together, took responsibility for shaping the idea of a Detroit Summer, which was modeled after Mississippi Freedom Summer. Mississippi Freedom Summer became the master analogy for the Detroit group and enabled the members to characterize their effort as a radical, direct, and imaginative response to injustice and dehumanization. Clementine Barfield, founder of Save Our Sons and Daughters (SOSAD), Paul Stark and Shea Howell of Detroit Greens and Detroiters Uniting (an anticasino gambling group), and James and Grace Boggs gathered at the Boggs's home in early December 1991. They wrote a letter inviting about 100 community leaders to discuss the idea on January 15, 1992, in honor of Martin Luther King, Jr.'s birthday and invoking the image of Freedom Summer.

That meeting, hastily rescheduled after a snowstorm, attracted over 60 individuals representing grassroots activists, the arts communities, public broadcasting, unions, educators, and environmentalists. They reflected the ethnic mix of Detroit and ranged in age from their late 20s to early 70s. This group expanded and contracted over the next 6 months. Almost everyone who joined did so because of his or her concern for young people and many were active in other community organizations that served youth. Almost everyone belonged to other community groups and represented established constituencies. This characteristic of bona fide groups (see Putnam & Stohl, 1990, 1996) brought energy, resources, and commitment to the new group.

The meeting was an open forum where people talked about creating something that would rekindle the spirit young people had demonstrated during the civil rights struggle. The group began to coalesce around the rhetorical vision of Freedom Summer, which became the group's master analogy and provided common ground for the members. With this sense of shared mission, the group moved cautiously ahead, exploring the possibilities of a program. Participants spoke of attracting a diverse group of young people that would reflect the racial and ethnic make-up of the entire city. They also talked about the limitations of programs that brought volunteers from elsewhere into such city endeavors. They had seen such volunteers pick up trash or paint houses while local youth made fun of them.

To counter this potential problem, the group agreed that Detroit youth needed to take a leadership role in any efforts. This led to a heated discussion of the merits of volunteer versus paid participation. Some thought that the only way to attract young people was to offer money. James Boggs, however, spoke persuasively in favor of volunteerism. Reminding people of Freedom Summer, he pointed out that the civil rights movement resulted from people struggling together to bring a vision to life, not from paid jobs. He argued that it was a disservice to foster the idea that youth should be paid for everything they did. Boggs thought that Detroit Summer should be an opportunity for youth to take responsibility for the larger community by contributing their hearts, hands, and imagination to rebuilding the city. The group ultimately agreed to make the effort voluntary. In the spirit of self-reliance, it then took up a collection among the attendees to establish some working funds. The participants divided into working subgroups and returned the following week with plans to invite 14- to 25-year-olds in the city and around the country to participate as volunteers on community projects.

Throughout this initial discussion and subsequent meetings, issues of race, the role of young people, social responsibility, and self-reliance were discussed in terms of practical actions that would create the framework for the program. The meetings were advertised in local newspapers and usually attracted 30 to 40 people; a stable core of about 15 people were present at each meeting to provide some continuity. Everyone was welcome to participate in the discussions. Out of these meetings, the basic direction of the program was established. The group explicitly decided that Detroit Summer would be multicultural, focus primarily on Detroiters, develop leadership during the course of engaging in action, work out differences collectively, look to each other for resources, create intergenerational ties, and promote the social consciousness of youth. The Detroit Summer group, thus, unified around a vision for collective action and created an "organic center" (Stohl & Putnam, 1994, p. 289) out of which new initiatives could be created and implemented.

The formal and informal structure of this group took shape in and from an interactive process. The following discussion shows, as Poole et al. (1985) suggested, that consensus was achieved by basing decisions on agreed-on principles.

Consensus Decision Making

Decisions were made informally after group discussion. Because the group had agreed to launch the program in July 1992, members felt an urgency that made decision making more important than unending discussion (see Sharf, 1978). At the same time, the shifting membership of the general meetings meant that issues and the decisions made about them were often brought back for discussion as new people joined the group. Tensions began to emerge between those who attended weekly and those who came irregularly. These tensions resulted from the problem of trying to socialize members at different points as the group simultaneously moved forward quickly with its task decisions. As Anderson, Riddle, and Martin (1999) made clear, fluctuating group membership requires incorporating new people into existing norms, while simultaneously acknowledging that these individuals have an effect on the functioning of the group. The pressures created by the short time period to complete tasks and the continuing emphasis in the city on the crisis of youth contributed to the group's willingness to develop structures and processes for listening to one another and making decisions through participatory, democratic processes that fostered a high degree of group-member commitment (see Poole et al., 1985). As Berteotti and Seibold (1994) observed, both group member "interdependence" and "coordination" are fostered when the task requires members to work with one another.

Although the fluctuating membership was problematic at times, it did enable the group to draw on and renew resources necessary to carrying out tasks. Newcomers were socialized, in part, through what became the ritual reciting of the group's history and purpose. Anderson et al. (1999) pointed to the important role that this type of communication process can play in helping a group to address tensions and create a shared culture.

Each meeting began with Grace Boggs providing a summary of why group members had come together and the key agreements reached thus far. This narrative, sometimes augmented by others, enabled participants to feel connected to the project and to see the progress that had been made. This communication practice, thus, helped to create a necessary balance between socialization and the ability of the collective to move forward with the tasks.

Within a few weeks, the group wrote a call seeking young people willing to volunteer; created an application process; handled logistics such as housing and transportation; and established committees dealing with media relations, programming, finance, and recruitment. These four committees were coordinated by a steering committee composed of representatives from the committees. Major policy decisions were made in biweekly open forums of the entire group membership.

Members of these committees drew on their own resources and community connections. Individuals and organizations donated photocopying, meeting space, telephones, and materials. A local youth theater donated a corner of its suite for an office, the public television station housed the first program meetings, and an Episcopal church offered space for larger gatherings. Community organizations and Wayne State University provided mailing and copying services. Individual committee members served as "boundary spanners" (Putnam & Stohl, 1990), obtaining resources from other organizations and helping to coordinate interorganizational activities.

Along with physical resources, participants who were parents or grandparents offered, on the basis of their previous community-building efforts, perspectives for decision making that were carefully considered by the group as a whole. At the biweekly meetings, people argued over the age limits for recruits, what types of projects and programs to support and create, ratio of city-to-outside youth, and supervision and rules for youth volunteers. Many participants framed issues in terms of their own experience, asking what it would take for them to be willing to send their own child to this unknown program.

Social Legitimacy

Out of these discussions, the question of how to establish legitimacy for the program became central. After much consideration, the group decided to ask well-established local groups identified with successful community activity to endorse the effort. SOSAD, Attic Theatre, Neighborhood Information Exchange, 4-H Urban Gardening, Core City Neighborhood, Warren Connor Development Coalition, Arab Community Center for Economic and Social Services, and the First Unitarian Universalist Church were among the local groups selected. These groups represented a broad ethnic and cultural spectrum; however, most were not known outside of the metropolitan Detroit area.

To establish national legitimacy, the group decided to contact nationally recognized activists. Instrumental in contacting individuals likely to be known on the national scale were James Boggs, a well-respected African American leader; Richard Feldman, who had maintained ties with leaders from the antiwar movement; and Clementine Barfield, whose organization for mothers was beginning to get national recognition as a symbol of antiviolence.

First among these prominent figures contacted were actors Ossie Davis and Ruby Dee, who had been friends of Boggs since 1963 and the publication of his text, *The American Revolution: Pages from a Negro Worker's Notebook*. Manning Marable, Ron Daniels, David Hahn-Baker, Richard Moore, and Cornel West joined soon thereafter. Ultimately, the national endorsers numbered 20 and reflected in many ways the multicultural vision of the program. They included 6 women and 14 men and 11 African Americans, 2 Asian Americans, 1 Native American, 2 Hispanics, and 4 European Americans. Organizational affiliation included the Southwest Network for Environmental and Economic Justice, the Greens, Institute for Policy Studies, National Wildlife Federation, and Workman's Circle. These endorsers were listed on the group's letterhead and in its leaflets. To maintain the group's ideological commitment to Detroit, local organizations were placed first in all publications.

By early June 1992, the coordinating group solidified its membership to about 25 people, all of whom were involved in various concrete tasks. They began a fundraising campaign and secured a commitment from the national Green movement for money to hire a full-time coordinator. Primary leadership was provided by Sharon Campbell, an African American woman from Wayne State University's Department of Urban Studies, and Shea Howell, a European American community activist working with Detroiters Uniting, WePros (anticrack house marchers), and national and local Greens. They were elected as cochairs at a general meeting and facilitated the biweekly gatherings. All policy decisions continued to be decided in the open forums on the basis of discussion and eventual consensus.

The membership, leadership, organizational structure, and public support were intended to reflect the values embodied in the rhetorical vision of Detroit Summer. Members' understanding of the legitimacy of the group was consciously tied to how it functioned (i.e., by democratic principles) and how it represented itself to the public.

In April 1992, the city of Los Angeles erupted in response to the Rodney King verdict. After decades of neglect, the plight of large cities was forced to the forefront of national consciousness. Although Detroit Summer emerged out of local community activism, the group was able to respond quickly to this national event by portraying Detroit Summer as a direct alternative for action to those who wanted to intervene in the fate of cities. The call the group issued for volunteers was headlined, "If You Want to Save Our Cities, Detroit's the Place to be this Summer." The introduction said:

> All over the country people are agonizing over how to rebuild Los Angeles after the days of outrage precipitated by the Rodney King verdict. But LA is only the tip of the iceberg. The same challenge is faced by other U.S. cities abandoned by the Federal government and by multinational corporations who invest overseas to make more profit with cheaper labor.... In Detroit, we have come to the conclusion that if our city is going to be rebuilt, it will have to be done by the people themselves, especially our young people. (Boggs, 1998, p. 7)

The text of the flyer drew on images of the past and provided a vision for the future, saying:

> In the spirit of Mississippi Voter Registration Project of 1964, Detroit Summer '92 will draw national attention to recivilizing our cities as the number one priority of our period. It will encourage young people at the local and national level to take responsibilities for our communities, our cities, and our country. It will create a fellowship between generations and make clear that the devastation of American cities is not "their" problem but "ours." It will let the world know that together we can overcome. (Boggs, 1988, p. 7)

The call resulted in many applications and the program began with about 60 volunteer youth, just over half of them from Detroit. Others came through the SOSAD network, in response to the leaflets that had been handed out at national labor and civil rights marches, and through personal contacts with professors at the universities and colleges of Antioch, Michigan, Bard, and Dartmouth.

The ideology of assuming social responsibility, engaging in democratic decision making, and creating multicultural, multigenerational connections was central to the decisions made by the steering group to include young people at every level of the program. The cohesiveness among members produced by this vision added to the sense of their individual and collective identification with a set of core values. It also had important effects on the structure of the group.

STRUCTURE: AN EVOLVING, FLEXIBLE ORGANIZATION

The pattern set in the early planning meetings continued throughout the program: Major decisions made in open forums became an integral part of the ongoing structure. However, meetings were no longer publicized; instead, the core of adults stabilized and expanded to include all the youth volunteers. Conscious efforts were made by the adults to recede into the background for the purpose of encouraging youth to speak; consequently, the youth became part of the planning and development of all subsequent efforts and, thereby, developed their leadership skills. Tracey Hollins, a 17-year-old African American volunteer who began with the first group of volunteers, wrote in 1995:

> One of the issues that was immediately decided upon was the incorporation of youth in the programming of Detroit Summer was a necessity. As a result, I and other Detroit youth were thrust into the world of leadership. We took on responsibilities of organizing, and recruiting youth locally and nationwide. From our biweekly meetings came new ideals of organization and cultural events that would be beneficial to the program and its participants. Also from these sessions came the statement of what we really are. Detroit summer is a multicultural, intergenerational youth program/movement designed to rebuild, respirit and redefine Detroit from the ground up! (p.1)

Critical to the development of the youth's leadership skills, especially their feeling that their actions were making a difference, were the community-based projects selected by the group. The initial steering committee agreed that projects should be visible, doable, and have broad-based community support. Using these criteria, the group selected projects for turning vacant lots into children's parks and neighborhood gardens, creating murals in neighborhoods plagued with graffiti, working with neighborhoods to organize efforts to reduce violence, and engaging in environmentally conscious activities.

The youth had a great deal of autonomy in making decisions about these projects. They were responsible for the organization and development of each specific project and shaped the discussions, workshops, and dialogues for themselves and for the group as a whole. Empowering the youth in this way contributed to the effort to include young people within the decision-making processes and structure.

Loose Structure

The desire for harmony among what had become a series of subgroups called for a flexible organizational structure. A loose operating structure evolved that stressed agreement and willingness between group members to work together on tasks. These became group norms.

At the same time, the large general meetings became difficult to sustain. People with other organizational responsibilities were unable to attend regularly and some individuals who had major disagreements with the direction of the group withdrew rather than create extreme tension or contest leadership. Meanwhile, new people continued to arrive and needed to be socialized. The general meetings continued to generate for participants a sense of excitement about the idea of Detroit Summer but became impractical as a method of making policy decisions or coordinating the various committees. The constantly shifting membership required renegotiation of decisions already made and repetition of the basic history of the group. The result was that a small group emerged to take responsibility for the day-to-day organization of the effort. As Anderson et al. (1999) suggested in their overview of group socialization processes, this process of constant assimilation of new members not only moved the group as a whole forward to its tasks but also produced a culture where initiative, flexibility, and open communication were essential.

Sharon Campbell and Shea Howell continued to cochair these small meetings, which included Donald Softly, who was responsible for selecting projects; Michelle Brown and Lawton James, who handled publicity; Clementine Barfield and Ray Cooper, in charge of recruitment; Paul Stark, who handled logistics; Grace Boggs, who worked on programming; and Jackie Victor, in charge of finances. Six African Americans, three European Americans and one Chinese American—six women and four men—ranging from their mid 20s to late 70s in age comprised the group.

Beginning in April 1992, they met weekly, both as a group and with other volunteers in subcommittees. Added to the group was Gwen Heard, as a full-time director for the project, and John Barfield, the son of the founder of SOSAD, as her assistant. Heard, Barfield, and Howell became the day-to-day leadership. They continued, however, to emphasize the autonomy of the youth, who were responsible for project organization and development and who were encouraged to shape and direct the educational and social programs.

Core Leadership With Youth Involvement

At the end of the first summer, the group of active adults and youth met to evaluate their efforts. They felt that Detroit Summer had accomplished its goals. Detroit Summer demonstrated that youth cared about rebuilding the city and, if given the opportunity, were more than willing to become part of that effort. The next question was whether to continue. In discussing this decision, the ideas of the youth volunteers were given the most consideration. Their expressed view of the experience affirmed their acceptance of the rhetorical vision that shaped the effort. Echoing the core values of the ideology, Tracey Hollins (1992) connected her volunteer work to her own personal development and to the development of the community when she wrote in the group's newsletter, *The Commitment*:

> When most people heard about Detroit Summer their initial statement was, "You don't get paid?" To them working for no money was crazy, and

volunteerism seemed to be a foreign language. They didn't understand that a smiling child's face and friends for life were better compensation than wages.

A paycheck continues to cloud the minds of young adults who have been taught that money is everything. Teens continuously walk the streets not noticing the trash and not caring about the graffiti. Most don't realize the importance of putting a piece of paper in its right place. They have kept the mentality that one person can't make a difference. Detroit Summer was the perfect cure. (p. 1)

Participants felt that their efforts altered the popular image of youth in the city. The youth felt that they were part of a new vision that offered a viable alternative to the money-driven perspective on community involvement. Furthermore, the projects made a visible contribution in the various neighborhoods: Vegetables and flowers grew in place of weeds, a ball field had been uncovered from a vacant dumping ground, and a mural stood out in sharp contrast to graffiti-covered walls. The slogan suggested by the participating youth for the coming summers was, "You can make a difference."

The group agreed to host the program for a second year but to establish no ongoing organization. Heard was returning to school, as was Barfield; Sharon Campbell had become pregnant and chose not to continue as cochair; Donald Softly had withdrawn prior to the arrival of the volunteers; and Ray Cooper was becoming increasingly ill due to complications from AIDS. Michelle Brown agreed to be the next year's cochair with Shea Howell, which would continue African American and European American leadership while the group decided how to proceed. James and Grace Boggs remained committed, as did Paul Stark, Jackie Victor, and several youth volunteers, including Tracey Hollins, Julia Pointer, Becca Dorn, Chris Shine, Michael Fueri, and Cara Graninger.

In preparing for the second Detroit Summer, the structure of the group remained flexible. Meetings were held in the late afternoon or on weekends so that participating youth volunteers could attend after school. Decisions about recruitment, programming, projects, and fundraising were based on both adult and youth input. The youth volunteers were encouraged to speak to their peers at schools and community forums. They worked with the adult members to design a brochure and flyers about the program and established the tasks that needed to be accomplished for another year. During this period, an unstated standard of membership in the group began to develop: Only those who actively worked with the program were encouraged to participate in its development.

About 50 youth were again recruited and new adult volunteers were also brought in to work on specific projects. John Gruchala, a community activist on the east side of the city, proposed building a community greenhouse; Jim Stone met with the southwest Clark Park citizens' group and agreed to work with a master artist on creating an elaborate sports mural;

local activists Jane Kyriakopolos and Hassan provided transportation for youth volunteers to and from project sites; and Gwyn Kirk, a feminist and peace activist from Antioch University who was connected to Howell and Boggs, volunteered to cook community dinners.

By the end of the second summer, the group decided to establish permanent offices in a local Unitarian church. Eden Winter, an adult volunteer, managed the office. A small group met monthly to coordinate ongoing fundraising and planning efforts, and to develop the next summer's program. This group included Joe Jones, a 23-year-old African American man who had volunteered the previous summer to supervise the group housing provided for out-of-town volunteers. Michelle Brown, Shea Howell, Grace Boggs, Eden Winter, Julia Pointer, Becca Dorn, Tracey Hollins, and Cara Graninger completed the group.

Large, open meetings were no longer held; instead, the group planned one large community meeting about 3 weeks before the beginning of the program to generate ideas and excitement, but responsibility for daily organizing shifted to the smaller group. It claimed its legitimacy from the full and public participation of the youth volunteers and the work they had accomplished.

At the end of the third summer, the core group of leaders decided that Detroit Summer was not going away. There was a strong working group of nearly 30 adults and 15 youth committed to continuing. At the evaluation meeting in the fall, this group decided to form a nonprofit organization. This shift in formal incorporation, however, had little effect on the informal structure of the organization.

Summer Volunteer Community Program

The decision-making and planning structure of this group now depended on two additional elements: (a) project-based work teams and (b) leadership development programs. Both were designed to encourage the development of youth leadership skills, provide opportunities for them to engage in democratic decision making, and enhance their communication abilities.

Projects, although proposed by community groups, were turned over to youth volunteer teams. Those teams had full responsibility for organizing, planning, and securing materials for their projects. Adult support was available if needed, but the projects were in their hands. If a vacant lot was to become a park, the youth teams decided how that would happen. The skills necessary for engaging in these activities—such as listening, evaluating ideas, organizing volunteers and neighborhoods, and structuring work—were developed through the course of actually working together on concrete, visible projects. During the course of planning and executing these projects, issues of race, class, and gender quickly emerged. To deal with these issues, youth volunteers who had participated in the program during previous summers provided leadership. Jackie Victor and Joe Jones were able to provide a link to the older community members who had initiated the program, and Julia Pointer, Becca Dorn, Chris Shine, and Cara Graninger, all returning youth volunteers and active planners, encouraged new youth volunteers to deal constructively with tensions as they arose. Social issues were especially potentially divisive, so older youth volunteers organized and conducted workshops and held special meetings to encourage the whole group to discuss these issues and to decide how they would be dealt with on an individual and collective level.

Weekly meetings open only to the youth volunteers were held. These meetings had little formal structure. Volunteers were encouraged to talk about what things were going well and what was proving difficult. These forums gave the more mature young people the opportunity to provide to the new youth volunteers advice on organizing and working together. Leadership, thus, emerged through these sessions on an experiential basis. Actions, and evaluation of and accountability for those actions, were enacted through the projects and discussion of the task and social processes.

This emergent group process placed real power in the hands of young people—they controlled the resources and made decisions about things that mattered to them. This democratic process, as demonstrated in other groups (see Poole et al., 1985), reinforced their participation in the larger group discussions.

This shifting of power was given a deeper dimension through the guided educational experiences provided by the structured intergenerational dialogues and workshops. Although there was no question that Detroit Summer was youth centered, early in the planning, members agreed that one of the limitations of the youth movement of the 1960s had been the communication gap between older and younger activists. Organizers of Detroit Summer were very conscious of age segregation in the communities of Detroit. To overcome this gap and provide opportunities for people of various ages to share experiences, they created intergenerational dialogues. In these dialogues, community leaders were invited to simply talk about why they had chosen to live their lives as activists. People talked in personal terms, sharing a sense of history through their experiences. The sessions stressed dialogue and emphasized that all of the group's members had important things to share and learn from one another.

For example, in one of the first dialogues on the civil rights struggle, activists who had been part of the early Student Nonviolent Coordinating Committee movement were asked to speak. Among them was Gloria House, who told of being arrested along with about six other group members in a small southern town, released at night, and forced off the jail property. As soon as they were off the property, gunfire erupted, killing the man next to her and injuring another. After telling the story she said, "You know when you see someone killed, it changes you forever."

When she was finished, several adults began to speak, but the facilitator of the dialogue, Ray Cooper, stopped them, saying simply, "Let's hear from the young people first." Into the silence that followed came the shaky voice of Devron, a 15-year-old exgang member from Fresno, California. He said, "I know. When I saw my cousin die, then I knew I had to do something different." From these two stories of tragic death, separated by more than 25 years in time, young people and adults were able to talk together about profoundly important and meaningful issues.

Although not all of the dialogues held achieved this sense of emotional power, they reinforced the premise that everyone had something to say and offer. As the dialogues developed, leadership was more and more formally given to the youth volunteers, who selected the themes and contacted speakers, framed the discussions, and became active participants. Although adult support was available, these sessions were primarily in the hands of young people.

STRATEGIES: BRINGING DIVERSE INDIVIDUALS TOGETHER

The stable leadership group developed a number of strategies to integrate new individuals, especially youth, into the program. Of central importance were the idea of community, the notion of social responsibility, and the need to address issues of race, class, gender, and sexual orientation in open and constructive ways. Commitment to these core values as demonstrated by completing practical tasks contributed to a richly textured sense of identity that enabled group members to find common ground within their differences. The culture of the group was conveyed, as in many groups (see Anderson et al., 1999), through rites, rituals, heroes, and stories. The group decided to highlight its values in the ritual of an opening ceremony.

Opening Ceremony

The first strategy on which the group decided was to create an event marking the beginning of each year that would socialize new volunteers into the vision of the group. The event drew on the master analogy of Freedom Summer to impart to the members the significance of their participation. It also served to demonstrate the broad-based support in the community that existed for these volunteers.

Several key features became almost ritualized in these opening ceremonies. First, the philosophy of the program was presented by one of the elders. For the first two summers, Jimmy Boggs, although ill with cancer, spoke about the origins of Detroit Summer. He talked about how people initially thought that the group was crazy for inviting young people to volunteer, the challenge for African American Detroit youth to share leadership with many different kinds of people who volunteered, and his hope that they would work together to better their communities.

A second recurring element of the opening ceremonies was the acknowledgment of the youth leaders. Volunteers from the previous years were given the opportunity to talk about their experiences, the meaning of Detroit Summer, and their hopes for the future. In this way, the youth volunteers who had demonstrated leadership abilities were given the visible support of the whole group. Becca Dorn (1993) reflected the leadership emerging among young people when she said:

> We all need to understand that we are not just entering a summer program, we are building a real movement. Like Freedom Summer, we are fighting a prejudice. Today's prejudice is against the inner-city population. It is against Detroit and other cities in crisis. Like the civil rights movement, we are fighting for the right to live in peace, and the right to go to the store or to school without fearing for our lives. We, too, are people from different generations, races, and economic classes, here together for a common goal .... In Detroit Summer, we will learn things that don't allow us to hide .... By the end of these 4 weeks, we will know that we can make a difference, and with that knowledge comes the responsibility. Once you know what you can do, you can't use any more excuses. You can't sit around and complain how these adults are screwing up our world. We become obligated to get off our asses and fix what we don't like.

Third, the opening ceremonies were a way for local communities to welcome volunteers and to give them a sense that they were supported and part of something larger than themselves. Key elders emerged to speak on behalf of the community. Jesse Thomas came to every opening ceremony and talked about the hope she gained seeing youth doing something constructive. In turn, young people talked about what it meant to them to be met every morning at their site by Thomas carrying shovels, rakes, flowers, and food. Young people said she made it impossible for them to feel tired or discouraged. Dorothy Garner, founder of the group that marched against crack houses, spoke powerfully of love and the need to value everyone in the community, lessons she had learned from the young people of Detroit Summer. Jimmy and Grace Boggs spoke of the importance of seeing Detroit Summer as part of a larger movement for social change and transformation. After Jimmy's death in 1993, a videotape made for his memorial service has been played at all of the openings but one. Finally, each ceremony culminated in a community dinner and entertainment.

Workshops on Movement and Vision

The second strategy that the leadership group decided was to hold workshops on social movements and new visions. Grace Boggs and Shea Howell developed these workshops to engage the youth volunteers in thinking expansively and creatively about the city. These workshops sometimes lasted an entire day, and the meeting room was filled with newsprint and charts that redesigned whole neighborhoods. Sometimes, as in 1998, they were an afternoon devoted to groups redesigning abandoned landmarks.

Workshop products were reproduced in the group's newsletters and brochures. For example, a list generated by young people about what constitutes a movement was included in recruiting materials and printed in newsletters to emphasize that Detroit Summer was more than a brief program. Under the heading, "What is a Movement?" it read, "a group of people getting together when they feel things are unjust, seeing things grow and making things different, change that comes with passion" (Boggs, 1998, p. 15).

Tours and Closing Ceremony

The third strategy the group enacted were tours of the city. Youth volunteers went to project sites, historical places, ecological sites that demonstrated good and bad environmental practices, and some of the neighborhoods that had preserved a particular ethnic or cultural heritage. These tours offered a way to talk about the history of Detroit and the significance of Detroit Summer in rebuilding communities. Previous volunteers facilitated these tours, pointing out favorite sites and discussing the program with new volunteers.

The fourth strategy was the closing bicycle tour and ceremony. In keeping with the ecological emphasis of the program, volunteers rode bikes donated by the county's parks and recreation department. They pedaled through the Motor City from site to site, stopping to hear the story from each group of volunteers about what the members had accomplished.

Following the bike tour was a closing ceremony. In contrast to the opening ceremony, the closing ceremony was an intimate gathering of youth volunteers, project leaders, and other adults who had worked closely together throughout the 4 weeks. The program at the ceremony was put together by the youth volunteers and was a time to share creative works, laughs, and commitments for the following summer. Since 1992, it has been held in a backyard near the church that houses much of the Detroit Summer activity. The ceremony provides a sense of closure for all the participants.

Sharing Stories

As Detroit Summer developed, its philosophy was shared through the telling and retelling of stories. These stories, told at opening ceremonies, dinners, and discussions, were shared by and among all the various types of volunteers. A 14-year-old was as likely to tell a story as was an 80-year-old. Although most of these stories were conveyed informally in conversation, some were written down in newsletters and other organizational documents, and some found their way into newspaper accounts of the program.

All of the stories shared supported the ideology and intent of Detroit Summer. Some centered on creating heroes of group members who demonstrated extraordinary commitment, dependability, boldness, and the willingness to encourage other people to become part of the enterprise of rebuilding the city. Although they emphasized individuals and their actions, the stories identified key values for the group as a whole.

Stories held up Jimmy Boggs as one of the founders. His presence in the first 2 years of the program contributed to a sense that Detroit Summer was more than a youth project; it was part of a growing movement to reclaim the city. During the second summer, so ill that he had to be assisted up the stairs to the meeting room with an oxygen tank to help him speak, he inspired the young volunteers and gave them the sense that they were part of history. After his death, his presence continued to be felt, both because young people often quoted him and because many of his writings and speeches were made part of the Detroit Summer text that was given to each volunteer. Because of Boggs and his reputation in the city, Detroit Summer was able to cast itself as radical, outrageous, and audacious.

Jesse Thomas was a central figure in another story. She had lived on the east side of Detroit for more than half a century. Saddened by the deterioration of her city and her block, she came to Detroit Summer for help in cleaning up the junk that she had to see every day. She quickly became a model of community member support. She met volunteers in the morning, worked with them in the heat of the day, and provided food and drink. Her strength and good humor astonished most of the youth, who came to call her "Superwoman."

The story was often told of how Boggs and Thomas combined to work the magic of Beniteau Park. For years, two old trucks sat in the middle of the lots located across the street from where Thomas lived. No one had been able to remove them and they posed a barrier to any serious clean-up of Beniteau Park. With the aid of a neighbor, Boggs managed to start both trucks and drove them off the field to the cheers of the volunteers present, who mowed the area, planted flowers, and built a sandbox and swings. In the fall, volunteers gathered to dedicate the new park. A group of crack dealers watched uneasily from a nearby house. Rather than ignoring them, Boggs called out to them to join the ceremony. He persuaded them that for their own self-respect they should join in the dedication. They did and, subsequently, became important in looking after the field in following years.

Many stories were also told about Gerald Hairston, a man of African and Native American ancestry, who has lived and worked on the east side of Detroit all of his life. He had spent the last 12 years working with a group of elders to create community gardens; they call themselves the "Gardening

Angels." Every morning, he met a group of youth volunteers, took them to neighborhood plots, and helped them to use found lumber, recycled bricks, and chunks of concrete to create beautiful gardens. Every one of the 100-plus gardens they constructed has a story. The one recounted most often is the use of gardens to attack crack houses. Hairston simply arranged to have the manure piles dumped next to their windows (Mindell, 1997).

The various murals created by Detroit Summer volunteers were not only beautiful, they helped to forge community. Stories of their construction were recounted each year. The first mural, done by Ray Jimanez, an artist and exgang member from Fresno, California, encouraged neighbors to work to save Clark Park. Howell recounted the history of this mural in the 1998 Detroit Summer reader, entitled *Building Community*:

> Ray was committed to doing public art as a way to inspire people in the community to work together, to see that they could create something beautiful.... While going down the street, Ray saw an older woman who reminded him of his mother back in California. He ran to catch up to her, and when she turned around, she looked exactly like his mother, only a few years older. It turned out she was his mother's sister who had left California for Detroit over twenty years ago. She had lost touch with her sister and her family. She invited Ray home to meet his cousins. One of them, Dave Campos, joined in on the mural project and became part of the Clark Park Coalition, a volunteer group organized to protect and preserve the park. Dave said, "If my cousin can come all the way from California to help make Detroit a better place, the least I can do is walk over to the park in my neighborhood." (p. 150)

The stories of the murals became a way to convey to new members the group's commitment to working with local community members, especially those least respected by the dominant culture. The story of the sports mural in 1993 was a reflection of the group's concern with young men in gangs. After graffiti was discovered all over the newly painted primer on the walls of a park building, Detroit Summer leadership

> decided to call together the gangs in the neighborhood to find out why this had happened. Dave Campos knew the leaders and set up a meeting for us. At the meeting, the gang members said they had not realized we were going to do a mural on the building (they thought it was just being painted white). They said they thought the murals were important for the kids in the neighborhood and even though they were rivals in many ways, they would not do anything to take away from the opportunity of the little ones to become involved.
>
> We reprimed the wall, let it dry a day and then started the design. The gangs were true to their word and some even joined in to help. (Howell, 1998, p. 151)

These stories conveyed the shared values and aspirations of the group. They helped members to see themselves as part of an important historical struggle, carrying on an activist tradition and creating something new to improve the lives of their fellow community members.

Gathering Support From Institutions

The success of the group was augmented by the fact that established institutions in Detroit began to seek it out and to look to it as a place to find youth who could serve as leaders and who had something special to contribute to the larger discussion of community issues.

In the first summer, Greenpeace sent a special youth film crew to take a few shots of the program for footage in a documentary it was producing about youth and the environmental crisis. After the visit, Detroit Summer became one of the featured programs in Greenpeace's videotape, *Get it Together*. The following winter, the Detroit Public Broadcasting Service did a documentary series on new work in the postindustrial era and focused on the ideas and lives of Detroit Summer volunteers. At the same time, the steering committee organized public events as a means of recruiting and encouraging young people to think more deeply about issues. Youth speakouts were held throughout Detroit, with Joe Jones and Julia Pointer serving as emcees. Issue-based radio and television interviews were held, including a 3-hour public radio broadcast on education conducted by Detroit Summer youth volunteers. Youth volunteers also became active in conferences and events around the city; for instance, in 1998, Becca Dorn and Julia Pointer provided the main speeches for the citywide International Women's Day celebration. These and other activities were carried on throughout the entire year and accentuated the perception of local community members that Detroit Summer youth had something special to offer the city.

Over the years, Detroit Summer received a good deal of publicity both from television and the print media, with articles appearing in everything from community newsletters to *The Times* of London. These articles enabled the members of this group to see themselves as doing something important not only themselves but for the city and the country. This sense of purpose was captured best in an article by Lessenberry (1997), when he contrasted Detroit Summer with the summer 30 years earlier when the city had been engulfed in rebellion:

> Detroit Summer's goals are both more and less modest. Building a community is, in many ways, vastly harder than fixing a single immensely difficult problem. But they are trying, and in an era when cheap cynicism too often passes for sophistication …. "We have learned that we really can do anything when the community comes together," Angela Jones, a sixteen-year-old Cass Tech junior told me …. Lest she sound like a sociology book, she quickly added, "It is extremely fun, too." (p. 11)

CONCLUSION

As this case study shows, the bona fide group perspective illuminates how a small group of volunteer political activists were successful in creating a youth force that, for 4 weeks every summer, worked on projects to improve Detroit neighborhoods. Anchored in a shared vision, shifting events, and membership changes were strengths that enabled what started as a temporary group to evolve into an ongoing and sustained organization. The success of Detroit Summer teaches us not only a great deal about the nature of small groups but also about the importance of such groups in rebuilding communities.

First and most important, natural political activist groups and organizations have to develop a shared ideology. A shared ideology serves as a guide to defining membership and making decisions and influences the structures and strategies of the group and/or organization. In the case of Detroit Summer, core values of communitarianism, democratic participation, and engagement of people at the community level shaped and continue to shape the organization and its development. The incorporation of the group into a formal organization was a major step in structuring the ideology and the rhetorical vision behind Detroit Summer.

Second, a flexible operational structure is essential for voluntary groups/organizations. An inherent part of the Detroit Summer structure has been the attempt and ability to continually incorporate new participants and perspectives within the dominant ideology and rhetorical vision. This flexibility has enabled the group/organization to attract physical and human resources. Moreover, as the initial group incorporated youth into its decision-making processes, a strong sense of identity with the program among all the participants evolved. In addition, the flexible structure enabled the group to respond to shifts in the larger social context. For example, in response to the Los Angeles uprising, the group repositioned itself from a general response to urban problems to an alternative for direct community action.

Third, strategies consistent with the ideology need to be designed to create and sustain members' commitment to the group's goals and group cohesion. In the case of Detroit Summer, a sense of members' identification with the group that was based on a perceived common ground permeates, for instance, the opening ceremony and, thereby, strengthened the ideology and its appeal. The opening ceremony, in which community leaders welcomed volunteer youth and consciously shared the core values of the group through stories and speeches, was a cornerstone of this program, and served as an important means of socializing new members into the group's values and norms. Other groups may find such practices useful for socializing their new members.

Fourth, to be successful in the long run, a volunteer group/organization needs to create a permanent structure for its core leadership. However, when such a structure begins to take shape, the group/organization risks reducing its flexibility and losing a sense of its ideology. In the case of Detroit Summer, although the core leadership has changed little in the shift from a completely voluntary group to a nonprofit organization, the transition to a more sustained, year-long program raises major questions about purpose, definitions of membership, the role of volunteers, and finances.

Fifth, when a permanent structure is created for a political activist group, a tension may well emerge between the institutional interests of those who value the permanent structure and those who identify with the group's ideology, particularly around the issue of adopting strategies. In the case of Detroit Summer, the shift from relatively large, open meetings to a smaller, more committed core group resulted in some individuals abandoning the effort as undemocratic.

Finally, a group/organization best gains members and maintains their loyalty to the degree that strategies are translated into traditions that give the group/organization an independent life and history separate from its past and current leaders and members. Any enacted vision that develops, therefore, needs to be tied to the group/organization rather than to the leadership to maintain the degree of flexibility that is Detroit Summer's strength. Paradoxically, however, in the case of Detroit Summer, these traditions reduced its flexibility to adapt to the rapid changes in the larger community and to position itself as offering a new way for youth to contribute to resolving the crisis in the city.

Our inspiring experience with Detroit Summer teaches us that people who are very different from each other can find ways to successfully combine their energies to achieve a common goal. Acting together, as a group, members of Detroit Summer created an ideology and rhetorical vision and developed structures and strategies to bring it to life. The lessons learned from this group serve, hopefully, as an inspiration to other bona fide groups.

REFERENCES

Anderson, C. M., Riddle, B. L., & Martin, M. M. (1999). Socialization processes in groups. In L. R. Frey (Ed.), D. S. Gouran, & M. S. Poole (Assoc. Eds.), *The handbook of group communication theory & research* (pp. 139–163). Thousand Oaks, CA: Sage.

Berteotti, C. R., & Seibold, D. R. (1994). Coordination and role definition problems in health-care teams: A hospice case study. In L. R. Frey (Ed.), *Group communication in context: Studies of natural groups* (pp. 107–134). Hillsdale, NJ: Lawrence Erlbaum Associates.

Boggs, G. (1998). *Building community, developing leadership*. Detroit, MI: Detroit Summer.

Bormann, E. G. (1972). Fantasy and rhetorical vision: The rhetorical criticism of social reality. *Quarterly Journal of Speech, 58*, 396–407.

Bormann, E. G. (1985). Symbolic convergence theory: A communication formulation. *Journal of Communication, 35*(4), 128–138.

Cheney, G. (1983). The rhetoric of identification and the study of organizational communication. *Quarterly Journal of Speech, 69*, 143–158.

Dorn, R. (1993, June). *No more hiding*. Speech presented at the Detroit Summer Opening Ceremony, Detroit, MI.

Hollins, T. (1992). The true meaning of Detroit Summer. In *The commitment* (pp. 1-2). Detroit, MI: Detroit Summer.

Hollins, T. (1995). Detroit summer trilogy. In *The commitment* (pp. 1–2). Detroit, MI: Detroit Summer.

Howell, S. (1998). Detroit Summer murals. In G. Boggs (Ed.), *Building community, developing leadership* (pp. 150–152). Detroit, MI: Detroit Summer.

Lessenberry, J. (1997, July 9). Detroit Summer then and now. *Metro-Times*, p. 1.

Mindell, A. (1997, July 11). Cucumbers from concrete. *Metro-Times*, p. 13.

Poole, M. S., Seibold, D. R., & McPhee, R. D. (1985). Group decision-making as a structurational process. *Quarterly Journal of Speech, 71*, 74–102.

Putnam, L. L., & Stohl, C. (1990). Bona fide groups: A reconceptualization of groups in context. *Communication Studies, 41*, 248–265.

Putnam, L. L., & Stohl, C. (1996). Bona fide groups: An alternative perspective for communication and group decision making. In R. Y. Hirokawa & M. S. Poole (Eds.), *Communication and group decision making* (2nd ed., pp. 147–178). Thousand Oaks, CA: Sage.

Sharf, B. F. (1978). A rhetorical analysis of leadership emergence in small groups. *Communication Monographs, 45*, 156–172.

Stohl, C., & Putnam, L. L. (1994). Group communication in context: Implications for the study of bona fide groups. In L. R. Frey (Ed.), *Group communication in context: Studies of natural groups* (pp. 285–292). Hillsdale, NJ: Lawrence Erlbaum Associates.

4

SELECTING A SCHOOL SUPERINTENDENT: SENSITIVITIES IN GROUP DELIBERATION

Karen Tracy
Christina Standerfer
University of Colorado at Boulder

Books that offer advice about "how to be a good school board member" (e.g., Ashby, 1968; Smittle, 1963; Tuttle 1958) treat selection of a new superintendent as the most important decision that school boards make. However, with the exception of a recent study by Eisenberg, Murphy, and Andrews (1998) on a related type of decision—a university's search for a provost—there is little empirical study of how groups make personnel decisions. Written guidelines about university search procedures, as Eisenberg and his colleagues noted, are largely prescriptive with regard to technical procedures. Universities are told what they should do when they confront this task; namely, organize a search committee, select a committee chair, develop criteria for the position, announce and publicize the search, screen the candidates, make a short list, and so forth. If universities follow these steps, the guidebooks imply, they are likely to arrive at a high-quality decision. This rational face is certainly one part of the decision-making picture; the play of power and simple muddling through are two other facets.

Eisenberg et al.'s (1998) study provides a beginning sense of the complexity of group selection decisions. What remains invisible, however, is how a decision to select a particular provost, or a superintendent of schools, is dependent on a prior decision: the process that is to be put in place to arrive at the final personnel choice. In this chapter, we examine this process by focusing on the talk that occurred across several school board meetings, in which, following extensive public participation and input from "experts," a board nonunanimously approved the search process it would use to select its next superintendent.

Schwartzman (1989) believed that researchers need to question what they take for granted at the start of a research project; specifically, she argued that researchers need to "walk into a social system backwards in order to see it and the forms that produce it in a new way" (p. 4). A "back-wards walk" for Schwartzman necessitated questioning her initial assumption that organizational meetings were primarily about making decisions and solving problems. As she asserted, meetings "may be most important in American society because they generate the *appearance* that reason and logical processes are guiding discussion and decisions, whereas they facilitate … relationship negotiations, struggle and commentary" (p. 42).

Similar to Schwartzman, our purpose is to take a backwards walk through a civic group's discussions. On the basis of a study of the talk at one community's school board meetings, we argue that the concepts, *decision* and *decision making,* which provide the starting point for much research on groups as currently conceptualized, are limited. These concepts hobble the gait of researchers seeking to map the communicative terrain outside the laboratory. To pose interesting questions about bona fide groups, we need to rethink these and other foundational concepts. Framing community groups' central activity as *deliberating,* rather than decision making, and drawing on the scholarly traditions that use that frame, we suggest, offers a promising way to look at group communication afresh.

We begin by reviewing and critiquing past theorizing about bona fide groups. We then provide background about the group we studied, the structure of its meetings, key events in its history, and "the decision." In the final sections, we show (a) what the meeting talk was doing, (b) how the decision was formulated on the agenda and within the talk, and (c) what this case suggests about the taken-for-granted concepts of decision and decision making.

BONA FIDE GROUPS: REVIEW AND CRITIQUE

In his historical reviews of group communication scholarship, Frey (1994, 1996, 1999) noted that the 1990s were a period of both stability and change. It is fitting, then, that the bona fide group perspective (Putnam & Stohl, 1990, 1996; Stohl & Putnam, 1994) is a product of that decade, for this perspective encourages group communication scholars to grapple with how groups create (and recreate) and define (and redefine) both themselves and the larger social and institutional contexts in which they function. Specifically, Putnam and Stohl (1990) argued that

> individuals, groups, and the larger social systems exist in a symbiotic relationship in which each contributes to the other's development and survival. This system of symbiosis is embodied in what we shall term bona fide groups, the criteria for which are stable but permeable boundaries and interdependence with immediate context .... By attending simultaneously to both criteria in their entirety, investigators can detect the associations among context, group deliberations, and message systems that remain obscured in traditional research. (p. 256)

In further explicating the defining criteria of bona fide groups, Putnam and Stohl (1990) noted that stable but permeable boundaries are created by group members' communication both inside and outside the group. Specifically, permeable boundaries are facilitated through connectivity to other groups, overlapping and often competing group memberships, relationships among group members in other contexts, and fluctuations in memberships caused by turnover, absenteeism, and/or rotating appointments. The second criterion of bona fide groups, interdependence with immediate context, refers to a group's relationships with external forces and constituencies concerning jurisdiction of tasks, temporal control, and resource dependency.

Stohl and Putnam (1994) later added a third criterion for bona fide groups: unstable and ambiguous borders. As they explained:

> This characteristic ... adds an important level of complexity to our initial formulation of bona fide groups. At one level, a group socially constructs a unified whole to differentiate itself from external boundaries .... At another level, groups continually change, redefine, and negotiate their borders to alter their identities and embedded context. (p. 291)

The bona fide group perspective provides a way to move group communication scholarship from the study of zero-history, autonomous groups constructed primarily for laboratory research purposes to the study of ongoing, naturally occurring groups, a move that we and many others regard as needed. However, several important questions remain about this perspective.

The first question concerns the term itself: *bona fide* groups. What is gained (or lost) by marking certain groups as bona fide and others as not? Putnam and Stohl (1990) used the term to denote a "category" of groups different from "autonomous ones or ones in field settings," which tend to lead researchers to focus on a "narrow range of behaviors" and ignore "environmental factors" that may impinge on a group's dynamics (pp. 248–249). Lammers and Krikorian (1997) suggested that the marker is meant to convey three things: (a) group members' good faith in their memberships—their beliefs that membership will be beneficial both to themselves and the group's productivity, (b) the groups' statuses as *actual* groups that occur in human society" (p. 18), and (c) the positioning of the intragroup communication within a larger social system. The marking of certain groups as bona fide, however, also connotes a need to do so. In other words, the implication is that research concerning "group communication" is the standard, and research involving "bona fide group" communication is a deviation from that standard. Consider how the argumentative burden shifts, for instance, when group communication research is divided into perspectives that study groups and those that study laboratory groups.

The marking also suggests that once a group is identified as a bona fide group, certain assumptions can be made about that group on the basis of its categorical label, and that research findings garnered from a study of a particular bona fide group may be generalized to other bona fide groups. Although this may be true of general characteristics of bona fide groups (those identified by Putnam & Stohl, 1990), we contend that it is important to take seriously the purposes and concerns of distinct kinds of bona fide groups. School boards, juries, and organizational work groups, to name just a few, differ in important ways from each other (see, e.g., Barge & Keyton, 1994, for an analysis of issues particular to one type of bona fide group, a city council, as well as many of the other chapters in the first edition of this text). If we want to understand how groups define and redefine their boundaries and borders within larger social contexts and how they create and recreate participants' roles and identities, we need first to conceptualize what is being studied as school board groups, organizational work teams, and other context specific groups. As Stohl and Putnam (1994) warned, "There is danger ... in moving from the laboratory to the field without careful consideration of how we study group communication" (p. 248). Studying natural groups means taking seriously the problems, practices, and issues that a particular category of group in its environment usually confronts.

A second question concerns how communication is viewed within the bona fide group perspective; that is, what is its function? Putnam and Stohl (1990) indicated that one of the ways in which stable but permeable boundaries are facilitated is through "communication between groups (i.e., connectivity)" (p. 257). Connectivity is understood, according to Lammers and Krikorian (1997), by paying attention to the linkages individual group members initiate and sustain both with individuals who are members of immediately related groups and those who are members of not-so-immediately related groups. Lammers and Krikorian also argued that such linkages may be measured through network analyses; that is, by assessing who talks to whom and how much. The implication here is that communication and information are synonymous. As is illustrated later in this chapter, we take issue with this view. Communicating, we show, creates information. To understand both the dynamics within a group as well as the group's relationship with its contexts, we need to look closely at a group's talk, considering both what that talk is doing and how that talk is creating "facts" and information.[1]

A third and final question for the bona fide group perspective concerns how borders and boundaries of groups are communicatively determined and how these borders and boundaries (and what may be within or outside them) impact the ongoing process of group deliberation. The criterion of "unstable and ambiguous borders" suggests that groups continuously construct, change, and renegotiate their borders, but where does all this constructing, changing, and renegotiating take place? What are the resources for it? We believe that it is not enough to say that a group is interdependent with its "immediate contexts"; it is also interdependent with its past and anticipated future contexts. Past issues, coalitions, alliances, and oppositions are not forgotten as groups move from one issue, problem, or decision to another but, rather, become shards and residue on the interactional landscape that may figure prominently (or surreptitiously) in other issues, problems, and decisions. The way to understand this intertwining of past, present, and future, to unpack boundaries and borders, to excavate decision shards and issue residue, is through a close look at the talk that occurs in groups. To do that, we now turn to the bona fide group we studied.

THE BOULDER VALLEY SCHOOL BOARD

The Boulder Valley School Board is comprised of seven people, each of whom is elected for a 4-year term, with half of the board up for election every 2 years. Following each election, the board selects its president and other officers. Board meetings[2] occur twice a month and are held in a large rectangular room in the school district's main office. Members are seated on a dais arranged in a semicircle, with each person's full name and office displayed. On one side of the dais is a table where the superintendent of schools and the district's attorney sit; on the other side is the board's recording secretary, as well as the podium where citizens stand to present their concerns to the board. Directly in front of the elevated dais is a long rectangular table where school administrators, teachers, or community

---

[1]Putnam and Stohl (1990) alluded to a need to study the talk of groups with regard to explaining group formation and cohesion: "The way group members coalesce internally stems not only from what gets imported and exported into the group, but also arises from what and how members accentuate elements from their environment" (p. 258). However, as this quote implies, communication between a group and its environment is primarily viewed as conveyable information. In contrast, we wish to emphasize the process of how group members construct themselves and their environment through their talk.

[2]The school board has two official public meetings each month. In addition to these meetings, there are work sessions, special meetings, and executive sessions.

leaders who are involved in a particular agenda item sit when that item is considered. Finally, there is a public seating area that accommodates roughly 80 people. Meetings are broadcast live on a local public television channel. During the time period that is the focus of this analysis, meetings began at 7 p.m. and often ran 5 to 6 hours in length.[3]

Boulder Valley, a medium-sized school district, is located in an affluent and growing area of the Western United States. Approximately 25,000 children attend its 54 different schools,[4] and the district's main city of close to 100,000 is the home of a research university that educates many of the teachers and administrators that staff its schools. Others in the county's 250,000-person population live in bedroom suburbs, smaller cities, and difficult-to-reach mountain towns. In addition to the county being geographically diverse, the dispersal of children in the district is uneven and in flux, with some areas growing rapidly and adding new families almost daily and other areas "graying," with dropping numbers of school children.

Who the members of this group are is by no means clear. Besides the seven elected officials, every meeting includes the superintendent of schools, the school attorney, and the recording secretary. In addition, people in certain roles—for instance, parents and teachers, community leaders, and school administrators—are always there, although which particular parents, teachers, community leaders, or administrators are present (and how many there are) depends on the issues that are focal in the meeting. In line with the bona fide group perspective, participants, in all of their roles, display multiple loyalties. For instance, in any meeting it is quite easy to find signs of board members attending to the constituents who elected them, to the other members of the board, to the school administrators with whom they work, or to the abstract ideals of "good education" and "the children" that members regard themselves as serving. To state the obvious, this school board, as is true of all school board groups, is a bona fide group.

The Structure of Meetings

Meetings of the Boulder Valley School Board began in a highly traditional and formulaic manner. Following a call to order by the board president, roll was taken for the seven members, everyone present pledged allegiance to

---

[3]This chapter is based on materials collected for a larger research project. Videotapes of meetings were collected over a 33-month time period; other materials included meeting minutes and agendas, articles and editorials in the local newspaper, district documents, and interviews with most school board members. Over the 33 months, the format of meetings, their typical length, and their start time changed several times. The meeting structures described in this chapter were the ones in place at the time that is the focus of this analysis.

[4]These numbers reflect school district statistics in 1996–1997; the number of schools and students has risen since then.

the flag, and the president explained (read aloud) the procedures for public participation. Following public participation, which often lasted more than 1 hour, the school superintendent gave a report and then there was "Board Communication," a time when each board member commented on any nonagenda issues about which he or she wished to speak. The group's written rules specified that a board member's communication should be no longer than 3 to 5 minutes, but that rule was frequently violated.

The next part of a meeting involved the board voting on the "consent grouping," decisions that district documents defined as "those items which usually do not require discussion or explanation as to the reason for Board action." Typical types of decisions included in consent groupings were approval of minutes from earlier meetings, personnel hires, equipment purchases and building remodeling projects at individual schools, and policies that a previous board discussion showed to be uncontroversial. Board members were permitted to identify items in the consent grouping that they wanted removed and given independent consideration. Following a vote on the consent grouping, and discussion and disposition of any removed items, the board moved to discussion and voting on the meeting's action items. Finally, the group addressed "discussion items," policy issues for consideration that would be returned to in subsequent meetings for a vote. Every issue on which a decision was made, with the exception of items put in the consent grouping, was required to be discussed in at least one meeting prior to the meeting at which a vote was taken. Public participation was possible at the start of each action and discussion item. Up to 10 people could give 2-minute comments before the board started its own discussion. The amount of public participation varied from agenda item to item. Meetings followed Robert's Rules of Order, although as Weitzel and Geist (1998) have shown for community groups, and as was true in this group, the degree to which these rules were adhered to fluctuated.

Important Pieces of the Group's History

In November 1995, Stephanie Hult, who 2 years earlier had campaigned and won on a back-to-basics and educational excellence platform, was selected as the new board president. Interpreting the results of the 1995 election as evidence of the public's desire for something different, Hult launched a series of high-visibility changes. Included among the changes that her board instituted was the "demotion" of the then-superintendent; the demotion involved moving the superintendent's seat at board meetings off the central dais to a lower side table. In the Spring of 1996, several months after this action, much commented on in public participation during board meetings and in letters to the city newspaper, the superintendent resigned. At that time, an acting superintendent was appointed for the 1996–1997 school year, and plans were made to search for a permanent superintendent for the following year. Around that same time (1995–1996 school year), a controversial personnel decision was made. Despite the protests of various individuals and groups in the school district, including several Board members, the Board voted to appoint to the position of chief financial officer a man who had worked in business but lacked experience in school systems. The lack of familiarity with school settings was the main reason for most parties' opposition to the candidate; however, from the Board majority's position, his experience in business (and not schools) was an asset that made him better qualified than most persons in this role.

During this first year of the Hult-led board, members often divided into two distinct blocs. Heated exchanges occurred between these blocs and votes became highly predictable, with the same people in the majority or minority. In these conflicts, the three members who comprised the minority were seen as taking positions that were sympathetic to teachers and school administrators. The board majority, in contrast, often talked about teachers as a "special interest group" whose influence needed to be resisted to improve the quality of education in the district. In their talk, each side framed the other in highly negative ways: The majority framed the minority as not caring about educational excellence; the minority framed the majority as elitist and failing to attend to ordinary student needs, especially the needs of ethnic minorities.

In Spring 1996, a group in the Boulder Valley community collected signatures in the hope of forcing a recall election of President Hult. The Recall-Hult group failed to collect enough signatures, but in the process, which garnered considerable newspaper attention, the sense that the school board was divided and uncivil became established as community "facts" (see Tracy, 1999). Subsequently, at the start of the 1996–1997 school year, one of the three-person minority resigned, citing as her primary reason the unwillingness of the board majority to listen to anyone else. The board appointed an interim member who espoused views consistent with the majority positions. The result was that controversial votes often split 5 to 2.

The Focal Decision: Approving a Process to Select a New Superintendent

The talk episodes on which we focus revolve around the decision to approve a process to select a new superintendent. The decision was made over two meetings, with pieces of the decision surfacing in three distinct agenda items. In the first meeting, the decision appeared in the consent grouping (for a vote) and later in that same meeting as a discussion item. At the next meeting, "the decision" was an action item that was up for a vote. These three segments of talk, approximately 70 minutes in length, are the focus of our analysis. Each segment was transcribed simply, attending to words, vocal particles (uh, uhm), restarts, and repetitions.[5]

The decision about the superintendent search process surfaced initially in the first consent grouping of the December (1996) meeting. Linda Shoemaker, one of the minority members, asked that the item "Approval and Acceptance of the Superintendent Search Committee" be removed from the consent grouping. Following a 10-minute discussion in which Shoemaker voiced concern about how the search committee was being selected, the board voted 6 to 1, with Shoemaker the dissenting vote, to approve the search committee. In that same meeting, when the group reached discussion items, the written agenda listed "Process of Selecting a Superintendent." In introducing the item, President Hult said:

> Thank you very much. The next item of the agenda is the process for selecting a superintendent. Tab number 14. Discussion? Board members? I don't know what we're discussing exactly. I think we already took care of the one item earlier. Yes?

Immediately, Don Shonkwiler, the board's vice president, proposed that the group discuss the timeline for actions and ask the consultant who was being hired to coordinate the search to attend the next meeting.

At the second December board meeting, this decision returned as an action item on the agenda labeled, "The Process for Selecting a Superintendent." Following public participation, the hired consultant, John Ceruli, reported on the steps that would be taken over the upcoming 6 months, and then board members discussed the issue among themselves, with the two minority members doing most of the talking. A vote was taken regarding approval of the search process. Shoemaker, again, was the sole vote against the proposed process.

ANALYSIS OF DELIBERATION ABOUT THE BOARD'S SEARCH PROCESS

Looking Backwards: What Was "The Decision"?

At first glance, this particular decision might not appear to be a decision at all. It is listed on the agenda as an "Action Item" (an item for vote) and simply

---

[5]Transcription was done simply with limited attention to timing and intonation information. No assumption can be made, therefore, that punctuation corresponds with intonation, although it frequently does (period = falling intonation, ? = rising intonation, comma "," = continuing intonation). Where symbols are used, they are the ones commonly employed in the Jeffersonian system used by conversation analysts (see Atkinson & Heritage, 1984): hyphen (wha-) indicates an abrupt cut-off; underlined word (<u>no</u>) indicates a stressed word; a word with degree symbols (°okay°) indicates a word said more quietly than the surrounding speech; a pair of equals signs (=) indicates one utterance latching onto another without a noticeable pause; (hh) marks exhalation sounds; (.) indicates a micro-pause of around .2 seconds whereas (pause) indicates a longer pause; comments between double parentheses ((audience laughter)) indicate a non-speech sound and comments in brackets [ ] are explanations of terms or persons.

described as "The Board of Education is asked to approve the process for selecting a Superintendent." When this item came up on the agenda, Board
President Hult stated, "Board members, there is a recommendation that the
Board approve the search process and budget [for selecting a new superin-
tendent] as outlined in the attached documents." Both the wording on the
agenda and the president's statement suggested that a decision had already
been made about how the selection process would proceed. It seemed almost a formality, a public display of consensus, before the selection process
began. Later in the meeting, when the board president was challenged by
minority board member Shoemaker concerning what the vote was actually
about ("We're voting on the process, the budget, and these names, is that
correct?"), she and Shonkwiler, the Board Vice President, made it clear that
they were voting on a package:

Excerpt 1: Voting on a Package

(Sh = Shoemaker, H = Hult, S = Shonkwiler)

1	Sh:	I have some questions, um, I guess clarification first. I as-
2		sume that these names are added to, um, what we are going
3		to be voting on here. We're voting on the process, the bud-
4		get, and these names, is that correct?
5	H:	We're voting on the process and the budget. Search process
6		and budget.
7	Sh:	Will we =
8	H:	= I guess the names are an inherent, uh, element of that (.)
9	Sh:	So we are voting on the names or-
10	H:	It's the whole thing we are voting on
11	Sh:	not-
12	H:	Yeah.
13	Sh:	Okay. So we (.) <u>are</u> voting on the names.
14	H:	Yeah. Yeah. I think so (pause) in effect. I mean, there's no
15		separate category for it but,
16	S:	It's part, it's part of the whole package.
17	Sh:	Well it just-
18	H:	Part of the whole thing.
19	S:	Part, part of the package.

Both the preceding exchange, as well as other talk that surrounded this
agenda item, contradicted the initial frame, implied in the president's
statement, that positions were harmonious and uncontested. Rather than
a nice, clean parcel that needed only to be approved, the talk revealed "decision shards"; that is, the group's talk revealed "the decision" as far more

complex, interesting, and messy than simply approving the process to select a new superintendent.

Figure 4.1 outlines how the talk of participants (board members, parents, leaders of the teacher's union, and several school district advisory
committees) made visible shards in this ostensibly simple decision.[6] As the
figure reveals, the framing of this action by the majority as simply a "yes/no"
decision was met by resistance on several levels. Minority board members
and representatives from the teachers union and the Multi-Ethnic Action
Committee questioned the make-up of the committee in terms of what categories of people were to be represented and how the actual committee
members would be selected. Other participants questioned what would be
the search committee's relationship to the community and to the board,
the reasonableness of the consultant who was hired to facilitate the selection process, the budget allocated to conduct the search, and even
whether the current board should be making the decision or whether that
decision should wait until after the upcoming election. Simply put,
through their discourse a number of participants worked to reframe "the
approval decision" as something other than an innocuous item on a long
agenda. These participants made visible that a lot (too much?) was being
put into this decision item, choices with which they disagreed had already
been made without enough discussion, and people were being denied a
voice in "smaller" decisions.

Decisions of the past had, thus, become fodder for the deliberation of the
present. Decisions ostensibly "made" in the past were showing up as points of
contestation. Moreover, there was a concern about how present issues would
affect future issues. Consequently, questions concerning the committee's
make-up led to future-oriented questions about the reasonableness of the
committee in relationship to both the community and the board: Would the
committee be fair? Would there be public dialogue concerning the finalists for
superintendent? Would the board ignore what the committee recommended?
As these questions were raised, they entered the deliberation flow. In other
words, the group communication was not only about the here and now of approving this process, it was about how the process would unfold. Minority
board members and many of the public participants were unwilling to let the
approval of the process go forward without forecasting what the decision "to

---

[6]With the exception of the last comment from the public participant, all comments came
from the December 18, 1996 meeting. The final comment about whether the selection
should be postponed came from a June 1997 meeting, in which the Board was deliberating
about the actual superintendent choice. Field notes, however, indicate that comments about
postponing the search for a new superintendent were also made several times by the minority members in meetings prior to the December selection meeting. The president of the
teachers union also made comments during the public participation at the beginning of the
December 18th meeting (on nonagenda items). The chair of the Multi-Ethnic Action Committee also offered comments during public participation after the consultant had presented
and before the Board began its official discussion.

Decision Shards   **Speakers/Comments**

Committee Make-Up	**Minority Board Member #1:**
Categories of representatives	On those categories we had media and I don't see a person from media there yet. . . . Also, we don't have a student in here anywhere. . . . I'd like to see somewhere along the line that we had a student representative in some part of this process.
	Minority Board Member #1:
	I still, at some point in time, would like students represented.
	Teacher Union President:
	It was not BVEA [teachers' union] who refused to accept our first recommendation for the BVEA representative to the superintendent search committee.
Self-selected vs. Board-selected categories	**Chair of Multi-Ethnic Action Committee [MEAC]:** Recently, MEAC provided the Board with specific, written recommendations for the process of hiring a superintendent, including that MEAC be represented on the selection committee. For many years, MEAC has participated on administrative hires, hiring committees, and we see no reason to change this highly effective and time-tested strategy for the inclusion of multi-ethnic communities.
	Minority Board Member #1:
	I look back on the process that we've already gotten to now that we haven't allowed those groups to choose their own representative.
	Minority Board Member #2:
	I guess am going to have to vote against this primarily because of the process. I just don't think it's appropriate for the Board President to appoint all 11 or however many we are going to have of these people.
Charges of tokenism/Past unfairness	**Chair of Multi-Ethnic Action Committee:** One ethnic racial person will not be able to represent adequately the diverse views and feelings of the multi-ethnic community and be effective in a majority situation.
	Chair of Multi-Ethnic Action Committee:
	An open, fair, and inclusive process will win back some of the trust that has been eroded by recent events.

FIG. 4.1.   Unpacking the approval of a superintendent selection process.
Continued on next page.

approve the process" meant. In doing so, they exposed parts of the group deliberation process that could easily have remained hidden. Specifically, they
revealed that the decision package to approve "the process, budget, and
names" was simultaneously a decision about how decisions were and should
be made in this particular group.

Perhaps the most interesting decision shards were those that questioned
John Ceruli (the consultant hired to oversee the selection process), the reasonableness of the money allocated for the selection process, and the timing

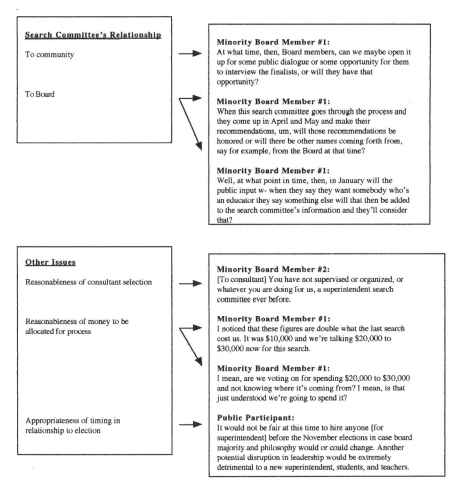

FIG. 4.1. *continued.*

of this action given the impending election. Raising these issues called into question the reasonableness of those in control of the board (those who had made the "small" decisions), as well as the reasonableness of those who sought to reveal the contentiousness of the current decision. Exposure of contention, however, did not change the vote: The superintendent process was approved. Yet, those unwilling to simply accept the process as a given brought to the surface sticking points (shards) about the process that would have otherwise remained buried. By exposing the pieces of the decision that were contested, they changed the meaning of the decision. Participants, thus, added "information" to the group decision-making process, but not information as it is usually conceived; what was added (discovered/uncovered) was information that could impact future decisions.

The Double Frame: Deliberation to Produce Information for the Future

Although the group's deliberation talk was complex, the decision choice was simple: whether each person was "for" or "against" approving the process. On this decision, the single "No" vote came from minority board member Shoemaker. Her comments on this agenda item began with the previously mentioned question about whether names were in the decision package:

Excerpt 2: Shoemaker's No Vote

(H = Hult, Sh = Shoemaker, S = Shonkwiler, C = Ceruli)

1	H:	Linda [calling on her to speak]
2	Sh:	I have some questions, um, I guess clarification first. I as-
3		sume that these names are added to, um, what we are going
4		to be voting on here. We're voting on the process, the bud-
5		get, and these names, is that correct?
6	H:	We're voting on the process and the budget. Search process
7		and budget.
8	Sh:	Will we =
9	H:	= I guess the names are an inherent, uh, element of that (.)
10	Sh:	So we are voting on the names or-
11	H:	It's the whole thing we are voting on.
12	Sh:	not-
13	H:	Yeah.
14	Sh:	Okay. So we- <u>are</u> voting on the names.
15	H:	Yeah. Yeah. I think so (pause) in effect. I mean there's no sep-
16		arate category for it but,
17	S:	It's part, it's part of the whole package.
18	Sh:	Well it just-
19	H:	Part of the whole thing.
20	S:	Part, part of the package.
21	Sh:	It seems to me that if we vote on the members of DAC [dis-
22		trict advisory council] and we <u>vote</u> on the members of our
23		real estate task force, we <u>certainly</u> should be <u>voting</u> on our
24		superintendent search committee.
25	H:	Wanna do it <u>name</u> by <u>name</u>, or d'you wanna do it as a lump
26		sum? Lump group.
27	Sh:	Lump sum is fine.
28	H:	Okay.
29	S:	hh move that we appoint the listed members to the task force
30		that was approved by the board at the last meeting.
31	H:	I just h- guess that would be just a friendly amendment (.) to
32		the motion.

33	S:	I stand corrected. That would be an amendment to the motion.
34	H:	°Okay° Great.
35	Sh:	°Okay° Now. Some questions for Mr. Ceruli, please? Um,
36		how many <u>searches</u> for superintendents have you conducted
37		in the past?
38	C:	Uh, w-
39	Sh:	Approximately?
40	C:	Our firm is a, ah, research and facilitation firm. So we have
41		not conducted a ah superintendent search. We've b-, been
42		in- involved with, um um, one particular search in Denver.
43		Uh, but what we do are <u>public process</u> and research and so
44		what were, ah what we've offered to do here and what we've
45		done thus far is, um, put together the parts of the public pro-
46		cess that would, uh uh, accompany this, um, and <u>all</u> of the <u>re-</u>
47		<u>search</u> and that it wh- th- it which essentially a search is. It is a-
48		it's an effort to, um, a- acquire the information you need from
49		these individuals and so that's what we would conduct.
50	Sh:	So the answer is that you <u>haven't</u>. ((laughs))
51		((Audience laughter))
52	C:	We, uh, that's right. That is the answer.
53	Sh:	Is that correct? ((laughs))
54	C:	That is the answer. Correct.
55	Sh:	That you have not, uh, <u>supervised</u> or <u>organized</u> or whatever
56		you are <u>doing</u> for us a superintendent's =
57	C:	Right.
58	Sh:	= search committee <u>ever</u> before.
59	C:	Uh, we've conducted searches for the, um, the scientific and
60		cultural facilities district, uh, executive director that's been
61		with them for 8 years. We, uh, assisted on the conducting of
62		the Great Outdoor Colorado search for their executive direc-
63		tor, so we have done executive director searches before. We
64		haven't done a search for a superintendent specifically.
65	Sh:	Uh-huh, I just wanted to clarify that. Um, I guess I'm going to
66		have to vote against this, um, primarily because of the pro-
67		cess. Um, I just don't think it's appropriate for the board
68		president to appoint all 11, or however many we are going to
69		have of these people, and I don't want to say anything nega-
70		tive about any of these people. Um, but I'm going to vote
71		against it 'cause I don't think these people are well represen-
72		tative of the community. They're not diverse and it doesn't
73		seem to me to be politically balanced.
74	H:	Well, I'm, I'm just going to have to respond to that, Linda. I'm
75		not appointing them. What happened is, I phoned every
76		board member who gave me a list of people. I have those

77   names and the lists as a matter of fact that I could show you at
78   any point, and I went through and compiled them, which is
79   what we had agreed upon that we would do. I compiled
80   them, and I took, I numbered people with the top, the num-
81   ber of times they showed up and, uh, those peo-, I then called
82   every board member and told them who got the most votes
83   in what category and who I'd be contacting for these posi-
84   tions so n-, these ones, these aren't my choices, these-, I
85   mean I contributed to the choices just as you did and every-
86   body and Sally [the other member of the minority] and any-
87   one else on the board. But, uh, th -this reflects, uh, majority
88   of the board's, uh, feeling on who should serve on the search
89   committee. And some of the people I know are on the com-
90   mittee are people that you had nominated and so it's, ah, I
91   think it's a fair committee and it represents the votes and the
92   input of every board member.

For analytic purposes, the exchange can be divided into three sections:
(a) lines 1 through 34, Shoemaker's questioning of the meaning of the upcoming vote; (b) lines 35 through 64, Shoemaker's challenge of Ceruli's
competence to do what he was hired to do; and (c) lines 65 through 92,
Shoemaker's account of why she would vote "No." If Shoemaker's actions
were interpreted through the focal decision—approval of the search process—we would likely "see" evidence of hidden agendas and the irrational-
ity of much of the talk in decision-making groups. Consider, however, what
becomes noticeable if we start from a different assumption: that people
and their talk are reasonable. The question that analysts then need to address is "Reasonable for what?"

Shoemaker's Questioning of the Meaning of the Vote.   A question can
do all kinds of interactional work. Although the most straightforward function is to seek information, a question frequently challenges and criticizes
(Tannen, 1984; Tracy, 1997). In lines 2 through 5, where Shoemaker questions whether committee members' names are to be part of the vote, it
seems possible that she is merely seeking information. However, when she
twice repeats the upshot of Hult's answer ("so we're voting on the names,"
lines 10 and 14) and then explicitly states why she regards it as unreasonable to not specify the committee make-up, to interpret her initial question
as a benign, noncritical "clarification" seems seriously off the mark. Hult's
response (lines 25–26) appears to acknowledge Shoemaker's criticism and
offer a solution. However, the choice she offers Shoemaker— "name by
name or lump group"—frames Shoemaker as unreasonable. Within the
context of the widely held group belief that school board meetings were al-

ready too long, a proposal to turn the approval process into a yes/no vote on 11 citizens, as well as all the other pieces of the process, implicates Shoemaker negatively. Stated differently, Hult's comment humors (silences?) a difficult member. That this comment was heard, and probably intended, as a putdown is underscored by Shonkwiler's proposal (lines 29–30) when he states, "Move that we appoint the listed members to the task force *that was approved by the board at the last meeting.*" In essence, the president's and vice president's comments work to frame Shoemaker as haggling over something that has already been decided and, therefore, as wasting time and being unreasonable.

Shoemaker's response, "lump sum is fine" (line 25), is interesting because it is at odds with an implication established through her prior questioning: that there was something troubling about the search committee's make-up. Allowing approval of the committee to be bundled into the "search process" decision would seem to be exactly the issue to which Shoemaker had earlier been objecting. Yet, at this juncture in the meeting, she pursues that issue no further, shifting her focus to other concerns. How, then, is it possible to see Shoemaker's talk as reasonable?

Models of group action often assert competing notions of good member behavior. For instance, members are encouraged to be vigilant and not to go along with the majority to avoid conflict (e.g., Janis & Mann, 1977). At the same time, however, members are expected to avoid actions that contribute to the negative reputation that meetings have come to have in Western society as ineffectual, a waste of time, tedious, and so forth (see Schwartzman, 1989). Put another way, participants face an interactional dilemma whenever they do not agree with where their group (as expressed by the majority) seems to be going. Particularly in groups that use majority rule rather than consensus, problematizing the group's direction but then agreeing with the group to continue toward it becomes a reasonable strategy for a person who knows that his or her position is in the minority. Such a move allows the member to simultaneously establish his or her reservations and yet to avoid being cast as the group's "problem." Shoemaker's talk certainly can be seen as functioning in just this way. Her talk is also indicative of both the unstable borders and permeable boundaries of this group: It frames her as a reasonable *minority* group member and, thereby, draws borders around a particular faction within the group. It also simultaneously frames her as a reasonable elected official and, thereby, demonstrates permeable boundaries by representing the constituents to whom she is responsible.

Shoemaker's Challenge of Ceruli's Competence. Shoemaker's next move was to challenge Ceruli's competence to be organizing the superintendent search process. In asking Ceruli how many superintendent

searches he had previously conducted (lines 35 through 37), and then tacking on that it would be acceptable for Ceruli to offer an approximate number (line 39), Shoemaker implies the reasonableness of expecting Ceruli's firm to have done a number of searches. In adding the word "approximately" to her initial question formulation, Shoemaker's question offers a "candidate answer" (Pomerantz, 1988), a guide about what kind of information is expected in the answer. Approximation of the number makes sense if one is dealing with relatively large numbers, say, at least 10 or 15. However, if it is expected that a person or firm has done only one, two, or perhaps three searches, it would be socially strange to ask for an approximate number. This is even more the case if a questioner expects that a person or firm may have done no searches of this exact type. Hence, Shoemaker's question is designed to imply the unreasonableness of hiring a person (or firm) who does not bring extensive experience conducting this type of job search.

Ceruli's nonfluent and rambling answer suggests his awareness of the implications of Shoemaker's question. Although Ceruli tries to reframe the experience he does have (lines 40 through 49), Shoemaker does not accept his reframing. Her summarizing of the gist of Ceruli's comment (line 50), as "the answer is you *haven't* [any experience]," offers an unfriendly, one could even say hostile, reading. A more neutral or sympathetic response would have been something like, "Although you haven't done a superintendent search before, you bring lots of experience in the needed job skills." Not only does Shoemaker respond unsympathetically but she also underscores it with her follow-up questions and, thereby, forces Ceruli to acknowledge publicly and repeatedly that he has no experience conducting a superintendent search. From Ceruli's point of view, it is hard to imagine that he did not see Shoemaker as deliberately trying to undermine (humiliate?) him in a situation where the group (i.e., the board majority) had already hired him.

If we raise the question concerning what group-level purpose Shoemaker's talk serves, a function does become apparent: Shoemaker's interrogation draws attention to the fact that some persons hired a consulting firm with questionable competence. Furthermore, her pursuit of this issue strongly implies that she was not part of that decision; either the decision occurred behind her back (because the majority favored it and did not seek her input), or it was made despite concerns she may have raised. Shoemaker's comments, thus, construct a version of recent events that make visible for citizens in the community (i.e., voters who are present at the meeting or watching it on television) that the board majority led by the president acted in a high-handed and/or questionable manner. That Shoemaker did not draw out other implications of Ceruli's lack of experience (such as firing the consultant) and summarized her reason for raising the issue as "just wanted to clarify that" (line 65), further suggest that her goal was to call into question those who had made the decision rather than re-open the decision for review. As in the previous segment where Shoemaker challenged the meaning of the vote, her questions to Ceruli give an indication of how "information" can be created for constituencies beyond the boundaries of a group.

Shoemaker's Explanation of Her "No" Vote.   Finally, consider Shoemaker's account of why she would be voting against approval of the superintendent search process (lines 65 through 73). Shoemaker's talk began with an implication that her "No" vote was being cast reluctantly. In saying, "I guess I'm going to have to vote against this," she implied that the action she is about to take was difficult, and that she was only taking the action because she "had to." She amplified her reluctance by highlighting how she did not want "to say anything negative about these people" (lines 69–70). The reason she was taking this personally difficult action was because she didn't "think it's appropriate for the board president to appoint all 11" members of the search committee. The members to be appointed, she argued, are "not well representative of the community," "not diverse," and "not politically balanced" (lines 67 through 73). Shoemaker's explanation, then, not only makes reasonable why she took an action that might be framed negatively by others—keeping the group from achieving unanimous agreement on an important decision—but also serves as a strong criticism of the board president.

President Hult's responding comment, "Well I'm, I'm just going to have to respond to that, Linda" (line 74), makes clear that Hult heard Shoemaker's comment as critical. Of interest, too, is that Hult also framed herself as speaking reluctantly. Hult said she "had to" respond; she was compelled by Shoemaker's talk to explain at length why Shoemaker's evaluation was unfair. Hult's description of polling all board members, in which she explicitly mentions that she called "Sally," as well as Shoemaker, illustrates how no detail of talk is purposeless. In mentioning Sally, the other person known to oppose the board majority, Hult further underscored that she solicited information from everyone equally. Moreover, the specifics she related about how she numbered each proposed candidate for the selection process and counted how many votes each person got offers a rather different picture of the process than the one advanced by Shoemaker. Rather than the selection committee being the product of the president's whim, as Shoemaker accused, Hult reframed the committee composition process as a fair and objective process in which every board member's opinion was represented equally. Hult's talk, then, does considerable work to display that she is a fair and reasonable leader in a situation where there is ongoing conflict. In doing so, Hult provides a different perspective from Shoemaker's. By emphasizing that each Board member, including even Sally, had a chance to participate equally in the earlier process, Hult's comments minimize the majority–minority opinion split within the group, and imply that equal treatment of each member is synonymous with fair treatment.

We regard both Hult's and Shoemaker's descriptions of the process to create the search committee as reasonable. As Hult noted, the composition of the committee was determined by using an objective, numerical aggregating process; hence, the process did insure equal representation. However, in a group that routinely split 5 to 2 in voting behavior, a logical upshot of giving each person an equal voice is to drown out minority voices. Thus, if majority and minority members favored different people for the search committee, it would be virtually guaranteed that using this process would result in no persons that only minority members favored making it onto the final list. Although strictly speaking, Shoemaker's characterization of the committee as "appointed by the president" was not accurate, the thrust of her criticism—that important voices were not included—was true.

In this particular context, where conflict lines had been clearly drawn and repeatedly enacted, Shoemaker most likely assumed (and it was probably true) that whatever she said would have no effect on the group's immediate decision. Her communication is, thus, best understood as an attempt to make visible to the Boulder Valley community a larger decision frame. In natural groups, an issue that is inescapably and always relevant is how well (e.g., reasonably, fairly, and tactfully) a member is doing the deliberation work she has been hired, appointed, asked, volunteered, or elected to do. That is, the talk that surrounds and enacts any group decision-making process can always be treated as "information" about a member's competence to be in the deliberating and decision-making roles that he or she inhabits. Applied to the Boulder Valley School Board, Shoemaker's conversational moves created "information" that was relevant to citizens in the community for the upcoming decision about who should be on the school board. In a nutshell, in working to display the problematic character of the deliberation actions and leadership of the school board majority, Shoemaker's talk was speaking to a decision she could potentially affect: the outcome of the next election. Put in the terms of the bona fide group perspective, Shoemaker's talk made visible to relevant constituencies the permeability of the boundaries of this group.

The Boulder Valley School Board Epilogue

In the November 1997 election, Hult and the two other members of the majority coalition running for re-election were defeated decisively. Two members from the old majority continued on the board. A division into majority and minority viewpoints and voting blocs became less sharp in the 1997–1999 board, but nonetheless continued.[7] The main difference in the board following the 1997 election was the change in which viewpoint was in the majority position. Shoemaker's viewpoint became the majority one and Shoemaker, herself, became the new board president.

FROM GROUP DECISION MAKING TO GROUP DELIBERATION

The preceding case of the Boulder Valley School Board raises questions about what group decisions are and how they get made. "Judging by most accounts," Poole and Hirokawa (1996) noted that "defining a decision is fairly straightforward. Decisions are assumed to be discrete events, clearly distinguishable from other group activities" (p. 9). However, as Poole and Hirokawa also admitted, most decisions involve "a series of activities and choices nested in choices of wider scope, rather than a single simple choice" (p. 9). That decisions are, in fact, activities embedded in other group activities remains invisible in much of the extant group communication scholarship. Part of the reason, as Frey (1996) explained, is that too many researchers continue to study laboratory groups comprised of students. Groups of students are asked to decide whether a defendant in a murder trial should be judged guilty (Kameda, Ohtsubo, & Takezawa, 1997), which parent should get custody of a child (Propp, 1997), and the by-now-infamous task of determining what supplies would be most important if a group found itself "Lost on the Moon" (e.g., Shelly, 1997). In giving clear-cut, discrete choices to groups in which members have no ongoing relationships with other members or outside constituencies to whom they are responsible and who will render evaluation, the group task is robbed of those features that make actual decision making so complex and interesting. It is not that this type of situation—a clear set of choice options to be decided by a group of people who are unrelated—never applies to actual groups; it does, but this kind of circumstance is by far the exception rather than the rule. It is time, therefore, for communication scholars to pose and answer questions about group decision making in the usual kind of contexts in which it occurs. Put simply, a conceptual reframing is needed to make visible what is ordinary in group decision making.

Conceptualizing what groups usually do as *deliberation* rather than as decision making, we suggest, will bring into focus important aspects of communication in groups. This vocabulary shift will facilitate desirable

---

[7]After the majority–minority split changed, members of the board who had previously been majority members engaged in discourse similar to that engaged in by former minority members, making visible in their talk the minority–majority borders and ensuring the permeability of group boundaries by creating information for their constituencies. As both Hult and Shoemaker independently told one of the authors in recent interviews, talk aimed at influencing the public's perceptions in future election decisions are part and parcel of being a minority board member.

change in several ways. First, if we take seriously the commonplace notion that language shapes how we think, then it follows that the vocabulary selected to frame research issues will draw attention to some features of a situation and away from others. In contrast to decision making, deliberation calls attention to a broader range of communicative action. In particular, it foregrounds the fuzzy, open-ended, issue- or problem-framing parts of communication that occupy so much of the talk in bona fide groups. In addition, deliberation legitimates as relevant a wider swath of possible topics and issues. That is, what is "on" or "off-topic" becomes a complex call, an assessment that groups often give considerable energy to debating.

An upshot of this vocabulary shift, for instance, is that many traditional concepts become more problematic, or at least need to be redefined. With respect to "hidden agenda," for example, if figuring out what are reasonable foci for group discussion is a legitimate activity for groups, then diagnosing a group member as having a hidden agenda becomes more difficult. From a deliberative viewpoint, it is not so much that group members (or the group as a whole) have hidden agendas as it is that group members accuse each other of having hidden agendas. Hidden agenda, thus, would be the name of a conversational strategy used by group members to legitimate a focus on some set of possible group concerns over others.

Besides drawing attention to problem framing, deliberation shifts attention away from choices about supposedly clear-cut matters toward discussion of policies. Groups make decisions, for instance, about where to eat or how to implement a policy; they "deliberate" about complex issues that meld technical matters with moral and social concerns. Deliberation and decision making are not mutually exclusive terms; they have conceptual overlap. Juries, for example, are routinely described as engaging in both deliberation and decision making. However, deliberation draws attention to a different range of the decision spectrum: Particularly important decisions, decisions that shape other decisions, and decisions in which "task performance and socioemotional concerns," to use current group communication language, are deeply woven together. To study group deliberation is to move away from conceptualizing decisions as either a matter of achieving task performance or building member relations. Studying deliberation, thus, means taking seriously the complexities with which people and tasks are, and must be, connected.

Moreover, although decisions may be made by individuals or groups (and, hence, the reasonableness of comparing individuals to groups), deliberation requires more than a single individual. Deliberation is fundamentally, not just possibly, a group activity. It is also a communicative activity that unites logic and emotion. March and Olson (1995) noted that "institutions organize hopes, dreams, and fears, as well as purposeful actions" (p. 33); the actions citizens take in community groups and larger political institutions "are expressions of what is appropriate, exemplary, natural or acceptable behavior according to the (internalized) purposes, codes of rights and duties, practices, methods, and techniques of a constituent group and a self" (p. 31). Bessette (1994) offered an especially useful description of deliberation. It may, he noted:

> be a largely consensual process in which like-minded individuals work together to fashion the details of a policy they all desire, or it may involve deep-seated conflicts over fundamental issues or principles. It may result in unanimity of view, where no votes are necessary; or it may reveal sharp disagreements that require formal voting to determine the majority view. (p. 49)

Studying deliberation rather than decision making would lead to research that considered (a) the consequences of formulating a group's focal decision one way rather than another; (b) ways to describe deliberative strategies so that task, emotion, and identity concerns were better fused; (c) how the treatment of members in past deliberative occasions might influence what a group does in future deliberations; and (d) the communicative strategies group members use to make salient future frames in which a current decision (or the interactional process and style in making a current decision) will be relevant. Figure 4.2 offers a visualization of how shifting from decision making to deliberation is likely to change what group communication scholars notice.

Finally, in addition to showing the value of deliberation as a lens for examining the communication of bona fide groups, our backwards walk though the Boulder Valley School Board meetings led us to another insight: Group decisions often revolve around how to make upcoming decisions. What occurred at the Boulder Valley School Board meetings—conflict about its group process—is a regular feature of group life. Many of the most important and contentious decisions that groups face involve establishing the criteria to put in place, or the process to use (e.g., sequence of steps, timing, and people to perform them), for making another decision. Looking closely at how groups deliberate about process is an especially promising area for future group communication research.

CONCLUSION

In this chapter, we have taken a close look at one school district's board meetings. In this look, we saw how participants constructed "the group" and its boundaries differently at different junctures in the deliberative process. At any moment in time the group that was invoked through a speaker's comments might be the two-person minority bloc, the seven elected officials, the board members plus district administrators, everyone attending the meeting, or some other set of persons. In addition to seeing

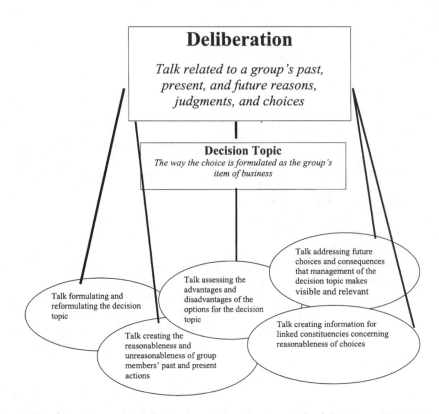

FIG. 4.2.   Reconceptualizing the communicative work of decision making in groups.

that the group's borders varied across time, our look made visible that the sense and sensibility of commentators' remarks frequently derived from linkages to and desired effects on outside constituencies. Simply put, this case study gives further evidence of the validity of the bona fide group perspective for understanding communication in naturally occurring groups.

REFERENCES

Ashby, L. W. (1968). *The effective school board member*. Danville, IL: Interstate.

Atkinson, J. M., & Heritage, J. (Eds.). (1984). *Structure of social action: Studies in conversation analysis*. Cambridge, UK: Cambridge University Press.

Barge, J. K., & Keyton, J. (1994). Contextualizing power and social influence in groups. In L. R. Frey (Ed.), *Group communication in context: Studies of natural groups* (pp. 85–105). Hillsdale, NJ: Lawrence Erlbaum Associates.

Bessette, J. M. (1994). *The mild voice of reason: Deliberative democracy and American national government*. Chicago: University of Chicago Press.

Eisenberg, E. M., Murphy, A., & Andrews, L. (1998). Openness and decision-making in the search for a university provost. *Communication Monographs, 65*, 1–23.

Frey, L. R. (1994). The naturalistic paradigm: Studying small groups in the postmodern era. *Small Group Research, 25*, 551–577.

Frey, L. R. (1996). Remembering and "re-membering": A history of theory and research on communication and group decision making. In R. Y. Hirokawa & M. S. Poole (Eds.), *Communication and group decision making* (2nd ed., pp. 19–51). Thousand Oaks, CA: Sage.

Frey, L. R. (1999). Introduction. In L. R. Frey (Ed.), D. S. Gouran, & M. S. Poole (Assoc. Eds.), *The handbook of group communication theory & research* (pp. ix–xxi). Thousand Oaks, CA: Sage.

Janis, I. L., & Mann, L. (1977). *Decision-making: A psychological analysis of conflict, choice, and commitment*. New York: Free Press.

Kameda, T., Ohtsubo, Y., & Takezawa, M. (1997). Centrality in sociocognitive networks and social influence: An illustration in a group decision-making context. *Journal of Personality and Social Psychology, 73*, 296–309.

Lammers, J. C., & Krikorian, D. H. (1997). Theoretical extension and operationalization of the bona fide group construct with an application to surgical teams. *Journal of Applied Communication Research, 25*, 17–38.

March, J. G., & Olsen, J. P. (1995). *Democratic governance*. New York: Free Press.

Pomerantz, A. (1988). Offering a candidate answer: An information seeking strategy. *Communication Monographs, 55*, 360–373.

Poole, M. S., & Hirokawa, R. Y. (1996). Introduction: Communication and group decision making. In R. Y. Hirokawa & M. S. Poole, (Eds.), *Communication and group decision making* (2nd ed., pp. 3–18). Thousand Oaks, CA: Sage.

Propp, K. M. (1997). Information utilization in small group decision making: A study of the evaluative interaction model. *Small Group Research, 28*, 424–453.

Putnam, L. L., & Stohl, C. (1990). Bona fide groups: A reconceptualization of groups in context. *Communication Studies, 41*, 248–265.

Putnam, L. L., & Stohl, C. (1996). Bona fide groups: An alternative perspective for communication and small group decision making. In R. Y. Hirokawa & M. S. Poole (Eds.), *Communication and group decision making* (2nd ed., pp. 147–178). Thousand Oaks, CA: Sage.

Schwartzman, H. B. (1989). *The meeting: Gatherings in organizations and communities*. New York: Plenum Press.

Shelly, R. K. (1997). Sequences and cycles in social interaction. *Small Group Research, 28*, 333–356.

Smittle, W. R. (1963). *The effective school board member*. Clawson, MI: Oakland Education Press.

Stohl, C., & Putnam, L. L. (1994). Group communication in context: Implications for the study of bona fide groups. In L. R. Frey (Ed.), *Group communication in context: Studies of natural groups* (pp. 285–292). Hillsdale, NJ: Lawrence Erlbaum Associates.

Tannen, D. (1984). *Conversational style: Analyzing talk among friends*. Norwood, NJ: Ablex.

Tracy, K. (1997). *Colloquium: Dilemmas of academic discourse*. Norwood, NJ: Ablex.

Tracy, K. (1999). The usefulness of platitudes in arguments about conduct. In F. H. van Eemeren, R. Grootendorst, J. A. Blair, & C. A. Willard (Eds.), *Proceedings of the 4th international conference of the International Society for the Study of Argumentation* (pp. 799–803). Amsterdam: SIC SAT.

Tuttle, E. M. (1958). *School board leadership in America*. Danville, IL: Interstate.

Weitzel, A., & Geist, P. (1998). Parliamentary procedures in a community group: Communication and vigilant decision making. *Communication Monographs, 65*, 244–259.

GROUP CONFRONTING CRISIS:
CONTEXTUAL EFFECTS ON GROUP
COMMUNICATION

5

IN THE MASK OF THIN AIR: INTRAGROUP AND INTERGROUP COMMUNICATION DURING THE MT. EVEREST DISASTER

Renée Houston
University of Puget Sound

I don't get paid to talk, I get paid to get them up the mountain.
—An expedition guide for Mt. McKinley (personal communication, February 12, 1998)

I think it is not so necessary that a guide chat good, but that he can climb good.
—Anatoli Boukreev, expedition guide for Mt. Everest (Boukreev & Dewalt, 1997, p. 45)

Mountaineers began the quest to climb Mt. Everest in 1922, but it would take another 31 years before Sir Edmund Hillary and Tenzing Norgay finally reached the peak's summit in May of 1953. Since that time, over half of the total attempts on the summit occurred within the 5-year time span of 1991 to 1996 (Coburn, 1997). Many of these attempts are commercial expeditions led by high-altitude veterans. After Dick Bass, at age 50, successfully scaled Mt. Everest with the help of expert climber David Brashears, the number of successful ascents on Mt. Everest by recreational climbers has increased more than threefold. As one survivor of the 1996 Mt. Everest tragedy put it, "Bass showed that Everest was within the realm of possibility for regular guys. Assuming you're reasonably fit and have some disposable income" (Krakaeur, 1996, p. 22).

The increasing number of groups on Mt. Everest has led to a type of "grid-lock" that creates the need for coordination within and between expedition teams. Tragically, 12 individuals who attempted to summit Mt. Everest in May of 1996 lost their lives—the worst single-season death toll since climbers began attempting to summit Mt. Everest over 75 years ago. This loss can be attributed to a variety of reasons: avalanches, blizzards, extreme temperatures, high altitude, unstable trail conditions, human error, lack of communication, complications due to lack of oxygen, and other reasons. The 1996 incident also clearly indicates how the interdependent mix of nature and human communication produced multiple fatalities on Mt. Everest.[1] The widespread media coverage of the ill-fated summit attempts during the 1996 climbing season generated numerous accounts of the events that occurred on the mountain from a variety of sources, including day-by-day radio reports from guides on the mountain, personal accounts, and interviews. Framed by the bona fide group perspective (Putnam & Stohl, 1990, 1996) and structuration theory (Giddens, 1984), it is my purpose to explore the intragroup and intergroup communication processes that occurred in the backdrop of this 29,028 foot, snow-packed, glacier-cut mountain with a grim mix of boulders, bulletproof ice, and nearly constant hurricane-force winds, and where the air is so thin that the higher functions of the brain—judgment, perception, and memory—fail (see Coburn, 1997). This analysis is intended to result not only in the discovery of structures emerging from group communication but also in how they are drafted into action to create unanticipated outcomes.

To accomplish this goal, I begin with a description of expeditions bound for Mt. Everest as a site for examining group interaction and provide a brief description of the May 1996 summit bid. I then explore the importance of understanding the context of group communication on Mt. Everest through the bona fide group perspective, which emphasizes the importance of studying the permeability of group boundaries and the interdependence of groups with their contexts. Moreover, given that expedition groups develop norms and rules for behavior in situ, I briefly review structuration theory and use it as an analytical tool to identify how groups on Mt. Everest develop certain communication and behavioral patterns within and between expeditions. It should be noted that the study covers one climbing season and focuses, in particular, on the events leading up to and including the May 10–11, 1996 disaster.

GROUP COMMUNICATION IN CONTEXT: MT. EVEREST EXPEDITIONS

To set up the context of the unique process of mountain climbing, in general, and Mt. Everest, specifically, I provide a brief overview of the nature of

---

[1]Avalanches, of course, may also cause mass fatalities.

Mt. Everest and the constitution of expeditions. The details include (a) the nature of expedition teams, (b) climbing costs, (c) ascension route details, (d) typical weather, and (e) expedition leadership. This section ends with a brief overview of the May 1996 summit bid.

The Nature of Expedition Teams

> In climbing, having confidence in your partners is no small concern. One climber's actions can affect the welfare of the entire team.
> —Krakaeur (1997, p. 37)

Beginning with the first attempts on Mt. Everest, most climbing groups are imbued with an ad hoc quality to them. Initially, mountaineers climbed Mt. Everest by hiring local people, known as *Sherpas* or *climbing Sirdars,* to help them carry supplies up the mountain. Over time, climbers, whose reputations were garnered by their "talent" of making it up the world's highest mountain, began creating their own expeditions to lead climbers inexperienced with Mt. Everest's terrain and perils. Although expedition guides may have a certain amount of respectability or charisma, their qualifications are not necessarily based on their leadership abilities but, rather, on their personal success in climbing Mt. Everest.

Currently, expedition teams typically consist of an expedition leader and a head guide, two to five "assistant" guides, several Sherpas, and, on average, 5 to 10 climbers. Despite Mt. Everest's reputation as a climb only for the very wealthy (see the following section on costs), clients range across economic classes and international borders, from elite doctors to local post office personnel. Because teams form on the basis of which expedition people join, individuals have very little knowledge of the skills and conditioning of their teammates. At best, participants may climb with a friend, although relationships between teammates do develop over time as they climb up and down the mountain, reaching higher and higher points each time as they acclimatize their bodies to the thin mountain air before their summit bid. Journalist Jon Krakauer (1997), who was a client in the Adventure Consultants expedition, realized at Base Camp that his Mt. Everest attempt would be the first time he would climb without a trusted and well-experienced friend. Krakaeur noted that "climbers are typically wary of joining forces with those whose bona fides are unknown to them" (1997, p. 38). One can imagine the initial tension felt by team members as they realize they must work together to coordinate resources, lay ropes, and provide emotional support as they face the overwhelming task of climbing Mt. Everest. As they move toward their goal, those better equipped, both physically and mentally, emerge and those less skilled realize they must rely on the expertise of their teammates for survival. The relationships between team members, thus, form on the basis of members' physical and mental preparedness.

Climbing Costs

Climbing Mt. Everest is beyond reach for many people, not merely because of the physical demands but also because of the cost of joining a guided team and paying the Nepalese government's climbing fee. The average cost of attempting to climb Mt. Everest is $65,000.[2] Because of the acclimatization schedule, a typical climb takes about 8 weeks, a substantial amount of time that potentially represents a lost opportunity cost. Although one might assume that only well-to-do clients could afford the climb, many different types of people make great personal sacrifices to raise the funds to achieve their dream of climbing Mt. Everest.

Ascension Route

Although a current trend in Mt. Everest climbing is to pursue new routes up the mountain, most expeditions follow the route carved out many years ago by the legendary Sir Edmund Hillary and his Sherpa Tenzing Norgay. Along this route, known as the Southeast Ridge Route, several camps are set up along the way. Starting from Base Camp (17,600 feet, more than 3 miles above sea level) climbers make their way through the Khumbu Icefall, a treacherous trek due to shifting ice, to Camp I (19,500 feet). From there, climbers cross the Western Cwm (pronounced "coom") stopping overnight at Camp II (21,500 feet) and then heading on to Camp III (24,000 feet). The trek from Camp III to Camp IV (26,000 feet) crosses a cliff of brittle limestone known as the Yellow Band. Camp IV, or the South Col, is the point from which climbers mount their summit attempt. The terrain from the South Col to the summit (29,028 feet) is known as the Death Zone, so called because the risk of death increases significantly. The best strategy on this last stretch of the climb is to get up and down as quickly as possible. This means climbers leave at 11:30 p.m., reach the summit around 1:00 p.m. the following day, and then quickly make their way back to Camp IV before the sun goes down.

Mountain Weather

Severely inclement, year-round weather makes attempts on the summit possible only a few times during the year. Although attempts are made during September and October, the best window of opportunity is during

---

[2]Several clients noted the sacrifices made to achieve their goal of climbing Mt. Everest. Costs may drop, however, if one secures a group oneself instead of using a guided group to cover logistics.

April and May. Of course, there is no guarantee that even in that window one will stand "on top of the world"; many climbers are forced to turn around for a variety of reasons, including bad weather or health. As they trudge back down the mountainside, they see their hopes and dreams of conquering the world's highest peak dissolve.

Leadership

Fee-based climbs place tremendous pressure on expedition leaders to get their team members up the mountain. In fact, the success of expedition guides is often measured by how many people they manage to escort to the mountain's peak. Given the characteristics of this group situation, where the skills of individual members vary greatly, leaders are in a particularly difficult position that often demands they pit their personal success and future employment against the safety of their expedition members.

The Summit Bid on May 10–11, 1996

In May of 1996, 12 expeditions set up camps at the base of Mt. Everest to attempt a climb from the Nepalese side of the mountain, the path Hillary and Norgay trod 43 years earlier. These teams consisted of an assortment of individuals who came from many different countries worldwide and who possessed a wide range of skills and experiences. Although all of these expeditions undoubtedly affected the intergroup experience on Mt. Everest that May, my analysis focuses primarily on the effects of intragroup and intergroup communication on expeditions led by Scott Fischer, Rob Hall, and the Taiwanese because of the media-centered attention on their attempts and because these teams experienced the greatest loss of life. In the following section, I review both the importance of understanding the characteristics of bona fide groups, focusing especially on the interdependent nature of groups and their contexts, and how group structure emerges, as proposed by structuration theory (Giddens, 1984). Context, in particular, is important because Mt. Everest expedition groups have little control over the site at which their communication takes place.[3]

THEORETICAL FRAMES FOR EXAMINING EXPEDITION TEAMS

Bona Fide Group Perspective

Since the 1990s, scholars have been invited to move beyond traditional ways of thinking about the study of group communication to consider the

---

[3]Although mountaineers cannot control the movement of the Khumbu Icefall or an oncoming storm, they do have some knowledge and understanding of the signs that lead to certain events, such as shifts in the ice field, avalanches, and so forth.

properties that "make a group a group." Specifically, scholars have been encouraged to study "bona fide" groups that have stable, yet permeable boundaries and are interdependent with their contexts. These characteristics are interrelated and influence intergroup and intragroup communication processes; hence, they are not mutually exclusive categories and, therefore, an illustration of one facet may overlap into another category. The bona fide group perspective, thus, focuses on how intragroup communication processes are related to (or affected by and affect) the external linkages and intergroup communication of contextually embedded groups. In the following sections, I apply the two central characteristics of the bona fide group perspective to the Mt. Everest expeditions of May 1996.

Stable, Yet Permeable Boundaries. The first characteristic of bona fide groups, as exhibited in the Mt. Everest expeditions, concerns the continuous negotiation of group boundaries as influenced by the rules and resources available to a group. As an example of permeable group boundaries, there were several instances where the leader of the Adventure Consultants (aka IFEE) expedition, Rob Hall, was consulted by the leaders and members of the other teams because of his role expertise. As Krakaeur (1997) explained, "People trudged over to our mess tent to seek Hall's advice" (p. 60).[4] Through his interactions at Base Camp with other groups, Hall worked to advance intergroup relations through dialogue and was able to influence other groups' patterns, as well as set shared guidelines for climbing the mountain. This intergroup influence would continue throughout the ascent, as groups were deciding on summit day whether conditions were, in fact, favorable for a summit push.

Interdependence With Context. The second characteristic of bona fide groups references the relationship between groups and their environments, as evidenced by such activities as intergroup communication and coordinated actions among groups. Group boundaries and the identity of groups are highly interdependent with the contexts in which groups are embedded. Within expedition groups, overlapping group memberships occur during escalation situations, which emerge when a group faces circumstances where costs have been incurred in pursuit of an objective that is highly unlikely to be accomplished, regardless of any future course of action undertaken (Staw & Ross, 1989). In such situations, "groups" don't survive within their original boundaries; they rearrange themselves by proximity into "survival" groups, which creates a feel of a larger group identity as climbers in general (expeditions in specific). Thus, under ex-

---

[4]By 1996, Hall had escorted 39 climbers to the summit, more than the total number of people who had summitted during the 20-year period following the first successful summit in 1953 (Coburn, 1997).

tremely unpredictable conditions, such as those common to Mt. Everest,[5] the membership of various groups changes in an effort to preserve the larger group of climbers. Group expedition membership, therefore, fluctuates according to the natural elements and conditions of Mt. Everest.

As a result of the volatile environment on Mt. Everest, escalation situations emerge that create tightly coupled groups (Weick, 1976). Expedition members, for instance, often have to step out of their group boundaries to rescue members of other expeditions. Overlapping group memberships occur during escalation situations, because in crisis, climbers need to rely on the links between the various expeditions to coordinate survival and rescue efforts. This tight coupling of groups produces a strong degree of loyalty to the whole in recognition of their interdependence. Moreover, as previously mentioned, expedition team members begin their quest with tenuous relationships at best and must develop norms and rules to guide their behavior. Drawing on Giddens's (1984) theory of structuration as a framework, I next explore how rules and resources drafted into action by the members of expedition groups are used to create interesting intersections between individual and group rules and resources in the context of the numerous expeditions attempting to summit Mt. Everest in May of 1996.

Structuration Theory

Since the 1990s, Giddens's (1984) structuration theory, which is often used as a conceptual tool to define and examine the foundations and processes of social organization, has evolved into several applications within the field of group communication research: microstructuration (Seibold, Poole, & McPhee, 1985); adaptive structuration theory (AST), in which structuration is merged with the information-exchange perspective (DeSanctis & Poole, 1994, Poole & DeSanctis, 1990; Poole & DeSanctis, 1992); and a morphing of the theory with self-organizing systems theory (SOST; Contractor & Seibold, 1993). The primary focus of these recent adaptations concerns how groups, or societies as a whole, produce and reproduce social systems through the application of generative rules and resources.

Social interaction, according to Giddens (1987), is based on three interrelated elements that produce and reproduce social interaction: (a) structure, (b) action, and (c) institutionalized practices. *Structure* refers to the "rules and resources" actors draft into and maintain in their actions. These *rules* make up generalizable procedures inherent in the "qualities of settings of actions agents routinely draw upon in the course of orienting what they do and what they say to one another" (Giddens, 1987, p. 215). During group communication, rules might emerge, for example, as statements

---

[5]From 1922 to 1996, Everest expeditions had approximately a 42% success rate; an individual climber has a 75% chance of surviving an Everest attempt (Coburn, 1997).

about how things ought to be done or how the group members should behave. Other structures emerge as a result of *resources*, or the materials and attributes available to a group, such as equipment and relationships. *Action*, then, is defined as how actors are able to create choices from the structures, or rules and resources, developed by the group. Over time practices may become *institutionalized* in the sense that they emerge from the interaction of action and structure and become "sedimented" across lengthy spans of time. Group structuration, consequently, emerges from the tension between internal group decisions and external environmental constraints. Accordingly, structuration theorists, in general, attempt to explain group communication processes by examining the rules and resources that are accessed and used by actors to create and recreate structures through a continuous, reproductive process. These three elements of structure (or rules and resources), action (whether intended or unintended), and institutionalized practices are common to most structuration theories and are recursively interrelated; this recursiveness is known as the *duality of structure*, a concept that underscores the notion that social systems act, but exist, only through their actions and the structures they build and, at the same time, are constituted by such structures. For example, when a structure is used in action, it is both a structure itself and a result of that action. Hence, action and structure can never be separated. Moreover, due to the recursive nature of the duality of structure, multiple structures may be enacted and changed concurrently.

Structuration, then, is the process by which social structures, obtainable from a variety of internal and external sources, are produced and reproduced in group life. Structuration theory provides a set of fundamental elements for analyzing group communicative practices. It also remains an important means for providing a conceptual boundary of how rules and resources shape communication processes (Houston, 1996).

AN ANALYSIS OF THE MT. EVEREST EXPEDITION OF 1996

To examine the communication processes that occurred during the May 1996 tragedy on Mt. Everest, I use a variety of sources. First, there are accounts from survivors who have participated in and/or observed the events that unfolded. Second, several media reports were released that contain interviews with survivors and observers. Third, transcripts of actual radio communication from Base Camp to the climbers, and vice versa, were made available on the World Wide Web day-by-day and, at times, hour-by-hour updates were provided on events as they unfolded on the mountain.

The individual narratives were initially divided into categories of rules and resources as described by structuration theory. The granularity of the resources category was divided into smaller units identified as members' knowledge or skill, previous experience, climbing attitude, money, and equipment. As I sorted account comments, several categories emerged beyond those initially anticipated using structuration theory. To some degree, the analysis emerged as a version of Glaser and Strauss's (1967) grounded theory method, which seeks to maximize a sense of discovery. Five categories grounded in the survivors' accounts emerged: (a) intergroup communication, (b) intragroup communication, (c) nature, (d) groupthink, and (e) escalation situations. This approach to understanding the Mt. Everest disaster revealed many complex relationships between natural and human phenomena (see Alder, 1997, for an analysis of the interplay between human interaction and natural conditions resulting in tragedy), especially the human communication factors that contribute to such tragedies.

Structures in Action: Resources, Rules, and Intragroup and Intergroup Communication

> Although we left the Col as members of three distinct expeditions, our fates were already starting to intertwine—and would become more and more tightly bound with every meter we ascended.
> —Krakaeur (1997, p. 165)

Resources in Action. Although successful summits of Mt. Everest depend on an individual's physical preparation, four basic resources, relied on by each expedition's climbers, are unanimously agreed on by climbers as necessary for success: (a) good equipment (e.g., radios, climbing gear, and weatherized clothing); (b) an acclimatization plan; (c) Sherpa support; and (d) bottled oxygen (at least for the novice climber). These resources fluctuate by expedition for a variety of reasons: the expedition guides' choice of equipment and supplies, their acclimatization plan, and the skill of the Sherpa team that assists expeditions in preparing the mountain, for example, by fixing ropes along the route and carrying supplies. The rate at which many of these resources are allotted is ultimately determined not only by the guides' assignment but also by individual needs and conditions on the mountain. Singularly, however, the mountain itself remains the site at which intragroup and intergroup interdependence emerges. The following discussion outlines the effects that planning and allocation of resources had on intergroup communication during the May 1996 Mt. Everest attempt.

One of the first planning actions in which intergroup communication emerged centered on the groups' reliance on the ropes that are typically fixed in advance of the climbers' ascent. Usually, a cooperative, intergroup approach is used to fix the ropes. This agreement is an important site for intergroup interaction given that all groups rely on this vital resource; it is an act of trust to rely on another team to fix the ropes along the route. In exchange for the preparation of the ropes, the designated expedition is paid $2,200 by every other expedition for its trouble.

As mentioned previously, ropes are fixed at multiple points through the Khumbu Icefall and along the route to the summit. During the May 1996 attempt, an agreement existed between five teams to cooperate in the fixing of ropes between camps III and IV (Boukreev & DeWalt, 1997). Because the guides anticipated that only a few ancient, tattered remnants of rope from previous expeditions remained along the summit ridge, the Mountain Madness and Adventure Consultants guides met before leaving Base Camp and created an agreement that their Sherpas would climb 90 minutes ahead of the clients and work collaboratively to fix the ropes. On the morning of the summit bid, however, no Sherpas left ahead of the expedition climbers. As the window of time to complete the summit attempt was closing with every moment the climbers waited, the lack of rope installation would be one of the many small, yet important, contributors to the overall tragedy. One survivor described the result of this obstacle:

> I ran smack into the first bottleneck ninety minutes after moving beyond the Balcony, at 28,000 feet, where the intermingled teams encountered a series of massive rock steps that required ropes for safe passage. Clients huddled restlessly at the base of the rock for nearly an hour while Beidleman [a guide]—taking over the duties of an absent Lopsang [a Sherpa]—laboriously ran out the rope. (Krakauer, 1997, pp. 175–176)

In hindsight, the Sherpas responsible for climbing ahead to fix the ropes claimed that two of the guides received information from another group that the ropes were already prepared. Furthermore, three of the guides, representing two of the teams, never heard of the change in plans (Krakaeur, 1997).

This confusion concerning the ropes reflects an intergroup communication problem of information dissemination, which as Scheerhorn, Geist, and Teboul (1994) discovered in their research, dominates the work of natural task groups. Clearly, a system of information balances and checks is important given that the multiple groups' work is so tightly coupled with the mountain context, and the success of the climb depends on advance preparation of the route. Furthermore, the lack of information dissemination that led to a life-threatening delay of the climb frustrated the team members; as one member noted, "Delays at the fixed lines were foreseeable and eminently preventable" (Krakaeur, 1997, p. 273).

There are three basic ways in which groups can communicate when climbing: (a) face-to-face, (b) over a radio, or (c) through Base Camp. The impact of radio equipment on intragroup and intergroup communication is especially noteworthy. As previously noted, the expedition guides' choices of equipment can have a critical effect on the success of the climb. Radios, in particular, constitute a crucial medium for communication with Base Camp and for coordination among team leaders and their clients on the mountain. One team member noted, "An experienced climber considers the state of his expedition's communications capabilities" (Boukreev & DeWalt, 1997, p. 62).

Poor radio equipment and a general lack of radio distribution affected both intragroup and intergroup communication on those critical summit days. First, the equipment model and number of radios available varied substantially by expedition based on the guides' choice. For example, one of the team members noted that the radios on the Mountain Madness expedition were "a joke ... a major misstep for him [the guide] to go over with those antiquated models" (Boukreev & DeWalt, 1997, p. 61). Second, not only did the older models present a problem but there were also too few of them; in fact, two of the Mountain Madness guides were not issued radios. When climbers on the mountain began having problems with fatigue, exhaustion, and other troubles, relaying information within groups, across groups, and to Base Camp to assist them was difficult, if not impossible.

The lack of ability to communicate frustrated the guides on the mountain. The following accounts, reported by Krakauer (1997), describe the frustrations of guides on the mountain. One guide noted, "Not knowing where Boukreev was on the route and not having supplied him with a radio so the two could communicate, Fischer headed down irked" (Boukreev & DeWalt, 1997, p.115) Another guide reported that "because neither he nor Beidleman had a radio, Anatoli had no way of knowing the true nature of the missing climbers' predicament, or even where on the huge expanse of the mountain they might be" (Boukreev & DeWalt, 1997, p.146). A third lamented, "He didn't have a radio, so there was no way to discuss the situation. It didn't even occur to me to grab his radio, too" (Krakaeur, 1997, p. 201). In all of these situations, climbers were in distress and the inability of the expedition guides to communicate both internally, as well as externally across groups, cost several lives on the mountain. In one instance, a guide who could have answered a call for help and delivered life-saving oxygen to a distressed guide and client above him, continued down the mountain oblivious to the situation because he did not have a radio. Attempts to coordinate rescue resources through base camps were also exacerbated by the poor communications equipment. For example, radio communication between Dr. Hunt at the Mountain Madness Base Camp and the guides and Sherpas of that expedition proved problematic. As Dr. Hunt became increasingly frustrated with the quality and quantity of information she was getting, she was forced to go over to the IFEE camp because it had better communications equipment that could provide her with more information (Boukreev & DeWalt, 1997).

Even when the communications equipment was considered satisfactory, accurate information dissemination was not guaranteed. As an IFEE guide noted, "My radio was malfunctioning. I was able to receive most calls, but my outgoing calls could rarely be heard by anyone" (Krakauer, 1997, p. 226). In this age of tremendous technological advances, it is easy to forget the efficiency of the radio as a communications tool. Furthermore, as this case demonstrates, people overlook the need to insure that a chosen communication channel is capable of carrying the message; people take for granted, even in a carefully orchestrated situation, the importance of communication and information dissemination as a tool for coordinated action. During this Mt. Everest ascent, however, it became clear that the various groups' communication was impaired by the erroneous assumption that members would always be able to reach any other member of their group at any time. This may have been due to the establishment of structures—systemic norms—that developed at Base Camp, where groups could easily consult with other groups and garner help through face-to-face communication. As a result, the groups left for the summit attempt with faulty assumptions and norms that could only be duplicated when they arrived at the next camp.

Even when face-to-face intergroup communication is possible, how the agreed-on structures are used in action (Giddens, 1987) can create dangerous climbing situations. As previously explained, an Everest summit attempt is only possible during the months of April, May, September, and October and, therefore, the window of opportunity is small. Because the last part of the climb—from camp IV to the summit—is the most difficult, time-consuming part of the ascent, climbers actually leave the night before the day they intend to summit. In addition, as previously discussed, given that all groups rely on the fixed ropes that are typically prepared in advance of the climbers, it is impossible for many teams to summit on the same day. As a result of these conditions, one intergroup coordinated action centers on an agreement as to when each group will summit on which days. Thus, every expedition "reserves" a date for a summit attempt.

In hopes of avoiding a dangerous bottleneck on the summit, the IFEE leader and guide held a meeting that included all the leaders of other expeditions (Krakauer, 1997). It was agreed that two expeditions—Mountain Madness and IFEE—would push for the summit on May 10. However, on the night of May 9, the Taiwanese team ignored the agreement and started out with the other two teams just after midnight. Further aggravating the situation, the Taiwanese expedition members bunched together and moved at a particularly slow pace and, thereby, created yet another bottleneck that made it impossible for faster climbers to pass them on the ropes (Krakaeur, 1997).

Part of the intergroup problem that was experienced on Mt. Everest that day was due to the fact that there was a lack of authority to enforce agreements; there existed no hard and fast rules or governing body. Although this intergroup agreement to allow only two groups to proceed that day (a structure/rule) was reached well before the summit day, the lack of adherence to that plan demonstrates that although agreed-on structures may be produced, it is how they are used in action that creates systemic disturbances in groups that reverberate through other groups. In this case, one group's action—the Taiwanese expedition's intragroup decision to also push for the summit that day—created a cumulative effect that produced an intergroup problem. Not only did the Taiwanese team create distress for their own members—one of them would eventually be rescued by another team not even attempting to summit that day—it also created many problems for the other teams as they were delayed in either their attempted ascent at the lines or even in climbing back down. As Krakauer (1997) reported, "Minutes after leaving the summit I reached the top of the Hillary Step, where I encountered a clot of climbers chuffing up the single strand of rope, and my descent came to an enforced halt" (p. 186).

As the problems discussed here reveal, it is difficult to monitor action on Mt. Everest. Even more distressing is the fact that there are few agreed-on rules in mountaineering. The following section further highlights the importance yet difficulty expedition groups face when they attempt to draft hard and fast rules into action. Of particular concern is the difficulty guides have in auditing clients' progress and in aiding them in times of distress. Guides seem to develop custodial relationships with their clients that gives the guides a strong sense of liability not only for clients' success in summitting Mt. Everest but also in terms of keeping their clients safe in an uncertain context.

Rules in Action. Generalizable procedures, routinely drawn on in the course of orienting what actors do and say to one another, were described by Giddens (1987) as rules. Such rules or structures are then used in action as choices that individuals create. In mountain climbing, few rules exist and even those rules are regularly contested by a variety of climbing philosophies. In particular, there exist two basic philosophies: the legalist and the situationist. Legalists argue there should be omniscient, rule-based decision making. Their perspective is motivated by the fear of bad publicity or lawsuits that could result from what would appear to be a lack of responsibility. In contrast, situationists argue that there is no way to create rules that cover every situation that may arise during a risky venture, such as the one Mt. Everest presents. Given the divisiveness of these philosophies, there are very few agreed-on rules expedition guides draw on to make decisions. The setting of rules, or lack thereof, depends entirely on a guide's reading of the situation at any given point in time. Of course, how climbers draft those rules into action may vary a great deal, which could diminish a guide's attempt at implementing structure.

Despite the lack of clear and agreed-on rules, there are a few common conventions most guides make use of when leading expeditions. One of the common rules employed by many guides is a predetermined time to turn around on summit day, regardless of whether the clients complete the climb. The turn-around time represents a choice of safety over success and is one of the few sedimented structures, or, as Gidden's (1987) would call them, institutionalized practices, of climbing. However, the practice of setting and/or adhering to turn-around times is actualized inconsistently across expeditions. Some guides assume their clients will turn around on their own, whereas others feel a sense of responsibility to enforce the turn-around time. Even when guides attempt to enforce this rule, it may be difficult to do when a team may have a quite lengthy physical spread between its first and last climber. Another problem in this situation is that although it is simple to agree on a time to begin descending Mt. Everest, enforcing that rule may dash the climbers' hopes and dreams, as well as their pocketbook. If climbers have not made the summit by the predetermined time and are compelled to turn around, they may feel defeated by the mountain and see themselves as having paid much for little gain. For example, Doug Hansen, a postal clerk, did not make the Mt. Everest summit in a previous attempt and returned to Mt. Everest in May of 1996 to fulfill his dream at great personal cost—a cost that would eventually include his life. Failed attempts also potentially affect a guide's reputation and, thereby, jeopardize his or her ability to recruit clients for future trips.

On the day of the summit attempt, Rob Hall and Scott Fisher, the guides for IFEE and Mountain Madness expeditions, respectively, never directly communicated an explicit turn-around time and policy for their clients. Ironically, all the climbers knew the philosophies of these two guides. Krakaeur (1997) explained Fischer's philosophy as:

> every climber has a set of guidelines he or she follows, little Stay Alive rules. One of Fischer's is the two-o'clock rule. If you aren't on top by two, it's time to turn around. Darkness is not your friend. (p. 146)

As for the summit day in May 1996, the plan was that two guides would alternately lead and Fischer would "sweep" from behind and turn around stragglers. Although Fischer's previously stated philosophy reveals the importance of having a turn-around rule, he never explicitly set a hard and fast turn-around time that day. As for the other Mountain Madness assistant guides, they felt they didn't have the authority to turn clients around. As one guide commented, "I didn't feel comfortable telling clients who'd paid 65k that they had to go down" (Boukreev & Dewalt, 1997, p. 200). This discomfort displays the tension that guides experience between guarding their clients' safety and trying to help them achieve that for which they have paid a great price—both economically and physically—to stand on the top of Mt. Everest.

From the first step toward the summit attempt, the guides' ability to turn around clients was impaired by a lack of communication. First, the oxygen-impoverished environment is simply a difficult setting in which to communicate. Clients and, for the most part, guides[6] wear heavy oxygen masks in order to breathe in the thin air. Second, the physical spread between clients and guides can grow quite large depending on the skills and physical conditioning of each individual climber. Third, the aforementioned radio problems further exacerbated the situation. Finally, the lack of explicit communication concerning turn-around times disturbed many of Hall's friends and colleagues. In interviews with Krakaeur (1997), they expressed "puzzlement at this uncharacteristic lapse of judgment. Why, they wondered didn't he turn Hansen around much lower on the mountain as soon as it became obvious that the American climber was running late?" (p. 224). Scott Fischer's lack of action would also be questioned by survivors; as one commented, "Fischer had not swept any clients back to Camp IV during the day because he's never made contact with any of them after Gammelgaard had parted from him early in the climb" (Boukreev & DeWalt, 1997, p. 154).

As survivors reflected on the happenings of that day, the pattern seen previously regarding the lack of articulating and enforcing a plan is reenacted time and again. The impoverished style of communication within groups, coupled with a lack of adherence to the plan, demonstrates how systemic enactment of structures can create crisis situations. One of the guides, talking about how confusingly the ill-articulated plan was put into action, said, "I was very surprised that people kept coming. I thought they would have either turned around on their own or by somebody else" (as quoted in Boukreev & DeWalt, 1997, p. 153). This guide's comment clearly reflects the lack of understanding as to whose responsibility it was to turn group members around—was it the leaders' responsibility or was it to be self-enforced? Furthermore, this comment represents just one of many that would be made that seem to suggest that the phenomenon of "groupthink" took place that day (Janis, 1982). *Groupthink*, as articulated by Janis (1982), proposes that groups under pressure to perform can make faulty decisions by ignoring or disregarding important information to preserve illusory unanimity. In this case, as multiple group members failed to turn around at a somewhat predetermined time, an illusion of unanimity appeared (Hirokawa, Gouran, & Martz, 1988; Janis, 1982). Many comments echo observations of such problems, perceived even in a hypoxic state, but they were never communicated as members trudged on to reach their goal of standing on Mt. Everest's summit:

---

[6]See Boukreev (1997) and Coburn (1997) for debates on guides' use of supplemental oxygen on Mt. Everest.

[A] few of the team members were still struggling with nausea and head-aches, but none were complaining too loudly, wanting to put the best picture on their condition. (Boukreev & DeWalt, 1997, p. 65)

Nobody discussed Fischer's exhausted appearance. (Krakaeur, 1997, p. 203)

I didn't really say anything to him ... he just sort of raised his hand. He looked like he was having a hard time, but he was Scott [Fisher] so I wasn't particularly worried. I figured he'd tag the summit and catch up to us pretty quick to help bring the clients down. (Krakaeur, 1997, p. 204)

It was as if there were an unspoken agreement .... None of us dare to acknowledge what was at risk here. (Krakaeur, 1997, p. 107)

[I] grew increasingly dismayed at the way the expedition was being managed, where logging on seemed to have a higher priority than logistics. (Boukreev & DeWalt, 1997, p. 94)

[It] became obvious to me the power that comes to you by being in a group. (Boukreev & DeWalt, 1997, p. 132)

These statements demonstrate an impoverished communication pattern typical of groupthink. The members of the various groups maintained a type of harmony as they enacted their goal of climbing Mt. Everest's peak, a harmony that failed to produce little, if any, concern for their own safety or for that of the others. As a result, group members failed to communicate their concerns despite what they observed; consequently, no team member turned around or was turned around by another member. Because members failed to articulate their observations of their teammates' physical condition, those who should have turned around failed to perceive the need to do so and simply kept trudging toward the summit.

Another symptom of groupthink is the relative lack of disagreement or conflict among members, which, in turn, strengthens the illusion of unanimity (Cline, 1990). With regard to the Everest expedition groups, conflict was avoided as group guides left dangling a decision about a precise turn-around time. This, too, was undoubtedly related to the tremendous pressure guides felt to get their clients up the mountain. Bryant (1997) noted that one of the expedition leaders even placed an ad that boasted a 100% success rate. Ultimately, none of the guides were able to turn around their clients for a variety of reasons: (a) lack of communication capacity through radios, (b) a wide physical spread between climbers, (c) faulty group communication norms, and (d) a type of groupthink that led to conflict avoidance rather than the enforcement of rules.

In the end, after many group members failed to turn around close to the somewhat preordained time, the climbers became trapped by a gale-force windstorm. Two guides and a client were caught somewhere along the ridge; another group was stranded in a bivouac on the mountain. One climber was simply never heard from or seen again. In total, there were 8 fatalities on May 10–11 and by the end of the season, the death toll reached 12. One climber summed it up simply, "It wasn't the storm that caused the problem, it was the time" (Boukreev & DeWalt, 1997, p. 227).

Implications

> The highest number on the summit of Mt. Everest at any one time was 30 on May 10th 1996, shortly after this many of those who reached the summit died as a storm suddenly closed in.
> —Adventure Magazine (2000)

This study examined the intragroup and intergroup communication process in escalation situations, with a particular focus on those fateful days in May 1996 on Mt. Everest. The results have several implications for the bona fide group perspective and for understanding the effects of rules, resources, and norms on group structures. First, the negotiation of intergroup boundaries shifts dramatically in crisis situations. Whereas expedition group identity typically develops initially due to the actions of the head guide, these preliminary borders crumble in crisis because group members need to rely on the links developed with other groups to coordinate survival and rescue efforts. This reorganization of groups into a tightly coupled system demonstrates the effects of the context on those embedded in it; the context leads them to recognize their interdependence as climbers rather than as members of a particular expedition. Ultimately, the context creates permeable group boundaries that allow expedition members a chance for survival.

Another standpoint from which to examine the permeability of boundaries is its effects on group identity formation. The source of group identification is often conceptualized as the sense of pride or belonging that members feel toward their group. Previous group research suggests that encouraging external threats is a constructive way to increase cohesion in a group (Ellis & Fisher, 1994). Ironically, as this case suggests, even in the presence of intergroup conflict, which would seemingly create a stronger bond within groups, the permeability of boundaries during crisis situations allows individual groups to band together into a single, large group. Thus, membership leapt from the singly constituted group to an overall identification with climbers as a whole. Scott (1997) argued, in a discussion of the diversity of identification levels as "targets," that a shift in targets is a function of identity and, therefore, "shifts in connection, perceived membership, and loyalty are perhaps best understood via the construct of identification" (p. 492). Under expedition crisis conditions, bona fide groups' identity target is not their primary expedition target but, rather, their larger survival group as climbers. This finding supports Putnam and

Stohl's (1996) argument concerning the importance of analyzing shifts back and forth between internal and external communication group processes as a foundation for understanding bona fide groups.

Another implication emerges from the observation that expedition groups lack structured norms or rules: Expedition group members, operating under circumstances in which there existed no predetermined or enforced guidelines, behaved in ways that created unintended consequences for both themselves and for other climbers on the mountain. The failure to create or enact explicit rules highlights the importance of creating and enacting structure in groups. Ill-defined norms or rules can spiral into a type of groupthink in which group members become overwhelmed by circumstances for which they have no resources or rules to draw on and, subsequently, do nothing except push toward the goal. In this case, groups of climbers hoping to gaze down from the world's highest peak systematically ignored signs and signals of trouble and had no explicit rules for how to deal with such trouble and, thereby, created an illusion of unanimity that led to a lack of what could have been life-saving communication.

CONCLUSION

Since the fatal season of 1996, many other climbers have gone on to conquer Mt. Everest, yet many others have died climbing that and other mountains. Just 1 year after surviving the 1996 disaster, both Anatoli Boukreev and Lopsang Sherpa lost their lives during a climb. In contrast, during June, 2001, the first blind climber stood on top of Mt. Everest. The triumphs and tribulations of climbing in expedition groups will remain an important site for examining group crisis communication. This study showed how groups in crisis situations that fail to create and sustain a communication-rich environment for its members can easily fall prey to a type of groupthink that can lead to a life-endangering situation. Furthermore, the lack of adherence to even an ill-defined plan demonstrates the importance of creating and enacting rules in such groups. In particular, group members in crisis situations are dependent on rules and resources, and when not available, create larger, unintended consequences impacting both individuals and the collective. Rules, resources, and structure are, thus, important foci for the study of groups in context.

This study highlighted, via the bona fide group perspective, the effects of the context on intragroup and intergroup communication. In summary, although the successful scaling of a mountain may depend on an individual climber's skills and expertise, in crisis situations, the permeability of group boundaries and effective intragroup and intergroup communication are critical to survival.

REFERENCES

Adventure Magazine. (2000). Everest climbing and Everest facts. (2000). *Adventure Magazine* [On-line]. Retrieved June 10, 1997 from http://www.adventure-mag.com/everest.htm

Alder, G. S. (1997). Managing environmental uncertainty with legitimate authority: A comparative analysis of the Mann Gulch and Storm King mountain fires. *Journal of Applied Communication Research, 25*, 98–114.

Boukreev, A. (1997). The oxygen illusion: Perspectives on the business of high-altitude climbing. *American Alpine Journal, 72*, 38–43.

Boukreev, A., & DeWalt, G. W. (1997). *The climb: Tragic ambitions on Everest.* New York: St. Martin's Press.

Bryant, M. (1997). Everest a year later: Lessons in futility. *Outside Magazine* [on-line]. Retrieved June 10, 1997, from http://www.outsidemag.com/magazine/0597/ 9705krakauer.html

Cline, R. (1990). Detecting groupthink: Methods for observing the illusion of unanimity. *Communication Quarterly, 38*, 112–126.

Coburn, B. (1997). *Everest: Mountain without mercy.* Washington DC: National Geographic Society.

Contractor, N. S., & Seibold, D. (1993). Theoretical frameworks for the study of structuring processes in group decision support systems: Adaptive structuration and self-organizing systems theory. *Human Communication Research, 19*, 528–563.

DeSanctis, G., & Poole, M. S. (1994). Capturing complexity in advanced technology use: Adaptive structuration theory. *Organization Science, 5*, 121–147.

Ellis, D. G., & Fisher, B. A. (1994). *Small group decision making: Communication and the group process* (4th ed.). New York: McGraw-Hill.

Giddens, A. (1984). *The constitution of society.* Berkeley: University of California Press.

Giddens, A. (1987). *Social theory and modern sociology.* Stanford, CA: Stanford University Press.

Glaser, B. G., & Strauss, A. L. (1967). *Discovery of grounded theory: Strategies for qualitative research.* New York: Walter De Gruyter.

Hirokawa, R. Y., Gouran, D. S., & Martz, A. E. (1988). Understanding the sources of faulty group decision making: A lesson from the *Challenger* disaster. *Small Group Behavior, 19*, 411–433.

Houston, R. (1996). The boundaries of change: An exploratory study of complexity theory, identity and computer-mediated communication (Doctoral dissertation, The Florida State University, 1996). *Dissertation Abstracts International, 57, 08A.*

Janis, I. L. (1982). *Victims of groupthink: A psychological study of foreign-policy decisions and fiascoes.* Boston: Houghton Mifflin.

Krakaeur, J. (1996, September). Into thin air. *Outside Magazine* [On-line]. Retrieved June 12, 1997 from http://www.outsidemag.com/magazine/0996/ 9609feev.html

Krakaeur, J. (1997). *Into thin air: A personal account of the Mt. Everest tragedy.* New York: Villard Books.

Poole, M. S., & DeSanctis, G. (1990). Understanding the use of group decision support systems: The theory of adaptive structuration. In J. Fulk & C. Steinfeld

(Eds.), *Organizations and communication technology* (pp. 173–191). Newbury Park, CA: Sage.

Poole, M. S., & DeSanctis, G. (1992). Microlevel structuration in computer-supported group decision making. *Human Communication Research, 19,* 5–49.

Putnam, L. L., & Stohl, C. (1990). Bona fide groups: A reconceptualization of groups in context. *Communication Studies, 41,* 248–265.

Putnam, L. L., & Stohl, C. (1996). Bona fide groups: An alternative perspective for communication and small group decision making. In R. Y. Hirokawa & M. S. Poole (Eds.), *Communication and group decision making* (2nd ed., pp 147–178). Thousand Oaks, CA: Sage.

Scheerhorn, D., Geist, P., & Teboul, B. (1994). Beyond decision making in decision-making groups: Implications for the study of group communication. In L. R. Frey (Ed.), *Group communication in context: Studies of natural groups* (pp. 247–262). Hillsdale, NJ: Lawrence Erlbaum Associates.

Scott, C. (1997). Identification with multiple targets in a geographically dispersed organization. *Management Communication Quarterly, 10,* 491–522.

Seibold, D. R., Poole, M. S., & McPhee, R. D. (1985). Group decision-making as a structurational process. *Quarterly Journal of Speech, 71,* 74–102.

Staw, B. M., & Ross, J. (1989). Understanding behavior in escalation situations, *Science, 246,* 216–220.

Weick, K. (1976). Educational organizations as loosely coupled systems. *Administrative Science Quarterly, 21,* 1–19.

6

CULTURE AND STIGMA IN A BONA FIDE GROUP:

BOUNDARIES AND CONTEXT IN A "CLOSED" SUPPORT GROUP FOR "ASIAN AMERICANS" LIVING WITH HIV INFECTION

Gust A. Yep
San Francisco State University

Sachiko T. Reece
Private Psychotherapy

Emma L. Negrón
Private Psychotherapy

AIDS, like other illnesses, presents cultural variables that affect all aspects of being ill. These include the labeling of symptoms, how or when pain or other symptoms are communicated and to whom, and the notion of what doctors and helpers are expected to do.

—Aoki (1993, p. 26)

The HIV/AIDS epidemic is spreading rapidly in "Asian American"[1] communities in the United States (see Aoki, Ngin, Mo, & Ja, 1989; Choi, Salazar, Lew, & Coates, 1995; Choi, Yep, & Kumekawa, 1998; Gock, 1994; Mandel & Kitano, 1989; Woo, Rutherford, Payne, Barnhart, & Lemp, 1988; Yep, 1993b, 1997, 1998a). In fact, Choi et al. (1995) observed that "the incidence of AIDS is increasing at a higher rate among Asian and Pacific Islanders than among Whites" (p. 115). This increase may be attributed, in part, to high-risk sexual behavior by "Asian Americans" (see Choi et al., 1995, 1998; Cochran, Mays, & Leung, 1991; Fairbank, Bregman, & Maullin, Inc., 1991).

In an extensive review of the HIV/AIDS problem in "Asian American" communities, Yep (1998a) argued that the AIDS risk reduction model (ARRM) is a useful conceptual framework for understanding health behaviors associated with HIV transmission and promoting efforts to eradicate such behaviors. As proposed by Catania and colleagues (1989, 1990), ARRM conceptualizes risk-reduction behavior as a fluid, rather than static, process. To change one's health behaviors, according to this model, individuals typically go through three stages: (a) labeling, (b) commitment, and (c) enactment. *Labeling*, the initial phase, is where individuals first recognize that their health behaviors are problematic in terms of being associated with the transmission of HIV (transmission knowledge), develop a personal sense of risk for HIV infection (personal susceptibility), and believe that HIV and AIDS are undesirable (social norms). *Commitment* is the stage when individuals attempt to decrease high-risk behaviors and increase low-risk practices by understanding risk-reduction behaviors (knowledge), their benefits (response efficacy), their degree of gratification (perceived enjoyment), their proper enactment (self-efficacy), and their endorsement by others (social support and group norms). *Enactment*, the last phase, occurs when individuals take direct action to reduce their high-risk behaviors by attempting to find solutions (help-seeking behaviors), acquiring the needed interpersonal (e.g., sexual communication) and behavioral skills to perform them, and enacting those solutions and skills (behavioral enactment).

After reviewing available research on "Asian Americans," Yep (1998a) observed that the majority of individuals in these communities are still in

---

[1]The term "Asian American" is a label of convenience used by a number of groups, including grassroots, community-based, and government organizations. We problematize this label by placing quotation marks around it to suggest that this is not a singular, natural, fixed, and/or homogeneous ethnic category. According to the U.S. Census Bureau, there are Asian and Pacific Islander groups from over 40 countries and territories, who speak more than 100 different languages, including Chinese, Filipino, Hawaiian, Japanese, Korean, Samoan, Thai, Vietnamese, to name only a few. "Asian Americans" are characterized by tremendous historical, geographical, social, and cultural locations and identifications, as well as by personal and collective oppressions; therefore, "Asian Americans" may be, according to Lowe (1996), more appropriately viewed as "a socially constructed unity, a situationally specific position, assumed for political reasons" (p. 82).

the labeling stage; a smaller group—namely, self-identified gay and bisexual Asian men and transgender and transsexual Asians—is in the commitment stage of the HIV risk-reduction process (Yep, 1993a). To facilitate movement toward the enactment phase, Yep (1998a) proposed four distinct, but interrelated, health communication intervention programs: (a) a general awareness program to promote the understanding that HIV and AIDS are problems within "Asian American" communities; (b) general information about HIV and AIDS to increase knowledge of HIV transmission, prevention, early intervention, and treatment; (c) an education program for groups with higher rates of HIV infection (e.g., commercial sex workers) to motivate them to change and to assist them in the acquisition of interpersonal (e.g., how to talk about safer sex) and behavioral enactment skills (e.g., how to put on and take off a condom); and (d) an education program for those who already have HIV or AIDS to disseminate information about early intervention, treatment, and medical updates and to provide them with psychosocial support. Although the first three types of communication programs have been implemented in "Asian American" communities (see, e.g., Yep, 1994, in press), educational and social support efforts for "Asian Americans" living with HIV infection have been largely ignored.

The purpose of this study is to examine communication processes that serve to promote education and offer social support for the "Asian American" population. More specifically, we use the bona fide group perspective to examine how culture and stigma affect group boundaries and the context of group life in a "closed" support group for "Asian Americans" living with HIV infection—a group in crisis characterized by the deadly nature of this disease and the societal stigma associated with it. To accomplish this goal, we divide the chapter into four sections. First, we propose a bona fide group perspective for the study of communication in support groups. Second, we describe and analyze emergent themes in a support group for "Asian Americans" living with HIV or AIDS. Third, we discuss the influence of culture on support group communication by examining and comparing the findings from the "Asian American" group we studied to findings from other HIV/AIDS-related support groups. Finally, we conclude with a summary and discussion of our findings and their implications for the study of communication in bona fide groups.

A BONA FIDE GROUP PERSPECTIVE FOR THE STUDY OF COMMUNICATION IN SUPPORT GROUPS

Support groups have proliferated during the past 25 years; Cline (1999) observed that "evidence indicates a burgeoning growth of social support groups as [U.S.] Americans search for a sense of community bounded not by streets and villages, but rather by shared experiences, symbols, and worldviews" (p. 516). In Western cultures, particularly in the United States, support groups are an important therapeutic modality that offers individuals help with acquiring information, giving and receiving social support, solving problems, and developing coping skills (see, e.g., Acevedo, 1993; Cline, 1999; Sullivan & Sherblom, 1995; Yalom, 1985). Group work is a cost-effective method for improving the psychological well-being of individuals in need (Vinogradov & Yalom, 1989) by fostering hope (Sullivan & Sherblom, 1995), fulfilling their multiple psychological needs (Chung & Magraw, 1992; St. John, 1992), improving their quality of life (Schaffner, 1990), and offering them social support (Cawyer & Smith-Dupré, 1995; Cline, 1999).

Most scholars have studied the internal processes of support groups as separate and independent from the larger contexts in which such groups are embedded. Support groups are, thus, traditionally treated as "containers" with rigid boundaries that separate the internal group dynamics from the personal, social, and cultural contexts in which these groups function. The bona fide group perspective, according to Putnam and Stohl (1990, 1996), Stohl and Putnam (1994), and Frey (Introduction, this volume), challenges this approach to the study of group communication by postulating that internal group communication simultaneously influences and is influenced by permeable and dynamic group boundaries and multiple contexts. This perspective, consequently, challenges traditional container models of group communication by highlighting three important characteristics of groups. First, bona fide groups are characterized by permeable, fluid, and socially constructed boundaries through participants' memberships in multiple groups, the conflicting role identities that result from such memberships, and their degree of belongingness, as well as the group identity formation that results from ongoing interaction with other members. Second, these groups have shifting borders as members continuously negotiate, clarify, reconstruct, contest, and change their individual and group identities and allegiances with other group members. Third, such groups are interdependent with their immediate contexts in the sense that there is a reciprocal relationship between a group and the environments in which it is embedded, as demonstrated through intergroup communication, coordinated actions among members, and a group's negotiation of autonomy and assignment of meanings to events.

Given these characteristics, support groups are a good example of bona fide groups. Support groups have permeable boundaries (e.g., participants are members of multiple groups—such as ethnic, racial, social class, sexual orientation, and gender communities—and group memberships evolve and change), shifting borders (e.g., participants constantly affirm, negotiate, and change their group identities and collective group identities are continually recreated and modified), and interdependence with their immediate contexts (e.g., participants continuously negotiate issues of privacy and secrecy related to disclosure of their HIV status in their personal, professional, and social lives outside of the group and group interactions are influenced by new medical developments).

These characteristics are created and sustained through communication. Communication is, thus, the essential foundation of support groups (Cline, 1999), and affects both the processes and outcomes of these groups. Hence, support groups form, develop, maintain, and change through communication processes. Similarly, communication plays a critical role in the affective, cognitive, and behavioral outcomes that members of support groups experience. In summary, "communication is essential to [the] power of support groups, and the degree of a group's effectiveness is in many ways contingent on how well communication goals are met" (Sullivan & Sherblom, 1995, pp. 246–247).

In the context of individuals living with HIV, Chung and Magraw (1992) observed that "group treatment provides peer support through sharing of experiences confronting the reality of illness and providing a forum in which to enhance coping with HIV-related problems" (p. 891). Support groups are invaluable because of their ability to decrease members' isolation through (a) sharing feelings and problems associated with a recent HIV or AIDS diagnosis; (b) venting emotions and experiencing catharsis and, thereby, enhancing their coping strategies; (c) discussing issues related to disclosure of their health status to significant others; and (d) sharing information about new medical discoveries and treatment modalities, among others (see, e.g., Adelman & Frey, 1997; Cawyer & Smith-Dupré, 1995; Coleman & Harris, 1989; Levy, Tendler, VanDevanter, & Cleary, 1990; Sullivan & Sherblom, 1995).

Although a number of researchers and practitioners (e.g., Aoki, 1993; Dworkin & Pincu, 1993; Jue & Kain, 1989; Yep, 1994, 1998a) have identified the need for culturally sensitive and appropriate communication in support groups for individuals living with HIV/AIDS, the interactional patterns among "Asian Americans" in support group settings have been largely unexplored. To partially fill this void in the literature, we conducted an exploratory study of an "Asian American" HIV/AIDS support group. In the following sections, we describe the group studied, examine how culture and stigma affect group boundaries and contexts, and identify other themes in support group interaction.

A SUPPORT GROUP FOR "ASIAN AMERICANS" LIVING WITH HIV/AIDS

The group for this study consisted of eight "Asian Americans" living with HIV infection (seven men and one woman). They were members of a "closed" support group (the group was constituted by these individuals af-

ter initial screening and no new members were allowed into the group after it was formed) that met every other week over a 6-month period—for a
total of 12 group meetings—and was facilitated by the second author, a licensed mental health professional. The meetings were held at a local private psychotherapy office in southern California and lasted 90 to 120
minutes each session. Six participants were HIV positive and asymptom-
atic; the other two were diagnosed with AIDS. They were all recipients of
services from a local HIV-related organization serving "Asian Americans."

The facilitator maintained detailed clinical records for each group meeting. These notes were carefully written after each session and included both
accounts of specific exchanges between group members, as well as clinical
observations and explanations of interventions. After receiving informed
consent from all of the group members, the content of group members' interaction reflected in the clinical notes served as the data for this study.

The data were content analyzed by the third author, a researcher and licensed mental health professional, who was not involved in the design or
delivery of the therapeutic services offered to the participants in the study.
The data were analyzed using the constant comparative method (Glaser &
Strauss, 1967; Strauss & Corbin, 1990), which requires that a tentative
typology be created on the basis of early observations and a coder then
continually refines these categories in light of new data until a more defi-
nite typology emerges from the entire data set. After initial coding by the
third author of the data from all 12 group meetings, all 3 authors worked
together to develop, refine, and reassess a typology of the themes that occurred in the support group interaction. Three main themes emerged: (a)
culture, (b) stigma, and (c) other themes.

Culture

In his seminal text on culture, Williams (1983) wrote, "Culture is one of the
two or three most complicated words in the English language" (p. 87). Culture encompasses both material products (e.g., books, artifacts, and visual
models of HIV) and nonmaterial meanings (e.g., cultural members' beliefs,
attitudes, ideas, and collective constructions of the HIV epidemic).
Through this lens, HIV/AIDS is both an epidemic of a transmissible deadly
disease and an epidemic of meanings and signification (Treichler, 1988). In
terms of meanings, Treichler (1992) argued that "AIDS continually escapes
the boundaries placed on it by positivist medical science and its meanings
mutate on a parallel with the virus itself" (p. 391). The effect of that double
epidemic, as Frey, Adelman, and Query (1996) noted, is that "AIDS is not
just creating havoc with body and mind, it has become a defining feature of
the body politic" (p. 385).

Consistent with the view of culture as fluid, continuously contested,
and ever-changing, Bell (1998), arguing from a Bakhtinian perspective,
suggested that culture is synonymous with dialogue:

> Culture, in this view, is the conversations we have and which we expect to have with various people in various places at various times; it is also the conversations we have which we did not expect with these various people in these various places at these various times. (p. 52)

This definition of culture focuses on its dialogic, creative, and improvisational nature. From this perspective, culture is characterized by contradiction, change, *praxis*, and wholism. First, culture is full of contradictions. For instance, Wat (1996) recalled his "coming out" experience to his parents, whose cultural upbringing made homosexuality a forbidden topic: "[My parents] hate queers, but they love me, even though I am gay" (p. 76). Second, ebbs and flows of change characterize culture; cultural change is more like a spiral than a straight line. For example, family members of a gay or lesbian child go in and out of the closet depending on factors such as the situational context, their relational connection to their son or daughter, and their own adjustment to the child's sexuality. Third, culture is characterized by *praxis*—that is, culture simultaneously constrains its members while providing them with opportunities to change the future of the culture. For example, Kang (1996) recalled the process of coming out to his mother, a Korean woman:

> I told her [that] I was gay … [and] she asked me how long I had been impotent. I tried to explain that my problem wasn't impotence, but that I wasn't attracted to women. But she assumed, because I told her I was gay, that I was impotent. (p. 87)

In this case, cultural views of homosexuality restricted the mother's behavior, but at the same time, Kang's open discussion of his sexuality was creating conditions for changes and, indeed, as he reported, his mother later appeared to be more accepting of his sexual orientation. Finally, culture is characterized by wholism, operating in multiple contexts (e.g., temporal and spatial); cultural members, therefore, interact with others from their respective historical, geographical, and social locations and identifications.

Some of the factors just described have been attributed to "Asian American" culture, which, according to Lowe (1996), is characterized by heterogeneity, hybridity, and multiplicity. *Heterogeneity* refers to differences and differential power relationships that exist among "Asian Americans"; for instance, "Asian Americans" come from different national origins, generational relation to exclusionary immigration laws, social class backgrounds, gender, and sexual orientation. *Hybridity* refers to the processes through which "Asian Americans" survive and invent different cultural alternatives within relationships of unequal power and domination; for example, many "Asian Americans" live with a mixture of traditional Asian and dominant European American cultural values. Finally, *multiplicity* refers to the ways in which "Asian Americans" are simultaneously affected by factors such as capitalism, patriarchical power, racial hegemony, and heterosexist ideology.

These characteristics suggest that "Asian American" cultures are diverse and varied. In fact, when asked about whether there is a general "Asian American point of view," Hagedorn (1994), a renowned Filipina writer and performance artist, noted, "I'm not so sure. Well, perhaps food. Love of food, and a certain sensibility regarding beauty. And I do think our cultures are steeped in traditions of grace and hospitality—we share that with other Asian Americans" (p. 179). Given the seemingly minimal shared values noted, there appears to be no singular "Asian American" perspective.

The diversity of "Asian American" voices and experiences is, thus, characterized by interplay and collision between race, class, gender, sexuality, and other factors (see, e.g., Aguilar-San Juan, 1994; Chin, 1997; Eng & Hom, 1998; hooks, 1990; Jordan & Weedon, 1995; Leong, 1996; Lowe, 1996; Manalansan, 1996; Reyes & Yep, 1997; Wat, 1996). To illustrate, Yep, Lovaas, and Ho (2001) recalled a situation they encountered in a restaurant in a San Francisco gay neighborhood:

> A young, attractive, well-dressed, and highly limerent gay male couple was seated at an adjacent table. One was "Asian American" and the other Euroamerican. When the "Asian American" finished taking a call on his cellular phone (it sounded like that he was a high-level executive), the two started a conversation. The Euroamerican recounted, "I talked to my mother on the phone today and I told her about us. She asked me about you … and I told her that you are Eurasian and she said, 'What? What does that mean?' I explained to her that you were Japanese and Italian but American … very American … with that strong Italian part of you. I also told her that you have a very good job." They smiled into each other's eyes, seemingly happy with the mother's approval. The server came by to explain the "specials of the day" sustaining steady eye contact with the Euroamerican as if he was the only customer at the table. The server returned several times and each instance he inquired about their meal through the Euroamerican without ever directing his gaze and speech to the "Asian American" partner. (pp. 154–155)

Yep et al. explained their observation of this seemingly simple incident as follows:

> In this intricate interplay of race, class, gender, and sexuality, the "Asian American" male becomes invisible. His Japaneseness is erased as he and his partner perpetuate the image that being Japanese is un-American. This is co-created by his partner's overt Eurocentrism ("very American … with that strong Italian part of you") and his own consensual silence. The Euroamerican also included a social class marker (his partner has a very good job) in the conversation with his mother almost as an attempt to equalize the status of his partner (given that being Eurasian was perceived as "less than"). Likewise, the interaction with the restaurant server makes the "Asian American" virtually and symbolically invisible. (p. 155)

Keeping the interlocking axes of race, class, gender, and sexuality in mind, we now turn to emergent themes that support group members expressed in the context of their interactions over the 6-month period of the group's life.

Cultural concerns were an important theme for this group; such concerns consisted of experiences and issues expressed by group members that were attributed to their cultural upbringing and heritage. Two important issues were attributed to "Asian American" cultural traits: (a) shame associated with HIV infection, and (b) an indirect mode of communication in face-to-face encounters when compared to their U.S. counterparts.[2]

Shame associated with HIV infection was consistently expressed by group members. Because HIV is associated with taboo subjects in "Asian American" culture, such as homosexuality, illness, and death, it is extremely shameful to contract the disease. The shame not only affects the individuals who have the disease but also their family and community. Infected individuals often feel responsible for contracting the virus and bringing shame to their family and/or community. One support group member, who is both gay and a person living with AIDS (PWA), reported that he experiences "double shame" because his AIDS diagnosis "is like a betrayal to my family who does not even know that I'm gay." Past research has found that shame is a powerful force in "Asian American" cultures (Aoki, 1993; Carrier, Nguyen, & Su, 1992; Chan, 1989; Chang, 1993; Hom, 1996; Yep, in press). Even reactions to a "single shame," such as a child coming out as lesbian or gay, can be difficult. For instance, Hom (1996) reported the case of Shigekawa, an "Asian American" mother residing in Hawaii, who recalled her reaction to her daughter's disclosure of her lesbianism:

> I was ashamed. I felt I had a lot to do with it too. In my mind I'm not stupid, I'm telling myself, I know I didn't do it to her. I don't know if it's only because I'm Japanese … that's the way I saw it. I felt a sense of shame, that something was wrong with my family. I would look at [my daughter] and just feel so guilty that I have these thoughts that something's wrong with her. But mostly I was selfish. I felt more for myself, what am I going to say? How am I going to react to people when they find out? (p. 44)

Abramson (1986) noted that although "'guilt' societies provide the opportunity for the atonement of one's sins … shame is a life-long burden" (p. 4), and this sense of burden was consistently expressed by support group members. As one member lamented, "We are living in shame." The feeling of shame, coupled with the desire to not bring embarrassment or

---

[2]To provide a more complete characterization of "Asian American" cultural traits, we make explicit our points of comparison to European American culture. This descriptive and analytical procedure is consistent with the method of "double description" in intercultural communication that Lee, Chung, Wang, and Hertel (1995) suggested.

loss of face and honor to oneself and one's social groups, was an ongoing theme expressed by members of this support group.

Another issue attributed to "Asian American" culture by support group members was the indirect mode of communication that was used in their daily interactions. Some members noted that they had attended but felt uncomfortable in non-Asian or ethnically mixed HIV support groups because the communication exchange was too direct. As one person explained, "Some of those [non-Asian] guys have a very aggressive attitude and express what they think without worrying about how others [in the group] might feel." An indirect style of communication was also preferred by support group members in their interactions with family members, with several support group members indicating that their families never talked about feelings openly. As one member said, "We show how we feel through our actions; we don't talk about those feelings." This indirect mode of interaction is consistent with past observations of "Asian Americans" (see, e.g., Aoki et al., 1989; Yep, 1994, 1998b). Wat (1996), for instance, noted that "Asian American" parents tend to use "it" to refer to homosexuality, as if uttering the actual word was too shameful and threatening. Similarly, support group members often used "it" to refer to HIV or AIDS, as if saying it out loud made it more real and more stigmatizing, a concern that pervaded the group and to which we now turn.

Stigma

Stigma may be viewed as a "social contaminant" (Pryor & Reeder, 1993, p. 264) that spoils the affected person's identity by labeling him or her as bad, inferior, perverted, shameful, dangerous, and/or deadly. According to Goffman (1963), there are four types of stigma: (a) abominations of the body (e.g., physical deformities); (b) perceived blemishes of personal character (e.g., drug abuse or homosexuality); (c) tribal odium (e.g., stigma assigned on the basis of HIV status, race, or religion); and (d) "courtesy stigma" (e.g., stigma attached to a partner of a PWA, regardless of the partner's serostatus). Individuals living with HIV or AIDS can potentially be considered "fatally flawed" (Douard, 1990, p. 37) in several of these areas (e.g., a known intravenous drug user from a minority community with visible symptoms of opportunistic infections associated with AIDS).

AIDS-related stigma refers to those reactions directed at individuals who are perceived to be infected with HIV, regardless of whether that is, in fact, the case (Herek & Glunt, 1988). Leary and Schreindorfer (1998) argued that the core of stigmatization is interpersonal disassociation: "People are stigmatized when they are viewed as possessing characteristics that constitute a basis for avoiding or excluding them" (p. 15). They proposed four bases of AIDS-related stigma: (a) threat to others' health or safety (e.g., perceiving HIV to be contagious); (b) violation of social and cultural normative standards (e.g., illegal drug usage); (c) perception of a person's failure to contribute to the social good (e.g., perceiving PWAs to be draining resources from society); and (d) creation of negative emotional and aversive reactions in others (e.g., feeling repulsed and uncomfortable interacting with PWAs). Although the foundations for AIDS-related stigma might have some degree of universality, how individuals manage such stigma is influenced by culture. For example, how PWAs talk about their health and illness is influenced by cultural styles of communication.

For stigmatized individuals to engage in daily social interaction with nonstigmatized others with minimal discomfort, they must learn to "pass" (Goffman, 1963, p. 42), the complex process of managing the dialectic of secrecy and disclosure (Petronio, 2002; Yep, 2000). During interactions that occurred in the "Asian American" support group, members discussed various ways in which they managed interpersonal and work-related secrecy and disclosure issues to minimize stigma.

In terms of interpersonal issues, support group members expressed concerns about the potential effects that their HIV diagnosis may have on their interpersonal relationships. Two common themes were discussed by group members: (a) disclosure and the "coming out" process and (b) social isolation.

Disclosure about one's HIV serostatus or AIDS diagnosis was a major concern for most support group members. Some openly gay members of the group indicated that telling others about their diagnosis was like "coming out all over again" (referencing their earlier experiences of disclosing their sexual orientation); for the "closeted" members of the group, sharing their diagnosis was akin to a "double coming out" (disclosing both their HIV status and sexual orientation). Although some group members recalled positive experiences associated with the disclosures (one said, "I felt a sense of relief and accomplishment," and another added, "It [the disclosure] made my relationship stronger ... and the [friendship] bond deeper"), they were still cautious about who, when, and what they told others. Some restricted their communication boundaries to protect themselves against rejection and stigmatization. Others did so to protect their significant others; as one group member noted, "I should not tell [that I have AIDS] ... so that at least I can protect people who are dear to me from feeling shock and distress."

The process of disclosure about one's HIV status, in general, is extremely difficult and complex (see, e.g., Greene & Serovich, 1996; Leary & Schreindorfer, 1998; Serovich & Greene, 1993; Yep, 2000). HIV/AIDS is a life-threatening, communicable, and chronic health condition; therefore, it is not surprising that people living with HIV do not readily inform others about their condition (Marks, Richardson, & Maldonado, 1991; Yep, 2000). Individuals living with HIV often experience, among other reactions, social stigmatization (Adelman & Frey, 1997; Clemo, 1992; Douard,

1990; Frey, Query, Flint, & Adelman, 1998; Herek & Capitanio, 1993; Herek & Glunt, 1988; Pryor & Reeder, 1993; Siegel & Krauss, 1991), denial (Earl, Martindale, & Cohn, 1991), extreme uncertainty (Adelman & Frey, 1994, 1997; Siegel & Krauss, 1991; Weitz, 1989), fear and anxiety (Fullilove, 1989; Gochros, 1992), isolation and emotional turmoil (Cherry & Smith, 1993; Morin, Charles, & Malyon, 1984; Moynihan & Christ, 1987; Newmark & Taylor, 1987), difficulties in interpersonal and intimate relationships (Cameron, 1993), abandonment and physical rejection (Mooney, Cohn, & Swift, 1992; Stulberg & Buckingham, 1988), and homophobia and discrimination (Anderson, 1989; Cameron, 1993; Rowe, Plum, & Crossman, 1988). In short, there are few, if any, domains of life that are not touched by an HIV or AIDS diagnosis.

Related to issues associated with disclosure of HIV status were concerns raised by support group members about the possibility of social isolation, whether self-created or imposed by others. A member reported in his first group meeting that "I started noticing that I was cutting myself off from my friends to hide my HIV status ... but I know that I cannot live in isolation." This ongoing struggle between social isolation and need for social support is often a result of the stigma associated with the disease. As Cline and Boyd (1993) noted:

> The dilemma faced by persons with HIV/AIDS is this: either risk becoming stigmatized by disclosing their condition, in order to take a chance on gaining the potential health benefits of social support or avoid being stigmatized by engaging in information control and nondisclosure, thereby losing the potential health benefits of social support. (p. 132)

This dilemma can be formidable and there are psychological consequences, such as loneliness and depression, associated with it (Leary & Schreindorfer, 1998).

One of the ways that people with HIV or AIDS manage this dilemma is by participating in support groups. In support groups, people can disclose things that might not be accepted or understood by those not living with the disease. One member captured well the sentiments of the other members: "I can say things about myself [in this group] that I am afraid to talk about in the real world."

In addition to concerns about relationships, support group members expressed concerns related to their work; such concerns included fear of loss of employment, benefits, and financial security directly related to stigma, homophobia, and unfriendly working environments for people living with HIV or AIDS. One member shared with the group her anxiety about the fear that her new employer, if he found out about her HIV status, would "cut off her health benefits" while she was undergoing job training. Another was concerned about whether he could keep his job if his employer became aware that he had AIDS because, in his words, "the setting is very conservative and homophobic." Two other members were concerned about leaving their current employment, despite their feelings of dissatisfaction and unhappiness with their work settings, because of the fear of loss of health benefits and financial stability.

Throughout the ongoing internal group dialogue about fears of personal and interpersonal rejection, discrimination, and social isolation, support group members listened to and shared strategies for coping with HIV-related stigma. Such stigma prompted members to re-examine their life goals and their health and well-being, concerns to which we now turn.

Other Themes

As members shared, supported, and, at times, challenged each other, other themes emerged during the group interaction. One theme involved members redefining their personal goals; this included both redefining their short-term, day-to-day goals and their long-term life goals. Some group members indicated the need to "live for the present moment," whereas others engaged in what Cawyer and Smith-Dupré (1995) termed *communicating to prepare*—engaging in talk that would help them to deal with the onset of illness and prepare for death more effectively. One group member noted that writing an autobiography was his "new life task"; others talked about the need for and logistics of writing a will.

Another dominant theme of group talk was, not surprisingly, related to members' concerns about their health and well-being. Three health-related issues were commonly discussed in the group: (a) concern about bodily changes, (b) information about new medications and side effects, and (c) discussion of alternative medicine and Eastern healing practices.

Support group members were, to varying degrees, concerned about changes in their health. For example, weight loss was perceived to be an important indicator of their condition. As one member indicated, "I did not used to pay much attention to my weight .... Now I worry when I lose a few pounds." The group members spent much time discussing currently accepted medical indicators of immune system functioning, such as T-cell counts, and much anxiety surrounded discussion of T-cell count results. One member echoed the sentiments of the group, "When my T-cell count went under 500 [the low end of the acceptable normal range], I felt that I got closer to AIDS, my end." Group members also used other ways of monitoring and assessing their health; for example, one member noted that he had difficulties accepting his recent AIDS diagnosis because "I am looking good .... [and] I am capable of doing things." Although physical appearance is not considered to be a medically accepted indicator of the progression of the disease, most members used it as a form of ongoing personal monitoring of their health. Once in a while, group members expressed frustrations about this daily monitoring of their health. For instance, the female group member told the group, on several occasions, that "I am too busy taking care of my husband [who is HIV-negative] …. He is not eating a balanced diet …. I am not worrying about HIV!" This episode also appears to indicate that, given her "Asian American" cultural upbringing and gender-role behaviors, too much concern for herself seemed to be inappropriate.

Group interaction was also characterized by discussion and sharing of information regarding current and new medications and their potential side effects. Although support group members did not express consensus about the value of these drugs, the sharing of such information appeared to serve an important function for these individuals. As one member indicated, "Although I am not currently taking any drugs [for HIV] … it is good to be able to learn and share information."

A final significant theme discussed in the support group was about alternative and complementary treatments for HIV. Some members discussed stress-reduction techniques; others shared information about Tai-chi, meditation, healing with imagery, and prayer. Discussion of traditional Chinese medicine was frequent; in particular, members shared their knowledge about "Chinese bitter melon" (*momordica charantia*) as a potential anti-HIV agent with low clinical toxicity. Although members differed in their beliefs about the value of these alternative methods of treatment, group interaction was facilitative—as opposed to inhibitive—of discussion of methods, such as these, that are generally not accepted by the conventional medical establishment. In fact, one of the group members, a physician trained in the West, displayed great ease and comfort discussing both mainstream and alternative treatments and did not appear to exhibit any conflicting role identities between being an expert in the Western medical model and being a member of a group that explored and sometimes endorsed alternative medicine. Perhaps this comfort is because support group interactions appear to be in line with the influence of the larger context of "Asian American" culture, as some of these alternative treatment methods are well accepted within Eastern healing practices.

THE INFLUENCE OF CULTURE IN HIV/AIDS SUPPORT GROUP INTERACTIONS

As the findings from this study show, culture was an omnipresent force that affected how support group members initiated, maintained, and negotiated relationships with other group members; sought, received, and provided social support to others; and worked with the ongoing struggle of HIV/AIDS-related stigma management both inside and outside the group. To put it in bona fide group terms, culture was a powerful influence on the internal discourse of this support group. The question must be asked, however, to what extent "Asian American" cultural values made the support group we studied unique and different from other HIV/AIDS-related support groups. In this section, we examine and compare our findings to those from other HIV/AIDS-related support groups.

The findings from the present study differ in some important ways from what has been found in past research. Some of these differences might be explained in terms of cultural differences of the support group participants. For example, Cawyer and Smith-Dupré (1995) noted that endorsement of alternative treatments for HIV or AIDS was perceived as "a violation of community" (p. 251) in the HIV/AIDS support group, consisting mainly of European American members, that they investigated. In contrast, one of the themes ("health-related issues") in the discourse of the "Asian American" support group was about alternative treatments, which were often perceived as acceptable by the members. One plausible explanation might be that the group found particular alternative treatment modalities (e.g., Tai-chi and meditation) to be culturally validating and consistent with Eastern healing practices. Another possible explanation for the open discussion of alternative treatments, also related to the influence of culture, might be the participants' strong sense of collectivism (i.e., supporting such discussion to maintain harmonious relationships in the group) and face needs (i.e., avoiding open disagreement in the group to preserve and maintain other members' projected public image) when compared to their non-"Asian American" support group counterparts.

Another departure from past research involves Cawyer and Smith-Dupré's (1995) finding concerning the importance of communicating to vent emotions—including overt and subtle expressions of anger—in the HIV/AIDS support group that they observed. Although members of the "Asian American" support group expressed frustrations and other "negative" feelings, such communicative acts were not dominant in the group's discourse. This finding appears to be consistent with Asian cultural values regarding the moderate expression of strong emotions in the presence of others (Aoki et al., 1989; Yep, 1998b). Interestingly, Chung and Magraw's (1992) study of HIV-positive, mostly European American, lower middle-class women in group therapy also differs from Cawyer and Smith-Dupré's (1995) observation, as communicating to vent emotions was not one of the primary themes in the group that they observed. Future research needs to ascertain more clearly the role of cultural values, including gender-role behaviors, in the expression of intense emotions in HIV/AIDS support groups.

Finally, members indicated during group discussions that participating in an all-"Asian American" group had several advantages. Because of perceived underlying similarities in cultural backgrounds, group members indicated that they felt, as one member put it, "much more comfortable than

in the other [ethnically mixed support] groups [he had attended]." Moreover, this degree of comfort based on similarity appeared to be especially
true of first-generation "Asian American" members. Related to this perception of cultural homophily, the group, as one member claimed, "allowed
them to come together with no tension and no worry of being misunderstood"; the result was the creation of a safe space that mobilized feelings of
common ground and cohesion. However, some differences due to gender-role expectations did occur in the group; for example, the sole woman
in the group expressed more concern about caring for her HIV-negative
husband than caring for herself, whereas most of the men expressed more
concern about caring for themselves than for others. It, thus, appears that
there may be a difference between "Asian American" women and men infected with HIV in this regard. Group members also seemed to have different cultural perceptions of their role in support groups when compared to
European American groups. For instance, a popular view for a "closed"
support group for European Americans is that of an oral contractual agreement in which all members explicitly agree to attend and participate in all
group meetings. In contrast, members of the "Asian American" support
group used the metaphor of a "family" (as opposed to a contract) to describe their group involvement and behaved much more loosely with respect to their own and expectations of others' punctuality and attendance.
Some members came late to group meetings; others did not see the need
to stop interacting at the designated end time.

Our research also indicates, however, that interactions among "Asian
Americans" in an HIV-related support group are similar to other such support group interactions. For example, Cawyer and Smith-Dupré's (1995)
study of communication in an HIV/AIDS support group found that members interacted in the group setting for purposes of healing and preparing
for the possibility of getting ill and dying. *Communicating to heal* refers to
the open expression of concerns and frustrations through the sharing of
common experiences and expressing empathy for those experiences. This
form of communication also characterized the group examined in this
study, as many communication episodes were enacted to share, support,
and validate group members' feelings of concern about shame, stigma, and
the struggle between expanding personal boundaries through disclosure
of their condition to important others in their life and restriction of such
boundaries through nondisclosure and either forced or self-imposed social isolation. *Communicating to prepare* involves members sharing information to enhance their sense of control over their health condition. In the
"Asian American" support group, this type of sharing occurred frequently
in the form of discussion of health-related issues—specifically, new medical treatments and their side effects. The findings regarding the discussion
of interpersonal and health-related issues are in line with those of Chung
and Magraw (1992), who, in their study of group therapy for HIV-positive

women, found that stigma, isolation, and medical issues were common themes discussed by the participants.

In summary, culture influences the internal discourse of support groups. Some of the differences that we identified in this study of an all-"Asian American" HIV/AIDS-related support group, when compared to non-"Asian American" support groups, seem to support this claim. However, HIV/AIDS-related support groups also share some fundamental similarities, regardless of the participants' cultural background. Because of the nature of HIV/AIDS-related illnesses and the social stigma attached to them, support group members come together to heal—by sharing and affirming each other's experiences—and to prepare—by disseminating information and discussing coping strategies—to enhance their sense of control over their condition and to minimize the effects of social stigma.

IMPLICATIONS FOR THE STUDY OF GROUP COMMUNICATION

As more and more people become infected with HIV, management of this physical condition has become an important social and medical concern. Moreover, HIV and AIDS have, in recent years, become chronic medical conditions, which means that individuals must learn to live and cope with their diagnosis (Chachkes, 1993; Yep, 2000). Within that context, the support-group setting has become an important and cost-effective modality to assist people living with HIV and/or AIDS in coping with their diagnosis and the dynamics of living with these chronic conditions. Although some research exists on communication in HIV-related groups (e.g., drop-in groups and support groups), this literature has largely ignored the cultural contexts (e.g., ethnic composition of such groups and cultural assumptions about group work) that affect such group interactions.

To address this need, we used the bona fide group perspective to examine how culture and stigma undergird interaction in a "closed" support group for "Asian Americans" living with HIV/AIDS. Our analysis identified several themes that emerged during the support group interactions, including cultural concerns, interpersonal and work-related issues, redefinition of life goals, and health-related concerns. Cultural concerns consisted of group members' experiences that were attributable to their cultural upbringing (in this case, being "Asian American"), including feelings of shame associated with HIV infection (and, for some, homosexuality) and indirect ways of communicating with others, in general, and about their medical condition, in particular. Interpersonal issues consisted of members' concerns about the potential effects that an HIV or AIDS diagnosis might have on group members' personal relationships, as reflected in the ongoing struggle between disclosure and social isolation. Work-related concerns ranged from fear of loss of employment and benefits to financial security and/or stress associated with working in an environment that was unfriendly and hostile to those living with HIV and/or AIDS. Redefinition of life goals referred to group interactions that dealt with both adjustment to day-to-day life and reprioritizing of long-range goals associated with the prospect of a curtailed life span. Finally, health-related issues focused on concerns about health and well-being, including feelings about bodily changes and information about new treatment modalities and alternative medicine.

The "Asian American" HIV/AIDS support group we studied illustrates well the principles of the bona fide group perspective—in particular, the interdependence of a group and its contexts. As Stohl and Putnam (1994) put it, "Natural groups capture the dynamics, fluidity, and complexity of the role that context plays in group experience" (p. 285). In this study, we focused on two contextual components—culture and stigma—and examined their interplay in internal group discourse. Both culture and stigma affected the internal communication of the "Asian American" support group; however, their effects were somewhat different. Culture influenced group members such that their discourse was in line with "Asian American" cultural values (e.g., use of face-preserving modes of interaction). In contrast, stigma affected internal group communication in the sense that much of the discourse attempted to counteract this particular cultural influence (e.g., by providing a safe space so that members could cope with and develop strategies against the stigmatizing and shaming cultural discourse used on them by those outside the support group). This ongoing interplay between these two important contextual factors of culture and stigma characterized the interactions of the "Asian American" support group we studied.

Although this research sheds some light on support group communication from a bona fide group perspective, much research remains to be done. For example, future research needs to consider how both processes and outcomes associated with support group interactions are affected by contextual factors, and vice versa. In terms of support group processes, future research needs to explore how factors such as gender (e.g., how women and men experience and cope with various illnesses), social (e.g., how societal perceptions of various illnesses affect individuals' experiences), and culture (e.g., how cultural values influence the way individuals perceive and cope with illnesses) affect communication in support groups (e.g., how those factors influence what interactional styles in support groups are perceived by members as being facilitative of sharing and healing). In terms of outcomes, future research needs to examine and assess the potential utility of support groups for changing the external contexts for members (e.g., reducing social stigmatization and enhancing the daily lives of those who are ill).

CONCLUSION

The bona fide group perspective is a useful framework for studying natural groups, in general, and support groups, in particular (Frey, 1994). With an emphasis on fluid and permeable group boundaries, shifting borders and group membership, and interdependence with the immediate physical, social, and cultural contexts in which groups are embedded, this "newly emergent" perspective (Gouran, 1999, p. 19) can increase our understanding of support group communication—in this case, to help "Asian Americans" manage the crisis of living with HIV or AIDS and counter the effects of social and cultural stigmatization. As our study demonstrates, no matter how "closed" a group (in this case, a "closed" support group) may try to be (e.g., in terms of restricting membership), in line with the bona fide group perspective, a group is never closed; it is always interdependent with and influenced by the contexts in which it is embedded.

REFERENCES

Abramson, P. R. (1986). The cultural context of Japanese sexuality: An American perspective. *Psychologia*, *29*, 1–9.

Acevedo, J. R. (1993). A group model for AIDS prevention and support. In J. W. Dilley, C. Pies, & M. Helquist (Eds.), *Face to face: A guide to AIDS counseling* (pp. 84–93). San Francisco: AIDS Health Project, University of California, San Francisco.

Adelman, M. B., & Frey, L. R. (1994). The pilgrim must embark: Creating and sustaining community in a residential facility for people with AIDS. In L. R. Frey (Ed.), *Group communication in context: Studies of natural groups* (pp. 3–21). Hillsdale, NJ: Lawrence Erlbaum Associates.

Adelman, M. B., & Frey, L. R. (1997). *The fragile community: Living together with AIDS*. Mahwah, NJ: Lawrence Erlbaum Associates.

Aguilar-San Juan, K. (1994). Linking the issues: From identity to activism. In K. Aguilar-San Juan (Ed.), *The state of Asian America: Activism and resistance in the 1990s* (pp. 1–15). Boston: South End Press.

Anderson, E. A. (1989). Implications for public policy: Towards a pro-family AIDS social policy. In E. D. Macklin (Ed.), *AIDS and families* (pp. 187–228). New York: Harrington Park Press.

Aoki, B. (1993). Cross-cultural counseling: The extra dimension. In J. W. Dilley, C. Pies, & M. Helquist (Eds.), *Face to face: A guide to AIDS counseling* (pp. 26–33). San Francisco: AIDS Health Project, University of California, San Francisco.

Aoki, B., Ngin, C. P., Mo, B., & Ja, D. Y. (1989). AIDS prevention models in Asian-American communities. In V. M. Mays, G. W. Albee, & S. F. Schneider (Eds.), *Primary prevention of AIDS: Psychological approaches* (pp. 290–308). Newbury Park, CA: Sage.

Bell, M. M. (1998). Culture as dialogue. In M. M. Bell & M. Gardiner (Eds.), *Bakhtin and the human sciences: No last words* (pp. 49–62). London: Sage.

Cameron, M. E. (1993). *Living with AIDS: Experiencing ethical dilemmas*. Newbury Park, CA: Sage.

Carrier, J., Nguyen, B., & Su, S. (1992). Vietnamese American sexual behaviors and HIV infection. *Journal of Sex Research*, *29*, 547–560.

Catania, J. A., Coates, T. J., Kegeles, S. M., Ekstrand, M., Guydish, J. R., & Bye, L. L. (1989). Implications of the AIDS risk-reduction model for the gay community:

The importance of perceived sexual enjoyment and help-seeking behaviors. In V. M. Mays, G. W. Albee, & S. F. Schneider (Eds.), *Primary prevention of AIDS: Psychological approaches* (pp. 242–261). Newbury Park, CA: Sage.

Catania, J. A., Kegeles, S. M., & Coates, T. J. (1990). Towards an understanding of risk behavior: An AIDS risk-reduction model (ARRM). *Health Education Quarterly, 17*, 53–72.

Cawyer, C. S., & Smith-Dupré, A. (1995). Communicating social support: Identifying supportive episodes in an HIV/AIDS support group. *Communication Quarterly, 43*, 243–258.

Chachkes, E. (1993). AIDS: Future directions for education and practice. In V. J. Lynch, G. A. Lloyd, & M. F. Fimbres (Eds.), *The changing face of AIDS: Implications for social work practice* (pp. 3–18). Westport, CT: Auburn House.

Chan, C. S. (1989). Issues of identity development among Asian-American lesbians and gay men. *Journal of Counseling and Development, 68*, 16–20.

Chang, R. (1993). *U.S. national Asian and Pacific Islander HIV/AIDS agenda*. San Francisco: Asian Pacific AIDS Coalition.

Cherry, K., & Smith, D. H. (1993). Sometimes I cry: The experience of loneliness for men with AIDS. *Health Communication, 5*, 181–208.

Chin, J. (1997). Currency. In S. Raffo (Ed.), *Queerly classed: Gay men and lesbians write about class* (pp. 179–189). Boston: South End Press.

Choi, K., Salazar, N., Lew, S., & Coates, T. J. (1995). AIDS risk, dual identity, and community response among gay Asian and Pacific Islander men in San Francisco. In G. M. Herek & B. Greene (Eds.), *AIDS, identity, and community: The HIV epidemic and lesbians and gay men* (pp. 115–134). Thousand Oaks, CA: Sage.

Choi, K., Yep, G. A., & Kumekawa, E. (1998). HIV prevention among Asian and Pacific Islander American men who have sex with men: A critical review of theoretical models and directions for future research. *AIDS Education and Prevention, 10*(Supplement A), 19–30.

Chung, J. Y., & Magraw, M. M. (1992). A group approach to psychosocial issues faced by HIV-positive women. *Hospital and Community Psychiatry, 43*, 891–894.

Clemo, L. (1992). The stigmatization of AIDS in infants and children in the United States. *AIDS Education and Prevention, 4*, 308–318.

Cline, R. J. W. (1999). Communication in social support groups. In L. R. Frey (Ed.), D. S. Gouran, & M. S. Poole (Assoc. Eds.), *The handbook of group communication theory & research* (pp. 516–538). Thousand Oaks, CA: Sage.

Cline, R. J. W., & Boyd, M. F. (1993). Communication as threat and therapy: Stigma, social support, and coping with HIV infection. In E. B. Ray (Ed.), *Case studies in health communication* (pp. 131–147). Hillsdale, NJ: Lawrence Erlbaum Associates.

Cochran, S. D., Mays, V. M., & Leung, L. (1991). Sexual practices of heterosexual Asian-American young adults: Implications for risk of HIV infection. *Archives of Sexual Behavior, 20*, 381–391.

Coleman, V. E., & Harris, G. N. (1989). A support group for individuals recently testing HIV positive: A psycho-educational group model. *Journal of Sex Research, 26*, 539–548.

Douard, J. W. (1990). AIDS, stigma, and privacy. *AIDS and Public Policy Journal, 5*, 37–41.

Dworkin, S. H., & Pincu, L. (1993). Counseling in the era of AIDS. *Journal of Counseling and Development, 71,* 275–281.

Earl, W. L., Martindale, C. J., & Cohn, D. (1991). Adjustment: Denial in the styles of coping with HIV infection. *Omega, 24,* 35–47.

Eng, D. L., & Hom, A. Y. (1998). Q & A: Notes on a queer Asian America. In D. L. Eng & A. Y. Hom (Eds.), *Q & A: Queer in Asian America* (pp. 1–21). Philadelphia: Temple University Press.

Fairbank, Bregman, & Maullin, Inc. (1991). *A survey of AIDS knowledge, attitudes and behaviors in San Francisco's American-Indian, Filipino and Latino gay and bisexual male communities.* Santa Monica, CA: Author.

Frey. L. R. (1994). Call and response: The challenge of conducting research on communication in natural groups. In L. R. Frey (Ed.), *Group communication in context: Studies of natural groups* (pp. 293–304). Hillsdale, NJ: Lawrence Erlbaum Associates.

Frey, L. R., Adelman, M. B., & Query, J. L., Jr. (1996). Communication practices in the social construction of health in an AIDS residence. *Journal of Health Psychology, 1,* 383–397.

Frey, L. R., Query, J. L., Jr., Flint, L. J., & Adelman, M. B. (1998). Living together with AIDS: Social support processes in a residential facility. In V. J. Derlega & A. P. Barbee (Eds.), *HIV & social interaction* (pp. 129–146). Thousand Oaks, CA; Sage.

Fullilove, M. T. (1989). Anxiety and stigmatizing aspects of HIV infection. *Journal of Clinical Psychiatry, 50*(Supplement), 5–8.

Glaser, B. G., & Strauss, A. L. (1967). *The discovery of grounded theory: Strategies for qualitative research.* Chicago: Aldine.

Gochros, H. L. (1992). The sexuality of gay men with HIV infection. *Social Work, 37,* 105–109.

Gock, T. S. (1994). Acquired Immunodeficiency Syndrome. In N. W. S. Zane, D. T. Takeuchi, & K. N. J. Young (Eds.), *Confronting critical health issues of Asian and Pacific Islander Americans* (pp. 247–265). Thousand Oaks, CA: Sage.

Goffman, E. (1963). *Stigma: Notes on the management of spoiled identity.* Englewood Cliffs, NJ: Prentice-Hall.

Gouran, D. S. (1999). Communication in groups: The emergence and evolution of a field of study. In L. R. Frey (Ed.), D. S. Gouran, & M. S. Poole (Assoc. Eds.), *The handbook of group communication theory & research* (pp. 3–36). Thousand Oaks, CA: Sage.

Greene, K., & Serovich, J. M. (1996). Appropriateness of disclosure of HIV testing information: The perspective of PLWAs. *Journal of Applied Communication Research, 24,* 50–65.

Hagedorn, J. (1994). The exile within/the question of identity. In K. Aguilar-San Juan (Ed.), *The state of Asian America: Activism and resistance in the 1990s* (pp. 173–182). Boston: South End Press.

Herek, G. M., & Capitanio, J. P. (1993). Public reactions to AIDS in the United States: A second decade of stigma. *American Journal of Public Health, 83,* 574–577.

Herek, G. M., & Glunt, E. K. (1988). An epidemic of stigma: Public reactions to AIDS. *American Psychologist, 43,* 886–891.

Hom, A. Y. (1996). Stories from the homefront: Perspectives of Asian American parents with lesbian daughters and gay sons. In R. Leong (Ed.), *Asian American sexualities: Dimensions of the gay and lesbian experience* (pp. 37–49). New York: Routledge.

hooks, b. (1990). *Yearning: Race, gender, and cultural politics*. Boston: South End Press.

Jordan, G., & Weedon, C. (1995). *Cultural politics: Class, gender, race and the postmodern world*. Oxford, UK: B. Blackwell.

Jue, S., & Kain, C. D. (1989). Culturally sensitive AIDS counseling. In C. D. Kain (Ed.), *No longer immune: A counselor's guide to AIDS* (pp. 131–148). Alexandria, VA: American Association for Counseling and Development.

Kang, D. (1996). Multiple-box person. In E. H. Kim & E-Y. Yu (Eds.), *East to America: Korean American life stories* (pp. 81–89). New York: New Press.

Leary, M. R., & Schreindorfer, L. S. (1998). The stigmatization of HIV and AIDS: Rubbing salt in the wound. In V. J. Derlega & A. P. Barbee (Eds.), *HIV & social interaction* (pp. 12–29). Thousand Oaks, CA; Sage.

Lee, W. S., Chung, J., Wang, J., & Hertel, E. (1995). A sociocultural approach to intercultural communication. *Howard Journal of Communications, 6*, 262–291.

Leong, R. (1996). Introduction: Home bodies and the body politic. In R. Leong (Ed.), *Asian American sexualities: Dimensions of the gay and lesbian experience* (pp. 1–18). New York: Routledge.

Levy, R. S., Tendler, C., VanDevanter, N., & Cleary, P. D. (1990). A group intervention model for individuals testing positive for HIV antibody. *American Journal of Orthopsychiatry, 60*, 452–459.

Lowe, L. (1996). *Immigrant acts: On Asian American cultural politics*. Durham, NC: Duke University Press.

Manalansan, M. F. (1996). Searching for community: Filipino gay men in New York City. In R. Leong (Ed.), *Asian American sexualities: Dimensions of the gay and lesbian experience* (pp. 51–64). New York: Routledge.

Mandel, J. S., & Kitano, K. J. (1989). San Francisco looks at AIDS in Southeast Asia. *Multicultural Inquiry Research AIDS Quarterly Newsletter, 3*, 1–2, 7.

Marks, G., Richardson, J. L., & Maldonado, N. (1991). Self-disclosure of HIV infection to sexual partners. *American Journal of Public Health, 81*, 1321–1322.

Mooney, K. M., Cohn, E. S., & Swift, M. B. (1992). Physical distance and AIDS: Too close for comfort? *Journal of Applied Social Psychology, 22*, 1442–1452.

Morin, S. F., Charles, K. A., & Malyon, A. K. (1984). The psychological impact of AIDS on gay men. *American Psychologist, 39*, 1288–1293.

Moynihan, R. T., & Christ, G. H. (1987). Social, psychological, and research barriers to the treatment of AIDS. In C. G. Leukefeld & M. Fimbres (Eds.), *Responding to AIDS: Psychosocial initiatives* (pp. 80–94). Silver Spring, MD: National Association of Social Workers.

Newmark, D. A., & Taylor, E. H. (1987). The family and AIDS. In C. G. Leukefeld & M. Fimbres (Eds.), *Responding to AIDS: Psychosocial initiatives* (pp. 39–50). Silver Spring, MD: National Association of Social Workers.

Petronio, S. (2002). *Boundaries of privacy: Dialectics of disclosure*. Albany: State University of New York Press.

Pryor, J. B., & Reeder, G. D. (1993). Collective and individual representations of HIV/AIDS stigma. In J. B. Pryor & G. D. Reeder (Eds.), *The social psychology of HIV infection* (pp. 263–286). Hillsdale, NJ: Lawrence Erlbaum Associates.

Putnam, L. L., & Stohl, C. (1990). Bona fide groups: A reconceptualization of groups in context. *Communication Studies, 41*, 248–265.

Putnam, L. L., & Stohl, C. (1996). Bona fide groups: An alternative perspective for communication and small group decision making. In R. Y. Hirokawa & M. S. Poole (Eds.), *Communication and group decision making* (2nd ed., pp. 147–178). Thousand Oaks, CA: Sage.

Reyes, E. E., & Yep, G. A. (1997). Challenging complexities: Strategizing with Asian Americans in Southern California against (heterosex)isms. In J. T. Sears & W. L. Williams (Eds.), *Overcoming heterosexism and homophobia: Strategies that work* (pp. 91–103). New York: Columbia University Press.

Rowe, W., Plum, G., & Crossman, C. (1988). Issues and problems confronting the lovers, families and communities associated with persons with AIDS. *Journal of Social Work and Human Sexuality*, 6, 71–88.

Schaffner, B. (1990). Psychotherapy with HIV-infected persons. *New Directions for Mental Health Services*, 48, 5–20.

Serovich, J. M., & Greene, K. (1993). Perceptions of family boundaries: The case of disclosure of HIV testing information. *Family Relations*, 42, 193–197.

Siegel, K., & Krauss, B. J. (1991). Living with HIV infection: Adaptive tasks of seropositive gay men. *Journal of Health and Social Behavior*, 32, 17–32.

St. John, M. (1992). Anti-body already: Body-oriented interventions in clinical work with HIV-positive women. *Women and Therapy*, 13(4), 5–25.

Stohl, C., & Putnam, L. L. (1994). Group communication in context: Implications for the study of bona fide groups. In L. R. Frey (Ed.), *Group communication in context: Studies of natural groups* (pp. 285–292). Hillsdale, NJ: Lawrence Erlbaum Associates.

Strauss, A., & Corbin, J. (1990). *Basics of qualitative research: Grounded theory procedures and techniques*. Newbury Park, CA: Sage.

Stulberg, I., & Buckingham, S. L. (1988). Parallel issues for AIDS patients, families, and others. *Social Casework*, 69, 355–359.

Sullivan, C. F., & Sherblom, J. C. (1995). Communication concerns for an AIDS support group. In L. K. Fuller & L. M. Shilling (Eds.), *Communicating about communicable diseases* (pp. 243–260). Amherst, MA: Human Resource Development Press.

Treichler, P. A. (1988). AIDS, homophobia, and biomedical discourse: An epidemic of signification. In D. Crimp (Ed.), *AIDS: Cultural analysis, cultural activism* (pp. 31–70). Cambridge: Massachusetts Institute of Technology Press.

Treichler, P. A. (1992). AIDS and HIV infection in the third world: A first world chronicle. In E. Fee & D. M. Fox (Eds.), *AIDS: The making of a chronic disease* (pp. 377–412). Berkeley: University of California Press.

Vinogradov, S., & Yalom, I. D. (1989). *Concise guide of group psychotherapy*. Washington, DC: American Psychiatric Press.

Wat, E. C. (1996). Preserving the paradox: Stories from a *gay-loh*. In R. Leong (Ed.), *Asian American sexualities: Dimensions of the gay and lesbian experience* (pp. 71–80). New York: Routledge.

Weitz, R. (1989). Uncertainty and the lives of persons with AIDS. *Journal of Health and Social Behavior*, 30, 270–281.

Williams, R. (1983). *Keywords: A vocabulary of culture and society* (Rev. ed.). London: Fontana.

Woo, J. M., Rutherford, G. W., Payne, S. F., Barnhart, J. L., & Lemp, G. F. (1988). The epidemiology of AIDS in Asian and Pacific Islander populations in San Francisco. *AIDS*, 2, 473–475.

Yalom, I. D. (1985). *The theory and practice of group psychotherapy* (3rd ed.). New York: Basic Books.

Yep, G. A. (1993a). First Asian/Pacific Island Men's HIV Conference, Los Angeles, California. *AIDS Education and Prevention, 5,* 87–88.

Yep, G. A. (1993b). HIV prevention among Asian-American college students: Does the health belief model work? *Journal of American College Health, 41,* 199–205.

Yep, G. A. (1994). HIV/AIDS education and prevention for Asian and Pacific Islander communities: Toward the development of general guidelines. *AIDS Education and Prevention, 6,* 184–186.

Yep, G. A. (1997). Overcoming barriers in HIV/AIDS education for Asian Americans: Toward more effective cultural communication. In D. C. Umeh (Ed.), *Confronting the AIDS epidemic: Cross-cultural perspectives on HIV/AIDS education* (pp. 219–230). Trenton, NJ: Africa World Press.

Yep, G. A. (1998a). HIV/AIDS in Asian and Pacific Islander communities in the United States: A review, analysis, and integration. In D. Buchanan & G. Cernada (Eds.), *Progress in preventing AIDS?: Dogma, dissent and innovation: Global perspectives* (pp. 179–201). Amityville, NY: Baywood.

Yep, G. A. (1998b). Safer sex negotiation in cross-cultural romantic dyads: An extension of Ting-Toomey's face negotiation theory. In N. L. Roth & L. K. Fuller (Eds.), *Women and AIDS: Negotiating safer practices, care, and representation* (pp. 81–100). Binghamton, NY: Haworth Press.

Yep, G. A. (2000). Disclosure of HIV infection in interpersonal relationships: A communication management of privacy approach. In S. Petronio (Ed.), *Balancing the secrets of private disclosures* (pp. 83–96). Mahwah, NJ: Lawrence Erlbaum Associates.

Yep, G. A. (in press). "See no evil, hear no evil, speak no evil": Educating Asian Americans about HIV/AIDS through culture-specific health communication campaigns. In L. K. Fuller (Ed.), *Media-mediated AIDS*. Creskill, NJ: Hampton Press.

Yep, G. A., Lovaas, K. E., & Ho, P. C. (2001). Communication in "Asian American" families with queer members: A relational dialectics perspective. In M. Bernstein & R. Reimann (Eds.), *Queer families, queer politics: Challenging culture and the state* (pp. 152–172). New York: Columbia University Press.

COOPERATIVES AND COLLABORATIONS:

COMMUNICATING AMIDST MULTIPLE IDENTITIES, BOUNDARIES, AND CONSTITUENTS

7

MULTIPLE IDENTITIES IN TEAMS IN A COOPERATIVE SUPERMARKET

John G. Oetzel
University of New Mexico

Jean Robbins
Barking Dog

Traditionally, most U.S. organizations have been organized in a formal hierarchy. Recently, many organizations are altering their formal structures to include teams and flatten hierarchies. One such alternative to the traditional organizational hierarchy is the *cooperative*, a business that is owned collectively and voluntarily by members who share in its benefits (Schaars, 1978). Groves (1985) articulated the triple thrust of cooperatives: economic, educational, and social. These three critical facets of a cooperative, particularly the economic and social, frame the dialectic of these groups/organizations. It can be argued that a sound business framework is necessary for the social concerns to be met, but the social (and, in some cases, socialistic) concerns undergird the assumptions and values of the cooperative group/organization (Groves, 1985; Schein, 1997).

The International Cooperative Alliance (ICA; 1995), an organizing body for cooperatives, articulates the values and principles in its "Statement on the Cooperative Identity." ICA defines a cooperative as an autonomous association of persons united voluntarily to meet their common economic, social, and cultural needs and aspirations through a jointly owned and democratically controlled enterprise. The primary values inherent in a cooperative include self-help, self-responsibility, democracy, equality, equity, and solidarity; other ethical values include honesty, openness, social responsibility, and caring for others. The principles on which cooperatives operate are guidelines for the implementation of the values into practice, and include (a) voluntary and open membership; (b) democratic member control; (c) member economic participation; (d) autonomy and independence; (e) education, training, and information for members; (f) cooperation between cooperatives; and (g) concern for community. The ICA document provides the framework for the mission statements created by cooperatives that ascribe to cooperative identity, including the cooperative studied in this chapter.

Although the ICA has existed for more than 100 years, cooperatives have garnered relatively scant research from communication scholars (for exceptions, see Cheney, 1995, 1997). This oversight is unfortunate, for the study of cooperatives is important because of the increasing concern for organizations to promote democracy. Cheney (1995) lamented that "surely one of the great ironies of the modern world is that democracy, imperfect as it is in the political realm, seldom exists in the workplace" (p. 167). A new trend in organizations is to increase employee democracy through programs such as employee involvement (Cotton, 1993), participation (Marshall & Stohl, 1993), empowerment (Conger & Kanungo, 1988), and self-managed teams (Barker & Tompkins, 1994; Cohen & Ledford, 1994). These programs, however, have been criticized because they not only serve to increase democracy but also increase responsibility, workload, and stress (Cheney, 1995). For example, Cheney (1995) explained that employee "empowerment" that provides a person with increased responsibility may also mean that the employee now has one and a half to two jobs. Moreover, another problem with these programs is that they are implemented within a hierarchical framework and ideology where workers serve the interests of management. In contrast, cooperatives are established and built on principles of democracy in the workplace. Studying cooperatives, thus, provides a timely and important way for understanding democracy in the workplace.

The cooperative (a grocery store) in the current study, like many cooperatives, is organized into teams to facilitate democratic involvement (and division of labor). However, a team structure does not always result in democracy. In some situations, teams result in more oppression and control over members than does a traditional organizational hierarchy (Barker & Tompkins, 1994). To understand whether and how teams result in democracy, we need to understand the multiple identities and paradoxes between these identities that exist within cooperatives. We employed the bona fide group perspective (Putnam & Stohl, 1990, 1996; Stohl & Putnam, 1994) to investigate how identity is constructed in the cooperative grocery store. This perspective "treats a group as a social system linked to its context, shaped by fluid boundaries, and altering its environment" (Putnam & Stohl, 1996, p. 148). In contrast to traditional "container" models of groups, the bona fide group perspective recognizes the importance of the influence of environmental factors on group members' communication and that groups also influence their external environments. In particular, this perspective examines the ways in which groups (re)define their boundaries (or identities) and negotiate relationships with their salient contexts in a fluid, processual manner. In essence, the bona fide group perspective offers a lens for seeing and shaping important aspects of group experience (Stohl & Putnam, 1994), for all natural groups display characteristics of bona fide groups (Putnam & Stohl, 1990).

The current study seeks to advance knowledge about the bona fide group perspective by studying teams in the NFC Cooperative Supermarket (a pseudonym). Specifically, we employ this perspective to understand the construction of multiple identities in this cooperative.

IDENTIFICATION AND IDENTITY IN THE NFC COOPERATIVE SUPERMARKET

NFC Cooperative Supermarket

We start by providing some background on NFC and its ideology. Specifically, we provide a brief history, discuss the organizational structure, and review the mission statement of the organization. This information provides a framework for the case study of multiple identities at NFC.

NFC is located in a medium-sized city in the southwest United States. It was incorporated in 1976 as a member-owned natural foods store, and has expanded from an initial membership of 300 households to over 7,000 households with annual sales in excess of $7,000,000. As the natural foods industry rapidly expanded (from approximately 7,000 retailers in 1994 to 22,000 in 1997), NFC, along with similarly organized cooperatives in the United States and Western Europe, found itself competing in a dynamic setting with "mainstream" businesses for both market share and qualified employees. Although many cooperatives in this industry have responded economically well to the challenges of aggressive growth of the industry, many others are experiencing difficulties that range from making decisions regarding expansion to closure. NFC is one of the few businesses organized on cooperative principles, within the supermarket industry, that demonstrates consistent profitability.

During 1990, as mandated by the board of directors, NFC adopted a team system in many areas of its organizational structure. The leadership of the cooperative was made up of a team of three persons who were required to provide expertise in areas of operations and finance. However, both the leadership group and the employee base lacked expertise in how to function in a team environment; one result of this lack of expertise was that, for a time, expenses grew much more rapidly than revenue. Consequently, the team structure at the leadership level was abandoned after little more than a year but the cooperative retains "team" as a pivotal unit throughout the organization. This structure is evidenced in the titles given to positions within the traditional hierarchy of NFC (e.g., Purchasing Team, Supervisory Team, Store Team Leader, and Department Team Leader).

NFC employs approximately 100 people to serve its 7,000-member households. The cooperative is organized in the following manner: (a) the membership elects a volunteer board of directors; (b) the board then hires and supervises the store team leader (STL); (c) the STL hires and supervises the operations manager (OM); (d) the STL oversees six nonrevenue-producing departments (membership, human resources, front end, accounting, janitorial, and marketing), each with a department team leader (DTL); and (e) the OM oversees eight revenue-producing departments (produce, bulk, deli/cheese, housewares, grocery, health and beauty aids, meat, and receiving), each with a DTL. The DTLs are responsible for all day-to-day operations for their departments, including hiring, corrective action, maintaining margin, scheduling, and purchasing. Team members are typically included in making decisions for the respective teams only insofar as the DTL invites their inclusion.

The framing of the context of NFC takes place within the continuing evolution of the ideology of ICA. This ideology continues to evolve in response to changes in the homogeneous organizational base of consumer cooperatives. ICA membership has broadened, both geographically and in terms of the types of organizations that are now included in its membership (Rhodes, 1996). This new diversity has the effect of moving the ICA ideological stance further away from a particular organizational form (the consumer cooperative). This ideology, as we show below, has become the focal point of identification for the cooperative movement and for NFC.

Identification at NFC

Identification is "the perception of oneness with or belongingness to an organization, where the individual *defines* him or herself in terms of the organization(s) in which he or she is a member" (Mael & Ashforth, 1992, p. 104). Simon (1976) explained that identification is important in organizations because through the process of identifying, individuals choose particular alternatives over others. For example, an individual who identifies herself or himself as a member of a team likely will make choices that emphasize the effects on the team as opposed to other alternatives (e.g., the organization as a whole or herself or himself). From an organizational perspective, member identification with the organization is beneficial in that it guarantees that choices made by employees will be consistent with organizational objectives (Tompkins & Cheney, 1983, 1985).

Tompkins and Cheney (1983) utilized Burke's (1969) theory of identification to explain the role of persuasion in identification processes. Burke explains his view of identification as "A is not identical with his colleague, B. But insofar as their interests are joined, A is identified with B. Or he may identify himself with B even when their interests are not joined, if he assumes that they are, or is persuaded to believe so" (p. 20). Tompkins and Cheney noted that when an organizational member is so inclined toward identification, he or she is receptive to persuasive communication by the organization.

Identification on the part of NFC employees with the cooperative system's ideology guides their expectations and behaviors. The democratic rhetoric frames the organizational setting and influences the discourse among employees and between them and members/customers. Democratic practices exist through communication, and such communication produces identification of individuals with the groups and organizations of which they are members (Cheney, 1995).

The overarching discourse that fosters the context for teams at NFC is a clear and compelling ideology presented in the form of a mission statement. NFC created its mission statement to reflect the ICA's statement. The mission statement (written on July 23, 1991) is as follows:

> NFC Co-op Supermarket strives for excellence in all we do. Our mission is to provide to our members, at the lowest price possible, exemplary customer service, environmentally sound products and the highest quality natural and organic food. We are committed to ethical business practices, participatory management and cooperative principles. Our intention is to provide to the entire community, through practice and education, a working model for a healthy, sustainable future.

This statement influences many of the assumptions about the organization and perceptions of the cultural norms held by employees. New employees are introduced to the mission statement at their orientation session. It is calligraphed and copies of it are taped on walls and pinned to bulletin boards throughout NFC. Pivotal employee assumptions about NFC's cultural norms are derived from this mission statement. Some of those assumptions include (a) NFC employees will work hard for worthy goals within a worthy organization; (b) NFC's goals are understood and shared throughout the organization, with clear guidelines that enable employees to reach those goals; (c) employees will be treated fairly by NFC; and (d) NFC is stable. The mission statement, as well as the organizational structure of the cooperative, provides some context for the study of team identity.

Identity in the Teams and NFC

There are two key characteristics of the bona fide group perspective for the current study: (a) stable yet permeable group boundaries and (b) interdependence of a group with its immediate contexts (Putnam & Stohl, 1990). Boundaries are preconditions of group identity or "groupness"; boundaries define what a group is and what it is not (Smith & Berg, 1987). Boundaries, moreover, simultaneously give meaning to belonging and not belonging. Once a boundary has been drawn, the possibility of relationship (e.g., group identity) emerges. However, boundaries are not pre-established structures that separate groups from their environments; they are socially constructed through internal and external communication among group members. A group identifies who is in the group and who is out via its labels and interactions about norms and expectations (Smith & Berg, 1987). These interactions serve to constantly define, negotiate, and redefine boundaries; thus, boundaries are permeable, dynamic, and fluid (Putnam & Stohl, 1996).

There are a number of potential boundaries and identities at NFC. *Identities* are relatively stable, enduring characteristics involving core beliefs, assumptions, and values that make up the self (Scott, Corman, & Cheney, 1998). Consistent with the bona fide group perspective, Scott et al. (1998) explained that identities are both a process and product of identification. Identities serve as anchors for individuals that influence their communication style and decision making; at the same time, identities are being created and recreated through interaction with others. Essentially, identity (and identification) is a dialectical process through which individuals link, via communication, with some groups/organizations and distance themselves from others. The identity construction process, then, is a paradox where perceived sameness and difference form the basis of both consensus and disagreement (Cheney, 1991).

A critical aspect of the permeability of identities can be the organizational context. Putnam and Stohl (1990) explained that bona fide groups are interdependent with their immediate context. *Context* refers to the ways in which a group depends on or contributes to the *environment*, which refers to an intergroup system that permeates and interfaces with the groups (Putnam & Stohl, 1990). Group boundaries shift through multiple memberships within the organizational context. For example, the supervisor of a team is a member of the team but may also be a member of the supervisory level or group. The organizational context influences the degree to which individuals experience identity with a particular group and whether individuals experience conflict from having to play multiple roles. In one organization, the team identity may be secondary to the supervisory identity, whereas another organization may regard both identities as deserving high status.

In summary, identities are created in internal communication between group members and external communication between group members and external others; in turn, these interactions are framed by the contexts within which a group operates. In the case of NFC, the organizational context includes its history, organizational structure, and mission. We seek to understand what identities exist at NFC and how these identities are constructed. Thus, the current study is guided by the following three research questions as framed by the bona fide group perspective:

> RQ1: What identities do NFC employees possess, and of what do the identities consist?
> RQ2: How are these identities constructed?
> RQ3: What are the consequences of the constructed identities for intergroup interactions at NFC?

METHODS

Data collection proceeded in two phases. Phase I consisted of in-depth interviews with various team members; Phase II consisted of short questionnaires completed by a sample of NFC employees. The interviewees and respondents to the questionnaire were two different samples, although it is possible that some interviewees also completed a questionnaire.

Interviews

Participants. Twenty-two employees at NFC from three levels of the organization were interviewed: the STL and OM, DTLs, and team members. Six of the interviewees were DTLs, 14 were teams members, and the final 2 were the STL and OM. The team members interviewed consisted of six members from the produce team, four members of deli/cheese, two members of front end, two members from grocery, and the remaining six were from various teams.

Interview Process. Nine open-ended questions were presented in a semistructured format to allow for probing (see Appendix). The questions were designed to investigate employees' perceptions of the organization and team identities (questions 1, 3–5), the construction of these identities (questions 1–3, 7–8), and relationships of the teams with other units in the organization (e.g., board of directors; questions 6–8). The second author conducted the interviews in an informal setting outside of the organization (e.g., at a coffee shop). She has a history with the organization, having been employed at NFC for 9 years and is still a member. She has developed a good relationship with many of the employees; this rapport led us to believe that interviewees would provide honest, detailed responses. Furthermore, she understood that sensitive issues would be discussed and that certain issues should not be made public. Thus, occasionally, she would stop the audiotape recorder and talk with the person in private before continuing the interview. The interviews ranged from 15 minutes to 3 hours. Identifying the organization by the pseudonym "NFC" and giving participants pseudonyms preserves their confidentiality.

Analysis of Interviews.   All interviews were tape recorded and transcribed by the interviewer (the second author). Transcriptions were then read and categorized by the first author, who has no direct ties to NFC. Responses were categorized in a manner consistent with the constant comparative method (Glaser & Strauss, 1967), which involves constantly comparing responses to determine goodness of fit to underlying themes (Lindlof, 1995). Using this method, responses are read and reread to ensure that categories are clearly defined and compose unique constructs.

The specific procedures the first author used to categorize the interview responses were as follows. First, transcriptions were read to get an overall flavor of interviewees' responses. Second, he loosely categorized responses on the basis of the two main characteristics and subfactors of the bona fide group perspective (Putnam & Stohl, 1996). Hence, responses were first labeled as being either a boundary issue or a context issue and then were characterized as a specific subfactor, such as an interpretive frame or intergroup communication, respectively. This initial sort was an attempt to understand the broad types of identity issues for NFC employees, as framed by the bona fide group perspective. Third, every response was reread and placed into original categories; this process was completed so as not to "force" the bona fide group characteristics on the data. This process revealed three distinct identities at NFC; hence, this step extended and solidified these categories that were loosely identified in step two. Each response could be placed into more than one category, but most responses were relevant for only one category. Fourth, the overall categories were mapped using the three research questions as a guide—that is, each category was placed under one, two, or all three research questions.

At this stage, the categories were determined by the first author to fit the research questions and the data well. Categorization of the data was then shared with the second author for confirmation. The categories were clarified and supplemented on the basis of this conversation; consensus was utilized to determine the final categories. The use of both authors to analyze the data was particularly advantageous in this case because one is an organizational insider, whereas the other is an outsider to the organization. The procedures used ensured that the outsider's view was not directly influenced by the organizational values and enabled the insider to help interpret the responses from the employees' perspective.

Questionnaires

Participants. Forty-nine of the 100 employees responded to the questionnaire, a response rate of 49%. This rate is very good given that, according to the OM, many employee surveys conducted by the cooperative have a response rate of approximately 15%. The relatively high response rate can be attributed to the rapport that the second author has with employees at the cooperative. The only background information we requested of the respondents was team membership. The team membership included: 11 front end, 4 accounting, 2 janitorial, 2 human resources, 4 bulk, 8 deli/cheese, 2 grocery, 7 health and beauty aids, 5 produce, and 1 each from 5 other teams.

Instrument and Procedures. The purpose of the questionnaires was to supplement and triangulate the interview data. The questionnaire consisted of three sections. First, to help answer the first research question, respondents were asked to complete a modified version of the Organizational Identification Questionnaire (OIQ; Cheney, 1983). The OIQ has demonstrated reliability (Cronbach alphas > .90) and validity (close parallel between OIQ items and answers to the open-ended question, "Do you identify with this organization?"; Cheney, 1983). The OIQ contains 25 items measuring a single factor; however, Cheney (1983) indicated that the OIQ can be shortened without serious damage. Thus, a 15-item version of the OIQ with targets to the team and the cooperative were included in the questionnaire. These items were measured on a 7-point Likert scale, with 1 being *very strongly agree* and 7 being *very strongly disagree*. The reliability of the OIQ was excellent in the current study: $\alpha = .94$ for the "store" version and $\alpha = .90$ for the "team" version.

Second, 14 items in the form of questions were presented to the respondents that investigated comfort level, socializing, competition, communication, and conflict, both within the team and with other teams (see Appendix). Questions focusing on the referent "within the team" were designed to answer research questions one and two; questions focusing on relations "with other teams" were designed to answer research question three. Each of the items was rated on a 5-point Likert-type scale, with 5 representing some form of strong agreement and 1 some form of strong disagreement. Finally, respondents were asked to identify their team membership.

The questionnaire was made available to all the employees at NFC by attaching to one biweekly pay packet a permission letter, the questionnaire, and a self-addressed stamped envelope. The staff newsletter from the previous pay period included a notice that described the study and informed employees to expect the attachments in their upcoming pay packet. Addi-

tional questionnaires were placed in the employee rest area. The questionnaire took about 10 minutes to complete.

RESULTS

The results are presented in two main sections. The data from the interviews are first discussed, followed by the results from the questionnaires.

Interview Data

Identities and Construction of Identities at NFC. The first research
question asked what identities NFC employees possess, and of what those
identities consist, whereas the second research question asked how identities are constructed. Considering these questions together, three distinct
identities were discovered: (a) an organizational identity, (b) a team identity, and (c) an organizational position identity.

The primary indicator that there was an organizational identity is the
fact that employees shared similar values. We speculated on discovering
this identity that individuals share the values that are reflected in the mission statement, and this speculation was partially confirmed. According to
respondents, the values of the cooperative include providing a sustainable
source of healthy food, cooperating with others to do work, being friendly
and responsive to customers and each other, and direct communication
with each other. For example, Tori, a cook on the deli/cheese team, said,
"Everyone tries to put out a good product and keep the customers happy. I
think that's the main one [value]." Matt, the produce DTL, noted two other
important values: "One is pride. We always want things to look good; leaving it [the work area] in good shape for the next shift. Cooperation [also] is
a big one. We all work together and try to help each other out." John, a produce team member, offered a similar sentiment, "I think the coop values
are to develop sustainable sources of healthy food, to buy and sell healthy
food, and to be a community marketplace where people are able to come
to a friendly environment in a cooperative way." Finally, when asked how
they deal with problems, most respondents reported that they directly discuss a problem with the other person. Trudy, a receiving clerk, noted, "I go
and approach that person constructively, just like I want them to do with
me." Nancy, the deli/cheese DTL, succinctly stated her approach, "I just go
directly to them."

The question of how organizational members come to share these values appears to be due to the development of a shared interpretive frame
derived from the expectations of what a cooperative should be. One indication of this shared interpretive frame is that the majority of respondents
chose to work at the cooperative for many of the same reasons. For instance, in response to why employees decided to work at NFC, Juanita, the

health and beauty aids DTL, reported, "I was going back into the workplace, and decided [to work at NFC] because of the values, the coop values—community-based, team oriented." Lisa, a maintenance team member, noted, "It's my lifestyle. I eat organic foods and think organically and ecologically. I think of the earth and I like people who are friendly—and that seems to be the coop." Kristi, a deli/cheese team member, summed up this perspective well: "I was attracted to NFC because of the perceptions that I had about it before I worked here." Many individuals, thus, entered this organization because its mission fit with their values.

Not everyone interviewed came to the cooperative for the values it offered; some focused on their own needs and experiences. Matt, the produce DTL, explained that he "was in school at the time and I needed money and I needed to cook breakfast. I came to the coop and saw the sign and it kind of just happened." Similarly, Jaime, the grocery DTL, noted, "It was basically a job choice. It was just a job." However, even for those not attracted to the coop initially because of its values, most tended to "buy into" the coop values and interpretive frame quickly and, consequently, decided to stay awhile.

Overall, the organizational identity of NFC serves as an interpretive frame for the members. Members share a number of important values both prior to their association with NFC and on the basis of their experience working there. Patty, a front-end team member, said, "When people challenge me with, like, 'You're still at the coop, why don't you work somewhere else?' and I think it has a lot to do with who I am here and cooperative principles. It is different [than other organizations]." Carmen, a deli-cheese member, offered:

> I think it's a privilege to have this kind of food in our city; and I've talked with people who've traveled all over the country and they say they haven't found anything nicer than what we have right here. As far as the looks, the produce, the quality, it's nice to be a part of that, even with all its problems.

The problems that Carmen alluded to focus on the inconsistency of how the values in the mission statement are put into practice. From our analysis, two notable values are absent: participatory management and low cost. As we discuss in more detail later, despite its claim to the contrary, NFC is structured as a hierarchy and does not practice participatory management. Employees also do not concern themselves with the cost of goods; they let management worry about it.

In addition to the overall identity for the cooperative, a second key identity is team identity. Although each team appears to have a unique identity, there are important differences in the strength of those identities. Three teams—produce, deli/cheese, and grocery—demonstrate a strong ingroup identity and tend to perceive themselves as separate from the rest of the store, whereas the other teams tend to have a weaker ingroup identity and perceive themselves primarily as members of the larger organization.

The produce team members interviewed reported that their team identity is very strong. Lana, one of the members, explained that the goal of the produce team is to have as much fun and get as much work done as possible. When probed about having fun, she said, "It's verbal—inside jokes. And it's all over the walls in produce, like our motto that 'Slime rides a fast horse' and our nickname 'Gang Green.' There's a close-knit group of people—a team." She also added, "My team catches me; they're my safety net if I'm confused or wrong." Kim, another member, supported these sentiments when she said, "We work so hard and we're a close-knit group. We laugh a lot and have a lot of fun, and so people say things like, 'You guys really have a lot of fun back there.'" The deli/cheese team also has a strong group identity. One of its members, Tori, noted, "I think we're pretty close. We all respect each other. We're buddies." Nancy, the DTL, stated, "I think it's [team relationship] really good. I like them. There's nobody here that I work with that I don't like. It's a really nice bunch of people." As Carmen, another deli/cheese member, explained, "We have fun once in awhile. We trip people sometimes [an inside joke], just doing silly things and talking, trying to make the job more fun." Further evidence of the strong ingroup identity in the deli/cheese team is that when a fresh slab of concrete was poured in the back of the store, the team members wrote in it "D.M.C. Forever"; D.M.C. refers to deli, meat, cheese, which used to be one department and now is two. Finally, the grocery department also has a strong ingroup identity. As Jaime, one of the members, explained, "The longer I've been here, the more appreciation I have for this department." Another member, Rosa, said of her team members' relationship, "It's good. We're mostly friends and it's cool."

All of the teams reported good relationships between team members, but only these three teams have a strong identity apart from the organization identity. One reason the members of these teams developed such a close personal bond and strong identity, whereas other teams did not, appears to be a physical location that allows for close, intimate, face-to-face communication. All three teams with strong identities have a physical location that sets them apart from the customers, to some degree, and encourages members to interact more frequently than what occurs in other teams. Specifically, both the deli/cheese and produce teams are situated along the back wall of the store. Deli/cheese has a kitchen and preparation area that is situated away from customers and a counter that separates team members from the rest of the store. Produce includes not only the display but also preparation and storage areas in the back of the store (away from customers). Grocery personnel also spend significant time in the back-stock areas. Because of these physical locations, members of these teams spend a lot of time talking with each other and much less time talking with customers or members of other teams. In comparison, other teams tend to spend more time talking with customers (e.g., front-end cashiers and information) or are isolated from their fellow team members (e.g., human resources and accounting). Patty, a front-end team member, stated, "I have little interaction with cashiers … and then the people I actually work with at the desk, we don't have much overlap time. We don't have a lot of speaking conversations, but we do have a journal and we communicate with the journal." Martha, a human resource member, lamented, "It's hard when you don't communicate face-to-face because you can't really understand the context of what's there." Thus, the physical location (and requirements of the job) affects team identity by facilitating or restricting the interactions of team members. The result is that those teams in which face-to-face communication occurs frequently develop a strong ingroup identity, whereas those teams that cannot interact do not.

The third identity discovered stems from the position employees hold within the NFC organizational hierarchy. Most of the front-line employees perceive themselves as distinct from the board of directors, the OM and STL, and even their DTL. Nancy, the deli/cheese DTL, explained how she feels about the board, "I generally don't feel good about them, I don't feel bad about them. I think the biggest problem is that they are very removed from what happens in the store. I feel they're on the outside looking in." The board is perceived as an entity that, as Juanita, the health and beauty DTL, noted, "focuses on membership and has forgotten about the employees." Our analysis revealed that the board is also perceived as lacking sound business knowledge, not really doing anything, and not interacting with employees. Matt, the produce DTL, reinforced the feelings of distance from the board and explained how the lack of direct interaction with the board led to these feelings:

> I think sometimes they're [the Board] a little clueless and that they're a little removed from what goes on, on a daily basis. There were a couple of ideas [to improve interactions with the Board]. One was to have meetings with the DTLs and the Board, but there was [only] one meeting, and the other was to have them work a shift in the store. I think it's a good idea, but it hasn't happened yet. I think they're a little out of touch. It's not how a business is [should be] run, but we try.

Many employees also feel distance expressed by upper management. Many believe that there is not enough communication between upper management and the teams and that when there is communication, it is not direct or supportive. For example, Martha, Karen, and Kim (members from various teams) all related a story about bonuses. The cooperative had traditionally given bonuses every year and the OM (Abby) and former STL (Sam) had always signed the note "Love A and S." However, one year, bonuses were not given because of lagging sales but no note was included in the employees' paycheck. Many employees did not find out why there was not a bonus until a few weeks later and resented that they did not receive a note.

The leadership structure of the cooperative also seems to create divisions along hierarchical lines. The DTLs have regular meetings with the OM and STL, and the OM and STL meet regularly with the board. However, other employees do not have any decision-making power and do not attend any of these meetings. As Frank, the bulk DTL, explained, "I think it [leadership structure] works for me as a DTL. I don't know if it works for the people who work for me. There's not a whole lot of direction from upper management for the so-called 'peons'." Frank also added that employees would like to have more direct contact with upper management because they do not see, and would like to see, the managers on the "front line." Patty, a front-end member, also noted the difference when she said, "There's definitely a separation between people who are in management and the employees. It's like supervisor meetings; nobody goes to supervisor meetings who isn't in a managerial position." Carrie, in accounting, further explained, "I feel like we're divided between the managers and the common folk-type of thing; like it's a contest almost." Martha, in human resources, addressed the DTLs directly: "As far as the DTLs, they aren't trained adequately. I think they get this attitude that they are above everybody else, and that creates more problems, because you know that if you're not a DTL, if you're not management, then you're powerless."

The ambiguity of the team structure at NFC also plays a role in the division between front-line employees and managers. Our analysis reveals that the word *team* is primarily a metaphor in NFC, in that the teams are a team in name only. As Kristi, from deli/cheese, explained:

> I don't perceive it as a team structure. It seems to be extremely hierarchical. It's called a team, but the managers make the decisions and we don't have any input .... The managers decide policy and make decisions about the product and clerks are given directives. My conception of a team is more group decision making.

Lisa, from maintenance, supported this position when she said succinctly, "The team structure is an illusion."

Organizational position is, thus, a third identity of importance for the employees of NFC. However, this is not an active identity in the sense of affecting daily interactions among employees, for employees do not hold meetings; only the upper administration does. This identity, therefore, is more latent than the organizational and team identities. It appears to influence only those interactions between employees and upper management or the board of directors.

Intergroup Relationships.   The third research question asked about the consequences of the constructed identities for intergroup interactions. The multiple identities, including the strong identity of some of the teams, have at least three consequences for relationships among the members of different teams: (a) indirect confrontation during conflict, (b) strong concern for one's own team, and (c) compartmentalizing the units (both departments and levels of the hierarchy).

First, although the organization's norms encourage direct communication and confrontation to resolve problems, five individuals, all from the grocery, produce, or deli/cheese departments, reported that they would go to their DTL if they had a problem with someone from another department. Carmen, from deli/cheese, stated, "I probably would go to my supervisor to discuss it. I wouldn't feel as comfortable with someone from another team." Lana, in produce, echoed the same feeling, "I would probably go to Karen [her DTL]. I would have trouble going outside the team because someone outside wouldn't understand the dynamic [interactions within the department]." The fact that all five people who reported using indirect methods are from these three teams perhaps indicates that the strong ingroup identity may encourage these individuals to construct "walls" between their teams and others.

A second consequence of team identification is that some individuals become concerned only with the welfare of their teams. This is evidenced by some DTLs tending to be concerned only with their department's numbers and not with the cooperative as a whole. For example, Rosa, the grocery DTL, noted, "When I get my financial stuff, I just look for my department, and if mine is doing good, that's all I care about." In addition, Karen, the former produce DTL, was against a wage policy that would allow employees to maintain their current wage if they joined a new team because it would have been perceived as unfair by her team members.

The third consequence, compartmentalization of the units, is reflective of both the strong identity of teams and the organizational position identity. Miguel, a produce team member, noted, "One thing I notice about the coop is that it's so compartmentalized. I mean the whole entire coop should be considered a part of the team, but the produce section seems to be more cohesive. It seems that's where the team spirit is concentrated."

It is interesting that this individual appears to be both advocating for and arguing against the compartmentalization of the store. John, a produce clerk, also recognized the separation of units when he stated, "I think we [produce team] are connected with the rest of the store because we try to assist customers, but we don't have any substantive connection [with other teams] that impacts on us." Lana, from produce, echoed this point when she said, "My focus isn't on sales. That kind of focus can actually inhibit sales." Essentially, her comment speaks to the way in which the teams

divide the labor and tend to take care of their own business and let management worry about sales. This division is especially prevalent between
groups with strong identities. For instance, cashiers sometimes have difficulty getting cooperation from other departments (e.g., with a price
check) because it is not perceived as a direct concern of those other departments. Therefore, coordination of the teams is accomplished through
management and rarely through direct discussion between members of
different teams.

Furthermore, neither the board of directors nor upper management en-
gages frequently in direct communication with the teams and, consequently, autonomy of organizational units is further encouraged. The
organizational culture of compartmentalization is, thus, reflected in these
interactions, and the lack of direct and supportive interaction between upper management (and the board) and the departments encourages the autonomy of the units/departments. Matt, the produce DTL, summed up the
feeling when he said:

> The overall structure—it's trying but it needs more work between depart-
> ments and with upper management. It's gotten better, but it needs work ....
> We could work together closer. It's a bunch of separate departments, and it
> doesn't really feel like a team of the whole store.

Questionnaire Data

The questionnaire data were analyzed in two ways. First, analysis of vari-
ance (ANOVA) was used to examine differences in the OIQ between
strong- and weak-identity teams. Second, descriptive frequencies were
then calculated for the remaining items. The items of this instrument
were summarized to create a composite score of organizational identity
and team identity (lower scores indicate stronger identity). Respondents
were divided into two groups on the basis of the findings regarding team
identity from the interview data: (a) grocery, produce, and deli/cheese
teams (strong-identity teams) and (b) other teams (weak-identity teams).
ANOVA revealed that members from strong-identity teams had a stronger
identification with their teams than did members of the weak-identity
teams, $F(1, 45) = 4.80, p < .05, d = .55$ (strong: $M = 2.40, SD = .64$; weak:
$M = 3.25, SD = 1.44$). There was also a slight, but nonsignificant, difference between these two groups on identification with the organization,
with strong-identity teams identifying slightly more with the organization
than weak-identity teams, $F(1, 45) = 1.73, p = .20, d = .37$ (strong: $M =
2.77, SD = .81$; weak: $M = 3.23, SD = 1.22$). These findings support the
conclusion drawn from the qualitative data that there is a difference in
the strength of team identity at NFC and its potential impact on identification with the organization.

Each of the remaining items on the questionnaire was analyzed individually. Respondents, again, were divided into the same two groups as explained above. The percentages of responses for each category of each item are displayed in Table 7.1. The data were not analyzed for statistical significance using chi-square analysis because that analysis requires a minimum expected frequency of five and because of the small sample size, many cells did not meet this expectation. Thus, the data were examined for general trends.

The two sets of teams show some similarities. For instance, there does not appear to be any strong distinction among the groups in terms of the amount of socializing during or outside of work or within or between teams. In addition, both sets of teams perceived very little competition between departments. Moreover, both sets of teams reported relatively similar comfort levels interacting with other teams. The amount of socializing within the teams appears to contradict earlier statements about the importance of location and face-to-face interaction. The distinction between the strong- and weak-identity teams, however, is likely the quality of the interaction, not just the amount of it. The fact that there is similarity in the perception of a low amount of competition is not necessarily surprising. Competition may not be prevalent but there may be a lack of concern for other teams by the strong-identity groups, as the interview data revealed. Finally, the similarity in high-comfort levels with other teams may be due to the overall organizational identity; that is, employees demonstrate a strong identity to NFC overall and, thus, this identity may lead to a high level of

TABLE 7.1

Percentage Responses to Questionnaire

	Produce/Deli/Grocery (n = 15)					Other Teams (n = 32)				
	5	4	3	2	1	5	4	3	2	1
Item	SA	A	N	D	SD	SA	A	N	D	SD
Comfort level with team	73	27	0	0	0	56	28	13	2	0
Comfort level with team leader	36	43	21	0	0	63	19	9	3	6
Comfort level with other teams	33	47	20	0	0	41	50	6	3	0
Willing to work for another team	20	33	20	7	20	41	16	25	13	6
Like to work for another department	0	20	27	13	40	23	19	19	19	19

Note. Percentages may not add up to 100 because of rounding.

comfort interacting with other team members. After all, individuals can be comfortable with others without being concerned for them.

There are, however, some differences in the responses that are consistent with the interview data. Members of the strong-identity groups, in comparison to those in weak-identity groups, reported a stronger level of comfort with their own team. Furthermore, there is a distinction in the items "willing to" and "like to work for another team/department." Twenty percent of strong-identity team members reported being strongly willing to work for another team, in contrast to 41% of weak-identity team members; similarly, only 20% of strong-identity team members reported either strongly or moderately liking to work for another team, in contrast to 42% of weak-identity team members. Another item that seemingly differentiated between the two sets of groups was whether there was good communication between teams: 53% of strong-identity team members disagreed or strongly disagreed with the statement, whereas only 9% of the weak-identity team members reported the same. These items appear to illustrate that these three teams have a strong ingroup identity and, therefore, their members may treat the team as more autonomous and separate from other teams than do members of the weak-identity teams.

One final difference worth noting is the comfort level with the team leader: weak-identity team members were slightly more comfortable with their team leader than were the strong-identity team members (63% strongly comfortable versus 36% strongly comfortable, respectively). Thus, formal leadership does not appear to be an important factor for the development of a strong ingroup identity.

DISCUSSION

The groups at NFC provide clarification of important characteristics of the bona fide group perspective and have theoretical implications for the perspective. In turn, the bona fide group perspective has practical implications for NFC. In this section, we discuss these aspects.

Bona Fide Group Characteristics at NFC

The bona fide group perspective helps to explain the construction and content of the identities at NFC. The first characteristic of bona fide groups is stable yet permeable boundaries. Three stable yet permeable identities were discovered at NFC: (a) organizational identity, (b) team identity (some strong and some weak), and (c) organizational position identity. Each of these identities is a dynamic and fluid boundary that influences the interactions of team members. That NFC employees simultaneously hold these three identities illustrates that groups are composed of members with multiple identities (Putnam & Stohl, 1990, 1996). The nature of organizational members' interaction depends on which identity or identities are salient within a given interaction. For example, if an employee is interacting with a customer, the organizational identity may be salient; if that same employee is talking with the OM, he or she may emphasize the organizational position identity.

The construction of the team identity, in particular, illustrates the concept of group identity formation in the bona fide group perspective (Stohl & Putnam, 1994). A strong loyalty among the members of the grocery, produce, and deli/cheese teams to their teams was demonstrated. The primary concern of these teams is with the success of their respective departments, as illustrated by the insular concern for the financial conditions of their departments. There is also a strong tendency for members of these teams to separate themselves psychologically from other teams. Furthermore, the loyalty demonstrated by these team members illustrates that group boundaries are socially constructed (Putnam & Stohl, 1990). These team members socially construct their group's identity through internal dynamics (e.g., inside jokes, team names, and having fun) that are facilitated by the group's physical location (i.e., the location of these three teams keeps them physically separated from the rest of the store and customers to a larger extent than other teams).

A second characteristic of the bona fide group perspective is the interdependence of groups with their contexts. At NFC, the context of the interpretive frame of the ideology of a cooperative affects the individuals and their identities; that is, the cooperative framework and organizational structure shape NFC's cultural norms. These norms affect the employees as they manage multiple identities (team, store, and organizational position). The three identities, in turn, provide the context in which group members interact within a multiplicity of overlapping frames that include their team and the organization. There is considerable overlap in the identities, but these identities also encourage potential paradoxical decision making at NFC, such as team-based versus organizational-favored decision making. As we noted, some of the individuals/groups emphasize decision making for the team, whereas others emphasize decision making for the organization (e.g., in line with the ideology of cooperatives); there was no direct evidence illustrating decision making for organizational position. However, the ideology seems to be an important reference point for all employees. The interpretive frame of the cooperative's values and principles, thus, serves as common ground for all employees.

Organizational ideology is not the only contextual feature that frames multiple identities of employees at NFC. The team and organizational positional identities have become constructed, in part, because of the inconsistencies between the mission statement and actual practices at NFC. One of these inconsistencies is the organizational structure/hierarchy at NFC. Specifically, cooperative principles of the ICA statement and NFC's mission statement emphasize democracy and equality. However, NFC is organized in a top-down hierarchy and, consequently, decision making is in the hands of a few organization members (i.e., board of directors, SM, OM, and DTLs). The structure/hierarchy of NFC promotes the autonomy of groups within NFC. For example, interviewees perceived the board of directors and the leadership structure as being distant from the actual team members, which encourages division of labor and autonomy in the teams. The general result is that the board oversees the leadership, the leadership takes care of the financial health of the entire organization, and the teams take care of their own work. Overall, there is a great deal of compartmentalization of the departments.

The autonomy of the various organizational groups also serves to perpetuate compartmentalization. Many employees blame the board and leadership for the lack of unification of the units. However, intergroup interactions in the organization also function to encourage group autonomy. For example, team members are not always willing to help out the members of other teams and DTLs have an insular concern for the welfare of their teams. Thus, the board and leadership likely believe that the autonomy of the units is "how it should be" and focus on policies and procedures that foster more autonomy. The cause of autonomy in the units is not possible to ascertain at this point; what is clear is that the intergroup interactions and the organizational structure serve to create and recreate an organizational culture that emphasizes autonomous units.

Theoretical Implications for the Bona Fide Group Perspective

The current study has several important implications for the bona fide group perspective. First, the findings illustrate how group identity and autonomy are constructed and what happens when groups attempt to treat themselves as separate "containers." For example, the strong-identity teams in the current study appeared to avoid direct confrontation with external team members and demonstrated an insular concern for their team. Furthermore, members of other units (specifically, upper management and the board) also demonstrated an insular concern and did not engage in direct communication with employees. Overall, the creation of autonomous groups appears to inhibit effective communication between units of an organization.

Second, the current study indicates several factors that influence the development of group boundaries. Specifically, physical location and organizational structure were identified as playing important roles in boundary construction. Multiple group memberships, overlapping memberships, and fluctuations in memberships, identified by Putnam and Stohl (1996) as factors that help create boundaries, are important, but imposed structural features (such as one's boss, where one works, and organizational hierarchy) sometime encourage or discourage the development of a strong group identity. These structural features are also socially appropriated in that group members create meaning for these features and share these meanings with other group members through interaction (Stohl, 1995). At NFC, for instance, the organizational structure is recreated and reinforced by the autonomy of the groups and, in turn, encourages autonomy of the departments. In the present conceptualization of the bona fide group perspective, organizational structure would fit under a group's negotiation of jurisdiction and autonomy, but perhaps it is a separate contextual factor worthy of more detailed consideration.

Implications of the Bona Fide Group Perspective for NFC

The current study has important social and business implications for those who work at NFC. Awareness and understanding of the group dynamics in this organization could aid employees at all levels to manage their employment at and identification with NFC to realize greater benefits for themselves, their teams, others who work there, and the organization. For instance, there is, for cooperatives, an "acute need to maintain a dynamic, self-reflective, and comprehensive communication system" (Cheney, 1995, p. 195). Parts of the status quo at NFC, however, are contradictory to some of the cooperative principles on which the organization is based. Specifically, the ICA statement of cooperative identity emphasizes democracy (among other principles), and NFC's mission statement explicitly states that it is committed to participatory decision making. However, participatory decision making is not the case in practice, for employees are not involved in making decisions unless the DTLs choose to involve them. Furthermore, as explained, the organizational structure and internal dynamics foster group autonomy, which run counter to the principle of cooperation.

Part of the inconsistency at NFC between mission and practice is that the cooperative is member-owned and not worker-owned. Thus, the board and leadership are more concerned with cooperative principles as they apply to the membership, not to the workforce. However, the dialectical nature of cooperatives—striving to find balance between economic and social concerns—would seem to necessitate an examination of the current situation by the employees and leadership of NFC.

Many employees view NFC at a crossroads. They have been committed to the cooperative because of the principles it espouses but are now questioning their loyalty to an organization that does not always value those principles in actual practice. Although the organization is economically healthy, many employees feel that the social ills may lead to some business problems. In particular, the organization needs to find employees willing to work for low wages. If the principles are not followed, turnover may increase as the demand for skilled employees in the natural foods industry increases. In summary, several paradoxes exist for employees at NFC: (a) the paradox of identifying with the cooperative mission but recognizing the actual practices that are currently in place, (b) the paradox created by the tension between organizational and team identities, and (c) the paradox of identity to the organizational position and separate responsibilities and to democracy and increased interdependencies.

Finally, the team structure at NFC needs to be questioned; indeed, NFC leadership may wish to consider reorganizing the structure. The team structure as presently operationalized does little to involve the workers and, moreover, serves to isolate teams. It may be better for the organization to abandon the team structure and acknowledge the use of a traditional hierarchy. Alternatively, and preferably, the team structure could be integrated into the decision-making hierarchy, such as by including employee representatives on the board or at supervisor meetings. This inclusion would help to create more permeable boundaries between the organizational levels and within the groups. Another possibility is to have employees rotate between teams to get a better sense of how the entire system works. Both of these suggestions would, hopefully, serve to increase the interdependence and coordination of the organizational units. Of course, it is relatively easy to make suggestions looking in from the outside. Ultimately, the members of NFC will need to work out identities and structures in a manner consistent with its principles.

CONCLUSION

The purpose of this study was to examine the teams at NFC from the bona fide group perspective. The findings revealed that the hierarchy of the organization and the interactions between groups result in groups that function as autonomous units. Despite the autonomy of groups at NFC, however, the organization is able to survive and thrive economically because of the underlying ideology of cooperative principles (although some principles have been abandoned) and the commitment to selling natural foods. The continuing struggle for NFC is to reflect on how to balance social and economic concerns; hopefully, this study provides some useful means to guide future decision making at the organization.

This study helps to illustrate several characteristics of the bona fide group perspective. The results demonstrate how groups construct multiple boundaries within a hierarchical structure at an organization that is grounded in cooperative principles. The findings also help to explicate specific factors that influence the creation of relatively autonomous units and what happens when groups attempt to treat themselves as "containers." The organizational factors extend the bona fide group perspective and demonstrate some paradoxical factors that face groups in these types of situations. Hopefully, future research in this and other organizational contexts will provide further knowledge of how groups create and manage multiple identities.

ACKNOWLEDGMENT

The authors thank Brad Hall for his constructive comments on an earlier version of the chapter. .

REFERENCES

Barker, J. R., & Tompkins, P. K. (1994). Identification in the self-managing organization: Characteristics of target and tenure. *Human Communication Research*, *21*, 223–240.

Burke, K. (1969). *A rhetoric of motives*. Berkeley: University of California Press.

Cheney, G. (1983). On the various and changing meanings of organizational membership: A field study of organizational identification. *Communication Monographs*, *50*, 343–363.

Cheney, G. (1991). *Rhetoric in an organizational society: Managing multiple identities*. Columbia: University of South Carolina Press.

Cheney, G. (1995). Democracy in the workplace: Theory and practice from the perspective of communication. *Journal of Applied Communication Research*, *23*, 167–200.

Cheney, G. (1997). The many meaning of "solidarity": The negotiation of values in the Mondragon worker-cooperative complex under pressure. In B. D. Sypher (Ed.), *Case studies in organizational communication 2: Perspectives on contemporary work life* (pp. 68–83). New York: Guildford Press.

Cohen, S. G., & Ledford, G. E. (1994). The effectiveness of self-managing teams: A quasi-experiment. *Human Relations*, *47*, 13–41.

Conger, J. A., & Kanungo, R. N. (1988). The empowerment process: Integrating theory and practice. *Academy of Management Review*, *13*, 471–482.

Cotton, J. L. (1993). *Employee involvement: Methods for improving performance and work attitudes*. Newbury Park, CA: Sage.

Glaser, B. G., & Strauss, A. L. (1967). *The discovery of grounded theory: Strategies for qualitative research*. Chicago: Aldine.

Groves, F. (1985). What is cooperation? The philosophy of cooperation and its relationship to cooperative structure and operations. *University of Wisconsin Center for Cooperatives* [On-line]. Retrieved December 2, 1998, from www.wisc.edu/uwcc/index.html

International Cooperative Alliance (1995). Statement of the co-operative identity. *International Cooperative Alliance* [On-line]. Retrieved December 2, 1998, from www.coop.org/menu/ icasite.html

Lindlof, T. R. (1995). *Qualitative communication research methods*. Thousand Oaks, CA: Sage.

Mael, F., & Ashforth, B. E. (1992). Alumni and their alma mater: A partial test of the reformulated model of organizational identification. *Journal of Organizational Behavior, 13*, 103–123.

Marshall, A. A., & Stohl, C. (1993). Being "in the know" in a participative management system. *Management Communication Quarterly, 6*, 372–404.

Putnam, L. L., & Stohl, C. (1990). Bona fide groups: A reconceptualization of groups in context. *Communication Studies, 41*, 248–265.

Putnam, L. L., & Stohl, C. (1996). Bona fide groups: An alternative perspective for communication and small group decision making. In R. Y. Hirokawa & M. S. Poole (Eds.), *Communication and group decision making* (2nd ed., pp. 147–178). Thousand Oaks, CA: Sage.

Rhodes, R. (1996). The role of ideology and organization in the ICA's survival between 1910–1950. *University of Wisconsin Center for Cooperatives* [On-line]. Retrieved December 2, 1998, from www.wisc.edu/uwcc/index.html

Scott, C. R., Corman, S. R., & Cheney, G. (1998). Development of a structurational model of identification in the organization. *Communication Theory, 8*, 298–336.

Schaars, M. A. (1978). Cooperatives: Principles and practice. In F. Groves (Ed.), *What is cooperation? The philosophy of cooperation and its relationship to cooperative structure and operations* [On-line]. Retrieved December 2, 1998, from www:wisc.edu/uwcc/index.html

Schein, E. H. (1997). Organizational learning as cognitive redefinition: Coercive persuasion revisited. *University of Wisconsin Center for Cooperatives* [On-line]. Retrieved December 2, 1998, from www:wisc.edu/uwcc/index.html

Simon, H. A. (1976). *Administrative behavior* (3rd ed.). New York: Free Press.

Smith, K. K., & Berg, D. N. (1987). *Paradoxes of group life: Understanding conflict, paralysis, and, movement in group dynamics*. San Francisco: Jossey-Bass.

Stohl, C. (1995). *Organizational communication: Connectedness in action*. Newbury Park, CA: Sage.

Stohl, C., & Putnam, L. L. (1994). Group communication in context: Implications for the study of bona fide groups. In L. R. Frey (Ed.), *Group communication in context: Studies of natural groups* (pp. 284–292). Hillsdale, NJ: Lawrence Erlbaum Associates.

Tompkins, P. K., & Cheney, G. (1983). Account analysis of organizations: Decision making and identification. In L. L. Putnam & M. E. Pacanowsky (Eds.), *Communication and organizations: An interpretive approach* (pp. 123–146). Newbury Park, CA: Sage.

Tompkins, P. K., & Cheney, G. (1985). Communication and unobtrusive control in contemporary organizations. In R. D. McPhee & P. K. Tompkins (Eds.), *Organizational communication: Traditional themes and new directions* (pp. 179–210). Newbury Park, CA: Sage.

APPENDIX

INTERVIEW QUESTIONS AND QUESTIONNAIRE ITEMS

Interview Questions

1. How did you decide to work at NFC?
2. How do feel about the team structure?
3. What's your relationship like with the team?
4. Can you name the team values?
5. Are the _____ team values the same as those of the rest of the store?
6. If you had a problem with a team member, how would you handle it?
7. What's your perception of the leadership structure at NFC?
8. What's your perception of the board of directors?
9. Is there anything you would like to add?

Questionnaire Items

1. What is your comfort level with your department team members? (High-Low)
2. What is your comfort level with your department team leader? (High-Low)
3. What is your comfort level with other department team members? (High-Low)
4. Would you be willing to work for another department? (Very Often-Never)
5. Would you like to work for another department? (Very Often-Never)
6. How often do you socialize (outside of work) with your team members? (Very Often-Never)
7. How often do you socialize (during work) with your team members? (Very Often-Never)
8. How often do you socialize (outside of work) with people who are members of other teams? (Very Often-Never)
9. How often do you socialize (during work) with people who are members of other teams? (Very Often-Never)

10. Do you think there is competition between your department and other departments?   (Absolutely-Absolutely Not)

11. Do you think there is a lot of conflict within your department? (Absolutely-Absolutely Not)

12. Do you think there is a lot of conflict between departments? (Absolutely-Absolutely Not)

13. Does your department have good communication among the team members?   (Absolutely-Absolutely Not)

14. Does your department have good communication with other departments?   (Absolutely-Absolutely Not)

CHAPTER

8

ENVIRONMENTAL COLLABORATIONS AND CONSTITUENCY COMMUNICATION

Jonathan I. Lange
Southern Oregon University

Since 1973, the year that marked the beginning of contemporary and formal environmental mediation processes (Bingham, 1988), there have been hundreds and perhaps thousands of attempts at resolving environmental conflicts through alternative dispute resolution (ADR) methods.[1] This trend will continue; in late 1998, the governors of the Western U.S. states all agreed publicly that such methods were the preferred way to resolve environmental disputes. These methods are known by various labels,

---

[1]Numerous elements inherent in natural resource conflict make it an especially contentious and difficult site for productive management. To begin, environmental damage is often irrevocable (Cox, 1982)—that is, there may be no reclamation or recovery from environmental harm. Species extinction is perhaps the most common and profound example of irrevocability. A second reason is that such conflicts rarely end: "Counter-environmental" forces can repeatedly try to achieve their aims, even after many failures. Hundreds of developments, from housing tracts to utility dams, illustrate how counter-environmental forces outlasted government administrations, overcame changed environmental protection laws, and, through sheer perseverance, eventually triumphed. A third reason for the special difficulties in environmental conflicts stems from the perceived choice between destroying the economic health of entire communities—dependent on extracting natural resources for jobs and commerce—and environmental destruction or degradation. Conflicts over forestry management in logging regions and communities typify this difficulty. Disputants find themselves in what Freeman, Littlejohn, and Pearce (1992) called "moral conflict," in which "participants not only differ about what they want, believe, or need, but also lack shared criteria by which to adjudicate their differences" (p. 312).   (*continued on next page*)

including *collaboration* (Gray, 1989), *environmental mediation* (e.g., Amy, 1987; Bacow & Wheeler, 1984; Crowfoot & Wondolleck, 1990), or more broadly, *interest-based* (e.g., Fisher & Ury, 1981), *integrative* (e.g., Pruitt & Carnevale, 1993), and *mutual-gains bargaining* (e.g., Friedman, 1994). The essence of these ADR methods involves disputants working together to achieve a mutually determined, constructively settled solution to problems, sometimes with the aid of a third party and sometimes on their own. Disputants focus on their commonalities as they engage in various communicative forms to achieve mutually defined goals.[2]

Environmental collaborations, as with many other multiparty ADR situations (e.g., community planning and policy controversies, interorganizational conflicts, intergovernmental disputes, international struggles, and product liability cases), can be understood effectively from the bona fide group perspective (Putnam & Stohl, 1996), as these collaborative groups are marked by "permeable and fluid boundaries and interdependence with context" (p. 149). As will be shown, participants in these groups demonstrate "multiple group memberships and conflicting role identities" that are expressed when they take on "representative roles" (p. 150). In addition, these collaborations are marked by "fluctuation in memberships" and extraordinary "group identify formation" (p. 150) processes. There is also a "reciprocal relationship between the group and its environment" (p. 153), as decision making in environmental collaborations often pivots on "directives from authority" (p. 165).

This chapter tells the "story" of one ongoing, nationally renowned environmental collaboration known as The Applegate Partnership. The story of this bona fide group is rendered through description of its *constituency communication*—the communication between the members of this group and those they represent. As will be shown, this communication process contextualizes the entire collaborative process. Representative-constituency communication, as well as intraconstituency communi-

---

[1](*continued from previous page*) Environmental disputants hold different world views, competing frames for defining conflict, and disparate principles regarding appropriate conflict management (see Littlejohn, Shailor, & Pearce, 1994; C. W. Moore, 1994). Fourth, environmental conflicts are often complex, involving multitudinous issues and stakeholders with vastly different types and degrees of involvement and participation. For example, a single water-quality dispute can cross local, state, and/or national boundaries; simultaneously evoke issues such as fishing, irrigation rights, logging effects, and waste disposal; and involve people whose livelihood depends on the outcome, as well as those who are unaware of the conflict (Susskind & Cruikshank, 1987).

[2]Of the various definitions of collaboration, Gray's (1989) is one of the more inclusive: Collaboration is "a process through which parties who see different aspects of a problem can constructively explore their differences and search for solutions that go beyond their own limited vision of what is possible" (p. 5). The essential aspects of collaboration include (a) interdependence of stakeholders; (b) differences dealt with constructively; (c) joint ownership of (i.e., agreement on) decisions; (d) collective responsibility for future direction; and (e) the emergent nature of the process. These characteristics are sufficiently broad to allow a wide variety of environmental collaborative methodologies.

cation processes, are investigated with respect to the nature of the (a) communication between collaborating disputants and the constituencies they represent; (b) communication within different constituencies; and (c) effects of constituency communication on the collaborative process, particularly with respect to how collaboration success or failure is shaped by these processes.

Constituency Communication

Although they do not use the term *bona fide groups*, communication and negotiation scholars have regularly called for increased inquiry into the critical, yet often overlooked role of negotiator–constituent relationships and communication (e.g., Pruitt, 1994; Putnam, 1985; Putnam & Jones, 1982; Roloff & Campion, 1987; Turner, 1992). The majority of extant literature on this role extrapolates from traditional labor-management negotiation and/or private mediation contexts, and a number of relevant, foundational concepts have emerged. Walton and Mckersie (1965) and Adams (1976), for example, described how "boundary spanners" (internal organizational negotiators and representatives) felt pressured to meet the expectations of both their constituents and the other negotiators. Colosi (1983) and Ancona, Friedman, and Kolb (1991) pointed out that constituents—what they called the *second table*—often have the ultimate authority over negotiated outcomes; their internal deliberations, therefore, are critical to any mutual-gains bargaining. A number of researchers have found that when negotiators were accountable to constituents, concession making took longer and the probability of reaching agreement was reduced (see Ben-Yoav & Pruitt, 1984; Senecah, 1997). Turner (1992) reviewed the differential effects that high- or low-constituent trust had on negotiators' behavior, and Friedman (1992) described how successful boundary spanners have to develop their own "subculture of mediation."[3] Finally, Pruitt and Carnevale (1993) likened negotiators to Janus-faced intermediaries, arguing that their fundamental communicative task was to present the views of their constituents to the other negotiators and the views of the other negotiators to their constituents.

A second related, and heretofore barely mentioned, problem domain involves *intraconstituency communication activity*—communication within constituencies—and its effects on the collaborative group process. Pruitt (1994), a prominent negotiation theorist, argued that researchers' inattention to intraconstituency communication was a serious omission because constituents can themselves be complex organizational entities, "involving individuals and groups who communicate and negotiate with

---

[3]In this phrase, Friedman used the term *mediation* in the denotative and broad sense: "to mediate or resolve differences by acting as an intermediary between two or more parties; to serve as a vehicle for bringing about [a result] or conveying information to others" (p. 162).

each other about the issues under discussion" (p. 219). Pruitt's "branching chain" model moved to eliminate broad distinctions between interorganizational and intraorganizational negotiations, by focusing, instead, on communication "networks" along a chain of intermediaries (links that represent stakeholders and constituencies). Carpenter and Kennedy (1988) provided a sharp illustration of the complexity and importance of constituent communication in the context of collaboration. They described a "Water Roundtable" collaboration that included two members who represented a 17-organization "environmental alliance." In this collaboration, discussions and negotiations *within the alliance* often took more time than reaching agreements at the Roundtable itself. Completion of those intragroup discussions was a prerequisite to the Roundtable's continuation, which clearly illustrates the importance and influence of intraconstituency communication.

   To further understand environmental collaborations from a bona fide group perspective, I describe below the case of The Applegate Partnership. After explaining the methods used and providing some background on the context, the Partnership's story is told by recounting critical events in its representative–constituency and intraconstituency communication processes. I conclude with a discussion of the extent to which the group succeeded, with particular attention to transformational conflict management processes.

METHODS, CONTEXT, AND BACKGROUND

Methods

Following a methodological tradition of case study in ADR, I focus primarily on a single case; however, this case is informed by an environmental communication research program that spans 12 years (e.g., Lange, 1988, 1989, 1990, 1993) and includes some work on environmental ADR (e.g., Lange, 1992, 1994, 2000). Throughout this research, and in the current case, I have steadily followed data-gathering and fieldwork recommendations offered by Lofland and Lofland (1995) and Spradley (1979, 1980). I have attempted to immerse myself in environmentalist, counter-environmentalist (i.e., timber industry), and natural resource agency (i.e., United States Forest Service and Bureau of Land Management) cultures in the three ways suggested by Lofland and Lofland: through (a) bodily presence, (b) extensive interviewing, and (c) examination of textual (e.g., written) materials. This immersion process has involved over 475 hours of participant observation of strategy and planning meetings, conferences, government hearings, benefit concerts and events, political demonstrations, and other gatherings held by various groups and organizations. The current case study also draws from 5 audiotaped intensive interviews with informants, averaging 90 minutes per interview; scores of informal interviews and discussions during shared car rides, lunches, and dinners; dozens of occasions when I engaged in member checks by asking informants for their interpretation of the events I was describing and interpreting; as well as participant-observational data gathered while acting as a third party (described later). Additionally, I have examined a wide range of artifacts about the collaboration, including (a) local newsletters, press releases, and miscellaneous publications written by representatives from different groups; (b) articles reported by the Associated Press, United Press International, and local daily newspapers; and (c) various analyses in the national popular "environmental press." Because of my greater participation with and observation of environmental constituencies, and because this case study essay focuses on *environmental* collaborations, there is more reportage of evidence from environmental groups than from the timber industry, resource agencies, or others. However, as will be demonstrated, the communication principles work similarly for each set of representatives and constituencies.

Context and Background

The formation of The Applegate Partnership followed a remarkable reduction of "timber harvest" (logging) allowed on national forest lands in the Northwest—lands managed by two federal agencies: the United States Forest Service (USFS) and the Bureau of Land Management (BLM). Owing to a number of lawsuits initiated and won by environmentalists, in which it was successfully shown that previous and ongoing timber harvests were violating environmental law, the "allowable cut" on Pacific Northwest federal lands was reduced by approximately 80% between the mid-1980s and early 1990s. Although the laws and issues are much more complex, the primary reason for the reduction was the combined requirements of the National Forest Management Act and the Endangered Species Act, which stipulated that federally owned habitats for threatened or endangered "indicator species" must be preserved. The effect was that logging on certain national lands almost ceased when the Northern spotted owl, a species whose health served to *indicate* the health of its Northwest "old growth" habitat, was identified by the federal government as "threatened." The resulting lack of available timber and subsequent layoffs, however, hurt the economy of Northwest timber-dependent towns, as well as the timber industry itself. Direct and indirect employment was negatively affected and the industry became desperate for aid.

These events represented an historic shift in the power relations between environmentalists and the timber industry. Prior to the mid-1980s, the industry (depending on its markets) had near-free reign in the amount of timber it extracted from national forests. However, when environmentalists became successful plaintiffs, they held the high-power role for the first time. All this served to intensify the already bitter enmity between the conflicting camps and led to two dramatic and competing information campaigns designed to sway public opinion, federal judges, and Congress (Lange, 1993). In 1992, President Clinton convened a conference to develop a plan that would attempt to accommodate the interests of all the parties, yet still follow the law (Walker & Daniels, 1994).

After surviving several court challenges, implementation of the Clinton Forest Plan began in 1994. The plan draws from *ecosystem management* principles, which represent the national resource agencies' philosophy and method for managing national forests (and grasslands). Extraordinarily complex, relatively new, and still evolving, ecosystem management elevates ecosystem health above all other forest uses. It also employs various kinds of collaborative public participation processes in making decisions about resource use. Part of the intent of ecosystem management is to achieve compromise and consensus between previously "warring" groups by developing collaborative partnerships that represent all stakeholders' interests fairly. The Clinton plan identifies 10 "adaptive management areas" (AMAs) where local bona fide groups—composed of individuals with competing interests—attempt to collaboratively identify mutually acceptable timber sales for recommendation to the agencies. Clinton's plan, however, did not satisfy everyone. As discussed below, ecosystem management, which allows for some continued logging on public lands, still remains the subject of passionate debate between and within the environmental, industry, and agency communities (for a nontechnical summary and critique of ecosystem management, see Devine, 1994).

THE PARTNERSHIP

The Applegate Partnership, based in the rural Applegate Valley in southern Oregon, is famous throughout the national forest management communities, as it served, in part, as a model for the public participation portion of the Clinton Forest Plan. Begun in 1993 as a local grassroots community effort, the Partnership consists of 10 board of directors and 10 "alternates." The original group was selected through extensive discussions during a series of "front-porch" community meetings. (The first meeting had 70 attendees; subsequent attendance dwindled into the 20s.) Board members were to represent all possible stakeholders and constituencies: environmentalists, timber industry representatives, federal resource agency personnel, ranchers, farmers, and other interested members of the 12,000-person Applegate community. Since 1993, members have met weekly to collaboratively plan the ecosystem management of the 500,000-

acre watershed that frames "The Applegate" in southern Oregon and northern California.[4]

The Partnership met for several months prior to announcing its formation to the press. When it did "go public," there was great hope, both at the local and national level. Regional residents were surprised to read, for the first time, newspaper headlines heralding cooperation: "Applegate Valley Edges Toward a Forest Truce" (Durbin, 1993), "Peace in the Forest" (Fattig, 1993a), "Partnership Serves as Model for Future Problem-Solving" (Fattig, 1993b), and "We Can Work It Out" (T. Moore, 1993). When Department of Interior Secretary Bruce Babbitt visited the Partnership, he said:

> It is an extraordinary promise that the antagonists—the people who have been fighting each other in the West for the last 60 years—finally lay down their weapons and say, "We're going to find a common ground, build confidence and generate solutions." ... That's pretty radical stuff that could change the world. (Fattig, 1993c, p. 1)

The Applegate Partnership "vision statement" made clear the group's mission:

> The Applegate Partnership is a community-based project involving industry, conservation groups, natural resource agencies, and residents cooperating to encourage and facilitate the use of natural resource principles that promote ecosystem health and diversity. Through community involvement and education, this Partnership supports management of all land within the watershed in a manner that sustains natural resources and that will, in turn, contribute to economic and community stability within the Applegate Valley.

It is important to note that approximately 70% of the Applegate watershed is either BLM or USFS land and, therefore, "owned" by the national citizenry; only 30% of the land is privately held. Thus, although local community residents are most affected, final authority on timber sales and related resource-utilization decisions still rests with the federal government. Clearly, as with other bona fide decision-making groups, all environmental mediations and collaborative attempts are significantly shaped by the structure or location of final decision-making authority (Bingham, 1988; Gray, 1989).

To locate my personal role, beyond that of researcher, I cofacilitated Partnership meetings (alternating with another facilitator.) As a cofacilitator, for approximately 1½ years between 1993 and 1995, every other week, I helped the Partnership organize and move through its meeting agenda, keep on task, adhere to communication ground rules, clarify process issues, take on a group role when needed (e.g., consensus testing and

---

[4]Board members are replaced by a vote, every 2 years, or when someone leaves, according to constituency (i.e., environmentalist, timber industry representative, or community member).

summarizing), and manage certain conflicts. I did *not* act as an official mediator or convener; I joined the Partnership as a facilitator, at members' request, as an unpaid volunteer, after the group was under way. This relationship placed me more toward the participant end of the participant–observer continuum, although I was acting as an outside agent (and am not a resident of the Valley). My formal facilitation ended in early 1995, but to this day, I continue to observe the Partnership's activity.

Partnership Representative–Constituency Communication

Given that representatives involved in collaborations can agree only to what their constituents allow (Ancona et al., 1991), one cannot overestimate the importance and potential influence of representative–constituency communication. Thus, members of bona fide groups composed of competing constituencies must pay an extraordinary amount of attention to this type of communication. Representatives and their constituents must continually clarify expectations, address strategy, discuss progress, and consider potential bargaining outcomes (Carpenter & Kennedy, 1988). Although describing organizational—as opposed to environmental—teams, Ancona (1990) went so far as to suggest that group members' management of external relationships with constituencies is a better predictor of group performance than is the quality of the internal communication of collaborating groups.

With regard to the current case, the first, most persistent, and most striking representative–constituency theme is the *extraordinary complexity of relationship structures* that characterize environmental collaborations. Each Applegate Partnership board member represents not a single constituency but a complex web of related groups, organizations, and stakeholders, many of whom have competing, or at least different, interests. To illustrate this relational complexity and associated representative–constituent communication difficulties, and how group members can be affected, some characteristics of and comments by two group members are offered below.

Tim is a 20-year Valley resident, a carpenter in his 60s, and a steady and major leadership force on the Partnership board.[5] He belongs to a variety of environmental groups, although his membership on the board originally stemmed from his representation of one, local group, Headwaters, which is the major environmental presence in southern Oregon. This organization is closely linked to other local, regional, and national groups with an interest in the collaboration; the national organizations include the Sierra Club, the Wilderness Society, Audubon, the National Wildlife Federation, the Sierra Legal Defense Fund, and others. It may be argued that because the Applegate watershed holds 350,000 acres of *national* land,

---

[5]Pseudonyms are used to protect people's privacy.

Tim represents millions of stakeholders who may (or even may not) be "national" environmental group members.

Putting those arguments aside temporarily, there are clearly multiple linkages among many constituency groups and stakeholders involved in this collaboration, which severely complicates negotiator representation. Tim must answer not only to Headwaters and to community members in the Applegate Valley but to interested intermediaries from all the other local, regional, and national groups. These parties may disagree among themselves and they may wish to give different advice to Tim on Applegate policy negotiations. As Tim lamented:

> It seems like it's a new thing every day. I have to continually deal with new challenges [to the Partnership], make new responses. There's so much paper and so much handholding. "Oh, Okay. How are you feeling now guys? Is everybody else okay? And how are *you* feeling?"

Alexandra's (Alex) full-time job is to represent to the public the Southern Oregon Timber Industry Association (SOTIA), the largest, local timber alliance. SOTIA is also connected to other local, regional, and national groups, from the tiny, local but vocal "Save Our Sawmills" to the imposing and robust (national) American Forest Alliance. Another energetic leader, as well as the youngest member of the Partnership board, Alex said:

> Well, my constituents get frustrated at the lack of results. They wonder if this is a good investment of time. People outside the area give me a lot of flak but if they're not here, they can't fathom the process, the patience, the grind of it all. They can't understand the work …. None of this is easy.

Thus, in environmental collaborations, the complexity and multiplicity of constituencies cause substantial stress for negotiators and complicate their negotiating tasks. A negotiator's position as a "Janus-faced intermediary" (Pruitt, 1994) is especially problematic in environmental collaborations, since there are thousands of potential constituents and stakeholders, who, because of their remoteness, cannot possibly comprehend what occurs at the "first table" (see Friedman, 1994).

The Partnership board members' relationships to the national constituencies leads to a second theme: the *inherent paradox* and resulting difficulty when localized, place-specific groups attempt to address issues of national concern, as so many environmental collaborations must do. Smith and Berg (1987) defined *paradoxes in group life* as those situations that group members experience (consciously or unconsciously) as both contradictory and circular, and note that the situation allows no escape from the resulting dilemma, although it can be managed through communicative behavior (see Barge & Frey, 1997).

In the case of ADR, the paradox develops out of the need to include all "stakeholders" in the collaborative deliberations. Gray (1989) defined *stakeholders* as "those parties with an interest in the problem .... Stakeholders include all individuals, groups, or organizations that are directly influenced by actions others take to solve the problem" (p. 5). Bingham (1988), Carpenter and Kennedy (1988), Gray (1989), and virtually every other ADR theorist and practitioner agreed that if collaborations are to succeed, it is vital that all stakeholders in the process be present or at least represented. This axiom holds for a variety of reasons, including (a) having relevant and varied expertise at the table, (b) leading members to develop psychological "ownership" of the problem, (c) creating favorable conditions for implementing emerging solutions, and (d) avoiding the possibility that excluded stakeholders might later undermine or sabotage the process or solutions.

Although the necessity of stakeholder presence makes intuitive sense and is supported by a reasonable amount of empirical evidence (e.g., Bingham, 1988; Wondolleck & Yaffe, 1994), identifying stakeholders in environmental collaborations can be especially problematic and paradoxical. For instance, the stakeholders who represented the "environmentalist" contingents in The Applegate Partnership were thoughtfully and carefully chosen and fit criteria for membership in collaborations, as outlined by Carpenter and Kennedy (1988).[6] However, this collaboration is about land on national forests; hence, it could be argued that someone like Tim represents more than just his local environmental constituents. In a sense, he also represents the members of national environmental organizations (e.g., the Sierra Club, Wilderness Society, and National Wildlife Federation), because they too have a stake in the management of the national forests within the Applegate watershed. Pushing this perspective further requires us to at least consider the idea that since this is national land "owned" by the citizenry, Tim represents millions of stakeholders who may not even belong to an environmental organization but who might care or be affected by how the land is managed. (The same can be said for Alex and her relevant constituencies.) It could further be argued that this *stakeholder paradox*—in which it is both impossible but necessary to have all stakeholders present or represented in an environmental collaboration— characterizes every dispute that involves national lands (Lange, 2000). It could also be said to exist, with fewer numbers of people to consider, in collaborations on state-owned lands. Going further, one might even suggest that this paradox holds in air-quality disputes, river-use conflicts, energy and toxic waste decisions, and just about any environmental controversy that has significance beyond the particular

---

[6]In particular, representatives must come from appropriate "interest" categories and subcategories (e.g., industry and environmentalist) and have specific individual attributes (e.g., be knowledgeable, have respect of their interest group members, and possess the ability to get along with members from different interest groups).

place in which it is debated. Some environmentalists and scholars (e.g., Nash, 1989) have even argued that environmentalists' constituencies include wildlife, trees, and other flora and fauna.

Clearly, defining stakeholders so broadly begs the question of stakeholder representation. In fact, Pruitt (1994) suggested that conceiving of constituency composition in this broad manner only takes one into chaos. However, as Gray (1989) noted, "The decision of whom to include is often a paradoxical one" (p. 69), as when conveners and participants must make choices about representation that cannot possibly satisfy the full stakeholder participation requirement. In the case of The Applegate Partnership, the practical effect of this paradox was that almost anyone could come to the table and claim the status of stakeholder. And this they did, as the group's desire to remain inclusive and community oriented evoked visits from not-so-cooperative interested parties—stakeholders both inside and outside the community—some of whom tended to impede the process. These stakeholders forwarded unrealistic suggestions (e.g., an innovative but wild type of air crane logging that took several weeks for the group to consider), required the group to go over old ground (to bring the newcomers "up to speed," often a time-consuming process), or disrupted the general cohesiveness of the group by engaging in behaviors that emphasized difference and conflict (e.g., reminding particular members of past injustices committed by the "other" party). As was evident in this and other cases, the stakeholder paradox makes already difficult group decision making even more demanding, if not impossible, as it undermines the forward movement of a group.

Perhaps the most important problem posed by these newcomer/non-board members was that they did not participate in the day-to-day creation of what Friedman (1992) called the "subculture of mediation." Juxtaposing them against those who *did* participate in the creation of this subculture illustrates the third theme for this type of bona fide group: a *shifting of alliances*. This shifting is a specific and particularly intense example of what Stohl and Putnam (1994) referred to as shifting borders in bona fide groups.

In his longitudinal case study, Friedman (1994) reported how labor-management teams that reached agreement developed rules and norms distinct from their constituent groups. Although the progress and outcomes of their work were public, the labor-management teams built their own "social space" that allowed for discovery of commonalities among members and promoted trust and relationship building. Like those bona fide groups, over time, board members of The Applegate Partnership developed their own subculture and negotiator "embeddedness," in which they cultivated predictive knowledge of how others would act. They knew that they would work together for the immediate future; soon, many of the groups' internal relationships expanded beyond the Partnership meetings (cf. Van Maanen,

1992). They shared a place (Kemmis, 1990)—the Applegate—where they held community potlucks, drank beer, flew observation planes, and walked miles of forest trails. They appeared together on conference panels, radio programs, and in geographically distant forums. They could soon predict what topics to avoid at the negotiating table, who would say what, when, and the unnecessary effects a particular announcement would have. They learned how to "lobby" each other outside the meeting room, began to share their concerns about constituency groups, and increasingly saw themselves as a unit. Each participant's identity now included "Applegate Partnership Board member," in addition to environmentalist, logger, or forest ranger. A newfound trust replaced the enmity they once held for each other.

Trust became a key word within this subculture; it permeated the group's press releases, "official" videotape, and internal discussions. When arguments began, members reminded each other to trust each other and look to their vision statement for guidance. Different members on occasion would travel around the country as guests of other would-be partnerships, and their presentations focused on the trust that had developed. Don, a grizzled sawmill owner, reported to the group members one night that although he still could not "tolerate" some of their constituency members, he trusted "each and every one of you to never do anything that would deliberately hurt me." This came from a man who, in his own words, once wanted to "ring every Goddamn environmentalist's neck." Although the Partnership continually faced serious substantive and process problems, its local subculture of mediation—developed out of members' shared commitment to the economic, environmental, and community sustainability of the Applegate Valley—was getting stronger.

Simultaneously, members' commitment to their constituencies was weakening. In addition to Tim and Alex, mentioned earlier, other members were experiencing difficulty conveying the Partnership group's work to their constituents, especially those outside the local community. Eventually, some members began to cast certain constituents as "superordinate enemies" (Sheriff, Harvey, White, Hood, & Sherif, 1961), as these once-conflicting parties were united by their shared difficulties with constituents. Board members started likening themselves to Israeli and Palestinian peacemakers, as they were encountering more difficulty and resistance from their regional and national constituents than from each other.

Some of these difficulties resulted from constituent resistance. Early in the collaboration process, timber industry personnel had ridiculed their board representatives for the lack of timber sale output. Don later admitted, "My industry friends say to me, 'Why would you want to sit down and try to reason with those assholes?'" Within the resource agencies, colleagues scorned Partnership representatives for spending so much time with nonagency personnel. One long-time agency employee, having suffered through years of lawsuits, warned his colleague on the board,

"They're [the other Board members] just going to screw you in the end." Even community members were suspicious early on, wondering what this "partnership" was "really up to." The most difficulty, however, came from the environmental activists.

Environmental constituents continuously hindered or resisted the collaboration process. At one early stage, the Sierra Club, concerned that the Partnership was undermining its activism, faxed a "Red Alert" to dozens of major environmental groups, denouncing the Partnership's activity. This action embarrassed Headwaters and its two board representatives, Tim and John. It required dozens of explanatory phone calls, faxes, memoranda, and meetings. When the dust settled, other obstructive activity followed. Headwaters' meetings were soon dominated by internal disagreement (within the constituency) about the Partnership's activity. Tim, one of the original and founding members of Headwaters, was in conflict with various staffers, and the others increasingly viewed John, a relative newcomer, with suspicion. When the Partnership was wrestling with the specifics of its first group-approved timber sale—named "Partnership One"—Headwaters was the least compromising constituency and the slowest to sign off. Eventually, Headwaters officially withdrew from the Partnership. After much discussion by the board members, it was decided that Tim and John would stay in the Partnership as representatives of different, smaller environmental organizations to which they each belonged.

Within the broader environmental community, the representative–constituency relationship faced other, regular challenges. At an environmental law conference, held at a university 200 miles north of the Applegate, where John was as a panelist, he was verbally attacked by a number of environmentalists. Offering yet another example of the group's shifting alliances and unstable borders, John told me after the conference that he was beginning to feel more comfortable with Partnership board members, previously adversaries, than he did with his own constituent friends and assumed allies. Perhaps the most difficult moment occurred after the Forest Service finally approved Partnership One, thinking it had full public support. Although the Service did have the Partnership's favorable recommendation, *other* environmental organizations, including one from the northern part of the state, filed a lawsuit that alleged inadequate environmental analysis and, consequently, held up the sale. This type of constituent activity angered Partnership members and served to further strengthen their subculture and new alliance.

The environmental constituents were resistant partly as a result of their newly achieved high-power position. One agency member went so far as to say, "The only reason timber people are at the table is because they don't have another choice." This statement represents the fourth theme: how *power disparities affect representative–constituency communication*. A number of scholars (e.g., Crowfoot & Wondolleck, 1990; Gray, 1989;

Susskind & Cruikshank, 1987) addressed difficulties that asymmetrical relationships can create for collaborating groups, including (a) how motivation to participate is affected, (b) how low-power parties can develop countervailing power, and (c) what can be accomplished in spite of continued power inequity. However, they barely consider how power differences contribute to constituency communicative behavior.

By mid-1994, some environmental constituents began advocating the dissolution of the Partnership, "now that the industry is going to have to obey the law," as one environmentalist put it. However, after the November elections of 1995, when Republicans captured majorities in both the U.S. House of Representatives and Senate, the power shifted back to the industry. Congresspersons were quickly initiating anti-environmental bills to preclude future litigation, loosen existing regulations, and open forests to increased logging. Within weeks, it was the *timber* constituency that started talking tough and reconsidering its participation in the Partnership. Alex, SOTIA's representative, warned that she no longer knew how long her organization would support Partnership activity without more visible results (i.e., successful timber sales). As she claimed, "They're wanting me to spend more of my time doing other things."

The reversal of constituency resistance demonstrates the relationships between power, dependence, and cooperation (Emerson, 1962). Specifically, when constituents are dependent on another party, they are more likely to cooperate and less likely to resist. However, the power shift described previously reveals something beyond that formulation: That power can shift so quickly serves as an implicit argument for the long-term utility or viability of partnerships and collaborations. This was demonstrated when it became clear that prior to the Congressional elections, environmental representatives had to fight through their constituents' resistance. They stayed at the table because of their shared sense of community, their commitment to the Partnership, and their belief that collaboration was the best *long-term* method for solving these conflicts. Their tenacity was repaid when, even after winning the elections, timber representatives chose to continue with the Partnership. As Don, a timber representative, said, "Just because we have more of our boys in Congress doesn't mean I desert."[7] Thus, although it

---

[7]Communication *between* constituencies is another story altogether that is beyond the scope of this chapter. It should be noted, however, that to the extent that the Applegate Partnership is representative, environmental collaborations are contextualized by an almost bizarre set of inconsistencies. Although collaborative efforts inherently involve previously conflicting constituents, negotiators at the environmental collaboration table represent groups whose intense conflict continues right through the collaboration. For example, as representatives from the timber industry, environmental groups, and resource agencies were attempting to collaborate on management of the Applegate watershed, constituency members from both the industry and environmental camps were simultaneously filing lawsuits against the agencies for illegal forest management practices in the Northwest. (The lawsuits alleged illegality in Clinton's Forest Plan, although for different reasons and from different perspectives.)   (*continued on next page*)

might make sense to resist collaborations if one party were guaranteed a stable, high-power position, the zero-sum nature of these disputes and the swing of the "political pendulum" preclude certainty of any coalition's ascendancy (Kemmis, 1990; Thurow, 1980). Members of future collaborations should keep in mind this shifting nature of power.

Intraconstituency Communication

Examination of communication *within* different constituencies exemplifies issues related to the potential outward influence of an environmental collaboration. This case reveals deep differences between constituents about the inherent value of this type of bona fide group, generally, as well as The Applegate Partnership, specifically.[8] Arguments about even participating in the collaboration went beyond the usual ambivalence or intraconstituency disagreement in labor-management negotiations. Within each constituency—whether that be timber, environmental, resource agency, or community member—there were continual intraconstituency disagreements on foundational issues such as whether the Partnership was worth the expenditure of time by representatives and constituencies, whether anything useful would ever come of it all, the legality of Partnership decision making, the likely decisional quality, and other matters. Because I spent more time with the environmental constituency, compared to the others, I offer representative illustrations of the arguments in which environmental constituents engaged, although similar kinds of arguments were manifested in the other represented factions as well.

Within the space of a year, the Partnership became the anvil on which the environmental community's internal politics were hammered out. Headwaters originally went out on a limb for the Partnership; its support put that organization in a new role as relatively moderate forest activists. This role evolved from the organization's local, on-the-ground experience that compelled its members to advocate "thinning" of small trees to im-

---

[7]*(continued from previous page)* In addition, both environmental and timber activists continued intense negative information campaigns against the other; they lobbied the public, Congress, and both agencies in an essentially competitive strategy. All this took place at the same time that in the Applegate (as well as in other partnerships in the West), timber, environmental, and agency "representatives" were attempting to find collaborative solutions to localized forest management problems. Somehow, collaborative representatives must manage the obvious inconsistencies, although on its face, it seems a fairly extraordinary set of incongruities. Although not uncommon in political affairs—as when trade sanctions against a country are enacted by an "ally"—it should be pointed out that these behaviors contextualized and affect all intraconstituency, representative–constituency, and internal representative communication.

[8]Although my access to the environmental constituency was highest, I also enjoyed extremely high and continual admission to the agencies, particularly to the local Forest Service, and moderately high access to the timber industry and community constituencies. The relative differences in access reflect my inclination and desire to focus on the *environmental* "side," particularly as I investigated intraconstituency communication.

prove forest health and prevent catastrophic fire. Headwaters adopted a "forest management" or "conservationist" stance, a position that contradicted the more radical or extreme environmentalists, who argued that any logging was to be resisted with whatever means were available. The more extreme environmental activists held a "preservationist," "zero-cut" position of no logging on any nationally owned lands. When I asked the president of Headwaters if her organization experienced pressure from the more radical environmental groups, or from the "nationals" concerned about "local control," at first, she demurred. Later, she admitted, "We've been bucking the tide on this from day one, and we defended it; we thought we could do it; we hoped it would work out, you know, we really did and we were just prepared to take the flak." Nevertheless, Headwaters eventually withdrew from formally participating in the Partnership.

Although Headwaters did come under fire from the press (e.g., Durbin, 1994; Fattig, 1994) and other environmental groups, Headwaters' staffers to a person explained their withdrawal as the result of *internal* communication and relationship issues. The president cited time requirements, lack of clarification on Partnership process, and the fact that, as she said:

> We didn't have our own shit together. There were these areas of fuzziness in our policies. We weren't sure just how much leeway to give Tim or John. And when John was going all over the country saying all these things that we couldn't agree with ... like, "When people come to the Partnership meetings they leave their constituencies behind," that kind of thing just drove us nuts.

This concern is reminiscent of "the short leash" on which, according to Friedman (1994), constituents like to keep their representatives.

Other Headwaters staffers, however, were less careful and more dramatic in explaining their decision not to participate. They reported that the Partnership was dominating their agenda, philosophical disagreements were incessantly and unproductively argued, anger was commonly expressed, and decade-long friendships and working relationships were nearly abandoned. One alternate Partnership board member claimed that Headwaters had been "poisoned" as a result of the collaborative effort. Another Headwaters member said that the internal disagreements "almost broke us up"; he believed that one of his colleagues (who eventually left Headwaters) would be willing to "destroy" him "over these issues."

Tracking the events at three consecutive, annual West Coast Ancient Forest Conferences further revealed intraconstituency communication problems. At the first annual conference, in 1993, speeches, panel presentations, and discussions stressed "involving the community" and bringing organized labor into the environmentalist camp. There was a spirit of hope, as scientists and the courts seemed to be lining up on environmentalists' side. It was at this first conference that I first saw the prototype artifact of the then-embryonic Partnership: a button with the capitalized word "THEY" circled and lined out in red (that is, the internationally signed negation of any "they"). However, 1 year later, at the second conference, some activists wore competing buttons that had the capitalized word "TRUST" negated with a red line.

The second conference was dominated by disagreement between those who favored preservation, a zero-cut policy, and nationalization of the issue and those who argued for conservation, thinning, and local community building. Panelists debated the merits and demerits of partnerships, zero cut, and the Applegate collaboration, as activists repeatedly asked themselves what they perceived to be the central question, "Can we be watchdogs and [collaboration] participants at the same time?" Several activists who had participated in collaborative attempts that had "failed" spoke vehemently against partnerships, warning of the dangers of co-optation, compromise, and a "coercive harmony." "It's our *public* [italics added] lands," argued one environmentalist, nicknamed the "Godfather of Zero Cut." "We wouldn't take the treasure out of Fort Knox or the Smithsonian to create temporary jobs. Why should we do it in the Pacific Northwest?" Those who had positive experiences with partnerships, however, argued for the potential for "improving forest health" and "transforming communities." They warned of potential losses and political backlash that radical positioning would cause. Eventually, these recurrent arguments surfaced in the press, with headlines such as "Disagreement on Consensus: Applegate Model Splits the Greens" (Pittman, 1994).

By early 1995, at the third annual West Coast Ancient Forest Conference, the collaboration debate was still in progress, but now the more radical voices argued for "retaining the moral high ground" (by refusing to compromise) and that zero cut was politically defensible. Drawing on butcher paper a continuum of political positioning, one environmental activist contended, "Zero cut should be seen as the middle position by the [Clinton] Administration. No cut on *private* [italics added] land should be our next move. The further to the left we go, the further to the left we pull the middle." This strategy—to "pull" the debate to the left—recalled the intention of the radical environmentalist group Earth First! (Lange, 1990); it was obviously at odds with those who defended partnership efficacy. One partnership supporter challenged the radicals' claim to moral superiority and their political strategy as he pled for a unified community:

> The moral high ground? What zero cut means is that people will just cut down more trees from Canada and Russia. What kind of moral high ground is that? ... Politically, all this means is that we'll see riders [backlash Congressional interventions], and the [counter-environmental] "Wise Use" movement will just solidify .... We need to reach out to local workers, and they'll stay in, but they'll eat up the environment before they die or lose

their wages. They'll eat it up …. It gets so personal. It's the thing that angers me the most. It's destruction of people who we're going to have to be working with for the rest of our days, local people that have really good hearts that may have a strategy that isn't quite "perfect." … We're all coming with our piles of crap, whatever they might be. They're not just about forest management, they're about politics. They're about every part; they're about how people live together.[9]

The internal dissension that occurred within constituency groups evolves from the stakeholder paradox described earlier: the collaboration requirement to do the logistically impossible—adequately represent millions of current and future human stakeholders, let alone nonhuman species as well. However, these intraconstituency arguments reveal an even more important difficulty, a collaboration affliction labeled the *mainstreamer paradox* (Lange, 2000), because, simply put, mainstream collaborative processes necessitate including constituents who will subvert collaborations. Although radical environmentalists, or other groups, may oppose collaborative efforts and refuse to participate, the inclusive nature of the process deems them stakeholders or constituents. Their status as constituents enables—in fact, compels them—to resist, albeit from the outside. Although the just-mentioned description focused on radical environmentalists, the same can be said of any extreme voice—that is, any stakeholder with immoderate intentions. The paradox, then, is that for environmental collaborations to achieve full stakeholder participation, a factor required for collaborative "success," they must by necessity include, even if only indirectly, those who will attempt to undermine that success.[10] Thus, the intraconstituency communication that contextualizes the Partnership, as revealed primarily through a description of the environmentalist camp, was marked not only by *complexity* but also by *inconsistent strategy*, *internal difference*, and *paradox*.

Although other scholars have noted that representatives' constituents have multiple interests (e.g., Carpenter & Kennedy, 1988; Friedman, 1994;

---

[9]In 1998, at the sixth annual Ancient Forest Conference, the debates described here were still being held, although less often and with fewer in attendance. Partnerships, by then, had become a "fact of life." By 1999 and 2000, at the seventh and eighth annual conferences, there was even less evidence still of such debates, although the issues are still argued to this day in various environmental and natural resource-oriented literature (see, e.g., Brick, Snow, & Van de Wetering, 2000).

[10]In fact, if those extreme voices within constituencies were fully intent on subverting or disrupting the process, they would do better to join the collaboration group and attempt to sabotage it from within. There was some suspicion among Partnership members that something like this was the case with one of the alternate board members, a Headwaters representative, who eventually dropped out of the Partnership after Headwaters' withdrawal. Prior to his leaving, he continually resisted the emerging subculture. Overall, the board managed internal dissent exceptionally well, but his defiance was taken as an intentional obstruction. My own judgment is that his intent was not to sabotage but that he simply had a less moderate position, with little inclination toward consensus decision making.

Gray, 1989), in the current case, these internal differences dramatically altered relationships and, according to one activist, nearly destroyed an organization (Headwaters). Perhaps such intensity results from constituency differences in environmental (as opposed to other types of) collaborations, given that this particular type evokes competing visions of morality, political strategy, and community. It is these types of collaboration, in particular, to which I now turn.

CONSTITUENCY COMMUNICATION AND ENVIRONMENTAL COLLABORATIONS

The story of The Applegate Partnership, as seen through the lens of representative–constituency communication, so far reveals a collaboration forced to confront an illusive set of challenges. The difficulties stemmed from (a) the complexity of representative–constituency relationships, (b) the paradox of local groups addressing national environmental concerns, and (c) the shifting alliances and changing power relationships that can surface within a collaborative domain. Focusing on environmentalist intraconstituency communication uncovered deep differences within the environmental community, unveiling the mainstreamer paradox of collaborations—the required inclusion of those who would seek to subvert the process. At this time, there are two remaining issues to consider to bring the story of the Partnership to a close, however temporary. First, I briefly discuss how well the Partnership stands up to extant criticisms of environmental mediations and, in the process, reveal yet a third paradox associated with these types of bona fide groups. Second, I conclude by considering how the Partnership is an example of *transformative* dispute resolution.

The Critique of Environmental Collaborations

Amy (1987), in a wide-ranging and comprehensive critique of environmental collaborations, warned against a spectrum of problems potentially inherent in these types of bona fide groups. These problems include (a) "co-optation" that distracts activists from morality-driven political organizing and litigating; (b) involuntary participation, which can sometimes be imposed by a government agency; (c) unequal power of participants, with environmentalists often on the short end; (d) unskilled or unprincipled mediators who may prejudice or unduly affect the outcome; and (e) losing sight of constituency or public interest when reaching an agreement becomes an end in itself.

How does The Applegate Partnership stand up to such a critique? Although Amy's (1987) well-taken points represent potential threats to the integrity of any environmental collaboration or mediation (cf. Bush & Folger, 1994), they are generally irrelevant to this partnership. Co-optation doesn't fit, as demonstrated by the lawsuits and other aggressive strategies simultaneously pursued by constituents; participation is voluntary and, therefore, not an issue; as was shown, power shifted back and forth between the industry and environmentalists (an argument in and of itself for the long-term viability of collaborative dispute resolution processes); the Partnership employs no mediator; and there is nearly unanimous consensus—both inside and outside the Partnership—that the agreements reached benefit members' constituents and the public.

Perhaps Amy's (1987) most interesting critique—and the one related most directly to constituency communication—is what he calls the problem of "unequal access." Amy argued that unequal access to the table, if present, can substantially discredit collaborative efforts, and goes so far as to say that "these inequities will *inevitably* [italics added] plague ... processes like environmental mediation" (p. 161). The inequities of which he speaks are illustrated by Headwaters' desertion from the Partnership and the subsequent charge by more radical environmental constituents that without Headwaters, the Partnership was a sham because there were then no "true" environmentalists on the board.

Partnership members responded to these charges by reiterating the fact that the board members were essentially the same people as before; it was just that those who had done so before no longer "officially" represented Headwaters. They further asserted that anyone could come to any meeting and express whatever he or she wished at any time and, as argued earlier, that even if stakeholders did not appear at meetings, board members were always taking into account—sometimes begrudgingly—the most extreme voices and positions, wherever they were expressed. Finally, it may be added that, by definition, there will always be those whose claimed role is to remain outside the political mainstream (Lange, 1990). The paradox for *any* bona fide collaborative group that succeeds at bringing radical constituents into the process results from the certainty that others—more radical—will inevitably come along to take the original critics' place outside the group (for more detail on this paradox, see Lange, 2000).

Transformation and Public Conflict Resolution

Radical critique notwithstanding, it would be difficult to argue with The Applegate Partnership's success in accomplishing the goals articulated in its "vision" (cited previously). Beyond that, the Partnership exemplifies a deeper, less tangible kind of accomplishment: what has been termed *transformative dispute resolution*. In her groundbreaking essay on negotiations and ADR, Putnam (1994) challenged "instrumental goals" as the exclusive motivation for entering negotiations, "individualism" as the driving force for negotiators' moves, and "rationality" as the expected and solitary model of any dispute resolution process. She extended the work of Folger and Bush (1994), who argued for a "transformative" orientation to negotiation, in which disputes provide the potential for growth in participants' empowerment and recognition. As Folger and Bush explained:

> Growth in *empowerment* involves realizing and strengthening one's capacity as an individual for encountering and grappling with adverse circumstances and problems of all kinds. Growth in *recognition* involves realizing and strengthening one's capacity as an individual for experiencing and expressing concern and consideration for others, especially others whose situation is "different" from one's own. Growth in both these dimensions is the hallmark of mature human development. (pp. 15–16)

Putnam argued for adding *relationship* and *relational development* to any consideration of conflict management processes, as well as a *dialogic* view that shifts the "goal of negotiation to building mutual understanding and to creating a forum for effective interaction" (p. 343). In a different, although related, model of transformative public conflict resolution, Dukes (1993) posited three categories: (a) an engaged community, (b) responsive governance, and (c) a capacity for problem solving and conflict resolution.

The Applegate Partnership can immodestly claim to possess all of these transformative dimensions, dimensions that are potentially attainable by other bona fide collaborative groups. In 1995, as I was ending my association with the Partnership and conducting some final interviews, I asked many of the board members whether they considered their endeavors successful. At that time, few timber sale agreements had been reached. It was instructive—and indicative of the relational and dialogic goals about which Putnam (1994) wrote—that so many board members pointed with pride to the admittedly simple and otherwise "wimpy" claim that "we're still meeting." Although it took them several more years to begin reaching agreements on ecologically sound timber sales (as well as other concrete achievements), at the time, they were proud of their relational transformation. As board member John said, "There's always going to be a lot of 'yes-butters,' but I see people talking who have never talked before."

With regard to constituent communication, evidence of Dukes's (1993) categories of transformative conflict management—engaged community, responsive governance, and a capacity for problem solving and conflict resolution—has steadily increased in the Applegate Valley throughout the 1990s, with the major impetus clearly stemming from the Partnership and its outreach. The earliest evidence was demonstrated during the penultimate Partnership meeting that I facilitated in early 1995 at the Applegate High School. The Partnership invited community members to discuss a number of water-related issues, including fishing, irrigation for farming, and flood control (as managed at the Applegate Dam). Federal and state agency officials (i.e., the U.S. Army Corps of Engineers and the Oregon Department of Fish and Wildlife) were asked to come and present information and answer questions. Close to 200 community members attended; critical information was exchanged, and by the end of the meeting, a new, local committee was formed to help with watershed-monitoring and restoration projects. Since then, the committee has had extraordinary success in promoting community-involvement projects, securing grants, and solving environmental and agricultural water-related problems.

More evidence of community building and transformation emerged later that year at the last meeting that I facilitated. It was an all-day retreat and "potluck" at a board member's house that overlooked the Applegate Valley, the location of the very first front-porch meeting where original board members were considered. It was attended at different times during the day by all board members and their alternates, a number of board members' spouses, more than a dozen USFS and BLM staffers and top managers, and a score of community members. Part of the purpose of the retreat was to identify specific objectives and to develop an agenda for the following 60 days. Another aim was to identify past failures and challenges, as well as opportunities that lay ahead. It was the third module, however, that was particularly informative. The members had decided to identify the successes of the past 2 years and listed the following: "changed community dialogue between neighbors," "more involvement with the agencies," "changed the way the agencies do business," "opportunity for community to come together," "great response to [community] tree-planting process," "building relationships," "great community response to the newsletter," "cooperation between groups," "education about issues and points of view," "gap is closing between constituencies," "brought private lands into process," "growing acceptance of land stewardship concept," and from many people, "the fact that we're still meeting." Other, more concrete successes were listed as well (such as various timber sales and other agreements); however, at that early time in the Partnership's history, participants focused primarily on the relational achievements.

Perhaps the best illustration of empowerment and recognition emerged during an interview I conducted just prior to the Partnership meeting held with Oregon's governor. The governor was about to travel the remarkably long and curvy two-lane road into the Valley to meet with the Partnership. Bonnie, a board member representing the community, explained how she was looking forward to meeting him:

> See, I'm not sure why. I've always been a farm-wife, you know, and never really had much influence in the community, and it seems since I've gotten into The Applegate Partnership, people are asking my opinion on so many things.

I love the people we're involved with. I have become so fond of Tim, whom I thought I would never, ever have anything to do with years ago because of his ideas and his stand on things .... And John, ... he was an environmentalist and he was my enemy and that's just the way I felt about it because of my stand here. [And now, the fact that we can] sit down and talk about all these things that hold our future, you know, right here, in this community and in these mountains, ... that's a miracle.

REFERENCES

Adams, J. S. (1976). The structure and dynamics of behavior in organizational boundary roles. In M. D. Dunnette, (Ed.), *Handbook of industrial and organizational psychology* (pp. 1175–1199). Chicago: Rand-McNally.

Amy, D. J. (1987). *The politics of environmental mediation.* New York: Columbia University Press.

Ancona, D. G. (1990). Outward bound: Strategies for team survival in the organization. *Academy of Management Journal, 33,* 334–365.

Ancona, D. G., Friedman, R. A., & Kolb, D. M. (1991). The group and what happens on the way to "yes." *Negotiation Journal, 7,* 155–173.

Bacow, L. S., & Wheeler, M. (1984). *Environmental dispute resolution.* New York: Plenum Press.

Barge, J. K., & Frey, L. R. (1997). Life in a task group. In L. R. Frey & J. K. Barge (Eds.), *Managing group life: Communicating in decision-making groups* (pp. 29–51). Boston: Houghton Mifflin.

Ben-Yoav, O., & Pruitt, D. G. (1984). Accountability to constituents: A two-edged sword. *Organizational Behavior and Human Performance, 34,* 283–295.

Bingham, G. (1988). *Resolving environmental disputes: A decade of experience.* Washington, DC: Conservation Foundation.

Brick, P., Snow, D., & Van de Wetering, P. (2000). (Eds.). *Across the great divide: Explorations in collaborative conservation and the American West.* Washington, DC: Island Press.

Bush, R. A. B., & Folger, J. P. (1994). *The promise of mediation: Responding to conflict through empowerment and recognition.* San Francisco: Jossey-Bass.

Carpenter, S. L., & Kennedy, W. J. D. (1988). *Managing public disputes: A practical guide to handling conflict and reaching decisions.* San Francisco: Jossey-Bass.

Colosi, T. (1983). Negotiation in the public and private sectors: A core model. *American Behavioral Scientist, 27,* 229–253.

Cox, J. R. (1982). The die is cast: Topical and ontological dimensions of the locus of the irreparable. *Quarterly Journal of Speech, 68,* 227–239.

Crowfoot, J. E., & Wondolleck, J. M. (1990). *Environmental disputes: Community involvement in conflict resolution.* Washington, DC: Island Press.

Devine, R. (1994). Management and the uncertainty principle. *Wilderness, 58,* 10–23.

Dukes, F. (1993). Public conflict resolution: A transformative approach. *Negotiation Journal, 9,* 45–57.

Durbin, K. (1993a, February 14). Applegate valley edges toward a forest truce. *The Oregonian,* p. D4.

Durbin, K. (1994, April 6). Forest group acts for independence. *The Oregonian*, p. B2.

Emerson, R. M. (1962). Power-dependence relations. *American Sociological Review*, *27*, 31–41.

Fattig, P. (1993a, February 14). Peace in the forest. *The Mail Tribune*, pp. 1A–2A.

Fattig, P. (1993b, February 14). Partnership serves as model for future problem-solving. *The Mail Tribune*, p. 2A.

Fattig, P. (1993c, March 28). Babbitt likes local project. *The Mail Tribune*, pp. 1–2A.

Fattig, P. (1994, April 2) Headwaters leaves forest panel. *The Mail Tribune*, pp. 1A–3A.

Fisher, R., & Ury, W. (with Patton, B). (1981). *Getting to yes: Negotiating agreement without giving in* (2nd ed.). Boston: Houghton Mifflin.

Folger, J. P., & Bush, R. A. B. (1994). Ideology, orientations to conflict, and mediation discourse. In J. P. Folger & T. S. Jones (Eds.), *New directions in mediation: Communication research and perspectives* (pp. 3–25). Thousand Oaks, CA: Sage.

Freeman, S. A., Littlejohn, S. W., & Pearce, W. B. (1992). Communication and moral conflict. *Western Journal of Communication*, *56*, 311–329.

Friedman, R. A. (1992). The culture of mediation: Private understandings in the context of public conflict. In D. Kolb & J. M. Bartunek (Eds.), *Hidden conflict in organizations: Uncovering behind the scenes disputes* (pp. 143–164). Newbury Park, CA: Sage.

Friedman, R. A. (1994). *Front stage, back stage: The dramatic structure of labor negotiations*. Cambridge, MA: MIT Press.

Friedman, R. A., & Poldony, J. (1992). Differentiation of boundary spanning roles: Labor negotiations and implications for role conflict. *Administrative Science Quarterly*, *37*, 28–47.

Gray, B. (1989). *Collaborating: Finding common ground for multi-party problems*. San Francisco: Jossey-Bass.

Kemmis, D. (1990). *Community and the politics of place*. Norman: University of Oklahoma Press.

Lange, J. I. (1988, November). *The rhetoric of "no compromise": The case of Earth First!* Paper presented at the meeting of the Speech Communication Association, New Orleans, LA.

Lange, J. I. (1989, November). *Toward a research agenda on environmental communication: "Indications" from the spotted owl*. Paper presented at the meeting of the Speech Communication Association, San Francisco, CA.

Lange, J. I. (1990). Refusal to compromise: The case of Earth First! *Western Journal of Speech Communication*, *54*, 473–494.

Lange, J. I. (1992, November). *New perspectives on collaboration: Environmentalists, timber industry representatives and the United States Forest Service*. Paper presented at the meeting of the Speech Communication Association, Chicago, IL.

Lange, J. I. (1993). The logic of competing information campaigns: Conflict over old growth and the spotted owl. *Communication Monographs*, *60*, 239–257.

Lange, J. I. (1994, February). *The forest conference: Prelude to a form*. Paper presented at the meeting of the Western Speech Communication Association, San Jose, CA.

Lange, J. I. (2000). Exploring paradox in environmental collaborations. In P. Brick, D. Snow, & S. Van de Wetering (Eds.), *Across the great divide: Explorations in collaborative conservation and the American West* (pp. 200–211). Washington, DC: Island Press.

Littlejohn, S. W., Shailor, J., & Pearce, W. B. (1994). The deep structure of reality in mediation. In J. P. Folger & T. S. Jones (Eds.), *New directions in mediation: Communication research and perspectives* (pp. 67–83). Thousand Oaks, CA.: Sage.

Lofland, J., & Lofland, L. H. (1995). *Analyzing social settings: A guide to qualitative observation and analysis* (3rd ed.). Belmont, CA: Wadsworth.

Moore, C. W. (1994). Mediator communication and influence in conflict management interventions: A practitioner's reflections on theory and practice. In J. P. Folger & T. S. Jones (Eds.), *New directions in mediation: Communication research and perspectives* (pp. 209–221). Thousand Oaks, CA.: Sage.

Moore, T. (1993, February 19). We can work it out. *The Capitol Press*, pp. 1–2.

Nash, R. F. (1989). *The rights of nature: A history of environmental ethics*. Madison: University of Wisconsin Press.

Oravec, C. (1984). Conservationism vs. preservationism: The public interest in the Hetch-Hetchy controversy. *Quarterly Journal of Speech, 70,* 444–458.

Peterson, T. R. (1988). The rhetorical construction of institutional authority in a Senate subcommittee hearing on wilderness legislation. *Western Journal of Speech Communication, 52,* 259–276.

Pittman, A. (1994, March 10). Disagreement on consensus: Applegate model splits the Greens. *Eugene Weekly*, p. 9.

Pruitt, D. G. (1994). Negotiation between organizations: A branching chain model. *Negotiation Journal, 10,* 217–230.

Pruitt, D. G., & Carnevale, P. J. (1993). *Negotiation in social conflict*. Pacific Grove, CA: Brooks/Cole.

Putnam, L. L. (1985). Collective bargaining as organizational communication. In P. K. Tompkins & R. McPhee (Eds.), *Organizational communication: Traditional themes and new directions* (pp. 129–148). Beverly Hills, CA: Sage.

Putnam, L. L. (1994). Challenging the assumptions of traditional approaches to negotiation. *Negotiation Journal, 10,* 337–346.

Putnam, L. L., & Jones, T. S. (1982). The role of communication in bargaining. *Human Communication Research, 8,* 262–280.

Putnam, L. L., & Stohl, C. (1996). Bona fide groups: An alternative perspective for communication and small group decision making. In R. Y. Hirokawa & M. S. Poole (Eds.), *Communication and group decision making* (2nd ed., pp. 147–177). Thousand Oaks, CA: Sage.

Roloff, M. E., & Campion, D. E. (1987). On alleviating the debilitating effects of accountability on bargaining: Authority and self-monitoring. *Communication Monographs, 54,* 145–164.

Senecah, S. (1997, February). *Dimensions of accountability: Compromise among state environmental groups in a legislative arena*. Paper presented at the meeting of the Western States Communication Association, Monterey, CA.

Sheriff, M., Harvey, O. J., White, B. J., Hood, W. R., & Sherif, C. W. (1961). *Intergroup conflict and cooperation: The robber's cave experiment*. Norman, OK: University Book Exchange.

Spradley, J. P. (1979). *The ethnographic interview*. New York: Holt, Rinehart, and Winston.

Spradley, J. P. (1980). *Participant observation*. New York: Holt, Rinehart, and Winston.

Smith, K. K., & Berg, D. N. (1987). *Paradoxes of group life: Understanding conflict, paralysis, and movement in group dynamics*. San Francisco: Jossey-Bass.

Stohl, C., & Putnam, L. L. (1994). Group communication in context: Implications for the study of bona fide groups. In L. R. Frey (Ed.), *Group communication in context: Studies of natural groups* (pp. 285–292). Hillsdale, NJ: Lawrence Erlbaum Associates.

Susskind, L., & Cruikshank, J. (1987). *Breaking the impasse: Consensual approaches to resolving public disputes*. New York: Basic Books.

Thurow, L. (1980). *The zero-sum society: Distribution and the possibilities for economic change*. New York: Basic Books.

Turner, D. B. (1992). Negotiator-constituent relationships. In L. L. Putnam & M. E. Roloff (Eds.), *Communication and negotiation* (pp. 233–249). Newbury Park, CA: Sage.

Van Maanen, J. (1992). Drinking our troubles away: Managing conflict in a British police agency. In D. M. Kolb & J. M. Bartunek (Eds.), *Hidden conflict in organizations: Uncovering behind the scenes disputes* (pp. 32–62). Newbury Park, CA: Sage.

Walker, G. B., & Daniels, S. E. (1994, February). *The forest conference as communication: Dialogue versus strategic control*. Paper presented at the meeting of the Western Speech Communication Association, San Jose, CA.

Walton, R. E., & Mckersie, R. B. (1965). *A behavioral theory of labor negotiations*. New York: McGraw-Hill.

Wondolleck, J. M., & Yaffe, S. L. (1994). *Building bridges across agency boundaries: In search of excellence in the United States Forest Service*. Research report submitted to the United States Department of Agriculture, Forest Service, Pacific Northwest Research Station, in fulfillment of USDA Cooperative Agreement #PNW 92-0215.

9

ON THE VERGE OF COLLABORATION: INTERACTION PROCESSES VERSUS GROUP OUTCOMES

Joann Keyton
University of Kansas

Virginia Stallworth
Memphis Child Advocacy Center

Increasingly, interorganizational or interagency collaboration is lauded as a means for addressing our nation's most pressing community problems. As Chrislip and Larson (1994) contended, "When collaborative initiatives are well executed, they achieve extraordinary results of unexpected dimensions" (p. 108). Many nonprofit organizations are finding it necessary to work with other nonprofits to respond effectively to financial pressures or competition from similar providers (Berman & West, 1995; Johnson & Cahn, 1995; Quinn & Cumblad, 1994; Stegelin & Jones, 1991). Other collaborations form to improve service delivery (Gray, 1989) or to offer a service or product that cannot be provided by an existing group (Stallworth, 1998). Although communities perceive collaboration as an innovative, positive means for addressing social problems, researchers and practitioners alike are still trying to discover the most effective means to create and sustain collaborative efforts.

A collaborative group is formed when representatives from different organizations come together to share decision-making responsibilities directed toward solving a mutual problem. In this chapter, we first examine defining characteristics of collaboration and then demonstrate how collaborations exemplify groups in line with the bona fide group perspective. The usefulness of such an approach is then addressed by analyzing the interactions of the Drug Dealer Eviction Program, a collaboration involving representatives from the District Attorney General's Office, Memphis Area Neighborhood Watch, Sheriff's Department, Police Department, and Crimestoppers, Inc. in Memphis, Tennessee. This collaboration, mandated by the District Attorney, was formed to encourage rental property owners to participate in a program designed to remove drug dealers from rental properties. Observations of both primary and peripheral meetings, review of public and organizational documents, and interviews with representatives from all units of the collaboration provide the data for the case. We conclude with an analysis of how this case illuminates and extends our understanding of the bona fide group perspective.

DEFINING COLLABORATION

Although the relevant literature reveals a lack of consistency in the definition of collaboration (see Stohl & Walker, 2002), there is movement toward a consensus on the critical elements to be included in a definition. Nearly all definitions identify a collaboration as a temporarily formed group with representatives from many other primary organizations. Representatives to a collaboration are referred to as *stakeholders:*

> those who are responsible for problems or issues, those who are affected by them, those whose perspectives or knowledge are needed to develop good solutions or strategies, and those who have the power and resources to block or implement solutions and strategies. (Chrislip & Larson, 1994, p. 65)

Ideally, all stakeholders should be represented by membership in a collaboration, although some scholars suggest that this is not necessarily the case as long as the consequences of nonrepresentation are considered (see, e.g., Wood & Gray, 1991). More important than full stakeholder representation is the notion that stakeholders who become collaboration members each acknowledge and agree that an issue confronts them (Gray, 1985).

Another issue of considerable importance is the degree to which collaboration members perceive themselves to be equal. Quinn and Cumblad (1994) viewed collaboration as a style of interaction among co-equal partners. Such equality is likely to be difficult to achieve, however, given that collaboration members represent organizations that differ in terms of budget, staff, status, power, and other things. Iles and Auluck (1990) maintained that one way for collaborative groups to address equity is by acknowledging the inequality of collaboration members.

A third membership issue centers on how organizational representatives join a collaboration. Members who join voluntarily are more likely to view collaboration as an effective means of solving problems. However, federal or state governments mandate many interagency collaborations, and some organizational representatives are asked to join collaborative efforts because their task expertise is essential to the completion of the work of a particular collaboration (Hargrove, 1998). When participation is forced or required, there may be less desire on the part of individual members collectively and less agreement among members that collaborative efforts are as worthwhile.

Nearly all definitions of collaboration recognize that both shared decision making and working toward a common goal are central to collaborative efforts (Gray, 1989; Yon, Mickelson, & Carlton-LaNey, 1993; York & Zychlinski, 1996). For the case analysis that follows, the *collaborative process* is defined as "a process in which two or more organizations engage in shared decision making and coordinated, joint action to address a common goal" (Stallworth, 1998, p. 6). As a result, a *collaboration* is defined as the group of stakeholders or organizational representatives that engage in a collaborative process.

Are Collaborations Groups or Organizations?

Collaborations, in many ways, are like task forces or commissions—groups with a restricted range of activities that interact over a limited period of time (McGrath, 1984). Collaborations, however, are unique in that participants are already members of other organizations that are aware of problems in their environment. Participants are not likely to join a collaboration unless they agree that a problem exists. However, without collaboration, these organizations remain an unorganized system and, as a result, are less powerful in taking effective actions because not all perspectives, positions, or resources are represented or available to them (Gray, 1989).

A second difference between a collaboration and other temporary task groups is the locus of power. The impetus to collaborate must develop from somewhere. Many collaborations in the nonprofit and government agency sectors must obtain funding to operate. The party that is first to become aware of a grant opportunity is likely to be the one to initiate a meeting of interested parties. Acting in the role of the collaboration's facilitator, leader, or convener, this member may initially possess more power than do other collaboration members. Even when potential funding does not drive the initiation of a collaboration, it is unlikely that all organizations represented are equal in terms of power, status, staff, budget, and political agenda. Differences in these types of characteristics can become powerfully persuasive within a collaboration and shift the locus of power in decision making toward inequity.

It is precisely these types of membership characteristics that amplify the difference between a collaboration and the more traditional view of a temporary task group. In a traditional task group, members are more likely to perceive and present themselves as a group, an entity, responsible for carrying out the actions on which group members decide. In a collaboration, members participate as, and by virtue of being, representatives of other organizations. Thus, the needs and requirements of members' primary organizations can easily influence their loyalty to the collaboration and, more important, their actions within the group. Divided loyalty is an important issue when collaboration members decide on a course of action and then must take that decision back to their primary organization to carry out task activity. Issues that arise and decisions that are made in these external environments can easily alter the goals and decisions agreed on by the collaboration.

Different from many traditional task groups, and particularly problematic in collaborations, is the opportunity for organizational representatives to the collaboration to change. Organizations that send representatives to collaborations are typically more interested in having their organizations represented than in creating stable membership for the collaboration. Thus, who an organization selects to represent it may change depending on the needs and resources of the primary organization rather than the needs of the collaboration.

One could argue that collaborations are better viewed as organizations rather than as groups; however, this position can be disputed on three grounds. First, although a collaboration has an identifiable task, essential resources (e.g., budget and human resources) are unlikely to be under the control of the collaboration itself as they are in an organization. The collaboration must draw on the resources of its members' organizations rather than exist as an autonomous, independent unit, although its task is distinct and separate. Second, members of a collaboration are evaluated through the reward structures of their primary organizations as opposed to outcomes generated by the collaboration, which creates differing, and perhaps, competing, member motivations for participating in the collaboration. Third, participants have task or job responsibilities to complete in their primary organization in addition to their collaboration duties and activities, which may hamper the quality or quantity of time allocated to the collaboration. Thus, a collaboration is a temporary group that lacks many of the standard structural elements and resources characteristic of organizations.

Collaborations as Bona Fide Groups

In other essays about nonprofit collaboration, scholars have generally relied on six theoretical perspectives: resource dependency, corporate social performance theory/institutional economics, strategic management/social ecology, microeconomics, institutional/negotiated order, and political theoretical perspectives (Gray & Wood, 1991; Wood & Gray, 1991). Although theories from these perspectives have enhanced understanding about the preconditions for collaboration, how resources and dependencies are distributed among collaboration members, and collaboration outcomes, none provide much insight into the process of collaboration—that is, how members communicate to enact or engage the collaborative activity. We believe that the bona fide group perspective is especially helpful in analyzing the collaborative process because of its focus on the communication influences that emanate from group membership and group environmental characteristics.

The bona fide group perspective illuminates membership issues, which are central to collaborations. Bona fide groups have permeable and fluid boundaries (Putnam & Stohl, 1996), and collaborations, by definition, are initiated to take advantage of multiple membership conduits. Not only does a collaboration's membership provide conduits for information flow between the collaboration and its members' organizations, it also provides information conduits between the represented organizations.

Four characteristics—(a) members from various organizations addressing a shared problem, (b) the potential imbalance of power, (c) divided membership loyalty, and (d) rotating organizational representation—place collaborations within the bona fide group perspective and its emphasis on permeable boundaries, shifting borders, and the effects of a group's contexts on its internal processes (Putnam & Stohl, 1996; Stohl & Walker, 2002). Besides creating a unique type of group, these characteristics create unique challenges for members of collaborations. Because these characteristics are located in the collaboration's membership, they are likely to influence members' participation and communication and, thereby, affect members' abilities to work effectively together.

Taking into account the unique characteristics within which collaborations work, collaborations are special types of groups whose process is best viewed from the bona fide group perspective (Putnam & Stohl, 1996; Stohl & Walker, 2002). From this perspective, the group dynamics internal to a collaboration cannot be divorced from an understanding of the external environment in which the collaboration exists. We now turn to a discussion of the collaborative process.

THE COLLABORATIVE PROCESS

According to Gray (1989), "Collaboration is essentially an emergent process rather than a prescribed state" (p. 15). Although they are temporary groups, collaborations develop like other task groups through a period of deliberation and decision making in preparation for a stage of task performance. Once decision making is complete, a collaboration can enter the performance phase by automating its task and, thereby, require only limited and infrequent interaction of collaboration members. Alternatively, a collaboration disbands because implementation following decision making is transferred to other individuals, groups, or organizations. In either case, the limited life span of a collaboration, coupled with members' attentions to their primary group and/or organization, may unconsciously create detrimental effects on how members view the necessity or urgency of communication in the development of a collaboration.

Four elements are essential to the success of a collaboration: (a) shared goal, (b) member interdependence, (c) equal input of participants, and (d) shared decision making (Stallworth, 1998). These elements are products of the reflexive relationship between the communication of collaboration members and the development of the collaboration's culture and operating procedures. When one or more of these elements is weak or missing, the collaborative process is seriously jeopardized. Although less central, issues of leadership, member motivation and maturity, and members' multiple roles and perspectives also mediate the success of the collaborative process. In the following sections, we examine each of these primary and secondary elements.

Communication

As explained previously, collaborations are open systems that interact within multiple environments. Interactions within a collaboration, consequently, influence other stakeholder systems. Ironically, issues from these other systems are often the impetus for the content brought before a collaboration. Likewise, standards from these other systems often are used to evaluate the effectiveness of proposed solutions within a collaboration. Even given these external influences, studies have found that internal communication structures and processes have significant influence on collaboration effectiveness (Taber, Walsh, & Cooke, 1979; Yon et al., 1993). Creating an effective communication network between collaboration members has been identified as the essential component for collaborative success (Stegelin & Jones, 1991). When established, the communication structure, or network, between collaboration members allows others outside the collaboration to view it as a complete and active entity (Stohl, 1995). Just as a communication structure signals to others that the collaboration exists, the communication structure provides the mechanism by which collaboration members create their own culture. Thus, the degree to which the communication structure exists draws a boundary for a collaboration and reinforces its distinctiveness.

Culture

Culture commonly refers to the values, norms, assumptions, and practices associated with a collective. Culture is a symbolic system that is "created through the interactions" of members of a collective (Mohan, 1993, p. 12). The development of a culture that characterizes a collaboration is important for two reasons. First, like any task group, a collaboration must develop a culture of its own that motivates members, establishes an effective social environment, and provides norms for accomplishing the task. Second, a culture unique to a collaboration can supersede tensions and conflicts that can occur when members rely on the cultures of their primary organizations when working in the collaboration. This type of cultural importation is well explained by the bona fide group perspective in its acknowledgment of the idiosyncratic interpretative frames members bring with them (see Putnam & Stohl, 1996) to a collaboration.

The longer a collaboration takes to develop a unique and strong culture to replace cultural importing from other organizations, the greater these tensions will be. As Yon et al. (1993) explained, "Institutions have different rules, regulations, policies, target populations, budgets, methods of supervision and evaluation, and operational language" that fuel power issues within a collaboration (p. 419). Thus, the extent to which a collaboration can form a culture that is unique to its members and activities, and one that is owned by all collaborative group members, may be central predictors of a collaboration's success.

Shared Goal

A common or shared goal is both an impetus and a requirement for a collaboration to exist (Quinn & Cumblad, 1994; Stegelin & Jones, 1991; Yon et al., 1993; York & Zychlinski, 1996). In fact, efforts to collaborate are unlikely to succeed unless the collaborative parties agree on the goal and have a common definition of the problem they are addressing (Gray, 1989).

Interdependence

In the literature on groups, *interdependence* commonly refers to the interactions that result from a group having a shared goal. Interdependence means that both group and individual outcomes are influenced by what all members do in the group (Brewer, 1995). Most often, collaborations are formed to accomplish superordinate goals, an activity too large or complex for one group member or one organization to handle (DeLamater, 1974). Hence, without interdependence, a collaboration, like any other group, cannot succeed (Gray, 1989).

In collaborations, high interdependency between the collaboration's members creates the reciprocity needed for mutual interests to be achieved through coordination and cooperation. As a positive force, cooperative interdependence required by the task to achieve the expected outcome can significantly and positively influence group members' motivation, performance, satisfaction, and learning, in addition to helping to establish positive group norms (Wageman, 1995). Conversely, some collaborations are structured through asymmetry, or attempts by one or a few members to manipulate or coerce others. When interdependence is perceived to be inequitable, collaboration progress is inhibited and success is limited (Logsdon, 1991).

Equal Input and Shared Decision Making

Bringing in many sources to share in the making of decisions is often seen as the answer to complex community problems because stakeholders have varying expertise relevant to solving such problems. However, equal input can be difficult to achieve due to the varying degree of perceived power and status among participants. It is precisely this difficulty that must be overcome for a collaboration to work democratically through shared decision making. Thus, collaborations need to develop processes and structures that allow and encourage all members to contribute and that prevent any one member from inordinately affecting group outcomes. Although connected, the presence of equal input does not per se ensure that decision making is shared; collaborations must develop and use decision-making procedures that are agreed to by all members and that represent the perspectives of all members.

Leadership

Despite the shared and joint characteristics required for collaboration, someone must convene and lead or facilitate a collaboration, as coordination of organizational representatives is necessary and vital. A leader's style, including his or her communication style, as well as his or her organizational representation, can significantly influence both the collaborative process and the collaboration's outcomes.

The degree of leader influence is often more pronounced in collaboration groups because whoever takes on the leadership role must also be a member of the collaboration. This dual role of member and leader may cause a leader to momentarily consider suppressing self-interests in favor of providing leadership for the group. Doing so, however, would negate representation of one of the collaboration's stakeholders. The other problem associated with the dual member/leader role is one of control. A leader who is controlling of the collaborative process can be as detrimental as a leader who is controlling of the collaboration's interactive content. Whether a leader is appointed, selected, or emerges, it is the leader's responsibility to balance both interests—his or her interest in facilitating the group's process and in representing an organization. When a leader can facilitate the process in such a way as to not sacrifice either interest, it is more likely that all members, including the leader, will have opportunities for equal input and shared decision making.

Group Member Motivation and Maturity

Stakeholders must be motivated toward involvement in a collaboration if it is to succeed. Most are motivated by a desire to solve an important problem; however, other motivations—such as political power, financial incentives, or desire to control outcomes—may be impelling forces for stakeholder involvement. In addition to being motivated, collaboration members must also possess a certain degree of maturity or political savvy to be effective in representing their organizations. Gray (1989) noted that varying levels of member maturity is a common problem within collaborations.

The Collaboration Ideal

The four elements of shared goal, interdependence, equal input, and shared decision making result from the culture of a collaboration, which, in turn, emerges from the communication of collaboration members. In an ideal collaboration, each element would develop early in the collaborative process and effectively contribute to the collaboration's success. In addition, collaborative members would be engaged in effective communication aimed at creating positive working relationships and establishing a unique and useful culture for their collaboration. Procedural norms developed in the early meetings of the collaboration would promote equal input and shared decision making and, thereby, create an effective culture. Both leader and members would balance the relational needs of collaboration members with the task demands of the group. As a result, the resources, skills, knowledge, and perspectives brought by members would benefit the collaboration's ability to produce innovative and effective outcomes. The following case provides an opportunity to assess this collaborative ideal.

THE COLLABORATION OF THE DRUG DEALER EVICTION PROGRAM

The Drug Dealer Eviction Program (DDEP) is a collaboration in Memphis, Tennessee, a city ranked as having one of the highest crime rates per capita in the country. The DDEP was organized and implemented in July 1997 as a way to help neighborhoods combat the presence of drug dealers in rental property and eliminate accompanying crimes. Working from a suggestion given to the previous district attorney by a local landlord, the District Attorney General of Shelby County (the county in which Memphis is located) started the DDEP after promising this initiative as one of his major priorities if elected. Modeled after a program in New York City, state legislation was drafted to create the necessary legal support to remove drug dealers from rental property.

Five organizations—Crimestoppers, Memphis Area Neighborhood Watch, the Memphis Police Department, the Shelby County Sheriff's Department, and the Shelby County District Attorney General's Office—are represented in the collaboration. Crimestoppers is a nonprofit, volunteer, civilian organization that offers rewards and anonymity to citizens who report information about crimes. On the basis of the number of arrests and convictions for cities its size, this organization is recognized as one of the three most successful Crimestoppers programs in the United States. The Memphis Area Neighborhood Watch was founded in 1984 to help prevent and reduce fear of crime through education and the organization of effective neighborhood watch groups. Today, the organization has over 350 volunteers and approximately 1,400 satellite neighborhood watch programs. The Memphis Police Department employs approximately 1,500 officers and 550 civilian staffers; the Shelby County Sheriff's Department employs over 2,000 people, including 546 deputies and 750 jailers. The Shelby County District Attorney General's Office employs 160 and handled about 110,000 new cases in 1999. Clearly, differences in size of organization, resources, political motivation, and community responsibility exist for the organizations represented in the DDEP.

The five organizations, and their representatives, needed to effectively integrate to pursue the collaboration's goal. Figure 9.1 depicts how each organization contributed resources and skills to the collaboration. Crimestoppers was invited to participate in the collaboration because of its success in involving the community in solving crime. For the DDEP, Crimestoppers was the mechanism through which citizens report suspected drug dealers. Generally, two members of Crimestoppers represented this organization in the collaboration. The police and sheriff's departments were charged with investigating the drug tips received through Crimestoppers. Generally, two Memphis police officers were assigned to the collaboration; however, no representative of the sheriff's department regularly participated. The Memphis Area Neighborhood Watch was involved in the collaboration because one of its employees helped with the DDEP's community relations. Generally, this and one other employee represented the Memphis Area Neighborhood Watch program in the collaboration. Finally, five representatives were present from the District Attorney's Office (the District Attorney, three Assistant District Attorneys, and a community relations staff member). The District Attorney initiated the collaboration and provided leadership by calling and leading the meetings. The Assistant District Attorneys oversaw the day-to-day administration of the DDEP and prosecuted alleged drug dealers.

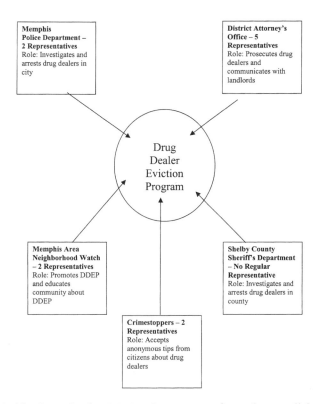

FIG. 9.1. The Drug Dealer Eviction Program configured as a collaboration.

In its initial stage, the DDEP had high public visibility because the collaboration was a campaign-promised initiative and the media gave particular attention to tracking such election promises. Moreover, the DDEP received regular news and editorial coverage because the collaboration's task was new and novel. The District Attorney General granted our access to the DDEP after a request was made to his office and all members of the collaboration were made aware of the research project. Each member of the collaboration was contacted by the research team to seek his or her agreement to respond to our requests for information outside the DDEP meeting environment. In this initial stage, data consisted of observations and interaction analyses of meetings and interviews with collaboration members. In the second stage of data collection, the District Attorney approved our requests for in-depth interviews with himself and with the three Assistant District Attorneys. Throughout the 12-month investigation, we also collected media reports and press releases about the DDEP.

Developing the DDEP

Since its initiation, the DDEP has always been referred to publicly as a collaboration; nearly all public and press documents include this reference about the program. Given that the program was an initiative of the District Attorney's Office, members representing that office in the collaboration were the leaders. Although the DDEP was configured after a similar program in New York City, logistics and local needs, as well as the fact that this was a new initiative in Memphis, created the need for members of the DDEP to meet on a regular basis as a group early in its development. Although the DDEP intended to meet monthly, meetings were frequently canceled and irregularly scheduled. At best, the DDEP met bimonthly. These early meetings focused on setting up procedures and systems by which the collaboration's task would be accomplished. Although citizens were already and regularly reporting drug tips to the police or through Crimestoppers, new state legislation allowed drug dealers to be evicted from rental property if convicted. Thus, the District Attorney wanted to specifically track drug tips of this type.

After the first few organizing meetings, procedural difficulties prompted the need for additional collaboration meetings. One participant said, "Most of the meetings are reactionary meetings to something [in established procedure] that is not going right." Others indicated that meetings were called when "glitches come up in our system." In this way, collaboration meetings were reactive rather than proactive. Interviews with collaboration members indicated that some procedural problems occurred because of the lack of frequent communication between collaborative members outside of DDEP meetings. Some members felt the need to meet more regularly, although other members did not. Thus, early on, a proactive/reactive tension appeared in the collaboration's interaction.

Although there were some periodic written reports, the collaboration did not substitute written communication for face-to-face communication. In fact, written communication within the collaboration was infrequent. Instead, collaboration members relied on one-to-one telephone calls and office visits to smooth out day-to-day operational problems experienced by the organizations. When meetings were called, no written agenda was offered ahead of time. Members of the District Attorney's Office presented the agenda at the meeting with no apparent input from other collaboration members.

Thus, in the early formation of the DDEP, communication was less frequent and effective than what was needed to develop a strong and unique culture for the collaboration. Interviews with organizational representatives indicated that several members evaluated the communication and task activity of the DDEP by the standards and expectations of their primary organizations. When asked to provide an evaluation of the DDEP, many members could not do so without making explicit comparisons to their representative organization's procedures and practices. Members' frustrations with the early meetings caused them to view the interactions of the DDEP negatively. Communication was further inhibited because some member organizations did not regularly send the same representatives to each meeting.

The lack of a unique and shared culture among DDEP members created credibility and trust problems for collaboration members. For example, one police officer said, "Police officers will listen to other police officers," implying that procedures developed in the collaboration would not carry sufficient credibility to be enacted by police who were not members of the collaboration. Another member of the collaboration confirmed this notion in an interview, stating, "Officers don't like non-officers telling them what to do." Rather than sharing with and learning from the unique perspectives brought to the collaboration by the various organizational representatives, collaboration members perceived their roles in the collaboration as one of protecting their organizations. Thus, the loyalty of group members was to their organization rather than to the collaboration, which affected the behaviors they demonstrated during the collaboration's interaction. In this sense, organizational representatives were never fully engaged as co-members of the collaboration.

The weakness of the collaboration's culture also prevented facilitative norms from developing. After a year of existence, the few norms that were in place encouraged negative, rather than positive, group processes and procedures. For example, as explained, meetings were called without an agenda and usually to react to some problem rather than to develop proactive policy and strategy. The one structural feature that perhaps most hampered the ability of the DDEP from developing a distinctive and positive culture was that the leader was the District Attorney. He was politically powerful and his management style was strong and decisive, which offered other members little opportunity to make contributions.

Even without the presence of an effective and strong group culture, the DDEP participants agreed on a common goal: They and their organizations were working together to evict drug dealers from rental properties. This common goal defined the purpose of the collaboration and was accepted enthusiastically by all members. Moreover, the goal required strong task interdependence between collaboration members, which all members independently acknowledged. The informational and legal steps necessary to evict a drug dealer from rental property could not be accomplished by any one of the member organizations working alone. In fact, the task interdependence required to achieve the stated goal clearly identified which organizations needed to be represented in the collaboration.

Despite the high level of task interdependence required, members did not have equal input into decisions made by the DDEP. Interviews revealed a lack of parity in perceived importance or status of collaborative members. Perceptions of inequity were also affirmed by the collaboration's unequal organizational representation; members representing organizations other than the District Attorney's Office were keenly aware of the representational imbalance.

Inequity was also evidenced in the collaboration's approach to problem solving. For example, early in the collaboration, a representative from the Memphis Area Neighborhood Watch suggested that drug tips be investigated in a more decentralized manner. Others blatantly dismissed her suggestion because she was neither a police officer nor a prosecutor. Later, when tip investigation was moved from a central unit to precinct officers, she received no credit for making the original suggestion. Rather than valuing the input from all group members, input from the functional experts was valued more highly, even when good suggestions were offered from nonexperts.

Obviously, the lack of equal input made it difficult to have shared decision making. Frequently, in these early meetings of the DDEP, only some members were consulted by the District Attorney about decisions that would affect the collaboration. For example, a subgroup of the collaboration decided that precinct-level police officers needed more education about the DDEP and brought this issue to a DDEP meeting. However, this subgroup decision was made without seeking input from the member charged with promoting the program. Seldom were decisions made with everyone present or with input from all collaboration members. Such decision-making strategies further prohibited a consensual culture from developing and kept trust among members at a minimum.

During meetings, the strong authoritarian leadership of the District Attorney minimized the interaction of the members. Moreover, the presence and autocratic manner of the collaboration's leader created a climate that did not allow the group to take time for more general and informational discussions. Changing organizational representatives from meeting to meeting limited the extent to which members of the DDEP could adequately understand the multiple roles and perspectives of each organization and further reinforced the effects resulting from the strong leadership of the District Attorney.

The influence of this strong leader was felt in other ways as well. Collaboration members noted in interviews that meetings and written reports were for the benefit of the leader rather than for the benefit of the collaboration's entire membership. The group's decision-making strategy also revealed the leader's strong influence. Although the leader rarely made decisions unilaterally, he always appeared to have the final word. Part of the leader's influence emanated from his preference for focusing on the achievement of outcome objectives rather than analyzing or discussing the process by which the group worked. This priority is best understood in political terms: The leader of the collaboration was an elected official, whereas other members were political appointees or employees of government and nonprofit agencies. Other members of the DDEP clearly understood the leader's political agenda and recognized and attempted to meet his need "to hear the numbers." Thus, interaction in the collaboration tended to be outcome rather than process driven.

Although the District Attorney realized that his office alone could not implement the objectives of the DDEP, other members were not treated as equals, their input was not always solicited, and decision making was not shared. Ironically, collaboration members contributed to these processes. They were accustomed to working on community issues within a political framework and perceived this state of affairs as normal. Rather than addressing the inequities of the collaboration, they were simply rationalized and accepted. For example, one member commented, "You don't have time to be that personable with the [leader] because he's real busy." Rather than address the problem of ineffectiveness directly, this member simply substituted the fact that the leader was busy and used this an excuse for both of their ineffective contributions.

Political inequities surfaced in other ways as well. After one meeting, the Memphis Area Neighborhood Watch representative was angry about the expectation other collaboration members held that she could automatically generate a crowd at community meetings at which the DDEP was being promoted. In another instance, police department representatives to the DDEP took DDEP procedural recommendations back to other officers but had little power over the acceptance or adoption of the procedures by those officers. These procedural and structural problems never received the full attention they deserved by the collaboration. Members were not willing to bring these issues up for discussion at DEEP meetings, as such discussion was perceived as distracting the collaboration and the District Attorney from focusing on the collaboration's agreed-on goals and outcomes.

Another political inequity resulted from who was not invited to join the collaboration. Although a local landlord prompted the DDEP, these community members were not represented as stakeholders in the collaboration. This was unfortunate because landlords were a critical link in accomplishing the DDEP's objective, as tip investigations could not proceed without the cooperation of landlords. The degree to which a landlord cooperated with the District Attorney's Office, therefore, affected significantly the extent to which the goal of the DDEP could be accomplished.

Initially, organizational representatives to the collaboration were told by one Assistant District Attorney that the DDEP was "their" program, implying that the collective owned the program and that the District Attorney's Office was there only to help with its administration. Observations of DDEP meetings and interviews with DDEP members, however, indicated that this collaborative structure was never fully realized. Because of his powerful position in mandating and leading the collaboration, the District Attorney was the most powerful and influential member. Despite this influence, the collaboration was successful in achieving its outcomes: Both drug tips reported through Crimestoppers and evictions of drug dealers from rental property increased during and immediately following the period in which the collaboration met.

Despite these gains, the internal structure established by the collaboration could no longer handle the number of tips in a time-efficient manner. In some ways, the collaboration was victimized by its success. At that point in time, interviews with DDEP members provided different perspectives on the collaboration and how it should be constructed and configured. The District Attorney repeated his desire that DDEP be a collaboration but expressed dissatisfaction with the time and energy required to make it work.

Alternately, the most senior Assistant District Attorney who first administered the program revealed that he believed that the District Attorney never really intended the DDEP to be a collaboration in which all members contributed equally. A new prosecutor hired to work solely on this project believed that, from an administrative point of view, there were too many glitches in the collaborative system and that moving responsibility for coordination and centralization of the task from the collaboration to one prosecutor was the answer. Even among those most powerful in the collaboration, there was no shared single vision about the DDEP. In response to the procedural and perceptual problems that marked the end of the collaboration's first stage, the District Attorney gave the new prosecutor full responsibility for leading the DDEP.

A Change in the Collaborative Structure

The initial stage in which the collaboration's structures and procedures were developed was quite distinct from its second stage. Once the DDEP was up and running, members of the District Attorney's Office tried to initiate changes in operating structures without inviting all members to meet and discuss issues face-to-face. At that point, day-to-day contact among collaborative participants was sporadic. Although leadership was centralized in the District Attorney's Office, there was no central DDEP member who communicated regularly with representatives from each participating organization.

As would be expected given the just-mentioned description, only weak rapport developed among the collaboration members; moreover, difficulties associated with relational issues started to erode what ties existed among collaborative members. Despite the apparent success of the DDEP, three specific performance issues had surfaced. First, tips about drug dealing in rental property that citizens routed to Crimestoppers were not being handled efficiently. Second, the police unit to which tips were being routed after being reported could not effectively handle the increased volume of activity. Third, the District Attorney and his staff began to question the viability and effectiveness of having the representative from the Memphis Area Neighborhood Watch office handle publicity and community relations for the DDEP. The result of these issues was that, after little more than a year of operation, the District Attorney restructured the DDEP. It was also at this point that the collaboration's work changed from being primarily intellective or decision making (i.e., creating how the DDEP would work) to tasks of repeated performance (i.e., handling drug tips; see McGrath, 1984). The District Attorney used this point in the development of the collaboration to impose a new structure on collaboration members.

Three specific changes were made. First, a new prosecutor (who was also new to the community) was hired specifically to organize the administrative procedures of the collaboration and lead it under the supervision of the District Attorney. Second, investigation of tips and complaints was moved from one centralized police unit to officers at the precinct level. Third, community affairs work associated with the DDEP was shifted from the Memphis Area Neighborhood Watch representative to a public affairs staff person at the District Attorney's Office, presumably to provide more direction for these efforts. As a result of these changes, the DDEP became even more centralized in the District Attorney's Office and less reliant on input from collaboration members. In essence, the new prosecutor acted as the functional expert responsible for moving a crime-related tip through the system and as the primary link between the District Attorney's Office and each of the collaboration members.

The effects of this structural change were striking. Previously, collaboration members perceived the DDEP as being community centered with tips being generated by informed, concerned, and involved citizens, and the DDEP collaboration as representing community, police, *and* prosecutors. In the reconfiguration, and from the perspective of the newly hired prosecutor in the District Attorney's Office, DDEP responsibilities began *after* a tip was reported to Crimestoppers. As a result, the scope of DDEP activity was significantly shortened. In the original structure, community involvement was considered a critical element and many DDEP activities were focused on increasing that involvement. In the new structure, community involvement was minimized, as the prosecutor focused only on moving a tip through the system once it was reported. By reframing the task in this way, the need for collaboration was effectively eliminated, as the revised task was perceived as being only the responsibility of the Assistant District Attorney. Thus, the focus of the DDEP changed from being community centered to being prosecutor centered.

Moving the responsibility for community relations from the Memphis Area Neighborhood Watch representative to another staff member of the District Attorney's Office further diminished the need for the collaborative team. Even if performance issues (e.g., lack of maturity and professionalism) needed to be addressed with the Neighborhood Watch representative, additional training or personnel replacement may have been more effective alternatives than removing a member and her organization from the collaboration. Rather than officially dismissing this member from the collaboration or formally reorganizing the collaboration, the member was simply ignored and not invited to DDEP meetings or other activities. This restructuring of the collaboration was detrimental, as the collaboration member from the Memphis Area Neighborhood Watch was in the best position to understand the connection of the DDEP to other neighborhood initiatives and crime-prevention promotions.

After the restructuring took place (see Fig. 9.2), the newly hired prosecutor admitted that, initially, she had no knowledge that the Memphis Area Neighborhood Watch was ever a part of the DDEP. Furthermore, the totality of her knowledge about the DDEP program and its members came from the District Attorney General and the senior Assistant District Attorney who initially administered the collaboration. Thus, performance and personality issues and power struggles among original collaboration members provided a framework of ambiguity for which the new prosecutor had no understanding and, therefore, could not handle. Consequently, whereas the representative of the Memphis Area Neighborhood Watch believed that she was central to promoting the DDEP, the new prosecutor believed that this member was only peripherally and indirectly involved. Their differing perceptions about membership and contributions to task activity made conversations between these two parties difficult and nonconstructive. The new prosecutor initiated interactions with other DDEP members, but she had ignored this member and her previous personal and organizational impact on the collaboration.

Finally, automation of the task (taking the report of drug-related tips through prosecution) appeared to be the primary objective for the new prosecutor. Although certain benefits would accrue from this shift in priorities (e.g., prosecutions and evictions would occur more quickly), the community-orientation element of the DDEP was significantly decreased. Although administrative and procedural gains were made, the reconfiguration dampened the commitment and motivation of collaboration members and the support of their organizations for the DDEP.

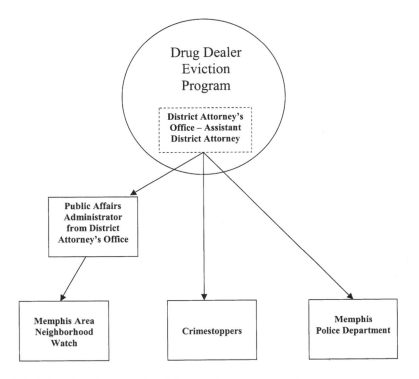

FIG. 9.2. The Drug Dealer Eviction Program reconfigured as a program under the auspices of the District Attorney's Office.

As one might expect, reconfiguring the DDEP as an automated task under the auspices of the District Attorney's Office rather than as a collaboration caused a new set of problems. After several months on the job, the Assistant District Attorney in charge lamented that communication with the other organizations was the most stressful part of her job. Of course, restructuring the DDEP effectively eliminated the best opportunity for communication between and among DDEP organizations. She also complained that there were regular tensions about who claimed ownership of the DDEP. In the collaborative structure, the DDEP belonged to all organizations involved, despite the powerful presence of the District Attorney's Office. In the restructured program, the lack of regular communication among organizational representatives to deliberate co-ownership made it easier for the District Attorney's Office to exert a demand for ownership.

In the final interviews, even the District Attorney indicated that the new structure was not effective. His particular concern was that the DDEP was not successful in attracting and maintaining the involvement of neighborhood organizations. Without the central involvement of the Memphis Area Neighborhood Watch, there was no grassroots link between the DDEP and local citizens. This was crucial, for without tips from citizens, the DDEP could not be successful.

Case Summary

Forming and promoting the DDEP as a collaboration established a set of assumptions and expectations among those invited to represent their organizations. Moreover, the potential for this group of representatives to succeed as a collaboration was apparent at about the time the DDEP experienced the three task-performance problems. Had organizational representatives been allowed and encouraged by the leader to meet face-to-face to work out these performance and implementation issues, the collaboration may have succeeded as it was originally designed.

The collaboration had two distinct and identifiable structures, one in which organizational representatives worked as a collective to identify and develop the collaboration's output and another that resulted from the distinct shift in power dynamics and was used to maintain and then automate the task. From a bona fide group perspective, such changes in group structure are considered normal given that the perspective acknowledges a group's interdependence with its contexts. In essence, the perspective explains these changes by acknowledging that a group does not remain static. A group and its task can "morph" relative to the influences and constraints of its external environments and internal processes.

The collaboration in its first configuration was technically successful according to the criteria suggested by the senior Assistant District Attorney (i.e., Did the DDEP make sense? Was the DDEP ethical? Were actions of the DDEP within the limitations of the statute? Were members of the community being treated well? Does the community know about the DDEP?). Meeting face-to-face as a group, the collaboration created and integrated new policies and procedures within existing organizational systems and structures to accomplish the collaboration's goal of convicting and evicting drug dealers from rental property. However, the District Attorney wanted the DDEP to produce a greater number of outcomes (both convictions and evictions), in part, because those outcomes would benefit the public but also, in part, to satisfy the political environment in which the DDEP existed. However, rather than using the interaction process of the collaboration to help the DDEP maximize these goals, the District Attorney believed that greater centralized control was the answer.

After its restructuring in its second stage, the DDEP appeared successful in that the overall incidence of crime was down in the city and county, the number of tips about drug dealing in rental properties was up, and more tips were resulting in arrests and convictions (nearly 300 convictions in 15 months as compared to less than 100 in the previous year). Some of this success, however, was due to increased task responsibilities on the part of the District Attorney's Office. The new prosecutor was personally perusing daily police log sheets for tips that could be channeled through the DDEP, whereas in the past, the prosecutor relied solely on tips called in by citizens to Crimestoppers. By going outside the collaboration's original system, the new prosecutor was able to add cases to the DDEP that otherwise would not have been counted as part of its activities. Although the success of the DDEP, in terms of the number of convictions and evictions increased, the collaborative group was used with less frequency because the links among collaboration members had been altered or eliminated. Had the collaboration members continued to meet as a group, they may have created additional opportunities for the DDEP to succeed.

Today, the District Attorney still sees the need for collaboration in his admission that as a task, ridding neighborhoods of drug dealers "is an impossible task to do alone." From an interaction perspective, the DDEP as it is configured today is more of an ongoing effort administered by the District Attorney's Office than a collective task administered by a collaboration. In the future, the District Attorney may have to rely once again on a collaborative model if he desires to accomplish the accompanying objective of restoring citizens' confidence in the criminal justice system at the neighborhood level.

DISCUSSION

Collaboration is a complex process that requires members to understand and embrace the role of communication in creating an effective group collaboration that relies on democratic practices. It is imperative that members be given, and that they devote, the time necessary to develop the type of relational ties that will support the collaboration's task activities given the permeable and fluid boundaries, shifting borders, and the group's interdependence with its multiply layered environments (Putnam & Stohl, 1996; Stohl & Walker, 2002). This case study reveals important implications for collaborations and bona fide groups as well as identifies questions for future research.

Implications for Collaborations

All salient stakeholders to a collaboration must be invited and encouraged to participate to ensure that their input is included and respected. Without such input, shared decision making is unlikely to be achieved. Although one member typically initiates the establishment of a collaboration, members should select their own leader and create procedures that facilitate the collaboration's activities. After a collaboration is established, members should consider rotating the responsibility for facilitation among group members. This practice would strengthen the skills of all members, as well as promote joint ownership, equal input, and shared decision making. These procedural and structural steps help to create member ownership of a collaboration, develop its own unique culture apart from collaboration members' organizational cultures, and sustain systemic changes and challenges.

Furthermore, the DDEP case suggests that collaborations are born of political aspirations and strategic motivations that cannot and should not be ignored. Numerous reasons for engaging in collaboration within the nonprofit community have been cited, including economic pressures, the need to reduce service duplication, the need for integrative treatment strategies and comprehensive services, fragmented service delivery, and multiple planning and funding bodies (Stegelin & Jones, 1991). Similar and other political challenges also arise in governmental and business collaborations.

Bringing political issues to the surface, instead of having them function potentially as hidden agendas, can create the opportunity for a collaboration to deal effectively with the challenges it faces. Dealing with power and political issues by subordinating the process or structure of a collaboration, or aborting or curtailing the collaboration's face-to-face meetings, is detrimental to the collaborative process. Regardless of the purpose, collaborations, by the very fact that they are comprised of members of various constituencies and organizations, are political and exist within these political realities; the most effective way to deal with these issues is in a direct manner.

Recognizing the political reality of multiple parties coming together in a collaboration suggests an important modification in the definition of collaboration presented earlier in this chapter. Accordingly, *collaboration* may be viewed as a process that brings power-differentiated parties together through interdependent activities, including shared decision making, for the purpose of achieving an agreed-on objective.

Implications for Bona Fide Groups

This case analysis also draws attention to three features of the bona fide group perspective (Putnam & Stohl, 1996). First, this perspective addresses the dynamic and fluid nature of a group, and this same framework could be useful for analyzing the type and development of group tasks. The work of bona fide groups is seldom about singular decisions; instead, it involves complex activities with multiple decision points. This is particularly applicable to collaborations, for collaborations are charged with generating integrated output—of information, decisions, problem solving, products, and services. The tasks of such a group are fluid in that not all of its tasks are decision oriented, or even well defined. Instead, a collaborative group will most likely engage in all four types of group task activities (McGrath, 1984) in trying to identify and achieve its outcomes: generating ideas, choosing among alternatives, negotiating conflicts, and executing or implementing ideas. The bona fide group perspective, thus, helps researchers to assess group tasks and activities for their fluid, rather than discrete, characteristics. Consequently, just as the bona fide group perspective has changed our view of groups (see Frey's introduction, this volume; Lammers & Krikorian, 1997; Putnam & Stohl, 1996), so may it change our view of group tasks.

Second, this case analysis illuminates ways in which groups, even those with no previous history, are never really without history and politics. When organizational representatives meet as a collaboration for the first time, members are not starting from scratch; rather, they bring with them the history and politics of their own organizations, as well as any positive and negative influences from their previous organizational history (as suggested by Lammers & Krikorian, 1997). Moreover, bona fide groups, such as collaborations, reside in a social and political milieu that is inescapable. A collaboration, thus, never has a fresh start or a clean slate. The bona fide group perspective acknowledges this history and suggests that those influences can, in fact, be stronger than any influences generated within the group itself (Putnam & Stohl, 1996). In the case of the DDEP, the collaboration could never overcome the power and politicism brought to the group by the District Attorney and his representatives.

Third, the bona fide group perspective highlights group processes and, specifically, why communication within a group changes as the group develops over time. Too often, groups are considered containers within which group members interact irrespective of the influence and constraints of external factors. The bona fide group perspective situates a group within its relevant contexts and requires researchers to both identify and track the effects of changing and embedded memberships and permeable boundaries.

Future Research on Collaborations

There are still, however, many questions that need to be answered. First, can the benefits of collaboration be achieved through a centralized, as opposed to decentralized, network? This question is particularly salient in the case of mandated, as opposed to voluntary, collaborations in which the convener is more likely to take on a powerful and influential role in the collaboration (Wood & Gray, 1991). Issues of authority, fairness, and trust are bound to surface whenever one party tries to establish dominance by organizing the administrative functions of a collaboration and, thereby, influencing the balance of power among collaborative members. Although a centralized administrative network may appear to be efficient in that it can streamline operations for a collaboration, such centrality may impose crucial constraints on the collaborative process.

Second, to what degree are effective interpersonal relationships among members important to accomplishing a collaboration's task or achieving outcome success? Clearly, group members' relationships influence a collaboration's task accomplishment (see Keyton, 1999), but the political and power inequities that exist among collaboration members suggest that group member assimilation and relationship building are more crucial and require more attention than in other types of task groups. Given that organizational representatives come with histories and politics of their own, as well as members' perceptions of the perceived histories and politics of other organizations and their representatives, collaborations cannot overlook this important developmental step.

Third, to what degree do collaborations need to evaluate their process in addition to evaluating their outcomes? Task-oriented criteria should be primary, but criteria for evaluating the process of how a collaboration works should not be ignored. In particular, an often-overlooked criterion is the degree to which the process of working together enhances the capability of members to work together in the future (Hackman, 1990); this should be considered, for it is unlikely that a collaboration could be successful for any length of time when its supporting relational processes suffer.

CONCLUSION

Collaboration is one way of organizing individuals, or representatives, as a group to address complex, shared problems. Helping both corporate and community partners, the number of collaborations appears to be increasing because of their ability to produce outcomes that are effective in resolving or managing problems. Collaborations are often touted as the panacea for public–private partnerships, as the means for achieving efficient use of resources in community and nonprofit organizations, and as the structure best suited to link governmental offices and agencies.

Collaborations are ad hoc groups in that they are formed for specific purposes, cases, or situations. The limited time frame for which most operate, however, does not mean that their members can communicate and perform effectively with improvised or impromptu procedures and structures. Practitioners should not mistakenly relate temporality with lack of attention to the process by which collaborations are formed and maintained. A collaboration's outcomes are inextricably linked to its interaction processes. It is not a zero-sum game.

REFERENCES

Berman, E. M., & West, J. P. (1995). Public–private leadership and the role of non-profit organizations in local government: The case of social services. *Policy Studies Review, 14*, 235–246.

Brewer, M. B. (1995). Managing diversity: The role of social identities. In S. E. Jackson & M. N. Ruderman (Eds.), *Diversity in work teams: Research paradigms for a changing workplace* (pp. 47–68). Washington, DC: American Psychological Association.

Chrislip, D. D., & Larson, C. E. (1994). *Collaborative leadership: How citizens and civic leaders can make a difference.* San Francisco: Jossey-Bass.

DeLamater, J. (1974). A definition of "group." *Small Group Behavior, 5*, 30–44.

Gray, B. (1985). Conditions facilitating interorganizational collaboration. *Human Relations, 38*, 911–936.

Gray, B. (1989). *Collaborating: Finding common ground for multiparty problems.* San Francisco: Jossey-Bass.

Gray, B., & Wood, D. J. (1991). Collaborative alliances: Moving from practice to theory. *Journal of Applied Behavioral Science, 27*, 3–22.

Hackman, J. R. (Ed.). (1990). *Groups that work (and those that don't): Creating conditions for effective teamwork.* San Francisco: Jossey-Bass.

Hargrove, R. (1998). *Mastering the art of creative collaboration.* New York: McGraw-Hill.

Iles, P. A., & Auluck, R. (1990). From organizational to interorganizational development in nursing practice: Improving the effectiveness of interdisciplinary teamwork and interagency collaboration. *Journal of Advanced Nursing, 15*, 50–58.

Keyton, J. (1999). Relational communication in groups. In L. R. Frey (Ed.), D. S. Gouran, & M. S. Poole (Assoc. Eds.), *The handbook of group communication theory & research* (pp. 192–222). Thousand Oaks, CA: Sage.

Johnson, P., & Cahn, K. (1995). Improving child welfare practice through improvements in attorney-social worker relationships. *Child Welfare, 74*, 383–394.

Lammers, J. C., & Krikorian, D. H. (1997). Theoretical extension and operationalization of the bona fide group construct with an application to surgical teams. *Journal of Applied Communication Research, 25*, 17–38.

Logsdon, J. M. (1991). Interests and interdependence in the formation of social problem-solving collaborations. *Journal of Applied Behavioral Science, 27*, 23–37.

McGrath, J. E. (1984). *Groups: Interaction and performance.* Englewood Cliffs, NJ: Prentice-Hall.

Mohan, M. L. (1993). *Organizational communication and cultural vision: Approaches for analysis.* Albany: State University of New York Press.

Putnam, L. L., & Stohl, C. (1996). Bona fide groups: An alternative perspective for communication and small group decision making. In R. Y. Hirokawa & M. S. Poole (Eds.), *Communication and group decision making* (2nd ed., pp. 147–178). Thousand Oaks, CA: Sage.

Quinn, D., & Cumblad, C. (1994). Service providers' perceptions of interagency collaboration in their communities. *Journal of Emotional and Behavioral Disorders, 2,* 109–116.

Stallworth, V. (1998). *Building a model of interorganizational nonprofit collaboration.* Unpublished master's thesis, University of Memphis, TN.

Stegelin, D. A., & Jones, S. D. (1991). Components of early childhood interagency collaboration: Results of a statewide survey. *Early Education and Development, 2,* 54–67.

Stohl, C. (1995). *Organizational communication: Connectedness in action.* Thousand Oaks, CA: Sage.

Stohl, C., & Walker, K. (2002). A bona fide perspective for the future of groups: Understanding collaborating groups. In L. R. Frey (Ed.), *New directions in group communication* (pp. 237–252). Thousand Oaks, CA: Sage.

Taber, T. D., Walsh, J. T., & Cooke, R. A. (1979). Developing a community-based program for reducing the social impact of a plant closing. *Journal of Applied Behavioral Sciences, 15,* 133–155.

Wageman, R. (1995). Interdependence and group effectiveness. *Administrative Science Quarterly, 40,* 145–180.

Wood, D. J., & Gray, B. (1991). Toward a comprehensive theory of collaboration. *Journal of Applied Behavioral Science, 27,* 139–162.

Yon, M. G., Mickelson, R. A., & Carlton-LaNey, I. (1993). A child's place: Developing interagency collaboration on behalf of homeless children. *Education and Urban Society, 25,* 410–423.

York, A., & Zychlinski, E. (1996). Competing nonprofit organizations also collaborate. *Nonprofit Management and Leadership, 7,* 15–27.

PART

V

GLOBAL GROUPS:

INTERFACING THE MACRO AND THE MICRO

10

INFLUENCES ON THE RECOMMENDATIONS OF INTERNATIONAL BUSINESS CONSULTING TEAMS

John C. Sherblom
University of Maine

International business consulting teams engaged in short-cycle projects ranging in duration from 7 to 10 weeks are increasingly common and important to business organizations that want to explore new markets, participate in entrepreneurial partnerships, or negotiate other business arrangements and opportunities in emerging economies around the world (Dawar & Frost, 1999; Garten, 1998; Yan, 1998). These consulting teams, however, face a number of important internal and external issues that affect their success, including developing a shared sense of purpose and group cohesiveness, confronting group communication challenges, and accomplishing their project goals. Specific challenges often include (a) being a zero-history group whose members are chosen primarily for their different areas of expertise and professional backgrounds; (b) having language and cultural background differences; (c) engaging in frequent or constant travel; (d) using communication technologies and computer-networking infrastructures that differ in sophistication and availability with geographic location; (e) having difficulties in maintaining adequate contact with home offices, client liaisons, and multiple other constituencies because of physical distance and time-zone differences; and (f) living and working together in conditions that are temporary and, at times, physically confining. Each of these factors poses a serious challenge to the consulting teams' overall working environments and, therefore, to their communication, decision making, and recommendations.

Although the recommendations made by these teams have important consequences for the long-term planning and growth of the companies for which they are consulting, little research has investigated the communication and decision-making processes in which these consulting teams engage to arrive at their recommendations. In this chapter, I use the bona fide group perspective to examine the multiple, simultaneous influences on the communication and decision-making processes of this type of team.

Putnam and Stohl (1990, 1996) identified bona fide groups as existing within larger social systems with which they have a symbiotic, interdependent, and dynamic relationship. From this perspective, bona fide groups have two important characteristics: (a) fluid, permeable boundaries and (b) interdependence with the immediate context (Stohl & Putnam, 1994).

Lammers and Krikorian (1997) extended the idea of boundary permeability beyond the individual members of a group to a consideration of group tasks, orientations, and goals that may change over time. Although the external environment does not determine the internal group dynamics, there is an interdependence between the external and the internal, across permeable group boundaries, which influences the social construction of a group's communication and decision making. This interdependence describes a reciprocal relationship between the group and its external environment. My purpose in this chapter is to analyze the nature of this reciprocal relationship across the permeable group boundaries and to explore the nature of this group-contextual environment interdependence as a subtle, yet important, influence on the decisions and recommendations made by international business consulting teams.

DESCRIPTION OF THE INTERNATIONAL BUSINESS CONSULTING TEAMS

The Teams and Their Projects

This study examines and analyzes the communication processes of 15 international business consulting teams as affected by the influences and constraints of their working environments. The team members were all living in the United States at the time that they participated in the consulting projects, but many team members were originally from other countries. The teams engaged in projects for both U.S. and non-U.S. firms. These projects took place in Argentina, Brazil, Belgium, Chile, the Czech Republic, Finland, France, Germany, Hungary, Italy, Indonesia, Israel, the Netherlands, Poland, Slovakia, Spain, Sweden, the United Kingdom, and Vietnam;

the firms consulted for were in the automotive, biotechnology, kitchen appliance, credit card, gas turbine engine, pharmaceutical, pulp and paper, silicon technology, steel, and vegetable seed industries.

The 15 teams involved a total of 65 members, with each team having between 3 to 7 members, and the two 7-member teams being composed of 2 and 3 person subteams. Each team and subteam contained one or more members who had some language facility and familiarity with the culture of the countries in which they traveled. Each team worked for a different corporation on a unique project that ran according to its own timetable of events, existed within a specific set of corporate expectations and constraints, and presented a special set of issues and concerns to be managed. The first team analyzed credit card acceptance rates in the United Kingdom. The second performed an analysis of a British company's corporate culture. The third developed short- and long-term capital financing plans for a Vietnamese steel corporation. The fourth worked on an automotive market analysis in various parts of Europe. The fifth investigated the electric-optical inspection and process-control measurement system opportunities for the pulp and paper industry in Finland, France, Germany, Sweden, and the United Kingdom. The sixth worked for a German company assessing the production value of the company's research and development projects that had been funded by European Community investments. The seventh, eighth, and ninth teams worked for different Israeli incubator companies to investigate the potential markets and uses for their developing technologies and inventions. Team 10 investigated opportunities for personal care pharmaceutical products in Indonesia, and Team 11 analyzed pharmaceutical product opportunities in Argentina, Brazil, and Chile. Team 12 examined the gas turbine engine market in Poland, Hungary, and the Czech Republic, and Team 13 analyzed the built-in kitchen appliance market in the these same countries and in Slovakia. Team 14 investigated the vegetable seed market trends in Belgium, France, Germany, Hungary, Italy, the Netherlands, Spain, and the United Kingdom. Finally, Team 15 examined the tourism potential of an Israeli national park.

I worked as a consultant charged with examining the communication needs, processes, and outcomes of these teams. I used four methods of analysis to undertake this task. First, I held focus groups with each team soon after it was formed and before it engaged in the consulting project and then again immediately after it returned from the project. Second, while the teams were engaged in their projects, I sent individual questionnaires via e-mail to team members that asked them to anonymously rate the communication within the team. The questions and rating responses appear in Table 10.1. Third, I analyzed the written report of one of the teams for evidence of explicit and implicit boundary and contextual interdependence influences

TABLE 10.1

Team Members' Ratings of the Teams'
and Team Members' Communication

In General, the Team can …	Mean Response	In General, Team Members are …	Mean Response
Clarify and Elaborate on Ideas	5.58	Honest	6.20
Agree on Standards and Procedures	5.57	Able to Provide Accurate Information	5.86
Test for Group Consensus on Issues	5.50	Action-Oriented	5.58
Initiate Discussions	5.38	Perceptive	5.58
Seek Information and Opinions of Members	5.36	Logical	5.56
Direct Conversational Traffic	5.34	Realistic	5.56
Suggest Procedures for Reaching a Goal	5.34	Organized	5.50
Avoid Simultaneous Conversations	5.33	Practical	5.50
Summarize Ideas	5.16	Focused	5.36
Express Feelings and Check Impressions	4.96	Insightful	5.34
Keep Discussion from Digressing	4.92	Informative	5.24
Ease Tensions; Deal with Difficult Matters	4.63	Decisive	5.20
Creatively Resolve Differences	4.54	Creative	4.98
Encourage Reserved Talkers	4.40	Stimulating	4.82
Control Dominant Talkers	3.87	Innovative	4.80
Take Members' Silence as Consent	3.41	Forceful	4.44
Allow 1 or 2 People to Make Decisions	3.16		
Concede to Unsupported Opinions	2.96		
Make Decisions by a Minority	2.28		

Note. Responses rated on a 7-point scale, ranging from 1 = *Never* to 7 = *Always*.

on its recommendations. Fourth, I examined the project notes, in-country reports, and final report generated by a second team for evidence of the influences of contextual interdependence on its decision making.

External Communication Challenges Facing the Teams

At the first focus group meetings, I became aware that the contexts within which these projects took place presented major challenges for the teams. One challenge was dealing with the language and culture of the country or countries in which the teams worked. Language and cultural differences were, of course, not as much of an issue for the two U.S. teams working in the United Kingdom. For other teams, however, language became a major hurtle, especially with regard to gathering information. For example, some of the project participants with whom the teams in Israel worked on incubator projects spoke Hebrew, others spoke Russian, and few were fluent in English. The team in Vietnam had only one member who spoke Vietnamese, which became a problem for the team during periods of time when this member was separated from the rest of the team. Several teams traveled through multiple countries and experienced several language changes. Using professional translators in their interviews with host business members became a challenge for some of these teams; translators were both expensive to hire and often unfamiliar with the industry and, therefore, with relevant technical terms, concepts, and processes. Although clients sometimes supplied knowledgeable translators, these translators were often perceived by team members to summarize information too much, minimize important information, and skirt sensitive areas in an effort to protect the company or the management team that had hired them.

The challenges posed by differences in language and culture sometimes presented unanticipated problems but they were usually not insurmountable. Other challenges were often more difficult to overcome. For example, teams sometimes felt isolated and undersupported by their corporate sponsor, in part, due to their distance from corporate headquarters (in terms of both geography and time zones), the asynchronous means of communication they used (e-mail and Web-based information exchanges), and the time constraints imposed by the nature of complex, dynamically changing, short-cycle projects that require frequent, rapid feedback. Effective discussion of rapidly changing project goals, expenses, and progress can be difficult through an asynchronous communication medium. Moreover, given time-zone differences, there was often as much as a 2-working-day delay in either direction, even between a simple information request and a response. The constraints of the asynchronous communication media utilized were often frustrating for team members, but were necessary because synchronous telephone or videoconferencing commu- nication was frequently impossible to use given time-zone differences, busy schedules, and a lack of available technology.

Several of the teams also experienced tight living conditions, by U.S. standards, with five members of one team living together in a small Israeli kibbutz guest quarters, another team staying in a small British home in an isolated town and at a distance from the local office, and other teams traveling frequently to new cities and countries and staying in hotel rooms. Indeed, some projects required constant travel, and these teams often did not stay in the same hotel for more than 1 or 2 nights. This constant travel, coupled with little or no client-provided office support for computers, telephones, photocopying, or faxing, made project management difficult and time consuming.

In addition, several of the teams had subteams with members located and working in different countries. Coordinating their work was difficult, especially given the relatively primitive telephone and computer-networking infrastructure available in some locations. Differences in the technological infrastructure and its accessibility in different countries also created difficulties, particularly for teams that traveled between countries with different electrical power and telephone quality and standards, such as the countries of central Europe.

One of the biggest challenges that the teams faced, however, was that while in the process of completing the projects, they often had to reconceptualize and rescope them in response to demands made by various external stakeholder groups. The in-country management team, for instance, frequently had a different opinion about the importance of and methods necessary for the completion of various aspects of the project than did those at corporate headquarters who had sponsored the project and initially briefed the team on its scope. When this disparity occurred, the project team, on landing in the country where the project was to take place, had to rethink and rescope the project to fit the expectations of the company's in-country management with whom they worked closely and on whom they relied for information. While doing this, they still had to communicate about the project in an acceptable manner with corporate headquarters for which they were producing the final project report. The combination of these influences created complex challenges for the teams.

TEAM COMMUNICATION, BOUNDARIES, INTERDEPENDENCE, AND CONTEXT

Communication Within the Teams

To judge how well teams were coping with the communication challenges associated with these influences halfway through the project, I sent the team members a questionnaire via e-mail and asked them to respond individually and anonymously to a set of 19 items on which they could rate the team's communication style and another set of 16 items on which they could rate team members. Table 10.1 presents the results of the team members' ratings. These results show that team members felt particularly comfortable in the team's ability to clarify and elaborate on ideas, agree on standards and procedures, test for group consensus on issues, initiate discussions, seek information and opinions of members, direct conversational traffic, suggest procedures for reaching a goal, avoid simultaneous conversations, and summarize ideas. Their ability to express feelings and check impressions, keep discussion from digressing, ease tension and deal with difficult matters, creatively resolve differences, encourage reserved talkers, and control dominant talkers were rated slightly lower. However, team members reported that they did not take members' silence as consent, allow one or two people to make decisions, concede to unsupported opinions, or make decisions by a minority. With respect to personal characteristics, team members perceived one another as honest, able to provide accurate information, action-oriented, perceptive, logical, realistic, organized, practical, focused, insightful, informative, and decisive. They also rated team members as relatively creative, stimulating, innovative, and forceful. These ratings suggest profiles of competent, professional team members who take their communication seriously and engage in it conscientiously.

Team Boundaries and Contexts

Prior to this electronic survey and before they left for their in-country project, I conducted a focus group with each of the 15 teams. Each focus group lasted approximately 1 hour, with team members spending the first 10 minutes individually filling out a short, written questionnaire and then spending the next 50 minutes as a group discussing the key issues that emerged from individual responses to that questionnaire. The focus group questionnaire directed their attention to four main issues. First, team members were asked to describe their project, how well defined and scoped it was at that point in time, and what needed to be done to achieve a sharper orientation. They also described areas of perceived ambiguity and uncertainty, and the challenges and complications they anticipated in working on the project. Second, they discussed their team in terms of how well they knew each other, their history of working together, what key areas of expertise they had on the team, any areas they believed were inadequately covered, and what challenges they thought they would face in working together. Third, they talked about their level of comfort with using the technology that was anticipated to be available in the country or coun-

tries to which they were going. Fourth, they identified their expected team
and project support needs while in-country and how they anticipated fulfilling those needs.

For some teams, an important topic was the challenge they expected to
face in living together in close quarters (by U.S. standards). Another topic
of concern was not having some needed expertise they would have liked
among their team members, such as greater language facility or cultural expertise, a team member with more background in a particular business
area (such as organizational behavior or marketing), or a member with
greater firsthand knowledge of the particular industry under study. For
other teams, the major concern was with the scope of the project growing,
shifting, or remaining unclear. Whatever the issue, the teams explored the
complexities and ramifications and discussed potential strategies they
could employ to face the challenge.

The second focus group session took place with each team immediately
after it returned from having completed the in-country information-gathering phase of the project and was preparing to produce the final
written report for the company. This focus group followed the same format
as the first session, except that each team member was asked to individually
list on paper the three most positive and worthwhile aspects of the project
and then to indicate the three most challenging, difficult, or surprising
things that happened during the project. Team members were also asked to
identify the biggest challenges they still faced in the project and in their
working together as a team, and to state how well the technology they had
available had worked and how well their team and project support needs
had been met during the project. These two focus group sessions helped me
to assess the teams' projects at key transition points in the process.

Table 10.2 shows that permeable, fluid boundary issues and interdependence with context were important areas raised by these teams during
the focus group sessions. Although many of these issues have both boundary and context interdependence aspects to them and cannot be cleanly
separated into one category or the other, it is useful to examine these issues and to separate them from internal team communication issues.

The issues identified as permeable, fluid boundary issues represented
30% of the anticipated, 34% of the positive, and 29% of the challenging issues raised by the teams. Even more important, interdependent context issues represented 70% of the anticipated challenges, 46% of the positive
responses, and 52% of the challenging ones, whereas internal team communication issues did not arise as anticipated concerns for the teams and
made up only 20% of the positive and 17% of the challenging responses. In
line with the bona fide group perspective, group boundary issues and interdependence with the environment issues were both anticipated and experienced as important influences by these teams.

TABLE 10.2

Frequency of Issues Raised Prior to and After In-Country Consulting Experience

Type of Issues Raised	Biggest Challenge Anticipated Prior to In-Country Consulting Experience	Most Positive, Interesting, Worthwhile Aspect Reported After Experience	Most Challenging, Difficult, Surprising Aspect Reported After Experience
Internal Team Communication			
Subteam Communication		21 (12%)	8 (5%)
Team Communication		3 (2%)	13 (8%)
Team Diversity & Expertise		11 (6%)	6 (4%)
Team Performance			
Total:		35 (20%)	27 (17%)
Permeable, Fluid Boundary			
Client Expectations	4 (7%)	6 (3%)	3 (2%)
Client Liaisons	4 (7%)	15 (8%)	16 (10%)
Corporate Culture	1 (2%)	38 (21%)	1 (1%)
City/Country Culture	5 (9%)	2 (1%)	4 (3%)
Effective Interview Setup	3 (5%)	2 (1%)	12 (8%)
Multiple Constituencies			8 (5%)
Total:	17 (30%)	63 (34%)	44 (29%)

continued on next page

TABLE 10.2 (continued)

Type of Issues Raised	Biggest Challenge Anticipated Prior to In-Country Consulting Experience	Most Positive, Interesting, Worthwhile Aspect Reported After Experience	Most Challenging, Difficult, Surprising Aspect Reported After Experience
Interdependence With Context			
Corporate Presentations		3 (2%)	1 (1%)
Industry (knowledge of)	3 (5%)	18 (10%)	3 (2%)
Information Collection	14 (25%)	17 (9%)	16 (10%)
International Business	2 (4%)	23 (13%)	10 (6%)
Language Translation		4 (2%)	8 (5%)
Living Arrangements		2 (1%)	19 (12%)
Refining Project Scope	10 (18%)	6 (3%)	10 (6%)
Technology Use	1 (2%)	1 (1%)	6 (4%)
Time in Country			
Travel (amount of)	9 (16%)	10 (5%)	10 (6%)
Total:	39 (70%)	84 (46%)	83 (52%)
Grand Totals:	56	182	154

Note. All percentages are column percentages and have been rounded to the nearest whole number so may not add to 100% due to rounding error.

Table 10.2 shows that the largest anticipated interdependent context challenges discussed during the focus group session prior to embarking on the project were with information collection (14 responses, or 25% of the anticipated concerns expressed) and refining the project scope (10 responses, or 18%). Comparing the most challenging, difficult, and surprising aspects with the anticipated challenges shows that refining the project scope proved to be an even larger challenge than anticipated (19 responses compared to 10) and that information collection was experienced as a challenge a little more frequently than anticipated (16 responses compared to 14), although the percentage of total responses offered is smaller for the post- than pre-experience in both cases.

A comparison of the items reported by the teams on returning shows that the most unanticipated or underanticipated challenges include establishing and working with client liaisons, effective interview setups, responding to the needs and interests of multiple constituencies, coping with language translation issues, and making effective use of the technology. Three of these challenges (working with client liaisons, effective interview setups, and responding to multiple constituencies) invoke permeable, fluid boundary issues. Language translation and the use of technology both highlight the team's dependence on and interdependence with the context. Even the aspects identified as the most positive, such as the corporate culture and the culture of the city and country in which the project takes place, focus on permeable, fluid team boundaries or, such as the knowledge of the industry and of international business gained, on the interdependent context in which the team works.

Having developed the communication competence of the consulting teams and their members, and documented the importance of group boundary and interdependence with context issues, case studies of two of the teams described earlier are presented in more detailed analysis. First, a case analysis of the recommendations made by one of the teams for a prospective joint venture between a U.S. company and a German company focuses primarily on the effects of permeable, fluid boundaries on their decision-making process. Second, a case analysis of a vegetable seed company newly created through the merger of three companies and existing with branches in eight countries develops the influences of contextual interdependence.

EFFECTS OF PERMEABLE AND FLUID BOUNDARIES ON A TEAM'S RECOMMENDATIONS

The first case analysis examines one team's report for a potential joint venture to be performed by two companies, a U.S. firm with significant market sales in Europe and a well-established German firm. The projected joint venture was designed to expand their operations in central Europe to the Czech Republic, Hungary, Poland, and Slovakia. The U.S. company has a strong market share in most central European countries, with excellent brand-image recognition, an in-depth knowledge of the local kitchen appliance and furniture markets, a strong network of retail trade partners, and an understanding of local consumer-buying preferences and attitudes. The German company is a leading kitchen furniture producer in several western European markets and offers a wide range of brands covering most market segments, while emphasizing the middle and high-end segments. It has a strong brand image, is a leader in state-of-the-art manufacturing and logistics operations, and is in a strong financial position.

Table 10.3 shows the list of recommendations made individually for each company and for their joint venture in each of the four countries. This table also shows that the team for each company in each country made different recommendations. Some of these recommendations are based explicitly on a standard set of criteria used to evaluate business opportunities in developing economies. These influences are presented first and represent boundary permeabilities that shape the team's decision making in ways that they explicitly acknowledge. Other influences, discussed thereafter, suggest additional, more implicit, and less clearly recognized boundary permeability characteristics.

The team's recommendations are explicitly influenced by political, economic, infrastructure, technology, and consumer analyses. The *political analysis* assesses the political risks to investment in a particular national market. For instance, in an environment of high political uncertainty, a firm might choose to partner with a domestic firm or license the sale of its products and services to a national organization rather than commit to a full-scale investment in manufacturing, distribution, and sales. The *economic analysis* provides a measure of the key economic forces that impact business strategy, such as inflation rate changes, per capita disposable income, and change in gross domestic product. The *infrastructure analysis* uses measures of age, reliability, availability, state of repair, and overall quality to assess the general level, sophistication, and reliability of a country's utilities, roads and railroads, and availability and quality of business services. The *technological analysis* examines the level of sophistication of telephone, computer, and other technological infrastructure and instrument development. The *consumer analysis* measures the level of sophistication and behavioral patterns of a country's consumers. The recommendations that result from these analyses are reported in Table 10.3. These recommendations show how the team's conclusions about the potential for market expansion into the Czech Republic, Hungary, Poland, and Slovakia are in some ways similar and in other ways different.

TABLE 10.3

Recommendations for a Prospective Joint Venture

	Czech Republic	Hungary	Poland	Slovakia
German Company Recommendations				
Advertising	X			X
Customer Relations	X			
Inventory			X	
Market Analysis				
Product Positioning	X	X	X	X
Retail Store Relations	X	X	X	X
Service				X
Trade Partner Relations	X	X		
Total Number of Recommendations	5	3	3	4
United States Company Recommendations				
Advertising				X
Customer Relations	X			
Inventory		X	X	X
Market Analysis	X		X	X
Product Positioning	X	X	X	X
Retail Store Relations				X
Service				X
Trade Partner Relations	X		X	X
Total Number of Recommendations	4	2	4	7
German–U.S. Joint Venture Recommendations				
Advertising		X		X
Customer Relations				
Inventory				X
Market Analysis	X	X		X
Product Positioning	X		X	
Retail Store Relations				
Service				
Trade Partner Relations		X		
Total Number of Recommendations	2	3	1	3
Grand Total of All Recommendations Made	11	8	8	14

In general, the consulting team concludes that central Europe provides a largely untapped market with growing economies and increased consumer spending power, and they make recommendations to the companies for the potential development of business opportunities in each country. Although these recommendations do not follow directly from the political, economic, infrastructure, technological, and consumer analyses, these analyses provide the rationale behind many of the recommendations. For example, the political indicators addressed by the team suggest that the Czech Republic, Hungary, Poland, and Slovakia are all relatively stable. This indicator, therefore, does little to distinguish between the countries but suggests the potential for developing product positioning and retail store relations in each.

On the basis of its economic analysis, the team makes different recommendations, however, for each country. The team expresses concern for the situation in the Czech Republic, as that country appears to be losing much-needed capital investment to Poland, where wages are lower. It is excited about Hungary's Western-oriented economy, which is successfully undergoing an extensive privatization of state assets and appears headed for European Union and NATO membership. Poland is also a fast-growing economy with declining interest rates, rapidly increasing wages, and rising business confidence. The team views Slovakia as having some risk of economic troubles, although official estimates predict a demand-led growth in household appliances. This economic analysis leads the team to recommend that one or more of the companies do a market analysis in each of the countries. Market analysis is more frequently recommended, however, for the Czech Republic and Slovakia. Hence, although all four countries appear to be in economic transition, the pattern of market analysis recommendations made for the U.S. company and for the joint venture suggests a greater concern for the economic transition in these two countries.

Analysis of each country's infrastructure also appears to affect the recommendations the team makes. The highway and railway infrastructures are identified as being relatively well developed in the Czech Republic. Hungary has made advances in the quality and reliability of its infrastructure. The electric, telecommunications, and broadcasting companies have been privatized, and the road system is widely viewed as more developed and better maintained than those of other East European nations; in fact, Hungary now serves as an important regional trade thoroughfare. Poland's infrastructure is unreliable but improving; for instance, the road system is poor but new highway projects are planned. Slovakia has a potential banking crisis looming, and the major highway systems are inadequate for business commerce, although there are plans to build a new highway system connecting the major Slovakian cities. These infrastruc-

ture analyses affect the team's recommendations for inventory maintenance. For Poland and Slovakia, where infrastructure is deemed of the
poorest quality, inventory becomes the greatest concern, appearing on
the recommendation list twice; in the Czech Republic, with a
well-developed infrastructure, it is of little concern and is not mentioned.

Technology is also undergoing rapid change in all four countries.
Technological advances vary widely in the Czech Republic, as there is a
substantial waiting period for new telephone installation, but cellular
telephone coverage extends across the country and provides a feasible alternative. There are also a surprising number of Internet hosts available
(3.95 per 1,000 people, which compares favorably with Western Europe).
Hungary's former state-owned telecommunications firm is now privately
owned and managed by a U.S.–German consortium with ambitious plans
to upgrade the inadequate system, including adding 600,000 new phone
lines. Where communications have been upgraded—especially in Buda-
pest, which has 49% of all telephones in the country, 50% of the retail
businesses, and 20% of Hungary's population (2 million people)—digital
systems appear more prevalent than in the United States. In Poland, the
telephone system consists mostly of an older technology with few
touch-tone facilities and it can be difficult to make telephone connections. However, digital cellular phone service is clear and reliable, and
business is, therefore, often conducted through the cellular network that
covers nearly all of Poland. In addition, plans to privatize parts of Poland's national telephone company are expected to upgrade the standard
telephone technology and bring Poland into the digital age. Slovakian
phone service is unreliable, and although there are plans for improve-
ment, there is little other modern technology currently available. Technology is, thus, undergoing rapid transformation in all four countries and
provides an important background to the team's overall business recommendations, but appears not to be an explicit characteristic for distin-
guishing among the countries.

Consumer analysis, however, does affect the company recommendations made for each country. The team's report indicates that there is a
boom in the consumer goods industries in the Czech Republic. With the
highest central European average salary and a salary growth rate of 9%
per annum, income growth and expectations for the economy make the
Czech consumers prime retail spenders. Although these consumers are
price conscious and want a good bargain, overall consumer spending is
increasing, and the kitchen is reported to be a focal point for such spending. A recent report suggests that 70% of free time is spent in the kitchen,
and an attractive kitchen is proudly shown to friends and neighbors. In
Hungary, the lackluster performance of the economy and a substantial
decrease in real wages has resulted in a consumer who is price sensitive.

The country's middle class is shrinking whereas lower and upper income segments continue to grow. In addition, these consumers do not view kitchen furniture and appliances as high-priority purchases; instead, the automobile remains the most dominant status symbol. Poland's consumers, in contrast, have increased purchasing power, as the average income has increased 30%, inflation has fallen, and salary and wage increases have outpaced increases in consumer prices. Polish consumers are well educated in terms of product features, styles, quality, and service, and have come to demand these characteristics in their purchases. In Slovakia, consumers are particularly concerned with service after the sale, environmentally friendly appliances, a brand's reputation for quality, and the available financing options. The consumer analysis, showing that Czech and Slovakian consumers have the spending power to consider more than price, leads the team to suggest recommendations for developing advertising and customer relations for both the German and U.S. companies in these countries. In addition, explicit service considerations, although appearing unique to Slovakia, may also be based, in part, on this consumer analysis.

In addition to these explicit effects of the political, economic, infrastructure, technology, and consumer analyses on the team's decision making, implicit influences on that decision making, such as the context and time within which the decisions are made, also show an effect that is of interest in the present analysis of group boundaries. Although Putnam and Stohl (1990, 1996) defined group boundaries largely by group membership issues, Lammers and Krikorian (1997) argued that sole reliance on membership as the principal boundary indicator of group stability, permeability, and identity is problematic. As mentioned earlier, they enlarged the parameters of this concept by suggesting other indicators of boundary change within a group, such as the introduction of new tasks, orientations, and goals. These changes occur within a particular time frame and context within which a group's decision-making processes take place. In the present case, evidence of a shifting orientation within the group over time is the team's decision to write two separate reports—one for each company. Each report contained confidential recommendations for that company along with a set of common recommendations for the joint venture opportunities. Neither company saw the other company's report. Given that the original explicit charge to the team from the companies' joint-venture management team was to generate one report that would be presented to each company, and given that generating two separate reports was substantially more work for the team and a difficult task to accomplish within the time constraints of the schedule, this decision marked an important introduction of a new task, orientation, and goal for the team. Writing two reports, however, allowed the team to better negotiate its separate and sometimes contradictory allegiance boundaries with each company. Generating separate reports provided the means for the team to communicate confidentially with each company, which became important to the team's ability to negotiate the simultaneous collaborative and competitive aspects of the boundary existing between the two companies. For although the companies had a tentative agreement to explore a joint venture, they still perceived themselves as two companies—competitors with separate identities, agendas, and goals. The permeable and fluid, yet stable, boundary between the companies and between the team and each of the companies became a major influence on the team's decision to generate the two separate reports.

In addition to the influence of permeable group boundaries on this team's decisions, the resulting pattern of recommendations made by the team introduces the second characteristic of bona fide groups as it suggests the influence of interdependence between the immediate context and the group's decision-making process. In the Czech Republic, most of the information-gathering interviews on which the recommendations are based took place in a dealership owned and operated by the German company; in Hungary, they took place in a department store office; in Poland, they occurred in a retail shop; and in Slovakia, they were performed in a local office of the U.S. company. These locations were chosen by the team for their availability and convenience to the interviewing task in each country. However, it is not too surprising, given the different immediate contexts of the interviews, that the greatest number of recommendations generated for the German company are in the Czech Republic from the interviews performed in its dealership and for the U.S. company in Slovakia, from the interviews performed in its local office. Interestingly, the greatest number of joint recommendations is also developed in these two countries, suggesting a conceptually energizing effect, as well as perhaps a company-biasing influence of the context on the team's recommendations.

Thus, this case analysis shows some of the explicit and implicit boundary influences on the set of recommendations made by an international business consulting team and introduces the concept of interdependence with the immediate context. Explicit political, economic, infrastructure, technology, and consumer analyses have a clear impact on the team's recommendations. However, implicit boundary and contextual influences, such as the boundary relationship between the two companies and the immediate context in which the information was gathered, also have important effects on the team's decision-making processes and recommendations. Thus, this case suggests at least three important sources of influence on the team's recommendations: the explicit analyses undertaken, the implicit company boundaries, and the immediate information-gathering context. The following case analysis develops and explores more fully the effect of context interdependence on a team's recommendations.

EFFECTS OF CONTEXT INTERDEPENDENCE ON A TEAM'S RECOMMENDATIONS

Putnam and Stohl (1990) argued that a second key characteristic of bona fide groups is their interdependence with external environments through the mutual influence that those environments and the group have on each other. Internal group processes, such as communication and decision making, are influenced by relevant contexts and, in turn, influence those contexts (Putnam & Stohl, 1996). For instance, importing information from outside a group is said to be critical to the group's phasic development, role coordination, communication effectiveness, and decision-making acceptability and implementation (Putnam & Stohl, 1990). Reciprocally, the present study suggests that a group's phasic development, role coordination, and communication effectiveness affect how that information is imported, contextualized, and used by the group in its recommendation-generating process.

Examination of the strengths and weaknesses identified by the consulting team that investigated the vegetable seed company with offices throughout Europe illustrates this interdependence of a group with its immediate contexts. This examination suggests that temporal points of timing and transition are important influences on the team's decision-making processes and their recommendation outcomes.

The team conducted 57 interviews with employees of a corporation created through the merger of 4 companies with offices and employees in 8 European countries. The consulting team of four individuals began their interviews in France and then split into two subteams. One subteam conducted interviews in Italy, Hungary, and Belgium, whereas the other subteam conducted interviews in Spain, the United Kingdom, and Germany; both teams then, while maintaining their subteam groupings, completed interviews in the Netherlands. In each interview, a team member asked the interviewee to identify the strengths and weaknesses of the newly merged company. On the basis of these interviews, the team generated a list of strengths and weaknesses for each interview and for each country, as well as a final overall list for the company. Table 10.4 shows the number of times specific company strengths were identified in the interviews; Table 10.5 shows the number of times specific company weaknesses were identified. The first subteam's results appear in bold; the second subteam's results are not bolded. In each table, an asterisk identifies a strength or weakness that appeared on the list for a country. The numbers in the second-to-last column show the number of interviews in which a strength or weakness was mentioned followed, after the slash, by the number of countries in which it was mentioned; a bolded X in that column identifies the strengths and weaknesses that appeared on the final list compiled for the company. The last column provides a novelty ratio generated by dividing the number of interviews in which a strength or weakness is mentioned by the number of countries in which it is mentioned. The purpose of these tables is to show the accumulation of information that the team uses to make its final list of recommendations to the company.

The strengths shown in Table 10.4, such as seed quality (mentioned in 23 interviews in 6 countries), brand equity (18 interviews in 7 countries), secure market share (26 interviews in 8 countries), and sales and distribution (22 interviews in 6 countries), are mentioned often enough and diversely enough, in terms of countries represented, to be obvious candidates for the final company list. However, on the basis of the numbers alone, it is unclear why such items as correct quantities and honest advertising (each mentioned in 2 interviews in 1 country), as well as product specifications and rapid response (each mentioned only once), make the final list, whereas competitor analysis (10 interviews in 4 countries) and good seed varieties (17 interviews in 7 countries) do not. Clearly, the final list is not created through a simple compilation of information or mathematical calculation of the frequency and diversity of strengths mentioned.

Examining the recommendation lists generated for the individual countries suggests other possible contextual influences at work. For countries in which few strengths are generated (fewer than 13), additional strengths are added to supplement that country list. These strengths appear to "bleed over" from the list of strengths identified in interviews done in a country either immediately before or after that country or in interviews being done simultaneously by the other subteam in another country. Honest advertising, for instance, appears on the country list for France but does not appear in any of the interviews conducted there. It does appear, however, in the interviews conducted in Italy immediately after the French interviews. Magazine/catalogue marketing appears on the lists for both France and Spain, but not in the interviews conducted in either country; it does appear, however, in an interview in Italy, although it does not occur on that country's list.

Interestingly, none of the bleed over of items occurs for countries with lists of strengths longer than 12 items, such as Italy, Hungary, Belgium, and the Netherlands, suggesting that bleed over occurs when it is necessary to add items to a list. Italy, Hungary, Belgium, and the Netherlands are also the countries in which the interviews are conducted by the first subteam (bolded in the table), suggesting that this subteam may have been both more prolific in identifying strengths and more assertive and influential in

TABLE 10.4

Interview, Country, and Final Company Lists of Vegetable Seed Company Strengths

Country:	France	Italy	Spain	Hungary	UK	Belgium	Germany	Netherlands	Final List[a]	Novelty Ratio[b]
(number of interviews)	(5)	(16)	(6)	(6)	(5)	(3)	(6)	(10)	(57)	
Production										
Competitor Analysis		6		1	*	2		1	10/4	2.5
Correct Quantities		2							2/1X	2.0
Honest Advertising	*	2							2/1X	2.0
Seed Quality	1*	15	2	2	1			2	23/6X	3.8
Marketing										
Brand Equity	1*	7*	1*	1		3*	1*	4*	18/7X	2.6
Four-Brand Strategy	4			3		1		2*	10/4	2.5
Magazine/Catalogue	*	1	*			1*		1*	3/3X	1.0
Product Performance		1		2		1			4/3X	1.3
Product Specifications						1			1/1X	1.0
Secure Market Share	2	8	3	4	2	1	1	5	26/8X	3.2
Seed Variety		2				1*			3/2	1.5
Worldwide Perspective								2*	2/1	2.0
Research										
Breeding Opportunities	1	4*	*	1	3		1	2	12/6X	2.0
Gene Pool/Biotech	1*	1*			1*			1*	4/4	1.0
Good Seed Varieties		1	1	5	2	3	3*	2	17/7	2.4
Taste Preferred		2							2/1X	2.0

Organization									[a]	[b]
American Image	1*	1							2/2	1.0
Brand Flexibility/Variety	1	2*	1	4		3			11/5X	2.2
Contact Processors		1		1*					2/2	1.0
Experience					1			1*	2/2	1.0
Financial Position	1		1	2				1*	5/4	1.2
Rapid Response	*	*				1*			1/1X	1.0
Responsive Agents	*	5*							5/1X	5.0
Sales and Distribution		13	1	2	1	1	3		22/6X	3.6
Service/Tech Support	1	1*	3	*	1	2*	2		10/6X	1.6
Size Market Presence		1*							1/1	1.0
Total Strengths	10	19	8	13	6	13	6	14		

Note. Countries are listed in the order in which interviews were conducted. Cell numbers show the number of interviews in which a strength was mentioned. *Indicates a strength that appeared on a country's list. X indicates a strength that appeared on the final company list. [a]Indicates the number of interview/country lists on which a strength appeared. [b]Provides a novelty-saturation ratio showing the number of interviews divided by countries in which a strength was mentioned.

TABLE 10.5

Interview, Country, and Final Company Lists of Vegetable Seed Company Weaknesses

Country:	France	Italy	Spain	Hungary	UK	Belgium	Germany	Netherlands	Final List[a]	Novelty Ratio[b]
(number of interviews)	(5)	(16)	(6)	(6)	(5)	(3)	(6)	(10)	(57)	
Production										
Germination	1	6	1			2*		2*	12/5	2.4
Seed Availability	*	6*			3*	2	*	2*	13/4X	3.2
Seed Information		2	1		3	1		3*	10/5	2.0
Seed Production	2	6	4		1		1	9	23/6X	3.8
Seed Quality	5	11*	1			3	1*	3	24/6X	4.0
Marketing										
Advertising Budgets		*	2	1			1		4/3X	1.3
Brand Image	1	2	1		*				4/3	1.3
Competitor Analysis		5			2*			2	9/3	3.0
Field Trials		1			*		*		1/1	1.0
Four-Brand Perception	1								1/1X	1.0
Media Use				1*					1/1	1.0
New Product Trials	2	9	2		1		2*	6	22/6X	3.7
Promotional Materials		9*		2	*				11/2X	5.5
Technical Product Info.		1		1				*	2/2	1.0

Research

										[a]	[b]
Breeding Methods		5	*		2*					7/2X	3.5
Breeding Productivity		6								6/1X	6.0
Communication of Sales	1		*		4				1	6/3	2.0
New Product Edge Loss		6	2*			3		1	6*	18/5X	3.6
Organization											
Brand Cultural Biases	1		*	2	1				2	6/4X	1.5
Bureaucracy			1	1					1*	3/3	1.0
Consolidated Brands		2	1						2*	5/3X	1.7
Corporate Identity	1*									1/1	1.0
Direct Contact Sales		3						1	5	9/3X	3.0
Lack of Technology			1	1		*				2/2	1.0
Payment Policies	4*		1							5/2	2.5
Price/Quality Ratio	2	8	1		3	1		2	1	19/7	2.7
Sales and Distribution	1		2*	1				1*	2	7/5X	1.4
Sales Structures								*	2	2/1X	2.0
Unclear Responsibilities									2*	2/1	2.0
Total Weaknesses	11	19	12	9	9	6	9	8	17		

Note. Countries are listed in the order in which interviews were conducted. Cell numbers show the number of interviews in which a weakness was mentioned. *Indicates a weakness that appeared on a country's list. X indicates a weakness that appeared on the final company list. [a]Indicates the number of interview/country lists on which a weakness appeared. [b]Provides a novelty-saturation ratio showing the number of interviews divided by countries in which a weakness was mentioned.

contributing items to the final company list, both directly through its own interview lists and indirectly through this bleed-over effect onto the list of the other subteam.

Table 10.5 shows the weaknesses identified in the interviews, country lists, and final company report. Many of the items on the final list, such as seed production (23 interviews in 6 countries), seed quality (24 interviews in 6 countries), new product trials (22 interviews in 6 countries), and new product edge loss (18 interviews in 5 countries), appear to occur due to the frequency and diversity with which they are mentioned. However, the country lists of weaknesses also appear to follow the same pattern as the list of strengths, with a bleed over of items from interviews conducted in other countries immediately before, after, or simultaneous to, appearing on some countries' lists. This bleed over adds items to the weakness lists of countries with fewer than 13 items. In addition, some items that should appear on the final list, on the basis of the frequency/diversity of mention principle, such as germination (12 interviews in 5 countries) and price/quality ratio (19 interviews in 7 countries), are missing, whereas advertising budgets (4 interviews in 3 countries) and four-brand perception (1 interview in 1 country) appear on the final list.

In addition to this bleed-over effect, being mentioned early in the interview process appears to have an important positive influence on an item making the final list. In this case, being mentioned in one of the first 21 of the 57 interviews conducted typically assists an idea in appearing on the final list; only the strengths of product specifications and rapid response, and the weaknesses of advertising budgets and sales structures, make the final list without being mentioned during one of these first 21 interviews in France or Italy. This finding of a primacy effect supports Gersick's (1988) argument that groups change predictably through phases of information acquisition and decision making. Gersick sees this predictable change as a punctuated equilibrium process in which a group initially frames an issue on the basis of the information imported into the group and the group's discussion of it at that time. Once established, these frameworks structure the issues and group discussions of them, unless the frameworks are explicitly dropped during a temporal transition period. The pace of a group's development of these frameworks and its need or willingness to change them are part of the complexity of the group decision-making process and a manifestation of the group members' ability to develop new ideas and problems, and to manage communication among themselves and with their external constituencies (Gersick, 1989). The pace and stage of a group's framework development affects how influential external constituents are in being able to introduce new ideas and concepts into the group's thinking. In the initial phase of group interaction and development, and during transition periods, group members' thinking is more easily and substantially influenced than during other phases (Gersick, 1989). The present pattern of results showing a primacy effect indicates the influence of such a punctuated equilibrium in the decision-making processes of this consulting team.

Although ideas that are mentioned early in the process and those that are endorsed by the first subteam (bolded in the table) are more likely to occur on the final list, two other influences are also somewhat predictive of an item appearing on the final list: an idea's frequency saturation and its novelty ratio. Frequency saturation is best illustrated by the company strength item of secure market share, which is mentioned in 26 interviews and in all 8 countries in which interviews took place. This item clearly occurs with more than adequate frequency to reach saturation of mention and appear on the final company list. In fact, all items that are mentioned in at least 20 of the 57 interviews appear on the final list. In addition to secure market share, these items include the strengths of seed quality and sales and distribution, and the weaknesses of seed production, seed quality, and new product trials. In these cases, the frequency with which the ideas are mentioned is a strong-enough influence for them to make the final list.

The influence of this type of saturation effect can be extended to other items on the final list as well, including all items having a novelty ratio higher than 3.0, as calculated by dividing the number of interviews by the number of countries in which they occur. The noted effect of this ratio suggests that, in addition to a saturation effect based on the total number of mentions across all interviews, an important influence on the team's decision-making process is the number of times an idea is mentioned in a particular country. Items that illustrate this novelty ratio effect created by a frequency saturation clustering in a country are the weaknesses of seed availability (13 interviews in 4 countries, novelty ratio = 3.2), promotional materials (11 interviews in 2 countries, novelty ratio = 5.5), breeding methods (7 interviews in 2 countries, novelty ratio = 3.5), and new product edge loss (18 interviews in 5 countries, novelty ratio = 3.6). These items can be compared with those that occurred frequently but did not achieve the same level of saturation within a country and did not make the final list: germination (12 interviews in 5 countries, novelty ratio = 2.4), seed information (10 interviews in 5 countries, novelty ratio = 2.0), and price/quality ratio (19 interviews in 7 countries, novelty ratio = 2.7). Thus, the clustering of the frequency of mention within a country appears to be an important influence on the salience of an idea. When an idea is mentioned frequently in a country in a short period of time, it appears to gain more salience in the team's discussion framework than an idea that is mentioned an equal number of times but over a more scattered set of interviews in different countries and over a longer time span.

In addition to this type of saturation effect, an almost opposite effect appears in the novelty with which an idea is mentioned. A number of ideas appear on the final list that occur in only 4 to 10 interviews in 3 to 6 of the countries in which interviews are conducted. Dividing the number of interviews by the number of countries in which they occur produces for these ideas a novelty ratio of between 1.3 and 1.7. The listing of these ideas on the final lists of strengths and weaknesses suggests a novelty effect. Such strengths as product performance (novelty ratio = 1.3) and service/technical support (novelty ratio = 1.6), and such weaknesses as brand cultural biases (novelty ratio = 1.5), consolidated brands (novelty ratio = 1.7), and sales and distribution (novelty ratio = 1.4), suggest this novelty principle.

It may be notable that these ideas appear in interviews in at least two of the first four countries (earlier than the interviews in the United Kingdom) and all but product performance occur again in interviews done in the Netherlands. This suggests that idea novelty may be assisted by primacy and recency influences that help place these ideas on the final list. In contrast, neither seed variety (novelty ratio = 1.5), which is listed as a strength in interviews in only one of the early countries and not in the Netherlands, nor brand image (novelty ratio = 1.3), which is listed as a weakness in interviews in three of the early countries but not in the Netherlands, make the final list.

Taken together, this pattern of results suggests that the influences on the decision to place an idea on the final list may be complex and depend, at least in part, on saturation, novelty, and the timing of the idea mentioned in the group decision-making process. A novel idea introduced during an early phase of the decision-making process, especially if it is reintroduced during a concluding phase, appears to have a greater potential to make the final company list than an idea that may be mentioned more frequently. The influence of idea novelty and saturation do not predict whether items will make the final lists. However, these influences combine with primacy and recency of mention, and, as previously discussed, the endorsement of the first subteam with its consequent bleed-over effect, to affect the team's discussion and decision-making processes. These combined influences produce a nonlinear, punctuated process by which items become recognized as important by the team and ultimately appear on the final lists.

Some ideas occur on the final list because of their overall saturation of mention, others because of their saturation of mention in interviews in a few countries, particularly when they are mentioned early in the interview process. Still other ideas may be included because their novelty sparks a team member's imagination, especially when they become salient during a key period of team discussion. Ideas that occur with only a mid-range frequency (novelty ratio between 2.0 and 2.5) or during the middle of the interviewing process, however, may appear mundane and, therefore, less important for inclusion on the final lists, or they may be simply forgotten during subsequent discussion of other ideas. Redundancy, without adequate saturation, may produce the perception that an idea is mundane and not of enough interest to be included on the final lists at the time when list-inclusion decisions are made.

In summary, ideas may maintain their salience through a saturation of mention, lose favor with the group by becoming perceived as mundane and ordinary, or be forgotten by the team. Although these influences do not describe the entire list-development decision-making process some ideas that achieve saturation of mention, or an early introduction and later rediscovery in the group discussion, appear to have a stronger potential for making the final company lists of strengths and weaknesses. Investigation of other groups should be conducted before firm conclusions are drawn, but the present data suggest complex, punctuated patterns of contextual influences on the final lists of strengths and weaknesses generated for the company by this bona fide international business consulting team.

CONCLUSION

The bona fide group analysis of these international business consulting teams suggests that permeable, fluid, yet stable boundaries and interdependence with the immediate contexts are substantial and important influences on the teams' communication, decision-making processes, and recommendations. The kitchen appliance team in the first case analysis identified political, economic, infrastructure, technological, and consumer analyses as explicit influences on their decisions and recommendations. Their decisions and recommendations, however, show the effect of other influences as well. The shift over time in the team's conceptualization of the report to be generated and of the type and quantity of recommendations to be made show the influence of the boundary contexts within which those decisions are made. These influences, although less recognized by the teams, appear to have an important impact on their decision-making process. Of particular interest here is the kitchen appliance team's perceived need to explicitly grapple with the complex boundary issues posed by having to report its findings to two companies that are intent on maintaining a competitive as well as a collaborative boundary between them.

The second case analysis explores the effects of immediate contexts on a team's decision-making and list-generating processes. List items might be thought to emerge systematically from the information gathered in interviews and summarized in the recommendation lists of those interviews and for each country. However, other implicit contextual influences—such as being mentioned early in the interview process, championed by a particular subteam, and mentioned with an adequate frequency yet with enough novelty not to become mundane to the team—appear to have an important impact on strengths and weaknesses that appear on the final lists as well.

Reports and recommendations made by international business consulting teams are increasingly important in their implications for the future growth and development of businesses worldwide. My purpose in this chapter has been to analyze some of the specific boundary and context influences on the recommendations made by those teams that were studied. Many of these boundary and context issues are explicitly recognized and accepted by the teams as important influences on their communication, decision-making, and recommendation processes; other influences are less recognized by the teams but no less powerful. The explicit and implicit influences document the complexity of bona fide group communication, decision-making, and recommendation-generating processes. These are competent professional consulting teams that generate recommendations on which international companies base their long-range future business plans and decisions. These important recommendations are affected by many influences, including explicit and implicit boundary factors. Other bona fide groups undoubtedly experience similar influences as well.

REFERENCES

Dawar, N., & Frost, T. (1999, March-April). Competing with giants: Survival strategies for local companies in emerging markets. *Harvard Business Review*, 119–129.

Garten, J. E. (1998, May-June). Opening the doors for business in China. *Harvard Business Review*, 167–175.

Gersick, C. J. G. (1988). Time and transition in work teams: Toward a new model of group development. *Academy of Management Journal, 31*, 9–41.

Gersick, C. J. G. (1989). Marking time: Predictable transitions in task groups. *Academy of Management Journal, 32*, 274–309.

Lammers, J. C., & Krikorian, D. H. (1997). Theoretical extension and operationalization of the bona fide group construct with an application to surgical teams. *Journal of Applied Communication Research, 25*, 17–38.

Putnam, L. L., & Stohl, C. (1990). Bona fide groups: A reconceptualization of groups in context. *Communication Studies, 41*, 248–265.

Putnam, L. L., & Stohl, C. (1996). Bona fide groups: An alternative perspective for communication and small group decision making. In R. Y. Hirokawa & M. S. Poole (Eds.), *Communication and group decision making* (2nd ed., pp. 147–178). Thousand Oaks, CA: Sage.

Stohl, C., & Putnam, L. L. (1994). Group communication in context: Implications for the study of bona fide groups. In L. R. Frey (Ed.), *Group communication in context: Studies of natural groups* (pp. 285–292). Hillsdale, NJ: Lawrence Erlbaum Associates.

Yan, R. (1998, September-October). Short-term results: The litmus test for success in China. *Harvard Business Review*, 61–75.

11

INDEXING THE POLISH TRANSFORMATION: THE CASE OF ECO-S FROM A BONA FIDE GROUP PERSPECTIVE

John Parrish-Sprowl
Indiana University-Purdue University Indianapolis

Much discussion has ensued since the 1980s concerning the nature, constancy, and pace of change, especially in organizational practices (see, e.g., Hammer & Champy, 1993; Hesselbein, Goldsmith, & Beckhard, 1997; Huber & Glick, 1995; Parrish-Sprowl, 2000). The phrase "Nothing is constant except change" is often repeated, particularly in the organizational context. This focus on change has raised several residual issues, perhaps most notably, the concepts of resistance to change and change management. Consequently, practitioners and scholars alike are interested in understanding the dynamics of large-scale change. In this chapter, the role of groups in the process of the social and economic transformation of the postcommunist countries is examined through a case study in the country of Poland.

Change and transformation processes are often examined from a broad macro level, often global or cultural in scope. Sachs (1993), for example, discussed at length (from a macro-economic perspective) the transformation of Poland's economy from that of a command and control to a free-market structure. Such an analysis helps us to gain insight into the big picture of change, but it is difficult to discern the nature of the change process from a more micro, personal level. Knowing that thousands of businesses were created in the first 5 years of Poland's transformation does not tell us much about the experiences of those actually engaged in enterprise formation. Thus, analysis from a macro-level vantage point shows that a transformation is taking place but does not reveal how the process unfolds in practice.

At the micro level, many scholars have examined developmental changes within groups; the research literature is filled with studies exploring group leadership emergence, other types of role development, and the evolution of group performance. Although such research offers meaningful information about internal group processes, it teaches us little about the role that groups play in larger organizational and societal transformations.

An alternative and complementary locus of study to the approaches just reviewed that potentially offers valuable additional insight into change and transformation is to focus on the reflexive relationship between the micro level of group processes and the macro level of the larger contexts within which groups function. The bona fide group perspective is one such framework that shifts our attention to this reflexive relationship and, thereby, offers great potential for expanded understanding of the group processes by which organizations and societies redefine their forms and functions.

Insight into large-scale organizational and societal transformation, thus, would benefit from the investigation of naturally occurring, bona fide groups (for other examples of such groups besides the ones included in this text, see the essays in Frey, 1994a, 1995). Because the privileging of a perspective necessarily illuminates some areas and shadows or blinds us to others, we miss with most traditional approaches to group research the critical links of groups to their larger social order. The historical use of analytical frameworks that treat groups as containers, to be studied as isolated entities, blinds us with respect to how group interaction is influenced by and, in turn, influences the broader contexts in which groups operate. As Putnam and Stohl (1990) and Frey (1994b) pointed out, this tendency to treat groups as containers divorced from their contexts is due, in part, to a body of scholarship built on studying zero-history student groups constructed in laboratories, which, by their very nature, have little connection to anything outside of that context. Consequently, to develop insight into the role of groups in large-scale change, we must step outside of the controlled laboratory environment and into the realm of bona fide groups.

As has been discussed elsewhere (e.g., Frey's introduction, this volume [see pp. 338, 401]; Lammers & Kirkorian, 1997; Putnam & Stohl, 1990, 1996), a bona fide group perspective creates a focus of equal concern on both internal group interaction and its relationship to the broader contexts in which a group operates. This approach allows us to view a group as both an ephemeral notion and as an enduring representation of a larger context (Lammers & Kirkorian, 1997). The former is possible because the perspective begins from a premise that challenges the very notion of "groupness," particularly with respect to viewing a group as having permeable boundaries and shifting borders; the latter evolves from the linkage of a group to the contexts in which its interactions occur, a recognition that establishes a group as a moment in a larger cultural conversation.

With respect to the change and transformation of Poland, the bona fide group perspective is especially enlightening. Although much has been written about the elections, level of foreign investment, privatization activities, and other macro-level indicators of this postcommunist transformation (see, e.g., Blazyca, 1994; Golebiowski, 1994; Gucwa-Lesny, 1996; Kolarska-Bobi'nska, 1994; Sachs, 1993; Weclawowicz, 1996; Wyznikiewicz, Pinto, & Grabowski, 1993), little has been done to analyze the process from a communication perspective and, even more specifically, from a group communication perspective. It is critically important that we understand the how (processes) and why (rationales for actions) to glean from these events insight into the enactment of change and transformation. A bona fide group perspective, with its inherent concern for linkages between a group's internal processes and its broader contexts is a particularly useful analytical framework for investigating the reciprocal relationship between the micro-level conversations that occur within groups and the construction of macro-level transformation. Thus, case studies of group conversations, particularly those groups whose primary purpose is to play a role in transforming contexts, can shine an intellectual light on the processes of creating a new organizational, national, or cultural order.

The following case study took place in Poland during the early years of the transformation from a communist country with a command economy to a democracy with a market economy. These events were triggered by the election of the first noncommunist government in post-WWII Poland. Following the Polish lead, communist governments all over Eastern and Central Europe began to topple, dramatically symbolized by the fall of the Berlin Wall in Germany. The shift in both governmental form and economic model in a relatively brief time frame as a consequence of the 1989 elections makes Poland an ideal laboratory for analyzing the role of naturally occurring groups in large-scale transformation. Because the postcommunist Polish government committed the nation to rapid and systemic change, every member of that society found himself or herself grappling with the process of reform in all aspects of his or her life. To create the necessary changes, Poles formed thousands of groups to develop businesses, social services, political parties, and issue advocacy movements. As I discuss in this chapter, these groups are the embodiment of the larger social change in one of the greatest political, economic, and cultural shifts in the modern era. To clarify the larger social context, I first present a brief discussion of the Polish transition, followed by a description of the particular group that is the subject of this case study. The discussion of the case and context focuses on the reflexive relationship between the two as illuminated by the bona fide group perspective.

POLAND IN TRANSITION

Virtually no one disputes the significance of the collapse of the former U.S.S.R. and the concomitant demise of the Eastern Bloc in the shaping of current global activities. These events not only underpin current international relations but they have also transformed the lives of the citizens of the postcommunist countries in profound ways that permeate every aspect of lived experience (see, e.g., Golebiowski, 1994; Kolarska-Bobi'nska, 1994; Malkiewicz, Parrish-Sprowl, & Waszkiewicz, 1994; Parrish-Sprowl & Engel; 2000; Sachs, 1993). It is of tremendous value not only for members of the changing nations but for everyone in the international community to learn from those who, through their daily interactions, are creating one of the greatest social transformations ever. To analyze this process, I first explain the Polish situation from the time of the Solidarity victory in 1989 to the time of the case examined in this essay. This is followed by a description of a group that met in a retreat to plan the actions of a newly formed company in Poland.

Although the Polish elections of 1989 are clearly a watershed event, they are best understood as a key moment in a long-term process. Poland had been undergoing political and economic change for several years prior to the victory of the Solidarity Trade Union. However, as Sachs (1993) pointed out, the communist government of Poland attempted to change by adjusting the system rather than by rejecting the old economic parameters in favor of a new approach. Throughout the 1980s, it became increasingly apparent that the assumptions behind the old system were flawed and that radical change was needed. In a policy labeled the Balcerowicz Plan, named after the new deputy prime minister for the economy, the Solidarity-led government instituted a rapid and complete shift to a market economy later described as "shock therapy" (Sachs, 1993, p. 42). This bold move created the conditions that could result in a transformation of Polish society, not only economically but politically and socially as well.

Poland was the first of the communist bloc European nations to initiate sweeping democratic and economic reforms and begin a process of rapidly converting to a capitalist economy. By 1993, it boasted a growing private sector, with 500,000 new companies coming into existence since the 1989 elections. It converted its currency and its economy gradually began to show signs of competitiveness in world markets. Exports were on the rise and along with 50% of its $33 billion in foreign debt forgiven, Poland's fiscal situation started improving (Sachs, 1993).

The first few years of Poland's economic transformation, however, were not a steady march toward development but, instead, were quite turbulent. Immediately following Poland's political shift, a steep drop in trade with the Soviet Union ensued. Industry suffered a 23% drop in 1990 and declined another 40% in the first quarter of 1991. Inflation, although down from a January 1990 rate of 250%, remained high at 48.5% for 1992 and 37% for 1993. Unemployment soared and Poland scrambled to privatize State enterprises. The country fell behind Hungary and Czechoslovakia in implementing reforms due to a political deadlock between the Finance, Privatization, and Industry Ministries (Schares, 1991). Poland's president at the time, Lech Walesa, turned to Western consultants for advice (most notably, Jeffry Sachs) and foreign investors to spur development. This shock therapy resulted in a nearly complete break with the communist system of the past; laws were enacted allowing a private banking system, the opening of a stock market, and guarantees of 100% fund repatriation for foreign investors in an attempt to lure their interest (Sachs, 1993; Tull, 1991).

Unfortunately, economic hardships, scandal, and corruption continued to eat away at the newly instituted system (Blazyca, 1994). Although a decommunization resolution was proposed by several members of the Sjem (the Polish legislature) in an attempt to remove from executive positions all former members of the communist elite, there were simply not enough experienced people with no communist ties prepared to take over quickly. Large State-owned companies trudging through this transitional period, reducing employee ranks and increasing productivity, fought against this corruption, as well as the lack of motivation and low confidence on the part of their staffs, in an effort to become competitive enterprises. Newly formed organizations faced the same problems as well and, although they did not need to engage in layoffs, they suffered from a system not designed to support the development of small business.

The tensions that existed in the people and economy of Poland in 1993 were not surprising considering that the country was undergoing an unparalleled redefinition of itself, metamorphosing from a "system" of a centralized, command economy to an increasingly decentralized economy with a free market (Kolarska-Bobi'nska, 1994). In Poland, such a shift in identity and lifestyle was of particular significance given the substantial role that tradition plays in the culture. Daily activities during the transition reflected long-practiced patterns of community life still devoid of modern consumerism. This aspect of Polish culture stands in sharp contrast to the U.S. experience. As one observer noted in 1990:

> Economics has become virtually the only lens through which we view developments in the former East Bloc. There's a great deal about Poland, ... that doesn't show up in the GNP [Gross National Product]. Family ties are strong. People eat at home, their foods are grown locally. There is not much packaging, litter or waste. People still read. Boom boxes don't disrupt the parks.

Shopping malls haven't replaced the traditional town center, which reinforces a sense of social cohesion and community. (Rowe, 1990, p. 21)

In addition to the 1,000-plus year history of the Polish culture, tradition
plays a strong role because it has been critical to the preservation of the culture when invaders have made a concerted effort to wipe it out (Davies,
1982). As such, internally inspired transformational shifts in cultural practices are far-reaching in their consequences for both national and personal
identities in Poland (Barber, 1995). In this case, because market economics
by their very nature reject tradition in favor of innovation and efficiency,
Poland faced an especially difficult transition.

By 1993, however, the intrusions of free-market/democratic activity had
begun to creep into Polish daily life (Blazyca, 1994; Gucwa-Lesny, 1996).
Advertisements were popping up all over where none had previously existed; people were able to access a vastly broader array of media; and
McDonalds, Pizza Hut, and other chain restaurants, along with several various other types of Western-style service providers, began to spring up in
major cities in Poland. With these changes came a new set of occupational
choices, alternative leisure activities, and new topics of discussion, along
with, on the downside, an increase in consumer waste.

Whereas it is one matter to declare that a society is now based on competition, supply and demand, and other capitalistic ideals when it previously
was not, it is quite another to embrace these concepts and practices and
change several generations worth of cultural and national experience. Poland had found itself, much like other countries in the former Eastern Bloc,
looking for answers to questions that no one had heretofore had to ask
(Sachs, 1993). Years of economic training in Poland had focused on how to
transform capitalism into socialism, not the other way around. Without a
reservoir of talent, expertise, and experience in how to affect such a transformation, the Poles faced a serious challenge with no guideposts along
the path. As the following case study shows, the lack of guideposts was
bound to affect the very groups that were working to change the system.

CREATING ECO-S

The group of people that I studied came together in September 1993 to
plan the activities of a newly formed recycling company. The company,
named Eco-S, had received a grant from the city of Wroclaw, Poland, to begin recycling efforts in various neighborhoods. Wroclaw is a large, industri-
alized metropolitan area with about 700,000 residents. It is located in the
southwest corner of the country and is one of the largest cities in Poland.
Because the communist government had engaged in virtually no environmentally sound practices, the problems associated with environmental
mismanagement took on special importance in postcommunist Poland.

Furthermore, as consumer waste, historically not a problem, began to develop as a result of growing consumerism, government officials felt the need to act. Rather than solving the problem via government intervention, as in the past, the city government of Wroclaw sought to have the issue of recycling addressed by private enterprise. Given that no companies offering this sort of service existed, because no previous market for such an enterprise had ever developed, new companies needed to be formed. By winning the grant from the city, Eco-S was in a position of some urgency, as the service would soon need to commence; yet the company did not exist as an operating entity. Because several decisions needed to be made, a group of about 10 to 15 people (the number changed at various times) went on a weekend retreat to Karpasz, a mountain resort village south of the city, to engage in strategic planning. I was invited along both to participate and observe.

This was my third trip to Poland and the beginning of a semester-long stay. During my first two trips to Poland, I conducted two seminars that were part of a multiunit communication series, which, in turn, was part of a larger United States Agency for International Development (USAID) program designed to offer technical assistance to Poles as they engaged in economic and political transition. The purpose behind the communication seminars was to acquaint the participants with the communication knowledge and skills necessary for the effective functioning of successful organizations in the new economic and political conditions of the country. The first session I conducted focused on organizational communication; the second covered negotiation and conflict. Participants in the seminar series included academics and professionals from a variety of backgrounds, all with a keen interest in communication. In those workshops, I met most of the people who would later be members of the Eco-S retreat group.

Following those workshops, which occurred in January and February of 1993, I was presented with the opportunity to spend the fall semester of that year in Poland, with the purpose of becoming further involved in change and transformation activities related to communication. Specifically, my activities included lecturing and developing communication curricula for two universities in Wroclaw, along with conducting workshops and consulting for various organizations. The leaders of the Eco-S group, as well as many of the others involved in the company, having met me at the seminars earlier in the year, knew that I would be interested in their activities. Consequently, the leaders told me that my participation in the retreat would present a valuable opportunity for all of us, so they extended an invitation to join them for the weekend.

Although pleased with this chance to engage in a participant-observational study of a unique group, given that I had almost no knowledge of the Polish language at the time, I questioned what I might do at such a gathering. The group leaders assured me that my presence would be useful and that I would be given constant translation of the proceedings as they unfolded. As it turned out, this worked well; because the sessions were, as described later, mostly lecture rather than discussion, the translator had a relatively easy time keeping me abreast of the proceedings. Armed with their assurances, I prepared to participate in the retreat.

Despite the fact that everyone was traveling from the same city, we arrived in many separate cars; given the cost of automobiles and gasoline relative to the economic conditions, this in itself was remarkable. I traveled with a Polish colleague whom I had met on one of my previous trips to Poland. In addition to being a member of the faculty at the Technical University of Wroclaw, he served as one of the principal members in the Eco-S project. Because I had not seen this area of the country before, we engaged in a sightseeing tour and the trip took about 6 hours instead of the normal 2 hours of a direct drive. In our conversation along the way, I discovered that all of the members of the retreat group knew each other from previous collaborations, although some were better acquainted than others. As discussed later, such collaborations between friends was a growing phenomenon in postcommunist Poland.

Many of the retreat group members had been university students together; some had been and still were professors at the Technical University of Wroclaw. Several of the younger participants had spent time in North America, some in the United States and others in Canada, and, consequently, Western practices were not totally unfamiliar to them. One common thread for all of the group members was some form of participation in opposition to the communist government that previously had ruled Poland. Given their backgrounds, all were supporters of the transformation of Poland to a democratic nation with a market economy. Some had been active in Solidarity, including a few with high-level positions in that organization; others had been active participants in underground radio broadcasting during the period of martial law in the early 1980s; and many had been student activists who had protested, written articles in underground papers, and engaged in various other oppositional activities. Through these activities they had collaborated in various ways in the past. Thus, the retreat group was simply a new collaboration that brought together friends and colleagues in their continued efforts to change Poland.

We arrived at the retreat hotel around 5 p.m. on Friday evening. We first rested and then had dinner as a group. After dinner, we walked around the area, following a trail until slightly past sundown. We then had a business session for about an hour and a half, followed by several hours of telling stories and drinking vodka. We turned in about 3 in the morning. Breakfast commenced at 8 a.m. and we then worked from 9 until 1 p.m., at which time we had lunch. After lunch, we went on an excursion, riding a chair lift to the top of the mountain. We then rested for about 2 hours. At about 6 p.m., we had dinner followed by about 2 hours of work. Again, as in the previous evening, work ceased promptly at 9 p.m. and socializing began, this time lasting until about 4 a.m. The next morning breakfast was served at 8 followed by a 4-hour work session. We then dispersed and returned to Wroclaw.

As this timetable reveals, over the course of the weekend, social activities comprised a much greater portion of the schedule than did work sessions. On one level, this privileging of social interaction reflected the friendship shared between the members of the group, but more important, for the purposes of this chapter, it also represented an approach to work that was consistent with the communist past when productivity was considered virtually a nonissue. Consequently, during the retreat, I occasionally found myself thinking that, for this group, work was a respite from walking, sightseeing, drinking, and dining rather than the other way around. This pattern of behavior, although manifested in ways consistent with Polish culture, was much more a reflection of postwar communist work patterns.

In contrast to the socializing activities, the work sessions were not highly interactive. They were led by the same person (with one exception) and were more in the form of lecture than discussion. Based on my observations throughout the weekend and subsequently during the semester I spent at the university, I believe that the leader, a professor at the Technical University of Wroclaw, was probably more familiar with this presentational form than a more highly interactive format and that this was probably the case for most of the participants as well. Consequently, very few questions were asked and almost no other comments were made. The first session (Friday night) consisted of an overview lecture explaining the genesis of Eco-S and describing the tasks that needed to be accomplished by the retreat group and the company leadership after the retreat. The material covered was presented by the leader in general terms and did not seem to prescribe a specific agenda. In subsequent sessions, this same pattern emerged; the lecturer presented the topic and proceeded to describe what needed to be done with few specifics given and little effort to create a specific action plan.

I found this approach to strategic planning to be quite different from my experiences with such group discussions in the United States. Given the backgrounds of the various group members, especially those members who had spent time in North America, I expected a much different pattern of interaction—one that stressed the sharing of the thoughts and perspectives of all of the members of the group. The type of interaction (or lack thereof) that characterized the work sessions, however, did not extend into the social hours; those, in contrast, were quite lively, with everyone engaged. Even at the times when one person was telling a story or joke, the others appeared more attuned to the speaker and demonstrated a greater readiness to participate afterward in an exchange with other members than they had demonstrated during the work sessions.

By the close of the weekend, several key points had been presented to the group for members' consideration but no action plan had been created. Moreover, members had no agenda for their participation in Eco-S after the retreat was over. Thus, although everyone was aware of the group's needs with respect to logistics, marketing, equipment, and other important matters, how they were to proceed was unclear after the retreat was concluded. Eco-S had somehow been launched but the future trajectory of the company was uncharted. Despite the uncertainty of the future, however, the weekend was declared a success by all of the members who shared their perspective with me, and we all went on our way.

DISCUSSION

The process of rapid, large-scale institutional transformation relies on the creation of multiple groups to accomplish the tasks that process entails; the actions of those bona fide groups are the lynchpin of this process. Although it is not necessarily essential for any given group to be successful in accomplishing specific goals or even in sustaining its existence, the success of a transformation as a whole depends on the establishment and subsequent work of such groups. In the case of Poland, the first wave of the shift to a market economy was accomplished by the creation of thousands of businesses by small groups of entrepreneurs. The establishment of a viable, decentralized economy was not predicated on the success of any particular business developed in this early period; however, without such group efforts, no market economy could come to exist in Poland.

The members of the group that I studied, although committed to the success of Eco-S, were not themselves necessarily committed to that particular group over the long term. In part, this lack of group commitment was due paradoxically to the permeable boundaries of the group. In all likelihood, without permeable group boundaries, several of the members would not have participated in this retreat, much less the founding of Eco-S. However, because of the permeable boundaries, most saw themselves as creators not sustainers of this company. All were employed elsewhere and they had no intention of relinquishing their positions. Such multiple occupational group memberships became common during the early stages of the Polish transformation period. As a result, many Poles were involved in more than one business startup. Thus, multiple group memberships serve as an important vehicle that both affords opportunities and sometimes creates constraints for the citizens in the transformation of their nation.

It is at the group level that the connection between macro and micro structures meet, serving similar purposes simultaneously, and the members of the retreat group were well aware of this reflexive relationship between macro-level accomplishments and micro-level efforts. The various members saw this group as one of many whose raison d'être was to effect the transformation. However, even as they set about the process of creating something new, the members of Eco-S tended to do so using familiar, historical discursive patterns. In other words, even while engaging in the endeavor to create something "outside of the box," the group members did so by relying on patterns created from within their historically familiar milieu. One example of such a pattern was the format of the working periods of the retreat. These sessions were invariably didactic, with the leader doing virtually all of the talking and the rest of the group engaged in very little discussion. This type of authoritarian approach to strategic planning retreats was much more characteristic of Poland's communist past than the contemporary practice of market-economy businesses in democratic countries.

Breaks were also frequent and generally rather long, given the short time frame of the retreat. This slow-paced approach to conducting business is antithetical to the typical efficient and productivity-focused sessions found in businesses within competitive economies. Competitive pressures tend to mitigate against such time-consuming group interactional patterns. Although most, if not all, of the retreat group members viewed the weekend as a success, virtually no organization in the United States would accept gaining so little from such a retreat, given the time invested in it. Thus, although this group was most desirous and at the forefront of change in Poland, the members tended to engage in the long-practiced discursive patterns that were no different from those born of their cultural and communist pasts.

Considering the outcome of their retreat, most traditional perspectives on group communication and decision making would view the members of Eco-S as ineffective in their performance. Indeed, some scholars might not see them as exhibiting the qualities of "groupness" at all, given the loose commitment to the group by most "members." From a bona fide group perspective, however, Eco-S is not only a group but a successful one as well. Because the bona fide group perspective shifts the focus from groups as containers to groups as embedded in larger contexts, such entities as the Eco-S group and the first wave of Polish businesses can be viewed in a new light. Each of these collective efforts may be considered to be groups, however brief their duration or how loosely people are committed to the group, when understood from a larger contextual perspective. The quality of groupness in the case of the Eco-S retreat group is as much derived from the process of societal transformation as it is from the internal dynamics of that particular group.

Putnam and Stohl (1996) asserted that "boundaries simultaneously separate and link groups to multiple contexts. Group members change, redefine, and negotiate their borders through (a) multiple group membership and conflicting role identities, (b) representative roles, (c) fluctuating membership, and (d) group identity formation" (p. 150). During the early years of the Polish transformation, people formed groups to achieve the national aims of instituting democracy and a market economy. As a consequence, many people belonged to multiple groups, which often produced conflicting role identities. "Members" joined and left groups with regularity and, consequently, group identification was ephemeral. Eco-S exemplifies this phenomenon. It would be a mistake however, to assume that commitment to and identification with the groups to which people belonged was weak. To the contrary, members' sense of affiliation with the groups to which they belonged was strong and their desire for success great. These qualities were derived from the national context and instantiated in group interaction. Hence, with respect to Eco-S, despite the outward appearance of a minimal sense of groupness, several of the members informed me that they were quite serious about the group and its purpose and felt a strong identification with the group. Their commitment and identification to Eco-S was based not on the group's immediate goal of developing a recycling firm but on being one important spoke in the wheel of progress toward the transformation of Polish society.

From the bona fide group perspective, the strategic planning process of the Eco-S retreat was a success. As Putnam and Stohl (1996) argued, "Typically, research on effectiveness treats decision quality as an objective attribute that surfaces at the time of the decision" (p. 163). They explained that a bona fide group perspective, in contrast, views decision making as an aspect of group interaction that takes place within larger contextual and temporal processes. Thus, from a traditional perspective of group communication, it would be nearly impossible to declare the retreat a success; however, when viewed as a contribution to the transformation of Poland rather than as an isolated event, it may be considered successful in that the retreat happened at all.

Taking a bona fide group perspective, thus, recognizes the importance of a contextual perspective in judging the success of any particular group decision-making process. In the case of the Eco-S retreat group, viewing the Polish situation as *merely* a social context or external factor misses the point; the retreat group was successful precisely because it reflected both the societal transformation that was underway and helped to produce it. When economists such as Sachs (1993) noted the success of the Polish transformation up to that point in time of the retreat, they were making macro-level claims on the basis of the actions of the many groups involved, such as the Eco-S retreat group. Without these group efforts, irrespective of their individual, long-term performance, the collective transformation would not have occurred. The quality of the decision making of these particular groups, then, has to be judged in the context of the societal transformation process of which they are a vital part, as opposed to viewing them as isolated group experiences.

The Eco-S retreat group was, however, simultaneously both successful and unsuccessful in achieving its aims. The members of the group could rightfully feel a sense of accomplishment with respect to contributing to the macro-level Polish transformation; they engaged in an activity (free enterprise) that was distinctly of the new order, and because they recognized their active participation in that new order, they felt good about the retreat. At the same time, the gap between their actions and what is necessary to achieve successful free-market performance remained substantial. Only later would the members begin to understand that disparity.

Finally, this case illustrates the importance of a bona fide group perspective for consultants as well as for researchers. During the early transformation period, Poles were frequently frustrated and angry with U.S. consultants because they felt that the suggestions and prescriptions being offered by those consultants were unnecessarily harsh in their implicit as well as explicit criticism of the Polish approach to economic and social change. Poles often felt that these consultants made no effort to understand their country or its culture. The effect in many cases was to slow down rather than speed up the rate of progress. The bona fide group perspective sheds important light on this potential problem. From this vantage point, anyone who wishes to intervene in such group processes needs to understand and appreciate the contexts within which such groups operate. For instance, a consultant should expect participants in such groups to engage in discursive practices that are familiar to them. In 1993, in the case of the Eco-S retreat group, as with most other Poles, the members were not familiar, much less proficient, with the conversational patterns that characterized successful business in a market economy (Parrish-Sprowl, 1994). The transformation process is as much as anything a learning curve associated with developing the ability to engage in a new discourse. The difficulty in developing the resources and practices necessary to progress on this curve was illustrated by the members of the Eco-S retreat group as they talked in ways familiar to them, even while attempting something new and different. Rather than engaging each other in a highly interactive format designed to move the group toward a defined strategic action plan, the group enacted discursive practices that reflected the historical, hierarchical, and rigid approach to group life with which they were familiar.

CONCLUSION

The process of enacting successful macro-level societal change and trans-formation is, indeed, difficult (Parrish-Sprowl, 2000). Developing an un-derstanding of that process necessitates, in part, a focus on the groups that, through their collective efforts, enact the new order. The dramatic events in Poland provide a historically unique opportunity to understand how changes at the macro level influence and, in turn, are influenced by changes at the micro level—in this case, in the groups that helped to forge those changes. As the analysis of these events reveals, a bona fide group perspective is particularly illuminating for two reasons. First, it illustrates the critical role that groups play in the process of systemic change and transformation. As such, this study illustrates the importance of under-standing groups not only within the contexts in which they operate but also as the embodiment of and genesis for those contexts.

Second, employing a bona fide group perspective in a study of the post-communist transformation context highlights the similarity between the traditional view of groups as containers and communism with its closed system and, conversely, the similarity of a bona fide group perspective with its focus on permeable group boundaries, shifting group borders, and the connection of groups to the larger contexts within which they are embed-ded and a free-market, open system. This comparison not only under-scores the important role that groups play in systemic change and transformation, it reminds us to be mindful that the perspective we take frames our sense of how things work and what constitutes meaningful and effective action. The study examined in this chapter shows that a bona fide group perspective can serve well to guide researchers, consultants, and group members as they struggle to understand, facilitate, and enact sys-temic change and transformation.

REFERENCES

Barber, B. R. (1995). *Jihad vs. Mcworld: How globalism and tribalism are reshap-ing the world*. New York: Random House.

Blazyca, B. (1994). *The economic consequences of post-communism in Poland*. Pais-ley, Scotland: Department of Economics & Management, University of Paisley.

Davies, N. (1982). *God's playground, a history of Poland*. New York: Columbia University Press.

Frey, L. R. (Ed.). (1994a). *Group communication in context: Studies of natural groups*. Hillsdale, NJ: Lawrence Erlbaum Associates.

Frey, L. R. (1994b). The naturalistic paradigm: Studying small groups in the postmodern era. *Small Group Research, 25*, 551–577.

Frey, L. R. (Ed.). (1995). *Innovations in group facilitation: Applications in natu-ral settings*. Cresskill, NJ: Hampton Press.

Golebiowski, J. W. (Ed.). (1994). *Transforming the Polish economy*. Warsaw, Poland: Warsaw School of Economics.

Gucwa-Lesny, E. (1996). *Four years after velvet revolution: Who is better off? Who feels better? In new socio-economic conditions*. Warsaw, Poland: Faculty of Economic Sciences, University of Warsaw.

Hammer, M., & Champy, J. (1993). *Reengineering the corporation: A manifesto for business revolution*. New York: HarperBusiness.

Hesselbein, F., Goldsmith, M., & Beckhard, R. (Eds.). (1997). *The organization of the future*. San Francisco: Jossey-Bass.

Huber, G. P., & Glick, W. H. (1995). *Organizational change and redesign: Ideas and insights for improving performance*. New York: Oxford University Press.

Kolarska-Bobi'nska, L. (1994). *Aspirations, values and interests: Poland 1989–94*. Warsaw, Poland: IFiS.

Lammers, J. C., & Kirkorian, D. H. (1997). Theoretical extension and operationalization of the bona fide group construct with an application to surgical teams. *Journal of Applied Communication Research, 25*, 17–38.

Malkiewicz, A., Parrish-Sprowl, J., & Waszkiewicz, J. (Eds.). (1994). *Komunikacja spoleczna w procesach transformacyjnych* [Social communication in the transformation process]. Wroclaw, Poland: Instytut Nauk Ekonomiczo-Spolecznych Politechniki Wroclawskiej.

Parrish-Sprowl, J. (1994). Organizational issues in Poland's economic transformation: A communication perspective. In A. Malkiewicz, J. Parrish-Sprowl, & J. Waszkiewicz (Eds.), *Komunikacja spoleczna w procesach transformacyjnych* [Social communication in the transformation process] (pp. 77–83). Wroclaw, Poland: Instytut Nauk Ekonomiczo-Spolecznych Politechniki Wroclawskiej.

Parrish-Sprowl, J. (2000). Communication, organizational management and industrial development. In A. A. Moemeka (Ed.), *Development communication in action: Building understanding and creating participation* (pp. 179–202). Lanham, MD: University Press of America.

Parrish-Sprowl, J., & Engel, E. P. (2000). The evolution of cybernetic civic discourse in post-communist Poland. In L. Lengel (Ed.), *Culture and technology in the new Europe: Civic discourse in transformation in post-communist nations* (pp. 239–252). Stamford, CT: Ablex.

Putnam, L. L., & Stohl, C. (1990). Bona fide groups: A reconceptualization of groups in context. *Communication Studies, 41*, 248–265.

Putnam, L. L., & Stohl, C. (1996). Bona fide groups: An alternative perspective for communication and small group decision making. In R. Y. Hirokawa & M. S. Poole (Eds.), *Communication and group decision making* (2nd ed., pp. 147–178). Thousand Oaks, CA: Sage.

Rowe, J. (1990, November). The stupidity of free-market chic in Eastern Europe. *Washington Monthly*, 20–26.

Sachs, J. (1993). *Poland's jump to the market economy*. Cambridge, MA: MIT Press.

Schares, G. E., (1991, April 15) Poland: The pain and the gain. *Business Week*, p. 54.

Tull, S. (1991, July 29). Who's who in the East. *Fortune*, 155–160.

Weclawowicz, G. (1996). *Contemporary Poland: Space and society*. Boulder CO: Westview Press.

Wyznikiewicz, B., Pinto, B., & Grabowski, M. (1993). *Coping with capitalism: The new Polish entrepreneurs*. Washington, DC: World Bank.

VI

MEDIATED GROUPS:

NEGOTIATING COMMUNICATION AND RELATIONSHIPS ELECTRONICALLY

12

HELP IS AT YOUR KEYBOARD: SUPPORT GROUPS ON THE INTERNET

Stewart C. Alexander
Veterans Affairs Center for Primary Care Health Services Research

Jennifer L. Peterson
University of Wisconsin–Milwaukee

Andrea B. Hollingshead
University of Illinois, Urbana-Champaign

Since the 1980s, people have turned increasingly to support groups for aid in coping with physical illnesses, addictions, and mental health problems (see Cline, 1999). In fact, over a 1-year period, approximately 3 to 4% of the U.S. population has used a support group (Kessler, Mickelson, & Zhao, 1997). The philosophy underlying most support groups is that people are able to deal most effectively with their needs or problems by coming together in a group with others who have similar needs or problems to disclose, listen, and learn (Yalom, 1985). Thus, members of support groups have the common goals of sharing information, offering and receiving emotional support, and releasing built-up stress. These groups are facilitated by individuals who have some experience with the problem or issue but are generally not therapists or health professionals (Borkman, 1990).

Traditionally, support groups have been loosely structured groups with less than 15 members that meet face-to-face. Recently, however, thousands of support groups have been established on the Internet. For instance, the results of a quick search on the Internet show over 100

Internet support groups for those living with cancer and their families alone. Internet support groups exist to deal with a large number of problems and issues, ranging from AIDS, rape, incest, shyness, addiction, suicide, and even such rare illnesses as male breast cancer. Many traditional face-to-face support groups, such as Alcoholics Anonymous and Parents Without Partners, have also established Internet support groups. The emotional benefits of participating in these mediated support groups are the major reasons why many health maintenance organizations, hospitals, and community health centers have started to investigate the feasibility of starting these support groups for their clients (Hawkins et al., 1997).

Internet support groups can take the form of *asynchronous groups*, which are groups where members do not necessarily read and send messages at the same time, such as a newsgroup (see Krikorian & Kiyomiya, chap. 13, this volume), or *synchronous groups*, where people meet at the same time to exchange messages, such as in a chat room. Unlike face-to-face support groups, Internet support groups have no specific meeting places or times and are open 24 hours a day, 7 days a week. Internet support groups are generally open to the public, although there are private groups that restrict membership and some asynchronous groups have a moderator who screens and edits the messages that are presented to the group. Perhaps most important, these groups provide opportunities to participate in a support group for those individuals who live in remote areas, are too sick to leave their homes, or want anonymity (Weinberg, Schmale, Uken, & Wessel, 1995).

Internet support groups provide an excellent opportunity to study groups from a bona fide group perspective. This perspective views groups as social systems interdependent with their contexts, shaped by permeable and fluid boundaries, and altering their environments (Putnam & Stohl, 1990, 1996). Internet support groups have permeable and fluid boundaries in that, in most cases, anyone can gain access to and contribute to them, and participants can simultaneously be members of multiple support groups. Members often bring information into these groups from sources outside the group. Moreover, because most Internet support groups are open to the public and easily accessible, researchers can study them.

In this chapter, we present a comparative case analysis of four Internet support groups that address a wide range of health-related issues: cancer, attention-deficit disorder, depression, and alcoholism. We examined these support groups from a bona fide group perspective, focusing on: (a) *membership and group boundaries*, in terms of how membership is defined in Internet support groups; (b) *intragroup communication*, with respect to how social support is provided in these groups; and (c) *intergroup communication*, or how these groups are interdependent with their context.

THE FOUR INTERNET SUPPORT GROUPS

The bona fide group perspective stresses the importance of understanding the background and history of the group that is studied. To that end, we present a brief description of the problem or issue that is the focus of each of the Internet support groups studied.

Alcoholics Anonymous (AA) is the method used most commonly to treat alcoholism, boasting more than 2,000,000 members worldwide (Cline, 1999). AA is free of medical and psychological advice (i.e., information provided by professionals who treat alcoholism), and focuses solely on helping individuals to deal with their alcoholism (Watson et al., 1997). AA members often report that the strength of AA groups is that through the sharing of personal stories, individuals are able to change their perspective on alcoholism as an illness (Wright, 1997). It is often difficult to observe and record AA groups because the organization assures anonymity to those who participate and its membership is never recorded and is often in flux (Kassel & Wagner, 1993); however, the Internet offers a unique opportunity to study AA support groups because all of the proceedings are conducted in public.

Attention-deficit disorder (ADD) is a newly recognized physical and mental affliction (Koziol, Stout, & Ruben, 1993). However, there is debate within the medical community as to what ADD is and how to treat it (see Bawden, 1993). Individuals who suffer from ADD and their loved ones often report feeling misunderstood by members of the general public (Parker, 1994; Thomas, 1991). In fact, members of face-to-face ADD support groups tend to report a high need for social support because of the perceived inability of societal members to completely understand and accept the disorder (Parker, 1994).

People with cancer often report that medical treatment alone is not enough for coping with cancer but do not feel comfortable expressing their thoughts and emotions to personnel in a hospital setting (Ford, Fallowfield, & Lewis, 1996). In fact, cancer patients' emotions are often the least discussed topic in a medical setting (Siminoff & Fetting, 1991). Therefore, people with cancer often participate in support groups. In general, an Internet cancer support group focuses on a physical problem for which a lot of information exists, but because that information is constantly changing and tends to be complex, it is sometimes difficult for people with cancer to understand (Sutherland, Lockwood, Tritchler, Brooks, & Till, 1991).

As in other support groups dealing with illnesses, understanding diagnoses and various treatments is an important component of depression support groups (Karp, 1992). Participants' disclosures about their experiences with various drugs and therapies and their need to rely on medical experts for their problem are central themes in face-to-face depression self-help groups (Karp, 1992). Internet support groups have also been shown to provide the same benefits for depressed individuals as do face-to-face support groups (Salem, Bogart, & Reid, 1997).

MEMBERSHIP AND GROUP BOUNDARIES IN INTERNET SUPPORT GROUPS

Groups change, redefine, and renegotiate their boundaries through multiple group memberships, conflicting role identities, fluctuations in membership, group identity formation, and representative roles (Putnam & Stohl, 1996). Group membership in face-to-face support groups is generally restricted, of course, to the relatively small number of people who attend meetings. It is much more difficult, however, for researchers to identify who is and is not a member of Internet support groups. Some individuals post messages often, sometimes daily or weekly; some post infrequently, perhaps biweekly or monthly; and some members post only once. For some Internet support groups, such as cancer newsgroups, there are often literally hundreds of people who post at least one message to the newsgroup.

Members' roles in a group are linked to their responsibilities within the group and to their identities outside of the group (Putnam & Stohl, 1996). Identities outside of a group may be influenced by a title, prestige, or status, among other characteristics, imported from outside the group. This is particularly true for Internet support groups, where imported identities are expressed in various ways. Members of Internet groups can identify their messages with their given names, a pseudonym, or no name to maintain a sense of anonymity. Members also express and develop identities through *signature files*, which appear at the end of messages and might consist of quotes, pictures, professional titles, or other defining information. For example, a physician who posts messages to an Internet support group might include a signature file containing a disclaimer indicating that the contents of the messages are not generated as part of a professional evaluation. Although this disclaimer serves to protect the physician from malpractice, it also reminds participants that this individual is a physician and, therefore, solidifies his or her role as a medical authority. However, physicians may enact various other roles in the support group, such as friend, family member, or a fellow person living with cancer. In contrast, there may be members of an Internet support group who choose not to make public their roles or expertise in other groups or contexts. Because postings are anonymous to some extent in Internet support groups, participants have more freedom to decide on the roles they will take within the group than they do in face-to-face support groups.

Research shows that a large percentage of individuals who subscribe to Internet support groups read messages by other members but never post messages themselves; these individuals are typically referred to as *lurkers* (Winzelberg, 1997). Lurkers rarely participate in surveys of newsgroup members; therefore, little is known about who they are and their motivations to read the messages of newsgroups. Hence, although lurkers are subscribers, it is debatable whether these individuals can be considered group members (McLaughlin, Osborn, & Smith, 1995).

One basic tenet of traditional support groups is that members must have firsthand experience with the issue or problem for which the support group is designed (excluding counselors and other professionals; Gladding, 1995). In addition to the person actually dealing with the issue or problem addressed by a support group, there are numerous friends and family members who also benefit from participating in a support group. However, because group boundaries are more permeable in Internet support groups than in face-to-face support groups, individuals who contribute to the interaction do not necessarily always have direct experience dealing with the issue or problem (Salem et al., 1997). Contributors to such groups may also include professionals who are interested in providing therapeutic assistance to members and vendors of products designed to treat the condition. A number of cases have also been documented of people pretending to be sick so they could join Internet support groups (see Grady, 1998). In this study, we examine issues related to group membership and boundaries; specifically, who are the participants of Internet support groups and what are their characteristics.

INTERNAL COMMUNICATION: HOW SOCIAL SUPPORT IS PROVIDED IN INTERNET SUPPORT GROUPS

As explained previously, individuals join support groups to give and receive support from empathetic others (Wright, 2000). Support groups, in general, provide members with opportunities to share their stories, find emotional support for dealing with important issues, develop a sense of empowerment, and seek advice and opinions on how to deal with situations from other individuals coping with the same issue or problem (Braithwaite, Waldron, & Finn, 1999). Social support is exchanged in such groups in at least four forms: informational support, esteem support, emotional support, and tangible assistance (Cutrona, Suhr, & McFarlane, 1990).

Informational support provides recipients with information to help deal with stressful situations. Informational support is offered by referring people to informational resources, summarizing and redefining the situation, and providing specific facts about the problem or issue. As one example of informational support, a posting to the Internet cancer support group read, "This site I found very informative for determining if information is accurate was http://www.quackwatch.com."

Emotional support deals with individuals' feelings, primarily in terms of relieving negative emotions and sometimes supplementing them with positive emotions. Individuals can express emotional support for one another by sharing their sorrow and regret, expressing understanding of the situation, or disclosing a personal situation that communicates understanding and lets another person know that he or she is not alone. People can also express a willingness to help, along with stressing the importance of closeness and love among group members, promise to keep another's problem in confidence, make attentive comments, and provide each other with hope and confidence. Providing someone with physical attention, such as a smile or a hug, is also a way to provide emotional support. In Internet environments, participants use a special type of symbol, called *emoticons*, to express emotion and communicate face-to-face nonverbal expressions in a medium where these cues are missing (McGrath & Hollingshead, 1994). Symbolic nonverbal communication, for instance, can welcome someone with a smile :) or support him or her with a hug ((((Joe))).

Esteem support is used to make others feel good about themselves by demonstrating respect through compliments, validation of opinions and beliefs, alleviation of guilt felt by others, and offers of encouragement. Previous research has shown that social support groups with higher levels of emotional support also have higher levels of esteem support (Gustafson et. al., 1993); this is not surprising given that individuals often attempt to make people feel better by providing support that conveys positive feelings or by trying to alleviate negative feelings. Of the four types of support, both emotional and esteem help individuals to change negative feelings to positive ones (Cutrona & Suhr, 1994). An example of esteem support from the AA Internet support group occurs when members commonly wish each other a happy birthday for the number of years they have been sober: "Happy 21st ... the applause you hear is from your higher power."

Tangible assistance provides recipients with direct help by offering to lend a helping hand in the form of, for instance, money, babysitting, or meals. An example of tangible assistance from the AA Internet support group is a posting that read, "I live in Seattle, too, so if you ever need a ride to a meeting or need to talk to someone (who is local), just send me an email and I will give you my phone number, ok?"

We expected that the four types of social support that would be predominant across the four Internet support groups (cancer, alcoholism, depression, and attention-deficit) would vary on the basis of three contextual factors: the nature of the communication medium, the type of illness, and the general philosophy of the group. First, because information about cancer treatments is continuously changing and because ADD is a relatively new disease about which few people know, we expected to see a high proportion of informational support in these two Internet support groups. Second, depressed people, in particular, often need a lot of emotional support and, hence, we anticipated a high proportion of emotional support messages in the Internet depression support group. Third, because the general philosophy of AA revolves around promoting high self-esteem, we expected a large proportion of esteem and emotional support messages in that Internet support group. Finally, because members are not physically co-present and are often widely geographically dispersed, we expected to find few instances of tangible support.

INTERGROUP COMMUNICATION: HOW EXTERNAL ENVIRONMENTS INFLUENCE INTERNET SUPPORT GROUPS

According to the bona fide group perspective, a group is defined through patterns of repetitive behaviors that become interdependent and structured (Putnam & Stohl, 1996). Although these patterns of repetitive behaviors can be examined through the communication that takes place within the group, internal group communication is also influenced by group members' links to external environments.

Intergroup communication refers to the frequency and pattern of interaction among individuals from different groups (Putnam & Stohl, 1996). People who seek help by joining Internet support groups typically are members of numerous other groups. For example, a person living with cancer who is a member of a support group might interact with members of other groups, such as family members, friends, members of a medical team, and other people living with cancer; each of these various groups may provide different informational and emotional support (Dakof & Taylor, 1990). Moreover, in comparison to face-to-face support groups, Internet support groups allow members opportunities for increased intergroup communication and boundary spanning. Because Internet support groups are more convenient than face-to-face meetings in terms of time and location constraints, members have more opportunities to participate in multiple groups. It is not unusual, for instance, to find the same message posted to multiple Internet support groups. In addition, there are frequent referrals or references to other support groups, web pages, or medical services. In this study, we examine ways in which Internet support group members are linked to their external environment and engage in intergroup communication as demonstrated in their references to additional sources of support.

METHOD

Two methods were used in this study: participant observation and self-reports. First, we collected and analyzed all messages posted over the same 3-week period from four Internet support groups: alt.recovery.aa (AA), alt.support.attn-deficit (ADD), alt.support.cancer (cancer), and depress.soundprint.org (depression). A total of 2,197 messages were produced during that 3-week period (425 messages in the AA group, 697 messages in the ADD group, 630 messages in the cancer group, and 445 messages in the depression group).

To analyze the collected messages, we employed both quantitative and qualitative methods of content analysis. Quantitative methods were used to examine the frequency and proportion of different types of messages; qualitative methods were employed to holistically examine the discourse with respect to the quality of the type of support posted to the Internet support groups. A total of three independent raters were used to code the messages of all four groups. As explained in the following text, each rater was trained to code for membership and group boundaries, intragroup communication, and intergroup communication. Interrater reliabilities were calculated for each Internet support group on all three main factors. All reliabilities exceeded Cohen's Kappa = .85.

After data collection was completed, we posted a message to each of the four support groups soliciting volunteers to answer a Web-based questionnaire that addressed members' participation patterns and satisfaction with that support group, as well as their use of other sources for social support. A total of 69 group members completed the questionnaire (18 in the AA group, 17 in the ADD group, 15 in the cancer group, and 19 in the depression group).

Membership and Group Boundaries

For each group, a list was created that contained the e-mail address of a member's name, if it was given, and the times and dates of each person's postings. Each posting was then examined for indications of what connection the sender had to the issue or problem being examined in the Internet support group. Seven basic categories emerged: those afflicted, family members, friends, doctors, advertisers, researchers, and unknown (unidentified). Some members were explicit about who they were and why they were participating in the group, such as the postings "I have a brain tumor" or "I am a friend of someone with leukemia." Signature files were also examined for possible identification of affiliation to the group. If a determination of a participant's association to a group could not be made, the participant's identity was coded as unknown.

Intergroup Communication

Intergroup communication was assessed by looking at the references made in postings to other support groups, nonsupport groups, organizations, or informational resources. Each message posted to the Internet support groups was also coded for referrals, which included any references to books, magazines, web pages, doctors, or medical centers, as well as directions to locate other Internet groups.

In addition, *crosspostings*, messages posted to any additional groups at the same time, were also recorded. Postings that included more than one address in the "To:" field of the message were counted as crosspostings, such as "To: alt.support.cancer, alt.support.cancer.prostate, alt.support.cancer.testicular ."

Intragroup Communication

We used Cutrona's Support Behavior Codes (Cutrona et al., 1990) to code for the four predominant types of social support: emotional, esteem, informational, and tangible. Because messages could contain none, one, or multiple types of support, each message was coded for the presence of each of the four types of support.

Satisfaction Questionnaire

The questionnaire was structured into three general categories (see Appendix 12.1). The first section asked general questions about how the person found out about the Internet support group, how long he or she had been a member, and what he or she liked the most and least about the Internet support group. The second section asked how satisfied the member was with the support provided by the Internet support group. The third section asked about other types of sources the person used to help deal with his or her problem or issue; specifically, whether the person relied solely on that Internet support group or also consulted other sources, such as the World Wide Web, self-help books, radio call-in shows, family members, friends, and/or other support groups.

RESULTS

The results for each group are categorized according to the tenets of the bona fide group perspective. By examining the membership and group boundaries, intragroup communication, intergroup communication, and satisfaction questionnaire results, a clear comparison of the groups can be made.

Membership and Group Boundaries

There were 108 participants in the AA group during the 3-week period. Most of the group members (75%) were alcoholics (see Table 12.1), although not all of them believed in the tenets of AA; some members even debated the merits of AA and the potential consequences in working within its paradigm.

One hundred thirty-four participants posted messages to the ADD Internet support group over the 3-week period. Participants were primarily people with ADD (40%) or family members (31%; see Table 12.1). Other members did not directly identify themselves with the disorder, and typically used the support group to discuss whether ADD really exists and to counter supportive messages sent to those who identified with the disorder. One interesting subset of members in this group was those advertising "folk remedies" for ADD (e.g., St. John Wart), advertisements for doctors who treat ADD, or pharmaceutical companies that manufacture Ritalin. All of these advertisements were framed as testimonials by individuals with the disorder who had used the products or doctors and found dramatic results. Many of these testimonials were questioned by the group members and many members took steps to determine who was and was not an advertiser by tracking down the name and mailing addresses of the person who posted the testimonial. These searches found that many of these postings originated from drug companies and doctors themselves.

The largest group, with 325 participants over the 3-week period, was the cancer group. Only 56 members were actually people living with cancer, which represented only 17% of the group's membership (see Table 12.1). There were actually more family members represented in the group (21.2%) than people living with cancer. The rest of the group members was composed of friends, doctors, and other individuals, such as researchers and advertisers. However, unlike the advertising in the ADD group, the advertisements in the cancer group were often straightforward advertisements for treatments, products, and even cures. One advertisement read, "We can cure your cancer for $1,000,000."

The depression group was the smallest with only 74 members. All described themselves as depressed individuals. Members indicated that they had been diagnosed and many of them indicated that they were seeking professional help for their depression (see Table 12.1).

Intragroup Communication

Informational Support. Surprisingly, the most common type of support provided by AA members was informational support (43%), typically expressed in the forms of teaching, advice, and referrals (see Fig. 12.1). Given that AA is a 12-step program, many of the informational support messages sought to teach other members how to perceive their situation within the steps of the program. For example, members often reminded one another that an alcoholic needs to take it "one day at a time, sometimes one minute at a time."

TABLE 12.1

Membership Across the Four Internet Support Groups:
AA, ADD, Cancer, Depression

	AA	ADD	Cancer	Depression
People Who Have or Are Experiencing the Problem				
Frequency	81	53	56	74
Percentage (%)	75	40	17	100
Family Members				
Frequency	6	42	69	0
Percentage (%)	6	31	21	0
Friends				
Frequency	7	6	15	0
Percentage (%)	6	4	5	0
Doctors				
Frequency	2	6	11	0
Percentage (%)	2	4	3	0
Advertisers				
Frequency	0	10	66	0
Percentage (%)	0	8	20	0
Researchers				
Frequency	0	0	37	0
Percentage (%)	0	0	12	0
Unknown				
Frequency	12	17	71	0
Percentage (%)	11	13	22	0
Totals				
Frequency	108	134	325	74
Percentage (%)	100	100	100	100

In accordance with AA ideology, members were also encouraged to provide personal testimonies as teaching tools for other members because, as one member put it, "There may very well be someone lurking on this group who is debating whether or not to give up the bottle. Your experience may be helping him or her right now." Members also provided a lot of advice for those who expressed inexperience with and hesitance about attending face-to-face AA meetings, such as "Show up early for meetings and help set

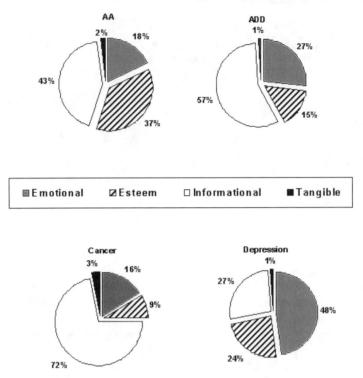

FIG. 12.1. Proportion of four types of social support by Internet support group.

up chairs—this will allow you to meet people informally" and "It might be scary at first but soon you will find yourself feeling safe and comfortable."

Informational support was also the most common form (57%) of support exchanged among members of the ADD Internet support group, and typically took the form of advice, teaching, and referrals. Informational support offered by ADD members was often provided in response to counter-information (i.e., information inconsistent with their beliefs surrounding ADD and its treatment).

One of the most discussed and debated issues in the ADD group was the use of the drug Ritalin for treating the disorder. Some members provided testimonials of the success of Ritalin, such as "My son reports that mental clarity is the main benefit to him from his recent use of Ritalin"; others reported on the failures of the drug, such as "Ritalin did nothing for me except make me feel more like a failure." Members often tried to help others understand and possibly accept their views on the role of Ritalin in combating ADD. For example, one member wrote:

No longer are defenses necessary, perceptions become more rational, the paranoia evaporates and life becomes far simpler once the attention-deficit disorder person learns about and can honestly and totally accept his or her own high-quality and very good self. We must look in, not out, if we are to find the answer to attention-deficit disorder. Ritalin certainly helps with the learning.

Others countered these stories of success with comments such as:

There is no consistent evidence to claim that Ritalin is any better than St. John Wort or other natural drugs to treat ADD. A "natural" drug is no better than a "synthetic" drug. Any drug is trying to "treat" a disease. The outside-in approach has always failed to improve the health of the American public. "Disease" is not caused by the absence of drugs, natural or synthetic.

Informational support was also offered in the form of testimonials or involved teaching members how to reappraise everyday situations. For instance, members typically offered advice to others on how to effectively make it through the day, such as "Routines are very important when you have a child with ADD or have ADD yourself" and "I find that making lists helps me make sure I don't forget to do anything when my mind starts to wander."

Informational support was also, by far, the most predominant type of support (72%) exchanged in the Internet cancer support group. The majority of the messages exchanged contained such support in the form of referrals, advice, teaching, and answers to specific informational requests. Advice to members was often straightforward and brief, such as "You should go to the doctor because the sooner the doctor catches it, the easier it is to fix" and "If it is indeed the lymph nodes that are malfunctioning, they should be examined by a qualified hematologist." Other types of informational support in the cancer group occurred in the form of posting recent research articles about cancer treatments for other members to read. Moreover, teaching as informational support was often used to counter empirical research or commonly held beliefs about the best treatments for cancer. For example, during a discussion of a human breast cancer study, one member wrote, "Do NOT let a single experiment in rats indicate what humans should do. There's a lot of data that needs to be obtained before recommending DHEA as a hormopreventative."

In addition to the wide range of informational support provided, many advertisers posted product information for pharmaceutical and homeopathic treatments. The inclusion of advertising, sometimes written in the form of testimonials from people living with cancer, probably made it difficult for members to judge the quality of the information provided in postings.

A large number of messages (27%) in the depression group also contained informational support. Members often helped one another by teaching and helping to reappraise situations. Typical of such comments were, "It IS just an illness, keep saying that" and "We are only human, but we battle depression which sometimes clouds up our judgments."

Esteem Support. Consistent with the main tenets of empowerment in AA, esteem support represented a large percentage (37%) of the support exchanged among members. Esteem support often appeared in the form of congratulations for remaining sober, which AA members refer to as their "birthday," the first full day an alcoholic has not had a drink. Offers of congratulations and encouragement were provided for members who had gone just 1 week without a drink as well as for members who had been without a drink for 50 years.

In the ADD group, esteem support constituted 15% of the support exchanged and was often offered in response to what another member had said concerning ADD and its treatments. Typical of esteem support were postings such as, "Applause, applause. Well said!," "You've already got some good ideas on how to handle the situation," and "You're making me think … very interesting comments!"

In the cancer group, less than 10% of the total amount of support messages exchanged constituted esteem support. Such support primarily took the form of thanking members for empathetic responses, as well as information and advice.

The depression group also had a high level of esteem support exchanged (24%). For instance, members often thanked fellow members for their support and praised them for their courage, insight, and honesty. Representative of esteem support were statements such as, "Mike, you are a gem!," "When I read your post Mary I was so proud of you," and "Please keep posting Allen—we love you and need you here!" Even at times when members expressed that they felt at their lowest, other members still offered them esteem support. For example, one member wrote:

> It's strange, I feel like I am REALLY being listened to and that feels REALLY good for a change. I haven't talked to any of you personally, or directly, and yet I feel close to you. You all seem very nice and concerned for one another. Thank you, everyone.

Emotional Support. The emotional support expressed in the AA group often came in the form of emoticons or expressions of willingness to listen and/or talk with another member. The most predominant emoticons were virtual hugs (((((HUG)))))) and smiling icons :).

In the ADD group, the second most common form of support (27%) was emotional support, typically expressed in the form of agreement with members about their perceptions of ADD. For instance, supporters of Ritalin often provided sympathy and hope to one another; messages such as, "Hang in there! It CAN get better," "There's a light at the end of the tunnel," and "I'm listening to you Nancy—talk to us" were typically offered to members along with emoticons to express nonverbal emotions (especially hugs and smiles).

Although emotional support was not as predominant in the cancer group (16%) as in the other groups, some emotional support was exchanged among the members. Emotional support was primarily focused on empathy, prayer, and wishes of good luck. These emotional responses tended to be brief, such as "Good luck with your friend" and "I pray she will quit smoking."

The primary support exchanged in the depression group was emotional support (48%), often found in the forms of offering sympathy, providing hope, and expressing affection. Members often would begin their postings with such emotional support as, "I hope everyone is doing well and holding on like I did through the latest crisis in my life" or "Good for you for participating, even though someone might be eavesdropping on you!" Members also ended many of their posts with emotional support expressed through emoticons (((((HUG))))) and references to future interactions, such as "I look forward to sharing more with you in the future."

Tangible Support. Tangible support accounted for a very small percentage of the support exchanged in all of the Internet support groups. It accounted for about 2% of all of the support in the AA group and was often provided by members who lived in the same region of the country, such as in offers of rides to meetings. There was almost no tangible support exchanged in the ADD group (four messages only). In the cancer group, tangible support was typically expressed in the form of offering other members their personal e-mail addresses and telephone numbers to correspond in confidence. Finally, almost no tangible assistance was evidenced in the messages exchanged in the depression support group (only 6 instances).

Intergroup Communication. The AA support group had a moderate number of referrals, mostly referring members to synchronous chat groups. When individuals expressed a concern about where to find AA groups in their area, members made referrals to local face-to-face AA groups, other Internet groups, Internet chat groups, and a number of books about AA.

The ADD support group had 47 referrals to outside sources. Most of these referrals were to other web pages supporting the members' view of ADD. Although most of the referrals were used to provide supporting evidence for members' views, a few referrals were for other Internet support groups that individuals could join to gain social support. For example, one message stated, "If you want support, go to alt.support.touretts because you will find no support here! Our group is designed for discussing attention-deficit disorder, not to provide support."

The cancer support group had a high number of referrals, reflecting the primarily informational style of the messages exchanged in this group. It was typical to find messages with referrals to multiple sources, or even a complete bibliography of sources, in the cancer postings, with web pages and other organizations comprising most of the referrals. The most common referral given was to resources that focused on the specific form of cancer, such as lymphoid cancer, about which an individual was asking information.

There were very few referrals to outside sources found within the depression support group. The referrals that did occur in the depression group were primarily to other Internet groups or web pages. For example, one member suggested that others might consider joining a chat group on America Online (AOL) to talk in real time when they felt severely depressed. However, this group was focused primarily on emotional health and support; there was not a large need to refer members to outside sources for information.

Satisfaction Questionnaire

Members of the AA Internet support group indicated that the group was only one of many sources they used for social support; other sources included face-to-face support group meetings, Internet synchronous chat groups, non-AA self-help publications, family members, and friends. Interestingly, members indicated that the Internet group allowed for, in the words of one member, an "opportunity to complain about group practices that is not available or tolerated at AA meetings." Although some members indicated that the best part of the Internet support group was the ability to challenge AA tenets, other members listed these challenges as the worst part of the Internet support group. For example, one member indicated that "there is a great deal of good, long-term, well-informed, caring sobriety in this Internet group; but you have to wade through a lot of crap to find it." The "crap" mentioned in the message referred to postings by members who did not believe in the tenets of AA. The conflicting responses to the questions returned by these 18 members might be one indication why these group members tended to report lower levels of overall satisfaction ($M = 5.33, SD = 1.68$) with this Internet support group as compared to the members of the depression ($M = 6.47, SD = .77$) Internet support group (see Table 12.2).

Unlike the AA group, members of the ADD group reported a lower level of satisfaction with all four forms of support, in addition to their level of

TABLE 12.2

Satisfaction With Types of Support

	AA	ADD	Cancer	Depression
Overall Satisfaction with Group				
M	5.33_b	3.88_c	5.93_{ab}	6.47_a
SD	1.68	2.00	1.10	.77
Amount of Information				
M	6.06_a	3.86_b	5.69_a	6.35_a
SD	.83	2.18	1.03	1.59
Quality of Information				
M	6.06_a	3.93_b	6.08_a	6.29_a
SD	.66	2.20	.86	.85
Esteem Support				
M	5.18_a	3.64_b	5.37_a	6.59_c
SD	1.33	2.47	1.25	.80
Emotional Support				
M	5.94_{ab}	3.71_c	5.15_a	6.82_b
SD	.83	2.27	1.34	.53
Tangible Support				
M	4.06_a	3.50_a	5.15_{ab}	5.88_b
SD	2.22	2.38	1.51	1.40

Note. Satisfaction was measured using 7-point scales (1 = *completely dissatisfied*; 7 = *completely satisfied*). Means in the same row that do not share the same subscript differ at $p < .05$ using the Bonferroni significance post hoc test.

overall satisfaction with the group ($M = 3.88, SD = 2.00$), compared to the other three Internet support groups. Perhaps this was due to the diversity of the ADD group in terms of those who did and did not believe in the diagnosis and treatment of ADD. When asked the best thing about the group, one member stated:

> If a new situation or possible treatment is presented to me, I know that I can get the kind of answers I trust from this group. Even the people who are "anti-ADD" who join in on the newsgroup discussions give a "devil's advocate" perspective that I personally need to hear.

Another member indicated "that there is no substitute for getting perspective and experience from real people who have 'been there & done that.'"

Although approximately half the respondents indicated that the ADD group was very useful, the other half was very negative about their experiences. For example, one person indicated that members "only received negative feedback and criticism. People would chastise me for allowing my young son to be using the medications that he needed to function at a decent level." Because many of the postings were very negative, some individuals surveyed later indicated that they no longer were part of this ADD group because of all the fighting, personal insults, and "general rudeness and apathy."

In general, the members of the cancer Internet support group were satisfied with their experience ($M = 5.93$, $SD = 1.10$). Members mentioned that one of the benefits was the wide array of information available from fellow members. Some members even stated that they used the group as a source of information because they mistrusted doctors and other members of the medical community. Information exchanged about alternative therapies, not necessarily supported by the medical community, was especially appreciated.

Members of the depression Internet support group were extremely satisfied ($M = 6.47$, $SD = .77$). They felt that the support group was "something I could turn to in times when I needed not to feel alone," that "the support is so freely given between the members," that "the people care about the other members," and that the group was "an outlet for people to express their opinions, beliefs, share their stories, and get them affirmed." When asked how to improve the depression Internet support group experience, members typically replied that there was nothing to change. As one member put it:

> I am actually shocked at how good this group really is—very mature most of the time. We take turns with support as we enter better periods, and seek support as needed. Can't imagine how this scenario could be improved, to be honest.

DISCUSSION

This study compared the communicative practices of four Internet support groups by using the bona fide group perspective to examine group boundaries, internal group communication, and external connections to other people and informational sources. This study extends previous work on Internet support groups by examining multiple groups simultaneously, both their internal communication and the ways in which these groups are interdependent with their context. The main empirical finding from this comparative case analysis was that Internet support groups have very different styles of communicating support and relating to their environment.

The findings from this study indicate that group membership and group boundaries could have important effects on group processes. In particular, members of the depression group, which had a homogeneous membership, seemed uniformly satisfied with the support exchanged in their group, whereas members of the other three groups were variably satisfied with their experience. In the other groups where the membership was more diverse, support seemed to be more informational and represented numerous perspectives. Further evidence to support this notion can be found in the satisfaction scores of the members of the ADD and AA groups, both of which had membership that was further divided by different approaches to treatment; the satisfaction scores in these two groups were lower than the scores of the cancer group, where the membership was diverse but not as divided. This finding implies that Internet support groups may be more satisfying to members when the membership is confined to those who actually have the condition and precludes a public forum. In this case, it would seem that a fluid and permeable boundary is not a desirable trait for an Internet support group but a challenge to overcome.

In agreement with previous research, an examination of the intragroup communication in these groups yielded an abundance of social support. However, previous research has found that Internet support groups generally have high levels of informational and emotional support. In the present study, not only was esteem support present in all four of the groups but each group had very different support processes. Given that each group developed its own way of exchanging social support, we cannot generalize across Internet support groups.

It is important to note that intragroup and intergroup communication were linked in these Internet support groups. All of the groups, except for the depression group, had a moderate to high number of referrals. By providing referrals to other sources for support, information, medical care, and so forth, members linked the group to external sources while at the same time provided informational support. Although the referrals indicate intergroup communication, they also demonstrated that some type of informational support was exchanged within the group (intragroup communication). In addition to this connection, crosspostings also indicated an exchange of information across groups; these crosspostings then became part of a group's intragroup communication and, thereby, demonstrated another important link between these two processes.

This examination of Internet support groups through the tenets of the bona fide group perspective indicate that although all four Internet support groups focused on health issues, the groups functioned quite differently and served different purposes for their members. The depression support group offered primarily emotional support to help members cope with the condition. The cancer group was very informational, and served as a first stop for many people in their search for informational support. The AA group was characterized mostly by informational and esteem support, and served as a supplement to face-to-face meetings. The ADD group was not supportive at all but, instead, developed into a discussion or debate about whether ADD actually existed. These unique support practices indicate that Internet support groups must be examined individually to truly understand the processes within these groups.

An interesting trend seemed to emerge regarding the relations among group size, membership, and social support. When groups were large and heterogeneous with respect to membership (see Table 12.1), their internal communication tended to focus more on information exchange than on emotional support. In contrast, when groups were small and homogeneous, their internal communication seemed to focus more on emotional support than on information exchange. The depression group, which was the smallest and composed almost exclusively of members who appeared to have depression, had the highest percentage of emotional support messages, whereas the cancer group, which was the largest and had the most diverse membership, was the most focused on information exchange. These results seem to parallel those observed in face-to-face settings that members of small groups are more intimate and disclose more personal information than members of large groups. More research is needed to investigate whether the observed relations among group size, membership diversity, and type of social support generalize across Internet support groups.

In addition to the specific findings, a strength of this study is the use of both quantitative and qualitative methods to examine Internet groups from a bona fide group perspective. Quantitative methods were used to examine the frequency and proportion of different types of messages, whereas qualitative methods were employed to holistically examine the discourse with respect to the groups' internal communication. To make valid claims about the differences between and similarities among groups, it is important to measure the same variables across groups. The bona fide group perspective also prescribes the importance of understanding a group from the perspective of its members, which involves asking about participants' views of their group and the group's relation to its external environments. This was accomplished via a questionnaire that was distributed to all four groups and contained both closed- and open-ended questions. The bona fide group perspective also points to key variables to consider when examining the reciprocal relation between groups and their environments. In this study, multiple group membership and intergroup relations were examined quantitatively and qualitatively through an analysis of the frequency and types of references to other sources outside the group in messages posted to the groups and in the crossposting of messages to other support groups. Through these crosspostings, members made their membership to other groups explicit. These practices may indicate how intergroup communication might influence and be influenced by the internal communication of the support groups.

The Internet provides researchers with a unique opportunity to study groups in their natural settings. Many face-to-face support groups, such as Alcoholics Anonymous, were previously off limits to researchers. Internet support groups, often being open to the public, provide researchers with opportunities to learn more about the functions and processes of social support provided by these groups. Moreover, because messages exchanged in Internet groups are text-based and archived, researchers can observe and code most of the messages exchanged among group members.

Although this study had a number of strengths, including a multimethodological approach and the examination of group processes for a fairly long period of time, it also had some limitations. First, the 3-week duration of the study represented only a small slice in the life of the four Internet support groups. Second, only a small proportion of participants in each support group completed the questionnaire and all were volunteers; hence, the responses from the questionnaire may not have accurately represented the opinions of all members of the four support groups. Third, it was difficult, if not impossible, to determine whether the "virtual" identity that members of the Internet support groups presented to their group was the same as their face-to-face identities. For example, it was not possible to know with certainty that participants who claimed to have a particular medical condition actually had it. In fact, it was discovered that some advertisers pretended to be people with the relevant condition in order to entice others to try their products or services. In face-to-face support groups, it is often easier to verify whether an individual member actually has a particular condition or illness, because, at least in some cases, others can visually inspect that member for signs of it. In addition, imposters often have to go to greater lengths to conceal their identities in a face-to-face support group than in an Internet support group, which may reduce the likelihood of such individuals participating.

This study also highlights some challenges and issues for researchers to address in the future. One challenge to researchers who study Internet groups is how to consider lurkers in the analysis and interpretation of the findings. Although lurkers never post messages to Internet groups, they can and do read the messages posted by other group members. Despite the fact that they were "never heard from" in direct messages, the group participants in this study who posted messages often pointed to the possibility of lurkers being present. By explicitly mentioning lurkers in messages, group members acknowledged lurkers' presence and established their existence within the group. Lurkers demonstrate the permeable boundaries of Internet support groups, and they deserve further research attention.

Another question is the degree to which face-to-face support groups resemble Internet support groups. Face-to-face and Internet support groups have never been directly compared, leaving many unanswered questions. The bona fide group perspective offers a valuable perspective for discovering and understanding the similarities and differences between these groups in that it takes into account a large amount of information about groups and how they function. An important next step would be to study multiple face-to-face support groups and their Internet counterparts in the same study.

A final direction for future research is the design of effective Internet interventions to improve the psychological condition of people with health problems. For instance, it is important to understand how people who have particular needs or problems discover Internet support groups. It may be the case that many people find them by searching for information about their need or problem on the Internet. Controlling who gets access may make it much more difficult for potential participants to locate Internet support groups. It is also important to understand support group participants' decisions about contributing to the discourse. Participants, for instance, may feel more comfortable lurking and learning about the group for a while before becoming an active contributor. This is, of course, much easier to do in a public rather than a closed forum.

CONCLUSION

All Internet support groups are not created equal: They differ from one another in their membership, the ways that they provide support to their members, and how they affect and are affected by their environments. The results of this study are inconsistent with early theorizing that hypothesized that computer-mediated communication was too "lean" a medium to support the exchange of messages that contained highly emotional content (see a review, see McGrath & Hollingshead, 1994). In contrast, the findings of this study demonstrate that members of Internet support groups give and receive social support and that these groups can and do develop a strong sense of group identity. This study is consistent with more recent research that suggests that computer-mediated communication in some situations (e.g., in groups where members communicate over a long period of time) can promote positive relational effects that are in some ways superior to those obtained face-to-face (Walther, 1995, 1996). The bona fide group perspective offers researchers an important theoretical framework for describing and examining communication processes both external and internal to groups. It is hoped that this partnership will lead to more important discoveries about Internet support groups.

ACKNOWLEDGMENT

We thank Elizabeth Strauss, who served as an undergraduate research assistant on this project, for her valuable help with data coding.

REFERENCES

Bawden, D. (1993). Predicting Ritalin response with neurometric testing: Case studies. In L. F. Leonard, C. E. Stout, & D. H. Ruben (Eds.), *Handbook of childhood impulse disorders and ADHD* (pp. 60–77). Springfield, IL: Charles C. Thomas.

Borkman, T. J. (1990). Experiential, professional, and lay frames of references. In T. J. Powell (Ed.), *Working with self help* (pp. 3–30). Silver Spring, MD: National Association of Social Workers.

Braithwaite, D. O., Waldron, V. R., & Finn, J. (1999). Communication of social support in computer-mediated groups for people with disabilities. *Health Communication, 11*, 123–151.

Cline, R. J. W. (1999). Communication in social support groups. In L. R. Frey (Ed.), D. S. Gouran, & M. S. Poole (Assoc. Eds.), *The handbook of group communication theory & research* (pp. 516–538). Thousand Oaks, CA: Sage.

Cutrona, C. E., & Suhr, J. A. (1994). Social support communication in the context of marriage. In B. R. Burleson, T. L. Albrecht, & I. G. Sarason (Eds.), *Communication of social support: Messages, interactions, relationships, and community* (pp. 113–135) Thousand Oaks, CA: Sage.

Cutrona, C. E., Suhr, J. A., & MacFarlane, R. (1990). Interpersonal transactions and the psychological sense of support. In S. Duck & R. Silver (Eds.), *Personal relationships and social support* (pp. 30–45). London: Sage.

Dakof, G. A., & Taylor, S. E. (1990). Victims' perception of social support: What is helpful from whom? *Journal of Personality and Social Psychology, 38*, 80–89.

Ford, S., Fallowfield, L., & Lewis, S. (1996). Doctor-patient interactions in oncology. *Social Science and Medicine, 42*, 1511–1519.

Gladding, S. T. (1995). *Group work: A counseling specialty* (2nd ed.). Englewood Cliffs, NJ: Prentice-Hall.

Grady, D. (1998, April 23). Faking pain and suffering in Internet support groups. *New York Times*, p. D1.

Gustafson, D., Wise, M., McTavish, F., Taylor, J. O., Wolberg, W., Stewart, J., Smalley, J., & Bosworth, K. (1993). Development and pilot evaluation of a computer-based support system for women with breast cancer. *Journal of Psychosocial Oncology, 11*, 69–93.

Hawkins, R. P., Pingree, S., Gustafson, D. H., Boberg, E. W., Bricker, E., McTavish, F., Wise, M., & Owens, B. (1997). Aiding those facing health crises: The experience of the CHESS program. In R. L. Street, Jr., W. R. Gold, & T. Manning (Eds.), *Health promotion and interactive technology: Theoretical applications and future directions* (pp. 79–102). Mahwah, NJ: Lawrence Erlbaum Associates.

Karp, D. A. (1992). Illness ambiguity and the search for meaning: A case study of a self-help group for affective disorders. *Journal of Contemporary Ethnography, 21*, 139–170.

Kassel, J. D., & Wagner, E. (1993). Processes of change in Alcoholics Anonymous: A review of possible mechanisms. *Psychotherapy, 30,* 222–234.

Kessler, R. C., Mickelson, K. D., & Zhao, S. (1997). Patterns and correlations of self-help group membership in the United States. *Social Policy, 27,* 27–46.

Koziol, L. F., Stout, C. E., & Ruben, D. H. (1993). *Handbook of Childhood Impulse Disorder and ADHD: Theory and practice.* Springfield, IL: Charles C. Thomas.

McGrath, J. E., & Hollingshead, A. B. (1994). *Groups interacting with technology.* Newbury Park, CA: Sage.

Parker, H. C. (1994). *The ADD hyperactivity workbook for parents, teachers, and kids* (2nd ed.) Plantation, FL: Impact.

Putnam, L. L., & Stohl, C. (1990). Bona fide groups: A reconceptualization of groups in context. *Communication Studies, 41,* 248–265.

Putnam, L. L., & Stohl, C. (1996). Bona fide groups: An alternative perspective for communication and small group decision making. In R. Y. Hirokawa & M. S. Poole (Eds.), *Communication and group decision making* (2nd ed., pp. 147–177). Thousand Oaks, CA: Sage.

Salem, D. A., Bogart, G. A., & Reid, C. (1997). Mutual help goes online. *Journal of Community Psychology, 25,* 189–207.

Siminoff, L. A., & Fetting, J. H. (1991). Factors affecting treatment decisions for a life-threatening illness: The case of medical treatment of breast cancer. *Social Science and Medicine, 32,* 813–818.

Sutherland, H. J., Lockwood, G. A., Tritchler, F., Brooks, L., & Till, J. E. (1991). Communicating probabilistic information to cancer patients: Is there noise on the line? *Social Science and Medicine, 32,* 725–731.

Thomas, S. F. (1991) Gaps, cracks, and craters. *Journal of Child and Adolescent Psychopharmacology, 1,* 251–254.

Walther, J. B. (1995). Relational aspects of computer-mediated communication: Experimental observations over time. *Organization Science, 6,* 186–203.

Walther, J. B. (1996). Computer-mediated communication: Impersonal, interpersonal, and hyperpersonal interaction. *Communication Research, 23,* 3–43.

Watson, C. G., Hancock, M., Gearhart, L. P., Mendez, C. M., Malovrh, P., & Raden, M. (1997). A comparative outcome study of frequent, moderate, occasional, and nonattenders of Alcoholics Anonymous. *Journal of Clinical Psychology, 53,* 209–214.

Weinberg, N., Schmale, J. D., Uken, J., & Wessel, K. (1995). Computer-mediated support groups. *Social Work With Groups, 17,* 43–54.

Winzelberg, A. (1997). The analysis of an electronic support group for individuals with eating disorders. *Computers in Human Behavior, 13,* 393–407.

Wright, K. B. (1997). Shared ideology in Alcoholics Anonymous: A grounded theory approach. *Journal of Health Communication, 2,* 83–99.

Wright, K. B. (2000). Computer-mediated social support, older adults, and coping. *Journal of Communication, 50*(3), 100–118.

Yalom, I. D. (1985). *The theory and practice of group psychotherapy* (3rd ed.). New York: Basil.

APPENDIX

Questionnaire

General Questions

How long have you been using the group?

How did you find out about this group?

What would you say is the best thing about this newsgroup?

If there were one aspect about this newsgroup you could change, what would it be?

Evaluation of Satisfaction With Group and Social Support

For the following questions please use the following 7-point scale:
  1. Completely dissatisfied
  2. Mostly unsatisfied
  3. Somewhat unsatisfied
  4. Neither satisfied nor dissatisfied
  5. Somewhat satisfied
  6. Mostly satisfied.
  7. Completely satisfied

How would you rate your satisfaction with this group?

How would you rate your satisfaction with the amount of information provided by members of this newsgroup?

How would you rate your satisfaction with the quality of information provided by members of this newsgroup?

How would you rate your satisfaction with how well group members provide you validation and make you feel less worried about your problems?

How would you rate your satisfaction with the group's ability to provide emotional support in the forms of empathy, understanding, and offers of hope?

How would you rate the group's offers of willingness to talk on the phone, e-mail you privately, or other forms of direct assistance?

Other Sources Used for Social Support

Have you or do you use any other support or chat groups online for dealing with alcoholism? If so, which ones?

Have you/do you use the World Wide Web for information for support on alcoholism? And if so, which ones?

Have you/do you use any self-help books for alcoholism? If so, which ones?

Have you do/you participate rail call in shows for alcoholism?   .

Have you/do you rely on family for support concerning alcoholism?
If so, who?

Have you/do you rely on your friends for dealing with alcoholism?
If so, which ones?

Do you have any other sources you use that are not listed here to deal with alcoholism?

13

Bona Fide Groups
as Self-Organizing Systems:

Applications to Electronic Newsgroups

Dean Krikorian
Cornell University

Toru Kiyomiya
Seinan Gakuin University

The new electronic interdependence recreates the world in the image of a global village.
—McLuhan (1962, p. 31)

PRELUDE: PURPOSE, PROBLEM, AND PLAN

Purpose

Group Internet technologies offer revolutionary ways to communicate: Chat rooms, newsgroups, bulletin boards, e-mail lists, virtual worlds, virtual clubs, group web pages, interactive games, buddy lists, desktop videoconferencing, and other group Internet technologies afford new and important ways to interact with others online. Online communication allows individuals to share common interests and to form community networks previously impossible due to spatial, time, or monetary constraints (Comer, 1997; Wellman & Gulia, 1999). Although there have been reviews of the social interaction of online groups (e.g., Fulk & Steinfield, 1990;

Hiltz & Turoff, 1978; McGrath & Hollingshead, 1994; Rice & Associates, 1984; Scott, 1999), group Internet technologies are so new that there has been little time to examine the processes, structures, and effects of their group communication.

Communication scholars historically have examined the nature of message processes (e.g., Berlo, 1960; Monge, Farace, Eisenberg, Miller, & White, 1984; Schramm, 1954; Watt & Van Lear, 1996) and network structures (e.g., Rice, 1982; Richards & Barnett, 1993; Rogers & Kincaid, 1981; D. F. Schwartz, 1968) and group scholars have explored dynamic (e.g., Bonner, 1959; Cartwright & Zander, 1968; Lewin, 1947) and developmental (e.g., Bales & Strodtbeck, 1953; Fisher, 1970; Poole, 1983; Tuckman, 1965) group processes. It is the intersection between communication networks and interaction processes that frames Internet group dynamic research via three general questions: (a) How do online groups network over time?; (b) How can message processes help to uncover the dynamics of online groups?; (c) How can communication theory help to explain online group interaction? In this chapter, we attempt to answer these questions by integrating communication process and structure research as a means to examine online group dynamics.

Problem

Online Internet groups grew rapidly in number in the span of only a few years during the mid-1990s (Hauben & Hauben, 1997). Due, in part, to improved accessibility, processing speed, and connect time, more and more people are meeting in groups online. As an example of this phenomenon, in August 1998, Yahoo.com introduced Yahoo! Clubs as a means for individuals to gather together in groups to discuss a common topic, using a combination of communication tools and functions such as group calendars, chat rooms, message boards, news, web links, and graphics. Within 4 months, there was an estimated 50,000 clubs online (the largest of which had about 2,000 members). By June 2001, the number of Yahoo! Clubs had swelled to over 500,000 (the largest of which had over 40,000 members),[1] representing a 10-fold increase in the number of clubs and a 20-fold increase in the number of members. Taken together, these increases can be viewed as a relatively high proportion of groups to members (1:2).

One can question, however, the make-up of these groups and, specifically, whether they are active or merely unoccupied shells of past interaction (see Spencer & Lawrence, 1998). As an example, Smith (1999) reported that 20% of all Usenet newsgroups (i.e., asynchronous text message groups) are uninhabited and that 43% are only partially inhabited (see

---

[1]These estimates were calculated by adding the total number of public groups accessible and members on Yahoo! Clubs.com in these time frames.

Dodge & Kitchin, 2001). We seek to chronicle newsgroup inhabitation from a bona fide group perspective (Putnam & Stohl, 1990, 1996). Using group dynamic topological mapping (Lewin, 1936) and self-organizing systems theory (Contractor & Seibold, 1993), a model of dying and declining newsgroups is developed based on qualitative observations. The goal of this research is to understand how and why online group activity declines by using communication constructs to explain such activity and by applying the results to prevent future occurrences. By understanding the communication processes in declining online groups, one gains insight into practical advice for groups struggling to survive.

Plan

The theoretical basis of this chapter traces the historical development and processual transformation of bona fide newsgroups as self-organizing (i.e., emergent structure) systems. Six sections are constructed to accomplish this goal. First, we explain the background of how the present study was conducted, from initial idea to final formulation. Second, the bona fide group perspective is briefly explained, focusing, in particular, on the concepts of group boundaries and interdependence of groups with their contexts. Third, Internet newsgroups are introduced and described as the context for the present study and explained as bona fide groups. Fourth, the research methods and data analyses employed are explicated, resulting in a specific model by which to examine newsgroups. Fifth, a general theoretical model is presented on the basis of four separate theoretical constructs using self-organizing systems theory. Sixth, a newsgroup death model is presented and used to advance six propositions and a hypothesis and to propose future directions and implications for the study of online groups. We, thus, explore message patterns of newsgroup interaction using a theoretical framework to examine communication activity over time. Our hope is that this analysis will not only illustrate a practical use of the bona fide group perspective but also provide insight into Internet groups, dynamic model development, and the communication theory-building process.

BACKGROUND

The genesis of this chapter began rather innocently with an undergraduate course (taught by the lead author in 1996), titled "Internet Communication: Theory and Practice." In that course, students were required to observe an Internet communication phenomenon and to describe it using theories covered in the course. One of the students, after hearing the instructor's lecture about a research study of bona fide surgical teams

(Lammers & Krikorian, 1997), wrote a novel and insightful essay on electronic newsgroups as bona fide groups that deserved further exploration.[2] As a result, we collected data over the course of 2 months to test the notion of newsgroups as bona fide groups. An initial version of this idea was presented at the Midwestern States Organizational Mini-Conference by the second author.[3] Although the constructs were not fully developed and the data were only partially collected at that time, key feedback was given by conference participants that helped us to better understand the concepts presented in that essay.[4] Most important, it became apparent that there was something bona fide about newsgroups. In this chapter, we seek to further understand the bona fide nature of these groups by focusing, specifically, on the stable, yet permeable nature of online group interaction.

THE BONA FIDE GROUP PERSPECTIVE

Background and Focus of the Bona Fide Group Perspective

As many of the chapters in this text indicate, the bona fide group perspective can be applied to a wide range of natural groups. As has been explicated elsewhere (see Frey's introduction, this volume [p. 401]; Putnam & Stohl, 1990, 1996), this perspective challenges static notions of "groupness" and the supposed fixed boundaries of a group's identity, by viewing groups as having stable, yet permeable boundaries and being interdependent with their contexts. This perspective provides insight into group development processes in natural contexts (Putnam & Stohl, 1990) and studies of bona fide groups have produced evidence of patterns of group dynamics as repetitive behaviors that become interdependent and interstructured throughout the life span of a group, as influenced by its contexts (see, e.g., Lammers & Krikorian, 1997). Hence, the notion of a bona fide group is simultaneously rooted in the social construction of group boundaries and the interdependence of groups and their contexts.

In this chapter, we focus on the permeable boundary region of Internet newsgroups as affected by internal and external forces impinging on those groups. As Weick (1979) observed, "Boundaries between groups and environments are never clear cut or as stable as many ... theorists think. These boundaries shift, disappear, and are arbitrarily drawn" (p. 132). We seek to illuminate the forces impinging on the group boundary region using endogenous (i.e., internal) and exogenous (i.e., external) message variables,

---

[2]Special thanks to Tara Brouilette for this insight.
[3]Mohammad Mdyusoff was also a coauthor of that essay.
[4]Special thanks to Linda Putnam for pointing out the role of intergroup communication in newsgroups and to George Barnett for noting the role of uncontrollable exogenous variables.

reflecting Putnam and Stohl's (1996) bona fide group factors of internal and external communication.

CONTEXT: DEFINITION AND CHARACTERISTICS OF NEWSGROUPS

> When technology extends one of our senses, a new translation of culture occurs as swiftly as the new technology is interiorized.
> —McLuhan (1962, p. 40)

In this section, we (a) provide details on the nature of Usenet newsgroups to frame the research presented in this chapter, (b) apply bona fide constructs to such groups, and (c) develop a model of bona fide newsgroups.

Definition of a Newsgroup

A *newsgroup* is defined as a topic-based online discussion group, also known as a distributed bulletin board system (Courtright & Perse, 1998; Levine, Baroudi, & Young, 1995). Newsgroups are the basic unit of the *Usenet*, the world-wide distributed discussion conferencing system that houses and distributes tens of thousands of newsgroups to all parts of the Internet (Deja News, 2001). Newsgroups are *asynchronous* in nature, meaning that messages are posted and responded to at different times. These messages, therefore, are viewed at the receiver's convenience, leading Preece (2000) to classify newsgroups as a "pull" technology in that newsgroup participants "pull" messages or articles off a centralized bulletin board system.

Importance of Newsgroups

Statistical data show that the Usenet has grown substantially over time. In June 1994, Usenet newsgroups averaged 67,344 articles (i.e., messages) per day and required 172 Kilobytes of storage space per day (Pfaffenberger, 1995). By October 1997, those numbers had grown to 850,000 articles per day and 8 Gigabytes of storage space per day (Spencer & Lawrence, 1998). Recent estimates list the number of Usenet users at 7.9 million, with 151 million messages per year (Weise, 2001). Other forms of newsgroups have extended their reach beyond Usenet; as noted earlier, most Internet clubs have message board features and many web pages are linked to specialized newsgroups in both public and private domains. These statistics and examples highlight the rapid expansion and increased popularity of group computer-mediated communication over the Internet, in general, and the importance and expansion of hybrid forms of newsgroups as an Internet communication medium, in particular. Moreover, as an interactive Internet medium, newsgroups rely on interaction for their maintenance and survival; if no one participates, a newsgroup will cease to exist. In the ensuing discussion, newsgroups are viewed as communication structures that emerge from the participation of their group members.

Structural Features of Newsgroups

Because of the emphasis on computer-mediated, asynchronous text, newsgroups have unique structural features. Each newsgroup has a name that captures the focus of the group. For example, in the "alt.fan.nysyc" newsgroup, the first identifier ("alt") describes the category of the newsgroup, the second identifier ("fan") describes the type of newsgroup (e.g., a fan club), and the third identifier ("nsync") specifies the topic (i.e., the musical group Nsync). People who are interested in a specific topic can easily find a relevant newsgroup using Internet browsers, such as Netscape or Microsoft Explorer, and search engines, such as Alta Vista and Google, that allow easy access to newsgroup messages. Once found, people can read and send messages by subscribing to the newsgroup.[5] Newsgroups are flexible in terms of membership, as members can sign on/off and join/unjoin whenever they like.

Newsgroups are divided into categories known as hierarchies. Standard newsgroups hierarchies are created via a formal voting procedure that requires at least 100 members voting for its creation (Pfaffenberger, 1995).[6] Standard hierarchies include (a) comp. (examines aspects of computers and computer use); (b) misc. (miscellaneous); (c) news. (Usenet administration and use); (d) rec. (recreation, hobbies, and sports); (e) sci. (the sciences); (f) soc. (social issues); and (g) talk. (dialogue about controversial topics). These formal newsgroups typically have rules of conduct and standard procedures (usually provided by the administrator of the group), although they can be moderated or unmoderated with respect to users and message content.

Alternative ("alt.") Newsgroups

The majority of newsgroups are more "informal" than formal and, therefore, do not fit into any of the standard hierarchies (Spencer & Lawrence, 1998). The most prevalent example of an informal newsgroup hierarchy is the "alt."

---

[5]Usenet newsgroups require joining a group to post messages; other groups, such as Yahoo! Clubs, require an ID (i.e., registration) to post messages.

[6]If 100 more (valid) yes/create votes are received than no votes and if at least two-thirds of the votes cast are in favor of creation, then a standard newsgroup can be created (Young & Levine, 2000).

or alternative newsgroup. *Alt. newsgroups* are defined as a wide-open discussion group on nearly any subject imaginable (Pfaffenberger, 1995). Anyone can create an alt. newsgroup and, unlike standard newsgroups, starting an alt. newsgroup does not require 100 member votes. Instead, only four steps are needed to create an alt. newsgroup: (a) determining a name, (b) posting a proposal to alt.config (news server administration), (c) waiting a week and reading comments on alt.config, and (d) establishing the online presence of the group (Young & Levine, 2000). Some of the most popular online groups are alt. newsgroups, accounting for 59% of all user activity via message-reads among the top 100 text-based newsgroups (Newsadmin.com, 2001).[7]

The alt. hierarchy was deliberately created to encourage the creative and spontaneous side of Usenet, which can be alternatively viewed as a potential strength or weakness (Pfaffenberger, 1995). Spencer and Lawrence (1998) paradoxically noted that whereas some alt. groups thrive on message activity, others exist "either because the proponents were unaware of the group creation process for the better propagated mainstream hierarchies or because they found the process too onerous" (p. 422). Their lack of formality also allows such newsgroups to be formed quickly in relation to fast-breaking news (Spencer & Lawrence, 1998). Because they are the most unmoderated type of Usenet newsgroup, alt. newsgroups strongly rely on members' active interaction. Given their informal characteristics and lack of substantial stable barriers for entry, alt. newsgroups are more bona fide than standard newsgroups, a topic to which we now turn.

Newsgroups as Bona Fide Groups

As defined earlier, a *bona fide group* is a natural group that has stable, yet permeable, boundaries and is interdependent with its contexts. We now apply each part of this definition to newsgroups, in general, and to alt. newsgroups, in particular.

Newsgroups Are Natural Groups. At the most fundamental level, activities in a bona fide group naturally emerge over time via the "good faith" of their members (Lammers & Krikorian, 1997). This certainly applies to newsgroups, as people decide to form a newsgroup because of a common interest. Alt. newsgroups, in particular, are naturally emergent because there are relatively few external rules necessary to create them. Moreover, members create the content of a newsgroup via the exchange of messages and the asynchronous nature of newsgroups provides flexibility in that exchange by allowing users to post messages at any time of day, across time zones, and without regard to large computing capabilities (because they

---

[7]Of the top 100 text newsgroup reads on January 10, 2001, 13,429 out of 22,610 were from alt. groups.

are text-based). Newsgroups are, thus, built from the ground up and emerge out of the flexible interactions of its members.

Newsgroups Have Stable Boundaries.   According to Putnam and Stohl (1990), boundaries denote who is and is not a member of a group. In Usenet newsgroups, there is a straightforward way to measure group boundary stability because individuals must subscribe to a newsgroup to post and reply to messages (i.e., participate). It is possible to be a *lurker*, a person who views but cannot post messages, but such a person should not be considered an active participant of the newsgroup, as a newsgroup consisting only of lurkers would cease to exist.[8] Thus, the stable boundary of newsgroup membership is defined here as those who participate. What differentiates a newsgroup from a bulletin board is the requirement of membership to post messages to the group. Moreover, newsgroups reflect text-based message exchanges, which require adherence to only one channel of communication (asynchronous text); this structure establishes boundaries for the type and content of newsgroup member communication.[9]

Newsgroups Have Permeable Boundaries.   *Permeability* refers to the fluid and dynamic boundaries in newsgroups, and can be ascertained by examining message patterns that occur in such groups. The permeability of a boundary region can be explained via differentiation of internal and external group communication. Internally, members post messages at different times and who participates in these groups fluctuates over time. Furthermore, members can stop subscribing to a newsgroup at any time, which would reflect a lack of communication from them. Externally, new members can join the group at any time. It is, thus, difficult to keep track of all the participating members of a newsgroup, as the group boundaries shift constantly over time.

Newsgroups Demonstrate Member Interdependence.   Members of a newsgroup respond to messages, which often leads to other responses. These interactions form and, in turn, are formed through interdependence of group members; sustaining communication through common message patterns, therefore, both gives rise to and reflects a strong interdependence among members. Interdependence can also be seen in the equal access provided to all members in that they receive the same messages at the same time via the Internet.

---

[8]Lurking can actually be determined in Yahoo! Clubs by denoting the number of "visitors" to a specified group and can also be measured via access to systems administration logs.

[9]In fact, most newsgroups frown on the use of graphics, except for the "alt. binaries" newsgroups. Often, when pictures (i.e., binaries) are posted on text-based newsgroups, they get scathing replies from members because of the relative space they consume.

Newsgroups Are Interdependent With Their Context. Newsgroups, as explained previously, are created on the basis of particular topics; members have a common interest in a topic and this, in turn, forms an environment for subsequent communication. Context, therefore, generates membership and message activities by providing a shared referent that interests all group members. The commonality of messages also depends on specified subjects about which members communicate. If there is no interesting subject, members will have nothing to talk about in the immediate context and the group may cease to exist. If there are many interesting subjects being discussed in a newsgroup, members are more active and the group will probably thrive. Meaningful subjects, or message topics, are, as a result, created by group members in context and are used as referents in ensuing group discussion. Day-to-day activities in newsgroups are, thus, produced and reproduced through recurring patterns of communication.

Summary and Model Development

Figure 13.1, Newsgroups as Bona Fide Groups Model, summarizes the previous discussion and illustrates how each bona fide group characteristic is evidenced in a newsgroup. The text boxes represent salient conditions that make a newsgroup bona fide. "Context" includes the topic-based (e.g., title of newsgroup) and subject-based (e.g., message header) nature of these groups, and references the group's interdependence with its external environments. The "Natural" box references the fact that these groups are naturally emergent and situated in real-life contexts. The "Stable Boundary" box reflects the necessary conditions of people subscribing to this type of group and the inherent structural limitations of newsgroups (e.g., text only). "Permeable Boundary" represents the fluid structure of these groups, especially with respect to how their membership and, hence, their size, fluctuates over time. "Member Interdependence" focuses on the network-tie interaction that occurs between members of newsgroups via message exchange.

Structurally, Fig. 13.1 represents an extension of the bona fide group perspective by simultaneously modeling and explicating the internal and external forces that affect newsgroups. Such a conceptualization is based on Lewin's (1936) topological representation of group dynamics as psycho-sociological forces that impinge on individual and group boundary regions. Figure 13.1, thus, integrates a Lewinian approach to modeling individual and group forces with Putnam and Stohl's (1996) notion of internal and external factors (i.e., forces) that affect bona fide groups.

Although Fig. 13.1 helps to illustrate newsgroups as bona fide groups, the particular characteristics of newsgroups need further exploration. The obvious question concerns the *specific* elements that make a newsgroup

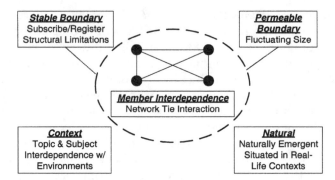

FIG. 13.1.   Newsgroups as Bona Fide Groups Model.

bona fide. To answer this question, we set out to examine, qualitatively, the salient characteristics of newsgroups. Of particular interest are the perceived communication activities and barriers to communication activities in newsgroup messages. In the next section, we describe the methods used to collect data about newsgroups that provide further insight into what is meant by a bona fide newsgroup.

RESEARCH DESIGN

Data Collection on the Internet

One of the unique characteristics of the Internet is the ability to record details of online interaction. The Internet is a public service and, hence, the material posted on it can be accessed by anyone. Moreover, in posting messages, individuals realize that the information they send can be read by anyone on the Internet. However, despite the opportunities to publicly examine the messages of Internet groups, there are some ethical issues about the protection of privacy of those communicating on the Internet that must be considered, especially in this early stage of such research. Researchers at the 2000 meeting of the Association of Internet Researchers in Lawrence, Kansas, addressed this question and concluded that collection of publicly available group data is considered to be an acceptable practice if the researcher does not participate in or manipulate the group discussion; that is, the role of a nonparticipant observer is ethically appropriate. The American Association for the Advancement of Science, however, reported that specifying the identity of groups can be detrimental, especially when messages can be traced back to the original user (Frankel & Siang, 1999).

We believe that individual and group confidentiality should be guaranteed when reporting data acquired from the Internet. Although the information is in the public domain, in keeping with other types of research, it is important to protect the identities of both individuals and groups. Researchers owe it to those discussing issues in a casual and frank manner on the Internet to protect their freedom of speech. By doing so, future researchers will more likely be able to collect data from the Internet. Hence, the identities of the newsgroups and their members are not specified in this study.

Data-Collection Procedures

The data collected for this study were obtained by accessing the Internet through DEC's Alta Vista service (http://altavista.com). Public services, such as Deja News (http://www.dejanews.com/)[10] or Netscan (www.netscan.research.microsoft.com), also could have been used to access the newsgroup information. Each service has its strengths and weaknesses; Alta Vista was chosen because of its ease in identifying newsgroup message activity. The general procedure for collecting data in this way is as follows: (a) access Alta Vista, (b) search Usenet, (c) enter the key words of the newsgroup topic one is looking for followed by SUBMIT, (d) click on a message from the newsgroup in which one is interested, (e) click on the newsgroup name, and (f) save all the messages. Alta Vista lists the number of messages posted for the past week, and allows sorting options by (a) date, (b) subject, (c) sender, and (d) message number. This procedure was performed for 26 separate alt. newsgroups chosen on the basis of the criterion that they represented a one-person "fan club." This criterion was used because we assumed that people might join alt. newsgroups with more than one person listed (e.g., a rock band) for different reasons (e.g., interest in different members of rock band), whereas an alt. newsgroup with a single person referenced would, by definition, demonstrate a common tie among members.

The first of two criteria stratifying alt. newsgroup one-person fan clubs employed three discernible genres: (a) authors, (b) musicians, and (c) movie figures. The first criterion, thus, examines contextual differences in alt. newsgroup fan clubs. For the second stratification criterion, groups were chosen on the basis of message numbers at the time of initial data collection. Our goal was to exclude from the sample both newsgroups that were extremely small and had little or no posting activity as well as newsgroups that were too large (and chaotic). As a result, three ranges of initial messages were chosen for the newsgroups selected: (a) 27–34, (b) 45–63, and (c) 80–122. These ranges were chosen because there were adequate distances between them and because they

---

[10]On February 12, 2001, Google.com acquired Deja News' Usenet archive.

proved relatively manageable with respect to gathering data over time. In summary, our research design consisted of identifying alt. newsgroup single-person fan clubs on the basis of newsgroup genre and newsgroup size, using a 3 × 3 factorial design of differing genre and size.

The data were collected at 6-day intervals, which allowed for the possibility of message deletion after a week (which was our experience in observing message-deletion patterns), over the course of 2 months. Six newsgroup message items were used in the analysis: (a) date, (b) subject, (c) sender ID, (d) total messages, (e) whether a message was posted to other newsgroups, and (f) number of newsgroups posted per message.

Analytic Method

After the third week of the data-collection process, a sample of the alt. newsgroup texts were assessed with respect to their communication activity. Six newsgroups (two from each genre) were randomly chosen and each individual analyst was given two separate newsgroups to examine (all newsgroups were analyzed at least twice). Analysts were undergraduate students in an Internet laboratory course who had no prior experience with newsgroups and, therefore, represented unbiased observers. Two analyses were performed. First, analysts were instructed to examine messages in their chosen newsgroups and to report the communication activity in those newsgroups. The instructions were purposively left broad to allow for multiple interpretations of the communication activity. After the fourth week of the data-collection process, analysts were given a general definition of *spam* as messages with no intrinsic "value" to a newsgroup and were asked to identify and elaborate on such posts. In this way, factors contributing to the decline of newsgroups could be examined in greater detail.

RESULTS AND DISCUSSION

This section reports the analyses of the alt. newsgroup texts, providing insight into how groups communicate online. The results are divided into two subsections that provide a rationale for two measures of newsgroup communication: communication activity and barriers to communication activity. Three selected analyses of communication activity are presented along with a discussion of their implications, followed by three selected analyses of barriers to such activity. We conclude this section with a discussion of the theoretical implications of the analyses, which leads to the development of a dynamic model of bona fide newsgroup communication.

Communication Activity Analyses

Analysis 1

I found that the newsgroup was used as a device to obtain things on the subject of MUSICIAN A's latest CD and a documentary that features MUSICIAN A's first release. I also found some interesting clips of how people felt about MUSICIAN A's music. I'd say 33% of it was informative and the other 67% of it were people looking for a common thread and using MUSICIAN A as a device to communicate with one another.

Analysis 2

On this newsgroup, I found conversations among fans of MOVIE FIGURE A. Users were writing to each other about different TV shows and movies. It was interesting to read their comments and views on what they thought was the moral issue or the "lesson" (if any applied) to the particular show of interest. It's interesting to know that anyone can just pick something of interest and chitchat with a plethora of other people about the subject. It opens the realization that everyone can make some sort of contact with whomever they want.

Analysis 3

The subject of my newsgroup was AUTHOR A. The newsgroup talked about a wide variety of things both relating and not relating to AUTHOR A's books. Some of the people talked about books of value (e.g., autographed and limited editions). Others simply conversed about their opinions of his books, characters, plots, etc. I also found that although the newsgroup members mostly discussed issues dealing with AUTHOR A's books, they also discussed everyday topics. It was interesting but not very informative. For the most part, they just chatted about a common hobby, AUTHOR A's books.

Communication Activity Discussion (Analyses 1–3)

These analyses reveal some interesting insights about the bona fide nature of alt. newsgroups. It should first be noted that the different genres elicited different types of topical discussion from their members: The first group discussed the latest albums, the second television shows and movies, and the third common books. These responses seem to indicate that the topic-based differentiation of these alt. newsgroups was reflected in the content discussed by the various groups. However, the topic of interest was not always important; it was often used simply as a vehicle by newsgroup members to elicit common threads. For example, as Analysis 1 revealed, people used Musician A as a device to open channels of communication about a wide variety of topical areas, demonstrating an interdependence among members that evolved beyond the immediate context of this particular alt. newsgroup. As noted in Analysis 2, members also spoke about different topics, such as movies and television shows related to Movie Figure A. In exploring how common threads occur, these analyses indicate that although alt. newsgroups often go "off-topic," such communication activity tends to be about a related area of members' interest. Individuals were free to participate in an ongoing topic or to create a new topic, and unique message patterns can help to distinguish members of newsgroups. For example, as shown in Analysis 3 of Author A's group, certain members varied their participation depending on whether the topics being discussed were book related, collectibles, and/or current events. The fluctuation of individual messages patterns provides an indicator of the permeability of the group and how individuals may develop group-specific roles based on their areas of expertise and interest.

Barriers to Communication Activity Analyses

Analysis 4

I thought it was interesting that one of the spams was actually an apology for the posting of topics that weren't related to the newsgroup. I guess it was nice of the organization to apologize, but it just created more garbage. Other spams that I found were related to money-making scams. I found an advertisement for software, a way to make money in the mail, and a way to buy my own London telephone number. The people who wrote these messages didn't care about MOVIE FIGURE B fans; they were mainly interested in sliding their ads onto the newsgroups in hopes that the fans would take time to read them. The spams that I discovered added a lot of garbage to the newsgroup. The spams also made it hard for me to figure out if the message I was reading pertained to MOVIE FIGURE B or not. I got very confused and had to read the entire spam before I realized that it had nothing to do with the newsgroup. Personally, if I were a MOVIE FIGURE B fan, I wouldn't go back to this newsgroup because it didn't contain much information on MOVIE FIGURE B.

Analysis 5

The thing that struck me the most was the fact that one spam would consistently elicit four or five responses, all requesting that the "spammer" not return to their board. These responses invite or evoke further conversation. The further conversation, of course, remains off topic. As many as six of the spams could have been avoided if the members of the board would simply ignore, or not be distracted by, the annoying spam of others and continue with the conversation that they are there for.

Analysis 6

When I read through the postings and would get stumped on a spam, I first read through it all. It was the same thing I did when I got my first chain letter on email. I read through all of the forwarded stuff, until I got to the main message that was being forwarded to everyone. When I got my next spam and saw that it was directed to a bunch of newsgroups, I read through the first two lines and then I quickly passed it up.

Barriers to Communication Activity Discussion (Analyses 4–6)

The second set of analyses reveals many interesting characteristics about spams and helps to determine the characteristics of off-topic newsgroup messages. First, as revealed in Analysis 4, advertisements are a constant source of spamming, as evidenced by the chain letters, money-making schemes, and software product marketing sent to newsgroups. The informational content of these messages is of low value to the members of these newsgroups because the messages do not pertain to the topic at hand. The result is that these messages can annoy members and make them not want to return to the newsgroup. Unfortunately, from the perspective of the interested members, the open boundaries of newsgroups seem to elicit such "junk" messages, as anyone can join an alt. newsgroup and they are less regulated than other newsgroup hierarchies. Advertisers, consequently, try to use alt. newsgroups as a mass medium to promote for free their product to a highly populated and/or targeted audience. However, as noted in Analyses 4 and 6, it was often difficult to identify when a message was a spam (although ways of handling spam are suggested). Moreover, as shown in Analyses 4 and 5, replies to spams are also often considered by members to be detrimental to the newsgroup, perhaps, as noted in Analysis 6, because such messages are often posted to multiple newsgroups. This phenomenon of *crossposting*, or posting messages to multiple groups simultaneously, warrants further exploration as a potential barrier to newsgroup communication activity.

Theoretical Implications and Summary

Analyses 1–3. Theoretical implications from the first three analyses provide a way to categorize the online communication of alt. newsgroups on the basis of commonly used concepts. Two characteristics, in particular, appear to relate to the nature of how individuals communicate within newsgroups: message participation and threads.

A *message* is defined as an individual article (e.g., text) posted to a newsgroup; *message participation* denotes the frequency of individual text communication to a newsgroup in a given time interval. From a network perspective, text communication encourages members to share opinions and ideas as a means to increase participation and, presumably, to develop status norms in online groups (see Sproull & Kiesler, 1991). Increased network use can also result in a saturation point that makes it economically and socially attractive for later adopters (Gurbaxani, 1990). The role of early opinion leaders in communication networks further uncover the processes by which saturation occurs (Rogers, 1971; Rogers & Kincaid, 1981). Leadership engaged in by individuals is an important factor in newsgroup formation and can be measured using individual message characteristics such as frequency or length. The relative frequency of messages posted by an individual—message participation—is the preferred measure of message length given the nature of brief message replies in newsgroups. We posit that the higher the message participation in a newsgroup, the more probable it is that the group will sustain itself over time; conversely, the lower the message participation in a newsgroup, the more likely it will decline. Message participation can, thus, be viewed as a means by which members exercise leadership to create a collective identity of a newsgroup.

The second characteristic of *threads* is defined as a group of messages with the same subject that constitute replies to an original message (Levine et al., 1995). For example, a response to an original message might be "re: Giants will the win Super Bowl." The "re:" specifies a continued thread to an original message; the second part of the thread signifies the *chain* of similar subject-heading messages. The more threads, the more potential for linking to others on the basis of a common referent. *Thread length* refers to the number of messages containing the same subject heading. High thread length indicates activation of message activities in a newsgroup with members feeding off each other's messages. As threads get longer, a newsgroup should thrive because of the strength of intragroup communication. The configuration of these structural patterns—such as the chain, Y, and circle networks (see Bavelas, 1950; Leavitt, 1951)—can be gleaned from the communication between members of a newsgroup. What is interesting in newsgroups is that the message headers form hubs around which members communicate. Rosen (2000) described network conversational hubs as key to the proliferation of "buzz" about a product; that buzz is facilitated around a common referent network hub. The density and configuration of the ties around network hubs tells much about a newsgroup, such as the core and periphery of a message network (Bienenstock & Bonacich, 1992).

Analyses 4–6. Theoretical implications from the last three analyses provide a way to categorize the barriers to newsgroup communication on the basis of the commonly used concepts. Two characteristics are identified and discussed as potential barriers to newsgroup communication: spams and crossposts.

On the Internet, as previously explained, spam is defined as a message that contains irrelevant content (Southwick & Falk, 1998). A spam is generally seen by newsgroup members as a form of online harassment but differs from a *flame* (an aggressive message or attack directed specifically at an individual or group) in that a spam is not topic or content based (Stivale, 1997). Spams are, thus, articles posted to a newsgroup that have little or no informational value. The analyses indicate that spams can be detrimental to a newsgroup's topic-based purpose and that an increase in spamming distracts newsgroup members. One possible heuristic would be to measure the informational value of a message as suggested by information theory (Shannon & Weaver, 1949). A simple, yet analogous, measure would be to take the inverse of the number of groups posted to in a message as the informational value of a specific message. Accordingly, we posit that the less the informational value of a message posted to a newsgroup, the more likely that message has an adverse effect on subsequent communication activity in that newsgroup.

The second characteristic, crossposting, as noted previously, refers to a message that is posted to multiple newsgroups. Such intergroup messages reflect external group communication (Putnam & Stohl, 1996). A. Schwartz and Garfinkel (1998) identified two (negative) forms of external communication on newsgroups: excessive crossposting and excessive multiposting. *Excessive crossposting* (ECP), also known as "velveeta," occurs when many newsgroups are specified in the same subject or header line and sent a message; *excessive multiposting* (EMP), also known as spamming, occurs when many newsgroups are sent the same message one at a time. The multiplication of EMP by the square root of ECP provides the Breidbart Index (BI), which is used to determine individual message overuse in newsgroups; a BI of 20 or higher indicates overuse (Spencer & Lawrence, 1998).[11] We posit that more crossposts result in reduced message activity within relatively unstable alt. newsgroups. Key to this idea is the nascent group developmental stage, in which the observed groups evidenced a relatively small number of initial messages (i.e., 27–122 per week). The extent to which newsgroups can withstand posting from other groups when their collective identity may not have been formed in a stable manner becomes a salient issue for emerging newsgroups. Crossposting, therefore, is seen as detrimental to a developing newsgroup's survival, as such messages do not differentiate newsgroups from one another and, thereby, threaten a developing newsgroup's identity.

In summary, message participation, threads, spams, and crossposts reflect communication activity and barriers to communication activity that take place in newsgroups. Message participation demonstrates an individual member's commitment to a newsgroup and, thereby, helps a newsgroup

---

[11]Although a useful rule of thumb, the BI is used to assess individuals' message behavior and, therefore, is not deemed applicable for tracking group processes.

to gain a critical mass and to foster a collective identity; threads are the responses to common message hubs that represent the strength of intranewsgroup identity; spams are messages with little or no informational value that constitute an external threat to newsgroup communication activity; and crossposts are intergroup threats to newsgroup communication activity. These concepts form the basis for a bona fide newsgroup model as a framework for understanding newsgroup communication.

The Bona Fide Newsgroup Model

Figure 13.2, the Bona Fide Newsgroup Model, depicts the bona fide characteristics of newsgroups. Message participation (MP) and threads (T) reflect newsgroup member interdependence and are modeled as internal (endogenous) factors. Crossposts (CP) and spams (S) characterize infiltration of the permeable boundary of newsgroup membership and are modeled as exogenous (external) factors. This conceptualization of newsgroups, thus, resonates with Putnam and Stohl's (1996) bona fide group "primary" constructs of internal and external (or boundary-spanning) communication. By elaborating on the details of the bona fide characteristics of newsgroups, Fig. 13.2, represents a more precise specification of the model proposed in Fig. 13.1.

Viewed in light of Fig. 13.2, alt. newsgroups have two strikes against them in their bid for survival: (a) lack of control over spams and crossposts and (b) lack of established threads and requisite message participation. Further examination of the model, however, reveals that the variables selected are grounded in a theory—self-organizing systems theory—which makes the model explanatory and not just exploratory. In the next section, we examine how self-organizing systems theory can be used to further explicate this model.

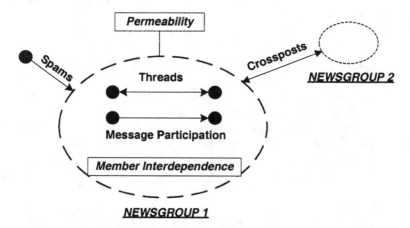

FIG. 13.2.   Bona Fide Newsgroup Model.

THEORETICAL PERSPECTIVE: SELF-ORGANIZING SYSTEMS THEORY

Bona Fide Groups as Self-Organizing Systems

A *system* is a collection of interdependent parts that is distinguishable from its surroundings by recognizable boundaries (Lucas, 2001). System boundaries, which are stable, yet permeable, can be used to define what is considered as being inside or outside of a group. A system's boundaries, as defined by exogenous and endogenous variables, thus, provides a way to operationalize the boundary conditions of a group.

Self-organization occurs when a system structure is robust and flexible enough to handle perturbations external to the system (Bierbracher, Nicolis, & Schuster, 1995). Consequently, a self-organizing approach examines the structural change processes of a system into an organized form by focusing on the interactions between components in a system in response to external variations. A *self-organizing system* changes its structure on the basis of its experiences and environment (Yovits, Jacobi, & Goldstein, 1962). Evidence of the importance of external forces is provided by Prigogine (1967), who noted that self-organization occurs in far-from-equilibrium (i.e., nonstable) conditions that dissipate (or slowly evolve) over time. He claimed that systems not only maintain themselves but also evolve into transformational structures using outside flows of energy. Similarly, Haken (1983) observed that lasers exhibit spontaneous fluctuations to different energy states as a result of external perturbations. Such "light avalanches" result from far-from-equilibrium conditions that reflect critical values of the combined actions of the individual components that comprise the system. Haken calls this process "synergetic" and provides the details by which a point of transition dissipates in relation to a system's external sources of energy. As a result, self-organizing systems are modeled such that endogenous and exogenous variations play critical roles in self-organization and system survival.

Bona fide groups organize on the basis of the relative interdependence (as demonstrated via internal and external communication) of members (Putnam & Stohl, 1996) and self-organization reflects the relative ability of a group to respond to external forces that threaten system stability. The study of self-organization seeks to uncover "the general rules under which such structure appears, the forms it can take, and methods of predicting to that structure that will result from changes to the underlying system" (Lucas, 2001, p. 3). The study of self-organization, consequently, employs a framework combining bona fide group processes of system stability and boundary permeability with internal and external communication activity. In the next section, we use this theoretical approach to develop a predictive model of newsgroup communication processes.

Self-Organizing Systems Theory (SOST) Model Development

In describing self-organizing systems from a group communication perspective, Contractor and Seibold (1993) specified four theoretical constructs as necessary, but not sufficient, conditions (i.e., they do not all
have to be present) of self-organizing: (a) autocatalysis, (b) mutual causation, (c) far-from-equilibrium (FFE) conditions, and (d) morphogenetic
change. As we explain, the first two conditions represent internal change
mechanisms, whereas the last two conditions represent external change
mechanisms.

Autocatalysis is evidenced when at least one of the components in a
system under study is directly influenced by another internal component. Autocatalysis can be viewed as the persuasive (one-directional)
component of SOST. For example, the presence of a key individual in a
group meeting can have direct influence on the actions of other group
members. Autocatalysis, thus, represents the endogenous reinforcement
of system behavior on the basis of individual change mechanisms
(Kontopoulus, 1993).

Mutual causation occurs when at least two components within a system influence each other reciprocally. The presence of "give and take" between components underscores the self-organizing generative mechanism
of mutual causation. Mutual causation occurs as a result of cooperative
communication emerging between elements in a system (Kontopoulus,
1993) and constitutes reciprocation between system elements, analogous
to the norm of reciprocity (Gouldner, 1960; Taylor & Altman, 1987) that
characterizes interpersonal communication processes. In group communication processes, mutual causation represents the interdependent ties
of group members.

Morphogenetic change occurs when a system experiences and responds
to random variations external to the system. Morphogenesis reflects the
change process of a current state of a system (Archer, 1982). This type of
change condition is random or chaotic in nature and, hence, is difficult to
predict. For example, a random event such as the unexpected loss of a key
group member can greatly affect group interaction and, consequently,
pose a threat to the group's established identity. This unexpected situation
is, of course, outside the control of group members, but it can substantially
alter the entire system. This type of random change, thus, tests the resolve
of a system as a whole.

Far-from-equilibrium (FFE) conditions occur when a system imports external energy, alters existing structures, and exports energy back out of the
system. FFE conditions have been explained as the way in which a system is
revitalized through expulsion of disorder back to the environment (Contractor, 1994; Contractor & Seibold, 1993). Intergroup communication is a

prime example of FFE conditions: As groups periodically interact, they change each other's characteristics. Such conditions can help to introduce a group to new ways of thinking, but they can also prove detrimental to a group's identity.[12] The alternative hypothesis, thus, warrants consideration: FFE conditions can *devitalize* a system when the system fails to effectively handle disorder. The fundamental assertion that we make is that a self-organizing approach can also be used to ascertain the conditions that lead to system extinction—that is, the lack of self-organization can be operationalized in devitalization processes. In the next section, we provide the self-organizing newsgroup model and apply it to newsgroup extinction.

The Self-Organizing Newsgroup Model

Figure 13.3 presents and illustrates the four theoretical conditions of SOST and forms the basis for examining the self-organization of groups. Autocatalysis and mutual causation are depicted as internal variations (endogenous variables), whereas morphogenetic change and FFE conditions represent external variations (exogenous variables). This model extends the explanatory potential of the bona fide newsgroup model (Fig. 13.2) by incorporating SOST constructs as theoretically based predictive elements of a dynamic system, and maintaining bona fide group conditions of boundary permeability and member interdependence.

Two main points should be emphasized about the model in Fig. 13.3. First, because alt. newsgroups are naturally emergent groups, endogenous variables are necessary for survival, whereas exogenous variables potentially undermine group identity and survival. The democratic nature of alt. newsgroups allows for their survival even beyond the sustenance of group activity (Spencer & Lawrence, 1998).[13] This phenomenon can be explained by the lack of control over exogenous factors combined with the lack of established endogenous ties. Second, in extending Fig. 13.2, Fig. 13.3 proposes operational-to-conceptual links between newsgroup and self-organizing constructs. More specifically, it is posited that (a) message participation is analogous to autocatalysis because of the importance of early opinion leaders and the degree of participation of individuals in news-

---

[12]Ashby (1947), who is credited with first coining the term *self-organization,* points out in later work (Ashby, 1960) that self-organization should be associated with the "good" of a system and frames the ability to self-organize with system survival. This bias could have led to Ashby's ultimate recapitulation of self-organizing systems as a field of study. We argue that assuming positive valence introduces a one-way bias into a self-organizing model.

[13]Spencer and Lawrence (1998) described the newsgroup tradition that "there is no such thing as a bogus group" and that group creation is resonant with free speech but group removal was not: "Alt. Groups just will not die except by exodus of any perceptible audience for the group—the empty shell of the group, however, will live on at far more sites than should be warranted" (p. 421).

groups, (b) threads are analogous to mutual causation because of their defining element of reciprocal message ties, (c) spams are analogous to morphogenetic change because of their random external nature, and (d) crossposting is analogous to FFE (in this case, the devitalization of less active alt. newsgroups) conditions because it represents intergroup communication. We now turn to an important extension of the model in Fig. 13.3—how naturally emergent communication can be used to predict the extinction of newsgroups.

Extension: The Newsgroup Death Model

The difference between the death and survival of alt. newsgroups can be explained as the relative lack of control over exogenous variables in such groups. Newsgroups that near extinction are in a negative spiral and cannot adapt or survive in the face of exogenous factors impinging on them. Newsgroup death, therefore, is modeled as a function of negative endogenous variables and positive exogenous variables (independent variables) compared to message activity (the dependent variable) over time. It should be noted, however, that the criterion for death is not absolute (it is highly unlikely that there will be zero messages in a group) and is operationally relaxed to that of near extinction (only a few messages).

Accordingly, four propositions predict the decline of communication activity in alt. newsgroups:

P1: As spamming increases, a newsgroup will near extinction. (Exogenous)

P2: As crossposts increase, a newsgroup will near extinction. (Exogenous)

P3: As thread length decreases, a newsgroup will near extinction. (Endogenous)

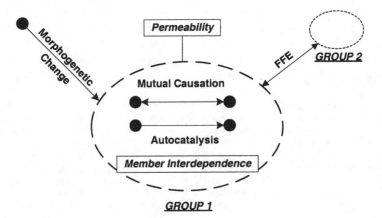

FIG. 13.3.   Self-Organizing Newsgroup Model.

P4: As message participation decreases, a newsgroup will near extinction. (Endogenous)

These propositions predict newsgroup death as a function of spams, crossposts, message participation, and thread length. Moreover, standardization of these variables (e.g., z-scores) allows for comparison between constructs in the above propositions. Each measure is operationalized as a ratio variable with respect to the population of group messages and can be viewed as network measures of newsgroup interaction (see Krikorian, in press). Network measures have similarly been used to study intergroup communication with respect to frequencies and patterns of interaction (Blau & Alba, 1982). Spams, crossposts, thread length, and message participation networks, thus, provide insight into the overall self-organization of alt. newsgroups. Moreover, because there are two positive and two negative factors, it is reasonable (at least at the outset) to incorporate the four standardized variables in a single model examining newsgroup extinction.[14] For subsequent points in time, the *newsgroup extinction factor* can be initially modeled as follows:

$$\textbf{Newsgroup Extinction Factor = } [\textbf{CP + S – MP – T}]_t \quad (13.1)$$

This measure takes into account the importance of the factors that prohibit the self-organization of newsgroups at particular points in time (t). If, say, a group evidenced a large number of relative crossposts and spams compared to thread length and message participation, the newsgroup extinction factor would be high.[15] The newsgroup extinction factor, thus, provides insight into the message activity of a particular newsgroup and it is initially posited that a high extinction factor would be indicative of a newsgroup in danger, as denoted by P5:

P5: A positive newsgroup extinction factor reflects a dying newsgroup.

By measuring change processes, the bona fide nature of newsgroups can also be further explored as changes in message structure over time. As newsgroups decline over time, we propose that they will be affected by the rates of change in self-organizing processes. By examining the rate of change of each of the variables over time, the model incorporates process

---

[14]Further refinement of the model that should occur after multiple observations of genre, size, and other segmentations of various types of online groups involves determining relative weighting of the factors.

[15]We further suggest that a standardization scheme be implemented that identifies newsgroups with extinction factors greater than zero and that qualitatively documents the communication activities of such newsgroups.

via momentum (i.e., a change in state). This change of state can basically be represented as follows:

$$\text{Newsgroup Extinction Rate} = \qquad (13.2)$$
$$[CP + S - MP - T]_{t2} - [CP + S - MP - T]_{t1}$$

This measure takes two reference points in time (e.g., a week or a month) and calculates change on the basis of the self-organization of a newsgroup. If, for instance, crossposts and spams are low for the month of June and high for the month of July, this would result in a high newsgroup extinction rate. It should be noted that this rate can be extended for multiple points in time and extrapolated to form more general (e.g., stochastic, lag-sequential) models. It can be initially posited that newsgroup extinction rates greater than zero suggests a newsgroup in decline, as indicated by P6:

P6: A positive newsgroup extinction rate reflects a declining newsgroup.

Combining P5 and P6 can help to assess the overall survivability of newsgroups; that is, positive extinction factors and rates can be used to predict whether a newsgroup will become extinct. By operationalizing the newsgroup extinction factor and rate, such measures can be compared to the number of messages at subsequent time periods, as described in the following hypothesis:

H1: If a newsgroup is both dying and declining, the number of messages for that newsgroup at a subsequent point in time will approach zero.

This hypothesis provides the means to assess a dying (P5) and declining (P6) newsgroup. If, for example, a newsgroup had a positive extinction factor for June and a positive extinction rate from May to June, that newsgroup would be predicted to be near extinction in ensuing months. The predictive element of H1 allows for testing of the model in an applied context and can be used to detect newsgroups in danger of extinction.

To summarize this section, we have proposed six propositions and a testable hypothesis by which to examine some of the factors that predict newsgroup death. We have, thus, provided a theoretical basis that moves the study of newsgroups as bona fide groups from explanatory to predictive research.

DISCUSSION

Four main points summarize the study of alt. newsgroups that we presented in this chapter. First, a bona fide group perspective was presented as a framework for analyzing electronic newsgroups, and reasons were offered as to why newsgroups have stable, yet permeable, boundaries and are interdependent with their contexts. Second, naturally emergent alt. newsgroups were explained and described using the bona fide group perspective. Third, qualitative analyses of alt. newsgroup messages provided insight into the nature of communication activity in such groups, resulting in the Bona Fide Newsgroup Model. Fourth, a self-organizing newsgroup model was proposed that incorporates dynamical theoretical constructs and the model was extended to predict the extinction of alt. newsgroups. We now discuss the limitations, practical applications, and future directions for research and then conclude with some final thoughts on what we have presented in this chapter.

Limitations

Several potential limitations are evident in terms of the work we presented in this chapter. The model, of course, needs to be tested, and some preliminary results are discussed elsewhere (see Krikorian, in press). Measurement techniques and analyses of the variables from that study will help to strengthen the validity of resultant models, particularly in identifying relationships between the self-organizing constructs (which are initially modeled as independent variables) and in accounting for potential multicolinearity effects. Second, the model is based on a particular type of group—alt. newsgroups—which may influence its overall applicability to other electronically based groups. Irrespective of the type of newsgroup (e.g., alt.), it is posited that natural, asynchronous electronic groups exhibit similar patterns of message decline. Third, the newsgroups we examined had small ranges of weekly postings and, therefore, were more susceptible to extinction. The relative size of a newsgroup (i.e., message posts) may also have affected the results found here. For example, smaller sized groups may be affected in an adverse manner by crossposts, whereas larger groups may benefit from them (see Smith, 1999). It seems more likely, however, that smaller groups would be more likely than larger groups to die off per se. Perhaps a bifurcation point exists between small and large groups as to the effects of crossposts and this point can be used to indicate a shift in newsgroup activity. Fourth, the selection of coders of the messages was from a convenience sample, although they were all inexperienced with newsgroups and only identified the communication activity of the alt. newsgroups. Selection of message analyses was determined by the frequency of responses and qualitative insight, and there is a highly subjective element in the latter criterion. We suggest that future research contain more points of observation and we encourage other models be developed to help us better understand various electronic groups, organizations, and systems in applied contexts.

Practical Applications

From an applied perspective, the Internet is a growing phenomenon in dire need of study as people continue to find new ways to express themselves electronically. Electronic newsgroups, in particular, offer a unique form of Internet communication that is ripe for examination. The initial indications from our study provide practical advice that reducing crossposts and spams and increasing message thread length suggest basic ways to combat newsgroup extinction. Increasing the scope of the methods, variables, models, and equations presented can help to understand the mechanisms by which online groups die and decline; by understanding such "failures to communicate," we gain insight into how to better communicate.

The work we reported here also offers a theoretical and methodological basis for using automated data-collection and software analysis tools to examine online group communication message processes. Groupscope, recently developed by the lead author, is one such tool that provides network analytic solutions for online groups and to explore various forms of online communication.[16] The tool can be used, for example, by corporate sponsors who have online groups on their Intranets, by marketing firms as indicators of public opinion, by the federal government for establishing policy on geographically dispersed asynchronous discussion groups, by administrators who determine newsfeeds and which groups are allowed access to them, and by members of online groups as indicators of their group's communication activity.

Future Directions for Research

Further applications of the theoretical model presented here could incorporate the study of e-mail lists, which should evidence less external message activity than newsgroups. These computer-mediated groups would, by nature, be more endogenous and, therefore, offer an excellent site for examining autopoeisis (i.e., self-generating processes) as a distinct form of self-organization (Barnett, in press; Mabry, 1999; Maturana & Varela, 1980).

As noted earlier, Yahoo! Clubs allow for message posting and thread communication, as well as chat, news, links, calendar, and photos. Yahoo! Clubs can be private (i.e., nonlisted) or public (i.e., listed). Private clubs are by "invitation only" and, therefore, represent a different type of online group than alt. newsgroups; public clubs, in contrast, have similar natural boundaries as alt. newsgroups in that anyone can join a public Yahoo! Club.[17] It would be

---

[16]For further information on this software product, contact Dean Krikorian by email (dk75@cornell.edu)

[17]On February 12, 2002, Yahoo! Club was merged with Yahoo! Groups. The integration of these two services yielded a similar structural format.

interesting to note the similarities and differences between public and private clubs, particularly those clubs that discuss a similar topic.

From a communication perspective, a most promising future direction is to explore the nature of thread communication. This would involve the analyses of links and nodes over time as emergent networks (Monge & Eisenberg, 1987) by examining the chain-like structures that emerge between individuals and among group members. Threads as "memes," or replications of extant message structures, may help to uncover these processes and offer a theoretic basis for such analyses (see Krikorian, Taylor, & Harms, 1998).

CONCLUSION

We began this chapter with a theoretical exploration of the bona fide group perspective as applied to electronic newsgroups. The construct of bona fide groups makes heuristic sense and has much potential for the study of the boundaries and contexts of natural groups. We extended the bona fide group perspective using self-organizing systems theory (Contractor & Seibold, 1993), which provided a means for examining the dynamic boundaries and interdependence of alt. newsgroup development and decay. The bona fide group perspective, especially when tied to other relevant theories and perspectives, thus, provides an important framework for exploring, understanding, and predicting group communication patterns on the Internet.

ACKNOWLEDGMENT

Portions of the theoretical bases of this chapter were presented at the 1998 International Communication Association Conference, Chicago, IL and the 1998 Alta Conference on Self-Organizing, Alta, UT. The authors would like to thank Mohammad Mdyusoff for literature review contributions to this essay.

REFERENCES

Archer, M. S. (1982). Morphogenesis versus structuration: On combining structure and action. *British Journal of Sociology, 33*, 455–483.
Ashby, W. R. (1947). Principles of the self-organizing dynamic system. *Journal of General Psychology, 37*, 125–128.
Ashby, W. R. (1960). *Design for a brain: The origin of adaptive behavior* (Rev. 2nd ed.). New York: John Wiley.
Bales, R. F., & Strodtbeck, F. L. (1953). Phases in group problem solving. *Journal of Abnormal and Social Psychology, 46*, 485–495.

Barnett, G. A. (in press). Introduction to self-organizing systems. In G. A. Barnett & R. Houston (Eds.), *Progress in communication sciences: Vol. 18. Self-organizing systems*. Greenwich, CT: Ablex.

Bavelas, A. (1950). Communication patterns in task-oriented groups. *Journal of Acoustical Society of America, 22,* 725–730.

Berlo, D. K. (1960). *The process of communication: An introduction to theory and practice*. New York: Holt, Rinehart and Winston.

Bienenstock, E. J., & Bonacich, P. (1992). The core as a solution to exclusionary networks. *Social Networks, 14,* 231–244.

Bierbracher, C. K., Nicolis, G., & Schuster, P. (1995). *Self-organization in the physico-chemical and life sciences* [Report EUR 16546]. Brussels, Belgium: European Commission.

Blau, J., & Alba, R. (1982). Empowering nets of participation. *Administrative Science Quarterly, 27,* 363–379.

Bonner, H. (1959). *Group dynamics: Principles and applications*. New York: Ronald Press.

Cartwright, D., & Zander, A. (Eds.). (1968). *Group dynamics: Research and theory* (3rd ed.). New York: Harper & Row.

Contractor, N. S. (1994). Self-organizing systems perspective in the study of organizational communication. In B. Kovaci'c (Ed.), *New approaches to organizational communication* (pp. 39–66). Albany: State University of New York Press.

Contractor, N. S., & Seibold, D. R. (1993). Theoretical frameworks for the study of structuring processes in group decision support systems: Adaptive structuration theory and self-organizing systems theory. *Human Communication Research, 19,* 528–563.

Comer, D. E. (1997). *The Internet book: Everything you need to know about computer networking and how the Internet works* (2nd ed.). Upper Saddle River, NJ: Prentice-Hall.

Courtright, J. A., & Perse, E. M. (1998). *Communicating online: A brief guide to the Internet*. Mountain View, CA: Mayfield.

Deja News (2001). *Usenet short course*. Retrieved January 3, 2001, from http://www.deja.com/ info/usenet_faq.shtml

Dodge, M., & Kitchin, R. (2001). *Mapping cyberspace*. New York: Routledge.

Fisher, B. A. (1970). Decision emergence: Phases in group decision making. *Speech Monographs, 37,* 53–66.

Frankel, M. S., & Siang, S. (1999). *Ethical and legal aspects of human subjects research on the Internet: A report of a workshop*. Retrieved January 5, 2002, from http://www.aaas.org/ spp/dspp/sfrl/projects/inters/report.pdf

Frey, L. R. (1994). The naturalistic paradigm: Studying small groups in the postmodern era. *Small Group Research, 25,* 551–577.

Fulk, J., & Steinfield, C. W. (Eds.). (1990). *Organizations and communication technology*. Newbury Park, CA: Sage.

Gouldner A. W. (1960). The norm of reciprocity: A preliminary statement. *American Sociological Review, 25,* 161–178.

Gurbaxani, V. (1990). Diffusion in computing networks: The case of BitNet. *Communications of the ACM, 33,* 65–75.

Haken, H. (1983). *Laser theory*. Berlin, Germany: Springer-Verlag.

Hauben, M., & Hauben, R. (1997). *Netizens: On the history of Usenet and the Internet*. Los Alamitos, CA: IEEE Computer Society Press.

Hiltz, S. R., & Turoff, M. (1978). *The network nation: Human communication via computers*. Reading, MA: Addison-Wesley.

Kontopoulos, K. M. (1993). *The logics of social structure*. Cambridge, England: Cambridge University Press.

Krikorian, D. H. (in press). The newsgroup death model: Self-organizing system results and implications. In G. A. Barnett & R. Houston (Eds.), *Progress in communication sciences: Vol. 18. Self-organizing systems*. Greenwich, CT: Ablex.

Krikorian, D. H., Taylor, J. R., & Harms, C. M. (1998, November). *Knotting by netting: Thread emergence in electronic newsgroups using network constructs*. Paper presented at the meeting of the National Communication Association, New York, NY.

Lammers, J. C., & Krikorian, D. H. (1997). Theoretical extension and operationalization of the bona fide group construct with an application to surgical teams. *Journal of Applied Communication Research*, *25*, 17–38.

Leavitt, H. J. (1951). Some effects of certain communication patterns on group performance. *Journal of Abnormal and Social Psychology*, *46*, 38–50.

Levine, J. R., Baroudi, C., & Young, M. L. (1995). *The Internet for dummies* (3rd ed.). San Mateo, CA: IDG Books.

Lewin, K. (1936). *Principles of topological psychology* (F. Heider & G. M. Heider, Trans.). New York: McGraw-Hill.

Lewin, K. (1947). Frontiers in group dynamics I: Concept, method and reality in social science: Social equilibria and social change. *Human Relations*, *1*, 5–41.

Lucas, S. (2001). *Self-organizing systems FAQ*. Retrieved January 5, 2002, from http:// www.calresco.org/ sos/sosfaq.htm

Mabry, E. A. (1999). The systems metaphor in group communication. In L. R. Frey (Ed.), D. S. Gouran, & M. S. Poole (Assoc. Eds.), *The handbook of group communication theory & research* (pp. 71–91). Thousand Oaks, CA: Sage.

Maturana, H. R., & Varela, F. J. (1980). *Autopoeisis and cognition: The realization of living*. Dordrect, Holland: D. Reidel.

McLuhan, M. (1962). *The Gutenberg galaxy: The making of typographic man*. Toronto, Canada: University of Toronto Press.

McGrath, J. E., & Hollingshead, A. B. (1994). *Groups interacting with technology: Ideas, evidence, issues, and an agenda*. Thousand Oaks, CA: Sage.

Monge, P. R., & Eisenberg, E. M. (1987). Emergent communication networks. In F. M. Jablin, L. L. Putnam, K., H. Roberts, & L. W. Porter (Eds.), *Handbook of organizational communication: An interdisciplinary perspective* (pp. 304–342). Thousand Oaks, CA: Sage.

Monge, P. R., Farace, V., Eisenberg, E. M., Miller, K., & White, L. (1984). The process of studying process in organizational communication. *Journal of Communication*, *34*(1), 22–43.

Newsadmin.com (2001, February 10). *Top 100 newsgroup readership*. Retrieved March 10, 2001, from http://www.newsadmin.com/top100reads.htm

Pfaffenberger, B. (1995). *The Usenet book: Finding, using, and surviving newsgroups on the Internet*. Reading, MA: Addison-Wesley.

Poole, M. S. (1983). Decision development in small groups III: A multiple sequence theory of decision development. *Communication Monographs, 50,* 321–341.

Preece, J. (2000). *Online communities: Designing usability, supporting sociability*. New York: John Wiley.

Prigogine, I. (1967). Dissipative structures in chemical systems. In S. Claesson (Ed.), *Fast reactions and primary processes in chemical kinetics* (pp. 371–382). New York: Interscience.

Putnam, L. L., & Stohl, C. (1990). Bona fide groups: A reconceptualization of groups in context. *Communication Studies, 41,* 237–247.

Putnam, L. L., & Stohl, C. (1996). Bona fide groups: An alternative perspective for communication and small group decision making. In R. Y. Hirokawa & M. S. Poole (Eds.), *Communication and group decision making* (2nd ed., pp. 147–178). Thousand Oaks, CA: Sage.

Rice, R. E. (1982). Communication networking in computer-conferencing systems: A longitudinal study of group roles and system structure. In M. Burgoon (Ed.), *Communication yearbook* (Vol. 6, pp. 925–944). Beverly Hills, CA: Sage.

Rice, R. E., & Associates (1984). *The new media: Communication research and technology*. Beverly Hills, CA: Sage.

Richards, W. D., & Barnett, G. A. (Eds.). (1993). *Progress in communication sciences: Vol. 12. Advances in the study of communication networks*. Norwood, NJ: Ablex.

Rogers, E. M., & Kincaid, D. L. (1981). *Communication networks: Toward a new paradigm for research*. New York: Free Press.

Rogers, E. M. (with Shoemaker, F.) (1971). *Communication of innovations: A cross-cultural approach* (2nd ed.). New York: Free Press.

Rosen, E. (2000). *The anatomy of buzz: How to create word-of-mouth marketing*. New York: Doubleday.

Schramm, W. L. (1954). *The process and effects of mass communication*. Urbana: University of Illinois Press.

Scott, C. R. (1999). Communication technology and group communication. In L. R. Frey (Ed.), D. S. Gouran, & M. S. Poole (Assoc. Eds.), *The handbook of group communication theory & research* (pp. 432–472). Thousand Oaks, CA: Sage.

Schwartz, A., & Garfinkel, S. (1998). *Stoppin and news postings*. Sebastipol, CA: O'Reilly.

Schwartz, D. F. (1968). *Liaison communication roles in a formal organization*. Unpublished doctoral dissertation. Michigan State University, East Lansing.

Shannon, C. E., & Weaver, W. (1949). *The mathematical theory of communication*. Urbana: University of Illinois Press.

Smith, M. A. (1999). Invisible crowds in cyberspace: Mapping the social structure of the Usenet. In M. A. Smith & P. Kollock (Eds.), *Communities in cyberspace* (pp. 195–219). London: Routledge.

Southwick, S., & Falk, J. D. (1998). *The net abuse FAQ*. Retrieved February 17, 1999, from http://www.cybernothing.org/faqs/net-abuse-faq.html#2.1

Spencer, H., & Lawrence, D. (1998). *Managing Usenet: An administrator's guide to Netnews*. Cambridge, MA: O'Reilly.

Sproull, L., & Kiesler, S. (1991). *Connections: New ways of working in the networked organization*. Cambridge, MA: MIT Press.

Stivale, C. J. (1997). Spam: Heteroglossia and harassment in cyberspace. In D. Porter (Ed.), *Internet culture* (pp. 133–144). New York: Routledge.

Taylor, D. A., & Altman, I. (1987). Communication in interpersonal relationships: Social penetration theory. In M. E. Roloff & G. R. Miller (Eds.), *Interpersonal processes: New directions in communication research* (pp. 257–277). Newbury Park, CA: Sage.

Tuckman, B. W. (1965). Developmental sequence in small groups. *Psychological Bulletin, 63*, 384–399.

Watt, J. H., & Van Lear, C. A. (Eds.). (1996). *Dynamic patterns in communication processes*. Newbury Park, CA: Sage.

Weick, K. E. (1979). *The social psychology of organizing* (2nd ed.). Reading, MA: Addison-Wesley.

Weise, E. (2001, March 13). Usenet users up in arms after Deja sale. *USA Today*, p. 3D.

Wellman, B., & Gulia, M. (1999). Virtual communities as communities: Net surfers don't ride alone. In M. A. Smith & P. Kollock (Eds.), *Communities in cyberspace* (pp. 163–190). New York: Routledge.

Young, M. L., & Levine, J. (2000). *Poor Richard's building online communities: Create a web community for your business, club, association, or family*. Lakewood, CO: Top Floor.

Yovits, M. C., Jacobi, G. D., & Goldstein, G. D. (Eds.). (1962). *Self-organizing systems*. Washington, DC: Spartan Books.

14

DOING "GROUPNESS" IN A SPATIALLY DISTRIBUTED WORK GROUP:

THE CASE OF VIDEOCONFERENCES AT *TECHNICS*

Christoph Meier
Fraunhofer-Institute for Industrial Engineering (FhG-IAO)

The possibility of hearing and at the same time seeing one or more persons at a remote location has been available for quite some time now. For example, the German Reichspost operated a public "Bildfernsprechdienst" (picture-phone service) between Berlin and Leipzig/Munich from 1936 to 1940. In 1964, the first commercial videoconferencing system (AT&T's "Picturephone") was introduced at the World Fair in New York City (Hart, Svenning, & Ruchinskas, 1995; Reuter, 1990). Since those early days, several new generations of videoconferencing equipment have been introduced that allow for meetings to be conducted via a two-way audiovisual connection between at least two physically separated sites. However, videoconferencing today is still a somewhat unfamiliar way of conducting business; for most people, it is a rather less familiar form of communication compared to, for example, using e-mail.

For the field of group communication, the study of video-mediated communication and distributed teams at work has, up to now, remained a relatively neglected area of research (for a recent overview of theory and research on communication technology and group communication, see Scott, 1999). This is unfortunate, as distributed project teams (often transcending organizational boundaries) and tools to support cooperation in distributed teams, such as teamware and groupware (cf. Chaffey, 1998), are becoming more and more common in the contemporary work experience. Studying collaborative processes and communicative practices of distributed work groups provides opportunities to understand such important issues as (a) the difficulties involved in developing a common ground that is indispensable for effective team cooperation, (b) the interplay of organizational identities and (multiple) team allegiances, and (c) the achievement of "groupness" in the course of task-related and nontask-related interaction.

In this chapter, I focus specifically on the achievement of "groupness" in the course of meetings conducted as videoconferences. The main argument I advance is that to appreciate groupness as it is locally and interactionally achieved by any bona fide group, we need to understand, in particular, the communicative situation—its particular logic and dynamics and its implications for joint activity—in which a group operates. Considering that almost 30 years ago Goffman (1972) issued a call to study the syntax of interaction and "moments and their men" rather than "men and their moments" (p. 3), this claim may perhaps appear to be outdated. However, it gains new relevance when the concern is not with the forms of unmediated face-to-face interaction to which people have long been accustomed but, rather, with the technically mediated forms of face-to-face interaction that have become possible over the course of the last few years. After all, it is not yet clear how unmediated face-to-face interaction differs from mediated interaction in the course of videoconferences; chance meetings via a video-window connecting, for example, the common room of two research labs; or encounters in a cyberworld where people move about and are represented by means of a more or less abstracted avatar (see e.g., www.cybertown.com).

Given this lack of knowledge, prior to asking how groupness is achieved in videoconferencing (or in any other technically mediated encounter), it is necessary to understand the inherent logic and dynamics of videoconferencing as a social situation. To achieve this understanding, I employ specific methods and apply particular concepts to a case study of videoconferencing. First, to study the particular logic and dynamics of a particular setting for interaction, interviewing and/or participant observation are not sufficient. Rather, it is necessary to analyze audiovisual records that preserve the details of the scenery as well as the realization, timing, and sequential structure of communicative actions.[1] Accordingly, this chapter is

---

[1]Although conducting interviews with those who have experience with videoconferencing may provide accounts of participants' impressions and experiences, it is difficult to get at the actual details of their activities in this way. *How* people do things is something they usually treat as uninteresting in the normal course of events; consequently, the details of their doings remain "seen but unnoticed"   (*continued on next page*)

based on the detailed analysis of a short stretch of interaction in a video-conference that was documented with videorecording equipment. Second, I explore how groupness is locally realized in that videoconferencing situation and use Goffman's concepts of footing and participation frameworks (i.e., the stance participants take toward any utterance or bodily communication) as analytic tools.

I start with a brief characterization of business group meetings, followed by a short discussion of videoconferencing as a new way of conducting such meetings and as a new environment for group communication. Following this introductory material, the videoconferencing group being studied is introduced, and an episode of one of its videoconferences is presented and analyzed in some detail, particularly with regard to the participation frameworks established. I end the chapter by pointing out how some of the situational features of videoconferencing have to be worked with and around when doing groupness in such a setting and conclude that videoconferencing is a particularly difficult environment for establishing groupness.

MEETINGS AS OCCASIONS FOR GROUP COMMUNICATION IN ORGANIZATIONS

Group meetings are an important and commonplace feature of life in contemporary organizations and they can serve numerous functions. They may be employed for disseminating information, soliciting feedback and tossing around ideas, solving problems and arriving at decisions, and/or solidifying support for decisions already arrived at and actions already taken (e.g. Kriesberg & Guetzkow, 1950). Workplace group meetings may be planned and prepared for, take place regularly without much planning, or be improvised ad hoc. Because such meetings often take up more time than people would like them to and frequently produce less satisfying results than were expected (see, e.g., Seibold & Krikorian, 1997), they have become the focus of much scholarly and popular work.

Looked at in terms of communication/interaction processes, group meetings can be considered, to use Wittgenstein's (1977) metaphor, a set

---

[1](continued from previous page)   (Garfinkel, 1967, p. 28). With regard to the study of group interaction, it has long been recognized (e.g., Bales & Gerbrands, 1948; Kendon, 1979) that merely sitting in and observing is not sufficient for understanding and reconstructing group processes, including the communicative processes involved, because it is virtually impossible to preserve the timing and sequential structure, as well as the identifying details, of communicative actions (Bergmann, 1985). For this, audiovisual recordings of the interaction are required, which provide a rich and permanent record that can be accessed and analyzed repeatedly (Grimshaw, 1982). I have discussed in some detail elsewhere (Meier, 1998) issues related to the authenticity or naturalness of any behavior that is observed in a systematic fashion, as well as issues surrounding the putative objectivity of an audiovisual record, and, therefore, do not touch on them here.

of established social forms bearing family resemblances, all of which are oriented toward:

- creating a boundary between the "in" and "out" of this particular activity and, thus, providing a way to distinguish, for example, between what is said informally in the pre- or post-meeting phase and what is discussed during the meeting;
- establishing a boundary between ratified participants and those not invited to participate (e.g., by means of gathering in a room and closing the door);
- maximizing opportunities for a joint focus of attention and mutual monitoring of all present, while, at the same time, making this joint focus and mutual monitoring mandatory (e.g., by means of limiting the number of participants and through seating arrangements in which participants are more or less evenly distributed around a table rather than forming separate clusters); and, in the case of more formal meetings conducted on the basis of rules of order,
- providing resources for ordering contributions in a specific way (e.g., through alternating slots for speakers arguing a pro or con position or by going "round the table"; see, e.g., Boden, 1994; Cuff & Sharrock, 1985; Meier, 1997; Schwartzman, 1989).

Looked at in terms of organizational processes, face-to-face work group meetings are "organizations in action" (Boden, 1994) and occasions where the missions of organizations are constructed, communicated, and confirmed (Schwartzman, 1989). They are also prime occasions for doing groupness in organizations, and it is in the course of such meetings that social relationships (e.g., work group memberships, alliances, and intergroup competition) are established and displayed. Whether meetings that are facilitated and mediated by communication technology, such as group decision support systems or videoconferencing systems, function in this way as well has yet to be established, a topic to which I next turn.

VIDEOCONFERENCING AS A NEW WAY OF CONDUCTING GROUP MEETINGS

A *videoconference* is set up by establishing an audiovisual connection between two or more participants at two or more physically separate locations. Early videoconferences were conducted by closed-circuit television, which was followed by several generations of videoconferencing equipment: elaborate corporate videoconferencing studios with broadband connections to other locations; more flexible roll-about systems operating on digital networks, such as ISDN, and moved on an as-needed basis into ordinary meeting rooms; or still more recently, videoconferencing add-on kits for the personal computer on the corporate work desk. There are purely software-based solutions requiring no such expansion cards available (e.g., White Pine's CUSeeMe or Microsoft's NetMeeting), and the most current development is videostreaming technology that allows for videoconferencing via the Internet.

Videoconferencing, as I use the term here, refers to conducting a work meeting using such equipment. It is a relatively new way of doing work that has been hailed for such benefits as reduced travel costs, reduced time away from the work desk, easier scheduling of meetings, and more timely outcomes. Despite these advertisements, however, the adoption of videoconferencing by organizations has been consistently more sluggish than projected (see Egido, 1990; Lautz, 1995).

Research on video-mediated communication dates back to the early 1970s when closed-circuit television began to be used in medical settings (cf. Parker & Olgren, 1984). That research emerged from diverse disciplinary origins (such as social psychology, organization science, and the study of computer-supported cooperative work), pursued different issues depending on the discipline from which it emerged, and only recently has been drawn together (see Finn, Sellen, & Wilbur, 1997). Thus, for example, social psychologists (e.g., Short, Williams, & Christie, 1976) have inquired into the consequences of video-mediated communication on interpersonal perception and the ability of groups to cope with cooperative and competitive tasks; organization scientists (e.g., Bronner, 1996) have studied the impact of videoconferencing on information processing and decision making; and researchers in the field of computer-supported cooperative work (e.g., J. S. Olson, Olson, & Meader, 1995) have investigated the role of the quality of digitized audiovisual information, along with the delays caused by signal processing, in the search for optimal cooperation support with minimal requirements for bandwidth and processing power.

Prior research on videoconferencing has led to some converging findings: Videoconferences are better suited to support such activities as informing team members than to negotiating controversial issues; they are, in comparison to unmediated face-to-face meetings, somewhat more difficult to lead and direct, with phases devoted to the organization of such meetings that are comparatively more extended; and, finally, there is a tendency in videoconferences for the development of such subgroups as "us here" and "them there" (Barefoot & Strickland, 1982; J. S. Olson et al., 1995; Sellen, 1992; Short et al., 1976; Weinig, 1997). It has also been pointed out that videoconferencing affects the way participants perceive each other; specifically, participants at the remote site(s) tend to be perceived as less sympathetic and less competent compared to participants in the same room (Storck & Sproull, 1995). However, other research results are equivocal (e.g., Finn, 1997; G. M. Olson & Olson, 1997); for instance, some studies report that problem-solving groups achieve better results in face-to-face interaction compared to videoconferencing, whereas other studies have found no significant observable differences, and still other studies conclude that better results are achieved via videoconferencing (Meier, 2000).

Although there exists a body of research on videoconferencing as a form of work meeting, a key issue from the point of view of group communication studies remains as yet unanswered: What are the implications of videoconferencing for group communication, group dynamics, and the realization of groupness? It is this issue that I address in the remainder of this chapter.

VIDEOCONFERENCING AS A NEW ENVIRONMENT FOR DOING "BEING A GROUP"

A *group* is commonly defined as comprising a limited number of members who interact repeatedly, have evolved shared norms and a describable communicative structure, and share a distinct social identity vis-à-vis outsiders (e.g., Graumann, 1994). With respect to the last characteristic, groups have long been regarded as distinct entities marked off from surrounding contexts by clear boundaries. Only recently, however, has it been appreciated that groups may not be stable social entities but, rather, amoeba-like; their boundaries and borders may be unstable, permeable, and ambiguous at multiple levels and change according to the salient contexts at hand (Putnam & Stohl, 1996; Stohl & Putnam, 1994).

One consequence of this revised view emerges immediately: If group membership and groupness cannot be taken for granted, we must look at the details of participants' doings—and, in particular, at the details of their communicative actions—to understand how groupness is accomplished. A second consequence is that any appreciation of the accomplishment of groupness turns on an understanding of the occasions and situations in which bona fide group members work together collaboratively. These occasions and situations may differ, for example, with respect to the organizational context at hand, the space and the furnishings available, or the information and communication technologies employed. In the case of the group to be discussed here, this involves an understanding of their regular videoconferences as a context for doing groupness.

On the basis of detailed analyses of audiovisual recordings of natural videoconferences, I have argued elsewhere (Meier, 2000) that the introduction of videoconferencing technologies in the workplace is likely to establish a collection of communicative forms bearing family resemblances. These family resemblances turn, in large part, on the technical features of videoconferencing systems and their consequences for interactional processes—the changed spatial ecology of the meeting rooms in which participants gather, the (in)ability of participants to establish eye contact with persons at the remote location(s), and the time lag resulting from analog-digital signal conversion plus signal propagation across distances. Thus, videoconferencing imposes a particular interactional context and accompanying dynamics that group members have to work with and around in their efforts to establish groupness. The result is that any joint focus of attention comprising all participants appears much more fragile than in a face-to-face group meeting. This occurs because the just-mentioned time lag occasionally throws off action coordination across sites. Once the interactional system becomes imbalanced during the course of a discussion (e.g., in the course of a controversial discussion at one location), it becomes very difficult for participants at the remote location(s) to get a word in again. Finally, communicative actions performed "here" (i.e., at the local site) come across less than fully transparent "there" (i.e., at the remote site); consequently, participants at the remote location(s), at times, appear to be uncooperative or even slow witted (see Meier, 2000). With these characteristics in mind, I now turn to analyzing a particular episode taken from a videorecorded videoconference group meeting. First, however, I introduce the setting where the recording was made.

GROUP VIDEOCONFERENCING AT TECHNICS

Until about January 1996, the approximately 12 members of the Customer Services Council (CSC) representing the Customer Services Division at Technics[2] (the German subsidiary of a large corporation operating internationally) used to meet face-to-face on a biweekly basis either at Karlsruhe, the company's German headquarters, or at Wesseling, the largest of several other company sites in Germany. This necessitated about half of the group flying to the other site at regular intervals to participate. Eventually, management decided to invest in the necessary equipment and conduct these meetings as videoconferences.[3]

---

[2]The name of the corporation and the names of participants and locations are pseudonyms.

[3]The equipment employed was a PictureTEL Concorde 4510 with optional electronic sound module (full-duplex, echo-cancelling, and noise reduction).

When I approached a member of the CSC in my search for a field site at which to conduct my research,[4] the group had been conducting its videoconference meetings for about 6 months. Following an initial research phase of about 3 months, during which I observed several videoconferences, four videoconferences and a face-to-face meeting were videotaped over the course of the next 5 months, totaling roughly 25 hours of audiovisual documentation. Thus, at the time of recording, the management group had been conducting its meetings as videoconferences for about 1 year.

The biweekly videoconference meetings began around 8:30 a.m. and usually lasted until between 12:30 and 2:00 in the afternoon. The official purpose was to coordinate the actions of the managers responsible for the various businesses within the Customer Services Division. Activities included a review of the minutes from the previous meeting, short statements about the current status of projects and "action items," discussion of current financial performance and possible measures of that performance, reports and presentations by either CSC members or invited guests, and discussion and decision making regarding issues ranging from advertising campaigns to work schedules. The meetings were videorecorded in toto, except for the discussions of current financial performance, which participants asked me not to videotape.[5] Figure 14.1 provides a view of the meeting room at Wesseling, in which meetings were recorded. The remote meeting room at Karlsruhe is available to the locally assembled participants (i.e., at Wesseling) via sound and the image on the monitor to the left; the monitor on the right displays either a control image of the group members at Wesseling (which allows them to check the image that is sent to Karlsruhe and whether their camera is positioned correctly) or, as is the case here, a slide presented via a document camera attached to the system but not visible in this picture.

An Episode: Assigning the Job of Taking the Minutes

The context for the episode that I look at in some detail is as follows. Around 8:30 a.m., a member of the group located at Karlsruhe set up a connection between the two videoconferencing rooms and participants gathered at both locations. As they gathered, separate communicative exchanges developed both among those at Karlsruhe and among those at

---

[4]Briefly stated, the arrangement between Technics and me was that my research would not cause any cost and that I would share results with the group (which were presented in January 1999). For a more detailed account of the establishment of this research relationship and the larger project of which this research was a part, see research reports nos. 1 and 2 at http://www.uni-giessen.de/~g31047.

[5]For a more detailed account of technical issues involved in videorecording videoconference interactions, see Meier (1998).

FIG. 14.1.   The videoconferencing room at Wesseling.

Wesseling. Johannes (located at Karlsruhe), the leader of this management group, made a first move toward starting the meeting by officially greeting the participants. He gave a short pep talk that mentioned some of the challenges that lay ahead, this being the first meeting after the Christmas/New Year break. He then welcomed a new member to the group (Heiner, located at Wesseling), and engaged in some talk with him about a meeting they both had attended the day before. Heiner replied by giving his impression of how that meeting went. This is where the transcript starts. Figure 14.2 provides an initial view of the scene and the names of participants.[6]

Transcript[7]

The transcript presented has been simplified for the purpose of this essay. The transcription convention employed follows the widely used notation

---

[6]According to company policy, participants address each other by first name and either an informal address term "Du" or a formal address term "Sie," depending on their respective relationship. Johannes is only partially visible, because the picture-in-picture mode of the videoconferencing equipment was activated in Wesseling, where the recording was made.

[7]Problems of representation involved in writing about the particulars of speech and bodily action are endemic in communication research; the numerous efforts to devise transcription conventions and the debates surrounding them bear witness to these problems. With the development of the World Wide Web (WWW) and concomitant software applications, it is now possible to provide an audience with much more direct access to the phenomena of interest. Although I cannot provide readers with access to the entire data base, a short excerpt of the audiovisual documentation   (*continued on next page*)

system developed by Gail Jefferson (see, e.g., Atkinson & Heritage, 1984). Interpunctuation marks are not used according to grammatical rules but represent actual intonation contours ("." indicating a falling intonation; "," a falling-rising intonation; and "?" a strongly rising intonation). Underlining indicates stress and degree signs ("°") indicate reduced volume. The beginning and ending of overlaps between utterances are marked by brackets ("[", "]"). Shorter pauses are noted as "(.)", "(-)", "(- -)", and "(- - -)", representing a just noticeable discontinuity and gaps of approximately 0.25/0.5/0.75 seconds, respectively. Longer pauses are represented by stating their length in parentheses (e.g., "(1.0)"). Commentary pertaining to the way a particular utterance is realized is noted below the respective line, with arrows marking onset and end (e.g., "<slowly, with relish >"); visible actions are also noted below their respective lines of talk (e.g., "Johannes turns toward his colleagues in Karlsruhe"). Shading is used to differentiate actions that emerge from the "far end," as seen from the place at which the recording was done. In cases where the local origin of a hearable utterance cannot be determined with any certainty, shading is intermittent. To keep track of the often multiple overlaps, lines that need to be read together have been marked off around line numbers and speaker identification.

---

[7] *(continued from previous page)* that is analyzed and discussed in this chapter is available for download on the WWW. This digitized videoclip is a compacted and edited version of the original documentation, but should nevertheless give readers a better idea of the episode analyzed than would any transcript. Given that personal names have been deleted from the videoclip, readers are advised to download the videoclip from the web page for this volume on the LEA Web site [http://www.erlbaum.com]. The file is in WinZip format for downloading, and readers can look both at the videoclip and the transcript to follow more fully the interaction. To view the videoclip, one needs to have Real Player G2 installed on one's computer; a basic version of this player can be obtained free of charge at http:// www.real.com. For the clip to play smoothly, the computer should be running on at least an Intel Pentium II processor (or equivalent). A command of the German language is helpful in listening to and viewing the videoclip, but is not a prerequisite, especially when the transcript is employed.

Code:	"Fast Learning" _ CSC2, 08:40:58_08:42:10
Event:	Videoconference at Technics between Karlsruhe and Wesseling
Date:	14/01/97 (Wednesday)
Time:	ca. 08:30_13:00
Recording:	Christoph Meier in conference room at Wesseling
Transcription:	Christoph Meier
Correction:	Michaela Goll and Holger Finke
Last modified:	14/01/1999

| 1 | | ((parallel zur Äußerung von Heiner Geflüster))
((whispering simultaneously with Heiner's utterance)) |
| 2 | Heiner | ne <u>gute</u>:: (—) Ausgangsposition jetz <u>ha</u>:bn.
are: : (— —) in a <u>good</u> position to <u>start</u> from. |

FIG. 14.2.   The participants at Karlsruhe (left) and at Wesseling (right) as they are positioned at this point in the episode.

3	Carla?	° °(⬛)° ° ° °(⬛)° °
4		(— ⬛ —)
5	Johannes	Okeh. ***All right.***
6		(- ⬛ - ⬛ -)
7		<<u>Super</u>. So. E dann fang wer <u>an</u>, <<u>Great</u>. ***Okay. Em now let's <u>begin</u>,*** <*Johannes from now on speaks noticeably louder than before*>
8		(- ⬛ -)
9		E: zunächst e:: (.) damit wer das ***Em first of all em:: (.) so that we***

10 Johannes n[ich   wieder   zu   spät   machn   ]
              d[on't   do   that   late   again   ]

11 Michael D. [°Könn (wir) des eigntlich au noch°   ]
               [°Can (we) ((no final verb)) this ((particle)) as well°]

                        |_____
                              |

            Michael D. points toward the television sets
                              |_____
                                    |

            Johannes turns toward his colleagues in Karlsruhe
            and remains in that position for some time

12 Johannes Wer   macht   das   [Protokoll,]
              Who is going to take the [minutes,   ]

13 ?   [sch::(   )]
                                            [(   )]

14   (1,0)

15 Johannes Wir hattn letztes mal gesacht glaub
              Last time I think we said

16   ich e: (_ _) alphabetisch,
              in em: (_ _) alphabetical order,

17   (-)

18 ?   °([   )°]
              °([   )°]

19 ?   [°(   ]   ) (Krause)°
                   [°(   ]   ) (Krause)°

20   (-)

21 Johann?   °(Krause) (war der letz[te)°]
              °(Krause) (was up las[t)°]

22 Johannes   [e:]:
                                      [em:]:

23   (- -)

24 Johannes Holger war der letzte,
              Holger was up last,

25   (- -)

26 Johannes Wer is jetz:
              Who is ((no sentence_final verb)) now:

27   (-)

```
28  ?           °°(        )°°
                °°(        )°°

29              ( - )

30  ?           °°(        )°°=
                °°(        )°°=

31  Johann                    =L:.
                              =L:.

32              ( - )

33  Michael D. °Lempp°
               °Lempp°

34              ( - )

35  Johannes  Ham mer ein (in) L,
              Do we have somebody (with) L,

36              (.)

37  Michael D. °Lempp°=
               °Lempp°=

38  ?                 =(°ehh°)
                      =(°ehh°)

39              ( - - )

40  Heiner     °eh[h°]
               °eh[h°]

41  Johann        [Le]mpp
                  [Le]mpp

42  ?          (   )[(
               (   )[(

43  Michael R.    [ ehh[  hh hh / hh      ]
                  [ ehh[  hh hh / hh      ]

44  Michael D.         [°heh heh heh [(wi]r    ham)°]=
                       [°heh heh heh  (with  Lempp )°]=

45  Johann?                        [(          )]=
                                   [(          )]=

46  Michael D.=[°(Mit Lempp) [ ei(nen] mit) [L.°]
             = °(We have)    (one)          L.°

47  Johann? =[(      ) Is   [ still.]
            =[(      ) keeps  silent.

48  Michael R.            [  °heh ]      [heh ]heh°=
                          [  °heh ]      [heh ]heh°=
```

```
49 Michael R.=°heh heh heh[ (heh)   °]
              =°heh heh heh[ (heh)   °]

50 Jürgen?                  [°L: M (O ] P Q) R°
                            [°L: M (O ] P Q) R°

51            ( - )

52 Johann     [ <R (wie) ] Rim:bech.>
              [ <R (like) ] Rim:bech.>
               <slowly, with relish >

53 Jürgen?    [(    )(bach)]
              [(    )(bach)]

54            ( - )

55 Johannes Raymbech.
            Raymbech.

56 ?          eh [h(eheh)(
              eh [h(eheh)(

57 Michael R.   [   N:ä::.    ] <Lempp w[ar doch oder ]
                [   No::.     ] <It was Lempp or
                                  <Michael R. starts up loud, then>

58 Johannes     [(          ) ]
                [(          ) ]

59 Heiner                          [  °(hhehh)°   ]
                                   [  °(hhehh)°   ]

60 Michael R.wie war  da(h)[s:. >]
             wasn't that   so:. >
             <decreases his volume    >

61 Christoph        [ hm[hm ]
                    [ hn[hn ]

62 Michael R.?           [°he]heheh°=
                         [°he]heheh°=

63 Johannes?                    =(Bitte was?)
                                =(Sorry what?)

64 Michael R.War das [nich     Lempp?]
             Wasn't  [it       Lempp? ]

65 Michael D.        [Rasemann °kommt] noch vor°
                     [Rasemann °precedes ((particle))]°

66 Michael D.°Rim[bach.°]
             °Rim[bach.°]

67 Michael R.    [E  Ra]semann.
                 [Em Ra]semann.
```

```
68                ( - )

69 Michael R.  Wie geht das denn damit.
                How would that work out.

70 ?          (a)(   [          [   )(
              (a)(   [          [   )(

71 ?                  [   (OH:[:)(
                      [   (OH:[:)(

72 ?                       [HAH HAH HAH[ HA:::.]
                           [HAH HAH HAH[ HA:::.]

73 Heiner                       [ hh hhh ]
                                [ hh hhh ]

                   |_____
                                          |

            Carla leans forward and beats on the table with her fists

74 Johannes ( )ie sacht aber (n)ix  =
             (she) doesn't say a thing=

75 ?                               =(  [
                                   =(  [

76 Michael R.                      [_e[hh          ]=
                                   [_e[hh          ]=

77 Holger                            [(Wenn die)]=
                                     [(If   she) =

78          ((weiter Lachen u. Stimmen in Karlsruhe))
            ((more laughter and voices in Karlsruhe))

79 Michael R.=[   ehh=
            =[   ehh=

80 Michael R.?      =heheheh(eh)                      ]=
                    =heheheh(eh)                      ]=

81 Holger   =[(jetz geschickt is sagt) [(die)     von ]=
            = (moves smartly now  she'll say)     von =

82 Michael D.                      [(da) haste (an_)]
                                   [  (what a_)

83 Michael R.?=[(          )]
            =[(          )]

84 Holger   =[(Rasemann,)] [(                    )]=
            =[(Rasemann,)] [(                    )]=

85 Michael D.              [Mein lieber Kolle:ge. (Da)]=
                           [My dear collea:gue. (What) =
```

```
 86 Holger   =[(   )]
              =[(   )]

 87 Michael D.=[  ha]ste aber wieder (G)lü[ck gehabt du.]
              =    (a)    lucky    turn    for    you. ]

 88 ?                                    [ heh heh heh ]=
                                         [ heh heh heh ]=

 89 ?          =((coughing))

 90 Johannes? Aber wie vorsich(tich) (      )=
              How   very care(fully)   (    )=

 91 ?                                    =ehih(heh heh)=
                                         =ehih(heh heh)=

 92 ?          =[(heh)]
              =[(heh)]

 93 Michael D.=[ Ich ] seh das nämlich grade
              =[  I    just noticed that

 94            [ Rasemann    steht    vor    Rimbach    ]=
              [ Rasemann    precedes    Rimbach    ]=

 95 Johannes [(            )    (der)    Rimbach    ]=
              [(            ) ((definite article)) Rimbach]=

 96 Johannes =(war) vorsichti [ch    n]e? =
              =(was)    careful wasnt he? =

 97 Carla?                        [ (o)( ) ]
                                  [ (o)( ) ]

 98            =((more laughter by several participants at Karlsruhe))

 99 Heiner?    [        (heheheh)            ]
              [        (heheheh)            ]

100 ?          ((sniffing/breathing?))

101 Johann?  (Was is los,)        wa[s is los mit dir.      ]
              (What's the matter,) what's the matter with you.]

102 ?1                              [      (heh   heh heh)   ]=
                                    [      (heh   heh heh)   ]=

103 ?1         =[ heh]]
              =[ heh)]

104 ?2         [ (ehe]he[heh](
              [ (ehe]he[heh](

105 Michael D.         [°(Jetz hab) ich (wieder) einen °=
                      [°(Now I have)  got   one credit° =
```

```
106 Michael D. = [°gut            du.°            ]
              =  °(again)((personal pronoun)) .°]

107 Burkhard =<[      Fast              lear]ning (is das) [( )]
             =<[      (That is)         fast    learning   [( )]

              <high pitch and loud but probably far away from microphone>

108 ?                                                  [(Ja )]
                                                       [(Yes)]

109 Heiner    F(h)ast [       learni[ng.      ]
              F(h)ast [       learni[ng.      ]

110 Michael R.        [° (hih hih [ hih)°]
                      [° (hih hih [ hih)°]

111 Johannes               [(Okeh)]      Also Carla,
                           [(All right)  so  Carla,

112           ( - - )

113 Johannes  es hat dich ( _ ) °erw[ischt,°]
              there is no ( _ )  ° escape,° ]

114 ?1                       [° (    ]    )°
                             [° (    ]    )°

115 ?1        [°(
              [°(

116 ?2        [(eh[eh heh heh)
              [(eh[eh heh heh)

117 Michael D.     [°(Da hab ich wieder einen gut)°
                   [°(Now I've got one credit again)°

118 Michael D. [    °(du.)°   ]
               [°((pers pron.))°]

119 ?         [° (         ][      )°]
              [° (         ][      )°]

120 Michael R.?            [hh hh ]
                           [hh hh ]

121 ?         °( [         ]   ) [(
              °( [         ]   ) [(

122 Michael R.     [Bitte,]
                   [Sorry,]

123 Michael D.             [°(Da) hab ich wieder°
                           [°(Now) I've got one°
```

```
124 Michael D. °einen [gut°        ]
              °credit again°       ]

125 Carla?          [°(        ]              )°]
                    [°(        ]              )°]

126 Johannes                       [      Gu]t.
                                   [All right.

127 Michael R.?([°
              ([°

128 Johannes   [E dann hab  ich [noch (.) (n)e  Frage ]=
               [Em now  I  still have(a)  question  ]=

129 Michael R.?            [°( ) (dhanke)  (heh)°]=
                           [°( ) (thahnks) (heh)°]=

130 Johannes =[Gibts  noch  Punkte ] für  die    Agenda?
             =[Are there  any other items for the agenda?

131 Michael R.?=[°(heh)(              )°]
              =[°(heh)(              )°]

132 Michael R. ((clears throat))

133           ( - - )

134           Ich würde  ganz  gern (1,0) mit draufpackn e::
              I would ((particle)) like (1,0) to   add  em:
```

"Us" Versus "Them" and Nothing New?

What transpired during this episode is that participants at both sites tried
to nominate for the task of taking the minutes persons who were located at
the other locale and shared a laugh in doing so.[8] The fact that several efforts
were made to dump an unattractive task on some person at the remote location is not really surprising, as prior research on videoconferencing has
revealed a tendency for the emergence of locally based alliances ("us" versus "them") and an increased likelihood of disagreement and conflict between the physically separated subgroups (Short et al., 1976; Weinig,
1997). Prior observations of this phenomenon, however, have been based
on the analysis of topically focused discussions, whereas the episode analyzed here preceded the introduction of the first agenda item and proper
"discussion." The episode occurred early in the meeting, with participants

---

[8]This can be observed for a first time when Michael D. softly mentioned his colleague
(Richard) Lempp, located at Karlsruhe, as a candidate (lines 33 and 37) and the ensuing
laughter (lines 43–44) when that suggestion was finally picked up on by a participant at
Karlsruhe (Johann, line 41). It can be observed a second time when Michael R., at Wesseling,
was brought up as a candidate by several participants at Karlsruhe (lines 52–56). Finally, after
Michael R. picked up on a softly spoken suggestion by his neighbor Michael D. and introduced Carla, at Karlsruhe, as a candidate (lines 67–69), several participants at Wesseling engaged in gestural and bodily displays of success.

engaged in the process of getting the event organized. Thus, the observation that participants team up on the basis of locality even prior to topically focused discussions confirms and extends previous findings.

What is more interesting, however, is that common linguistic procedures that have been identified in previous research as means of establishing such interactional teams as "us" and "them" were not employed here. As Lerner (1993) and Kangasharju (1996) have shown, such practices include addressing corecipients as an association (e.g., "What have *you* guys been doing?"), casting oneself as a spokesperson and employing the pronoun "we" (e.g., "Hey, *we* have got good news!"), joining the production of an ongoing conversational action (e.g., completing an utterance another person has begun), and aligning oneself with another in an argument by providing a source marker (e.g., "I fully agree *with Eva* with respect to ..."). In the episode analyzed here, no such practices were employed by participants; there was neither talk about "we" or "you," nor were there any argumentative alliances openly established in the ways just mentioned. Therefore, to understand how this episode unfolded and conveyed a sense of teaming up, we need to look elsewhere; specifically, we need to look at the participation frameworks established by participants.

Working the Participation Frameworks

In seeking to go beyond the rather crude concepts of *speaker* and *hearer* taken for granted in much of the research on language, Goffman (1981) noted that participation in an interaction is not a matter of either "speaking" or "listening." He pointed out that the role and stance taken by those involved in an interaction can be differentiated into more specific footings. For instance, a hearer can be listening attentively, eavesdropping furtively, or overhearing by chance; similarly, a person speaking can express his or her own original thoughts or merely animate someone else's words and phrases. Recognizing such differences, Goffman suggested the concept of *participation frameworks*, the stance participants involved in an encounter display vis-à-vis an ongoing utterance, as a tool for analyzing talk-in-interaction.[9] In discussing participation frameworks, Goffman noted that persons in a social situation, such as a group meeting, are usually expected to be ratified participants (although there may, of course, also be nonratified eavesdroppers or overhearers). However, not all of the ratified meeting participants need be the addressed recipients of any particular utterance; addressed recipients are spoken to specifically (e.g., by means of bodily orientation or address terms employed), which establishes an expectation that they (rather than any other person present) respond.

---

[9]Levinson (1988) attempted to systematize and elaborate on Goffman's categories but encountered criticism, for example, by Hanks (1990). I do not wish to go into any detail here about this discussion but merely wish to draw attention to the utility of the concept of participation framework for analyzing group communication.

In applying the concept of participation frameworks to the beginning of the episode reported previously, the following can be observed. Although Johannes was oriented to the television sets that are part of the video-conferencing system for most of Heiner's contribution, he turned away from the screen as he began to initiate his move toward officially starting the meeting (line 7). As he began to ask who was going to take the minutes, Johannes turned his upper body toward his colocated colleagues at Karlsruhe and subsequently remained in that position for some time. By doing so, Johannes treated those gathered at Karlsruhe as the addressed recipients of his utterance and, thereby, indicated that he expected them to respond. It comes as no surprise, therefore, that participants at Karlsruhe subsequently took a more active part than their colleagues at Wesseling in determining who was to take the minutes. Participants at Karlsruhe produced several softly spoken utterances, at least two of which addressed the question posed by Johannes (lines 19 and 21).

During these exchanges, those gathered at Wesseling, in contrast to their colleagues at Karlsruhe, conducted themselves in a manner that can be understood as "doing 'being off the hook'" for the moment. This is particularly obvious with Michael R., who was taking a sip of coffee and, in so doing, cast himself as not being implicated by Johannes's request. His colocated colleague Heiner, who began to take notes, proceeded in a similar way. The fact that participants at Wesseling did not complain about the utterances by those located at Karlsruhe being spoken softly (and, therefore, difficult to pick up not only for the transcribers but, presumably, for those at Wesseling as well) contributes to this impression that they took a "wait-and-see" stance toward things that were going on at Karlsruhe at that time.

Having established that Holger Krause took the minutes last time, Johannes again asked who was next in line (line 26), and Johann announced that "L" was the next letter in the alphabet (line 31). Michael D. (at Wesseling) then softly uttered the name "Lempp" for the first time (line 33; he did so again in line 37). Shortly thereafter, Johannes asked whether there was somebody whose last name began with "L" (line 35). His question may have been prompted by his not having heard the utterance by Michael D. If, indeed, he did not hear this utterance, this is in all likelihood due to two technical features of the videoconferencing system.

First, the technical set-up in the meeting rooms at Technics consists of two PictureTEL Concorde 4510 rollabout systems with enhanced audio components. The two sites are linked by two European-standard ISDN-B-channels, providing a bandwidth of 128kb/s. The electronically enhanced audio module limits the sounds amplified and transmitted to the other location. While a particular person speaks, sound from other directions in the room (i.e., from other persons gathered around the table) and from the other location is amplified and transmitted only once it passes a certain threshold value both with respect to its length and loudness. Thus, a short, softly spoken utterance may be amplified and transmitted to the other location only if the directionally sensitive microphones are not currently "logged on to" another speaker in the same room or at the other location.[10]

Second, because the videoconferencing system employed is based on digital signal processing (analog sound and images are digitized locally, transmitted, and converted to analog signals again at the far end), there is a time delay of about .25 to .27 of a second (one way) in reaching the remote location. Consequently, actions become audible and visible at the far end about a quarter of a second after they have actually been produced locally; the same is true for any responding action, which is also delayed by a quarter of a second. Sticking, for the moment, with the turns just examined, the implication is that what happened at Wesseling, as shown in the transcript in lines 31–35, can be reconstructed to have emerged in a different way at Karlsruhe[11]:

<1> detail 1, as recorded at Wesseling

31	Johann	L:. *L:.*
32		(–)
33	Michael D.	°Lempp° *°Lempp°*
34		(–)
35	Johannes	ham mer ein (in) L, *do we have somebody (with) L,*

<2> detail 1, as reconstructed to have occurred at Karlsruhe

31	Johann	L:. *L:.*
32		(– – –)
33	Michael D.	°Le[mpp°] *°Le[mpp°]*
34	Johannes	[ham] mer ein (in) L, *[do] we have somebody (with) L,*

---

[10]Due to this technical feature, potential next speakers, especially when they are located at the remote site relative to the current speaker, always find themselves at a disadvantage when it comes to self-selecting for a next turn at talk (cf. Sacks, Schegloff, & Jefferson 1974). Participants themselves, at times, also do not appear to have a good feel for which utterances are transmitted to and heard at the far end and which ones are not. There were several instances in the recorded materials where utterances that were clearly meant to be appreciated only locally were nevertheless heard and commented on by participants at the other location.

[11]The videorecording and the transcript provide a valid representation of how things became audible and visible only for the site at which the recording was done. For participants at the remote location, actions emerged in a different way and, therefore, both the recording and the transcript are somewhat misleading. Ideally, videoconferences should be recorded at all the locations involved.

Taking into account the time lag involved, the reconstruction shows that, for the participants at Karlsruhe, the utterance by Michael D. was more delayed relative to the utterance by Johann (line 31) and was also overlapped by the beginning utterance of Johannes (line 34). If the utterance by Michael D. was amplified by the microphone at all, it may not have been available to participants at Karlsruhe due to its overlap with the beginning of Johannes's utterance.

Returning to the softly spoken utterances made by Michael D. in lines 33 and 37, the way in which he produced them deserves mention. He remained absolutely immobile, looked neither toward the television sets nor toward any of the persons gathered around the table at Wesseling but looked, instead, at papers spread out in front of him. How his utterance is to be interpreted is not completely clear. On the one hand, he may have been making a guess, addressed—by means of its reduced volume—exclusively to participants at his location, about who those at the remote site would nominate as next in line for taking the minutes. In that he repeated his utterance, however, he may also have been insinuating to his colleagues at Karlsruhe who should be nominated, without making himself discernible (for those located at Karlsruhe) as the author and principal of this move (cf. Goffman, 1981). When the guessed or insinuated name eventually was mentioned at Karlsruhe, those gathered at Wesseling engaged in displays of amusement (beginning with Michael R. in line 43 and immediately followed by Michael D. in line 44; judging from his bodily comportment, Heiner also appeared to have joined in).

Who is the butt of the laughter at Wesseling at that moment, whether it is only Richard Lempp or the entire group at Karlsruhe, is not entirely clear. At any rate, Johann commented curtly on Richard's comportment (line 47) and also oriented his body toward the television sets (i.e., toward colleagues at Wesseling) at the end of his utterance. By commenting on Richard's conduct, Johann may have attempted to provide a "new laughable," to establish Richard as the butt of the laughter and to join those gathered at Wesseling in their display of amusement. Providing such a new laughable has been described as one way of transforming a "laughing at" environment into a "laughing with" environment (Glenn, 1995). Johann's boss Johannes appeared to be joining this effort as he also briefly turned toward the television sets (and, thereby, toward colleagues at Wesseling) and grinned.

There is no clear evidence, however, that participants at Wesseling picked up on what may have been efforts to create an environment of "the rest of us at Karlsruhe laughing with you at Wesseling." There is yet another feature of video-mediated interaction that may be responsible for this particular moment turning out this way. With respect to face-to-face encounters, Goffman (1961) observed that "for the participants this involves ... an eye-to-eye ecological huddle that maximizes each participant's opportunity to perceive the other participants' monitoring of him" (pp. 17–18). That is, in face-to-face interaction, people perceive acutely when and by whom they are looked at and monitored and they may, accordingly, develop stage fright. In videoconferencing, however, with direct eye-to-eye contact impaired (due to the angle between the camera and television screen) and the limited resolution of the picture rendering subtle changes in facial expression difficult to detect, this ability to perceive the monitoring activities of persons at the far end is significantly reduced (at least with those systems currently available commercially). In addition, gaze, gesture, and other bodily actions have been shown to lose much of their power for coordinating interaction in video-mediated encounters (Heath & Luff, 1993). Therefore, the conversational move made by Johann (and the supporting one made by Johannes) may not have been sufficiently transparent to solicit a response by those at Wesseling (on the issue of transparency of actions across a videolink, see Meier, 2000).

Jumping ahead a few lines, there is a point at which Michael R. (at Wesseling) was nominated as a candidate for taking the minutes and tried to fend this off (see lines 52–64). Michael D., his colocated neighbor, then announced that "Rasemann precedes Rimbach" in alphabetical order (line 65). This was immediately taken up by Michael R., who resubmitted this point as a question to those at Karlsruhe. Again, it is worthwhile to look at how Michael D. proceeded. After the first few syllables of his utterance, he noticeably reduced the volume of his voice, turned toward Michael R, and, thereby, treated him, rather than those gathered at the remote site, as the addressed recipient of his utterance. By performing these conversational moves, Michael D. cast himself as "not arguing with the colleagues at Karlsruhe" but, rather, as "assisting his colocated neighbor in getting off the hook," a point he tried to capitalize on several times later in this episode (see lines 105 and 107; 118; 124–125).

Michael D. was not the only person who could be observed to design his talk so as to selectively target meeting participants as addressed recipients, although he did this rather frequently. It is noteworthy that the participants to these videoconferences rather frequently produced utterances that were designed for different configurations of recipients and, thereby, established varied participation frameworks. They appeared to capitalize on (and perhaps play with) the fact that the videoconferencing system employed was not able to seamlessly link together the physically separated subgroups. Their utterances were (a) produced in a manner accessible for all participants on both sides and not addressed to any one location or person in particular (e.g., Johannes in lines 5–10); (b) produced in a manner accessible for all participants at both sites but specifically designed for and addressed to participants at the remote site(s) (e.g., Michael R. in lines 57 and 60); (c) designed for and addressed to participants at the local site and, thus, not/not easily accessible to participants at the remote site(s) (e.g., Holger in lines 77, 81, and 84); and (d) designed for and addressed to particular persons (rather than all of them) at the local site (e.g., Michael D. in lines 105 and 107; 118; 124–125). Moreover, to achieve these participation frameworks, bodily orientation and subtle differences in voice quality (pitch and loudness) appear to be important means.

Temporarily Splitting Up for Displaying Amusement

Jumping ahead again, I want to look at the moment when Carla was nominated by Michael D. and Michael R. to be a candidate for taking the minutes. Immediately following the utterance by Michael R. ("Wie geht das denn damit"/"How would that work out"; line 69), participants at Karlsruhe turned away from the television sets and toward Carla, who was seated in the back of the room. When loud laughter emerged from those gathered at Karlsruhe, participants at Wesseling initially focused on the television sets and the action taking place there. Subsequently, however, they engaged among themselves in commentary on the successful defense and, thereby, established a focus of attention separate from the one at Karlsruhe. For example, Holger turned his face toward either Michael D. or Michael R. as he began his utterance in line 81, and Michael D. also turned toward Michael R. as he began his comment in line 82. This split into two separate foci of attention is somewhat similar to the moment following the projection/insinuation by Michael D. discussed previously.[12]

Participants at both sites, in dealing with some potentially humorous moments, established a local focus of attention, sharing laughter with their locally assembled colleagues and displaying their amusement primarily toward them. Moreover, laughter and having fun at one location did not seem to carry over to the other locale. For example, following the guess/insinuation made by Michael D. at Wesseling (lines 33 and 37), its uptake at Karlsruhe (line 41), and the ensuing laughter at Wesseling (lines 43–44), there was no audible laughter coming forth from those at Karlsruhe. In fact, when Michael D. dwelled on the apparently funny side of this (lines 44 and 46) and, thereby, elicited a further show of amusement from his colocated neighbor Michael R. (lines 48–49), Jürgen (at Karslruhe) resumed in a rather sober voice the business of determining who might be in line for taking the minutes (line 50). He, thus, did not appear to be in sync with respect to the interactional mode in which his colleagues at Wesseling were still operating (and vice versa). Similarly, when those gathered at

---

[12]In that earlier sequence, shortly after Johann uttered "Lempp" (line 41), Michael R. (at Wesseling) began to laugh and, subsequently, Michael D. and Heiner (also located at Wesseling) oriented away from the television screens and toward him. At the same time, at Karlsruhe, several participants (Johannes, Burkhard, and Arnulf) turned toward their colocated colleague Richard.

Karlsruhe began to roar with laughter (lines 71–72), there was only a little laughter at Wesseling, which was delayed in its onset and much softer (cf. Heiner in line 73 and Michael R. in lines 76 and 79–80).

These observations suggest that in videoconferencing, when some amusing development occurs, it is rather difficult for the participants at the two (or more) locations linked together to maintain a single focus of attention and to remain synchronized with respect to the interactional mode in which they operate. More often than not, a tendency for *schisming* (i.e., the splitting up of a single interactional strand, such as a conversation, into multiple independent stands running in parallel; cf. Egbert, 1993) suggests itself. This tendency can, by the way, also be observed in passages of the videoconference meeting devoted to topically focused discussions (cf. Meier, 2000).

Providing Interpretations of the Conduct Displayed

A final observation on the episode discussed here has to do with the interpretations of the conduct of participants provided by some of the persons present. Following the roaring laughter at Karlsruhe after Carla had been "found out" to have been gambling on getting away without having to take the minutes as the next person in line alphabetically, Johannes pointed out the circumspect way in which Michael R. at Wesseling had conducted himself (lines 95–96). This led to a second round of laughter at Karlsruhe (line 98), after which Johann (presumably) challenged Michael R. regarding his conduct (line 101). Michael R. did not respond, however. Instead, Burkhard provided the next utterance (line 107) and his statement "(that is) fast learning" can be understood to provide an epigrammatic interpretation of the conduct of some of the participants in this episode. Given that this division of Technics had established a special task force charged with promoting a fast-learning organization, and given that Johannes had, in a previous videoconference meeting, expressed his strong concern about this issue, Burkhard's interpretation of the prior discourse presumably ties to a concern shared by most members of the group. Burkhard's physical orientation toward the television sets and his voice quality[13] both suggest that this utterance was designed to be heard at both locations. In fact, Burkhard's interpretation was immediately picked up on, both at Karlsruhe and at Wesseling. At Karlsruhe, some person confirmed this with a "yes" (line 108, although this is not beyond doubt), and at Wesseling, Heiner provided a repeat of this formulation (line 109). Judged by the voice quality in which these reactions were produced at either location, they were, however, not designed for the benefit of recipients at the remote locations. Thus, what can be understood as an effort by Burkhard to align members at both sites was, again, appreciated separately at both locations.

---

[13]The utterance sounds as if it was produced in a rather loud fashion although it did not come across loudly to those gathered at Wesseling, which may be attributed to the fact that Burkhard was positioned disadvantageously relative to the microphone and its current "logging."

CONCLUSION: DOING GROUPNESS IN VIDEOCONFERENCING

Taking a bona fide group perspective and viewing groups as not so much stable social entities but rather amoeba-like, with unstable and permeable boundaries changing according to the context at hand, raises an important issue: exactly how participants to an encounter achieve groupness and how they establish their groupness as a social fact that is recognized both by members and nonmembers. In pursuing this issue, the details of actual communication processes—such as who is and is not addressed in talk, who is and is not implicated in an utterance, and how a laughing-at or a laughing-with situation is established—are of prime importance. Focusing on the details of communication processes, in turn, demands the documenting of authentic interactions in their real-time sequential structure and the detailed analysis of any audiovisual records thus generated. Taking this as my point of departure, I have argued that to appreciate how and how clearly participants demonstrate their groupness turns on an understanding of the interactional dynamics of the group situation in which they find themselves, be it for the purpose of doing collaborative work or for some other purpose.

Doing groupness in business meetings is obviously implicated by such aspects as who is and is not invited, who can and cannot offer resources for a project, or the dress code adopted by participants. Above and beyond such aspects, how the interaction itself is conducted also plays an important role, in particular, the various participation frameworks that the participants establish in the course of their interaction. This is true not only for discussing business but also for lighter moments, such as the episode examined in this chapter. In that episode, the togetherness and interactional synchronicity that participants appeared to achieve was limited; in the process of nominating a participant for the job of taking the minutes, an "us-versus-them" dynamic clearly emerged,[14] an effort to transform a "them laughing at us" situation into an "all of us laughing together" situation was not successful, and an effort to tie an interpretation of the entire scene to a concern presumably shared by all participants ("fast learning") did not bring about a joint conversational focus.

The efforts of the Customer Services Council members at Technics to do groupness have to be appreciated, however, in light of the videoconferencing situation and its specific properties. Technical features of the videoconferencing system employed have to be taken into account, such as the time lag involved, the electronically enhanced and somewhat unpre-

---

[14]There are, however, limits to the sportsmanship and the "we win, you lose" approach participants displayed in the episode discussed here. This becomes particularly clear when, along with Carla's display of "being found out," participants at Karlsruhe shared laughter among themselves rather than brooding about "having lost the game."

dictable microphones, and the limited resolution of the television screens. These technical features result in specific interactional dynamics that group members have to work with and around when doing groupness. In particular, these interactional dynamics are characterized by a very fragile focus of joint attention and reduced participation opportunities for those at the "far end" relative to any current action "here." Moreover, action co-ordination is thrown off, occasionally, due to the time lag involved. Finally, communicative actions provided "here" are sometimes less than fully transparent to members located "there." As a consequence of these fea-tures, efforts to establish interactional synchronicity across both sites and, thereby, to establish togetherness, are quite likely to fail. Such together-ness, it turns out, is frequently displayed locally in each of the two meeting rooms, and, in particular, when it comes to expressing fun and amuse-ment. Videoconferencing, therefore, provides a rather difficult environ-ment for doing groupness in a way that encompasses all participants at all locations. It is an environment that renders efforts to establish groupness potentially ineffective and fosters the establishment of the two (or more) locally based subgroups of "us here" and "them there."

These findings provide some initial useful starting points for offering advice to members of bona fide groups participating in videoconferences. First, the tendency for the emergence of locally based subgroups and an "us-versus-them" dynamic may not be much of a problem if videoconfer-ence group meetings are conducted only occasionally. If, however, those assembled in one meeting room during a videoconference work together closely anyway and then meet with other such locally or functionally based bona fide groups, this polarizing dynamic may, in the long run, undermine trust and collegiality, and, consequently, effective cooperation. This is a particular problem with videoconferencing, as informal one-on-one talk prior to or following the end of a such a meeting is hardly possible across the video link (Meier 1999). Therefore, to provide those working together frequently via videoconferencing with the opportunity to develop into a mature group or team, it is important to conduct some meetings face-to-face, even if this does not appear to be necessary for getting the work done.

The just-mentioned problems pertaining to the limited transparency of conduct of group members at a remote site and the "us-versus-them" dy-namic may well apply to other types of bona fide groups. Distributed pro-ject teams formed to achieve a well-identified goal in a limited time frame, with members often belonging not only to several different teams but, at times, to different organizations, are a particular pertinent case in point.

Finally, an obvious implication concerns group members' media com-petence. Understanding the particular dynamics of a technically mediated situation of communication and collaborative work is, of course, a first step toward appropriate conduct and making good use of the technological resources available. This applies not only to videoconferencing but to other forms of technically mediated cooperation, such as the use of groupware to support distributed project teams. Members of both distributed and technology-dependent bona fide groups and organizations, thus, have to develop media competence; they have to become competent users knowledgeable about the features and functions of the technical systems they employ in their day-to-day work, and they, as well as organizations in general, have to build up knowledge with respect to the (long-term) consequences of the use of such technical systems and the scenarios of use for which they are most suitable.

ACKNOWLEDGMENT

The work reported here has been conducted under the auspices of a grant by the German Research Foundation (Be 1107/3-1). I thank Joerg Bergmann, Michaela Goll, Holger Finke, and Ralf Bundschuh for discussions and help with the transcription work. I also thank the members of the Customer Services Council at Technics for their trust and support.

REFERENCES

Atkinson, J. M., & Heritage, J. (Eds.). (1984). *Structures of social action: Studies in conversation analysis*. Cambridge, UK: Cambridge University Press.

Bales, R. F., & Gerbrands, H. (1948). The interaction recorder; an apparatus and check list for sequential content analysis of social interaction. *Human Relations, 1*, 456–463.

Barefoot, J. C., & Strickland, L. H. (1982). Conflict and dominance in television-mediated interactions. *Human Relations, 35*, 559–566.

Bergmann, J. R. (1985). Flüchtigkeit und methodische Fixierung sozialer Wirklichkeit: Aufzeichnungen als Daten der interpretativen Soziologie [Ephemeral social reality and its methodic documentation: Recordings as data in interpretive sociology]. In W. Bond & H. Hartmann (Eds.), *Entzauberte Wissenschaft. Soziale Welt, Sonderband 3* (pp. 299–320). Göttingen, Germany: Schwartz.

Boden, D. (1994). *The business of talk: Organizations in action*. Cambridge, UK: Polity Press.

Bronner, R. (1996). *Entscheidungs-Prozesse in Video-Konferenzen. Eine empirische Untersuchung der Leistungsfähigkeit moderner Kommunikationstechnik zur Bewältigung komplexer Management-Aufgaben* [Decision-making processes in videoconferencing. An empirical study on the potential of modern communication technology for assisting with complex management tasks]. Frankfurt A.M., Germany: Peter Lang.

Chaffey, D. (1998). *Groupware, workflow and Intranets: Reengineering the enterprise with collaborative software*. Boston: Digital Press.

Cuff, E. C., & Sharrock, W. W. (1985). Meetings. In T. A. van Dijk (Ed.), *Handbook of discourse analysis: Vol. 3. Discourse and dialogue* (pp. 149–159). London: Academic Press.

Egbert, M. (1993). *Schisming: The transformation from a single conversation to multiple conversations.* Unpublished doctoral dissertation, University of California, Los Angeles.

Egido, C. (1990). Teleconferencing as a technology to support cooperative work: Its possibilities and limitations. In J. Galegher, R. E. Kraut, & C. Egido (Eds.), *Intellectual teamwork: Social and technological foundations of cooperative work* (pp. 351–371). Hillsdale, NJ: Lawrence Erlbaum Associates.

Finn, K. A., Sellen, A. J., & Wilbur, S. B. (Eds.). (1997). *Video-mediated communication.* Mahwah, NJ: Lawrence Erlbaum Associates.

Finn, K. A. (1997). Introduction: An overview of video-mediated communication. In K. A. Finn, A. J. Sellen, & S. B. Wilbur (Eds.), *Video-mediated communication* (pp. 3–21). Mahwah, NJ: Lawrence Erlbaum Associates.

Garfinkel, H. (1967). *Studies in ethnomethodology.* Englewood Cliffs, NJ: Prentice-Hall.

Glenn, P. J. (1995). Laughing at and laughing with: Negotiations of participant alignments through conversational laughter. In P. Ten Have & G. Psathas (Eds.), *Situated order: Studies in the social organization of talk and embodied activities* (pp. 43–56). Lanham, MD: University Press of America.

Goffman, E. (1961). *Encounters: Two studies in the sociology of interaction.* Indianapolis, IN: Bobbs-Merrill.

Goffman, E. (1972). *Interaction ritual: Essays on face-to-face behaviour.* London, Allen Lane.

Goffman, E. (1981). *Forms of talk.* Philadelphia: University of Pennsylvania Press.

Graumann, C. F. (1994). Die Forschergruppe. Zum Verhältnis von Sozialpsychologie und Wissenschaftsforschung [The research group. On the relationship between social psychology and studies of science]. In W. Sprondel (Ed.), *Die Objektivität der Ordnungen und ihre kommunikative Konstruktion. Für Thomas Luckmann* (pp. 381–403). Frankfurt A.M., Germany: Suhrkamp.

Grimshaw, A. D. (1982). Sound-image data records for research on social interaction: Some questions and answers. *Sociological Methods & Research, 11,* 121–144.

Hanks, W. F. (1990). *Referential practice: Language and lived space among the Maya.* Chicago: University of Chicago Press.

Hart, P., Svenning, L., & Ruchinskas, J. (1995). From face-to-face meeting to video teleconferencing: Potential shifts in the meeting genre. *Management Communication Quarterly, 8,* 395–423.

Heath, C., & Luff, P. (1993). Disembodied conduct: Interactional asymmetries in video-mediated communication. In G. Button (Ed.), *Technology in working order: Studies of work, interaction and technology* (pp. 35–54). London: Routledge.

Kangasharju, H. (1996). Aligning as a team in multiparty conversation. *Journal of Pragmatics, 26,* 291–319.

Kendon, A. (1979): Some theoretical and methodological aspects of the use of film in the study of social interaction. In G. P. Ginsburg (Ed.), *Emerging strategies in social psychological research* (pp. 67–91). New York: Wiley.

Kriesberg, M., & Guetzkow, H. (1950). The use of conferences in the administration process. *Public Administration Review, 10,* 93–98.

Lautz, A. (1995). *Videoconferencing: Theorie und praxis für den erfolgreichen Einsatz in Unternehmen* [Videoconferencing: Theory and practice for successful implementation in corporations]. Frankfurt a.M., Germany: Institut für Medienentwicklung und Kommunikation.

Levinson, S. C. (1988). Putting linguistics on a proper footing: Explorations in Goffman's concepts of participation. In P. Drew & A. Wootton (Eds.), *Erving Goffman: Exploring the interaction order* (pp. 161–227). Cambridge, UK: Polity Press.

Lerner, G. H. (1993). Collectivities in action: Establishing the relevance of conjoined participation in conversation. *Text, 13*, 213–245.

Meier, C. (1997). *Arbeitsbesprechungen—Interaktionsstruktur Interaktionsdynamik und Konsequenzen einer sozialen Form* [Work meetings—interactional structure, interactional dynamics and consequences of a social form]. Opladen, Germany: Westdeutscher Verlag.

Meier, C. (1998). Zur Untersuchung von Arbeits- und Interaktionsprozessen anhand von Videoaufzeichnungen [On investigating work- and interactional processes based on videorecordings]. *Arbeit. Zeitschrift für Arbeitsforschung, Arbeitsgestaltung und Arbeitspolitik, 7,* 257–275.

Meier, C. (1999). Die Eröffnung von Videokonferenzen. Beobachtungen zur Aneignung eines neuen interaktiven Mediums [The opening of videoconferences: Observations on the appropriation of a new interaction medium]. In E. Hebecker, F. Kleemann, H. Neymanns, & M. Stauff (Eds.), *Neue Medienumwelten. Zwischen Regulierungsprozessen und alltäglicher Aneignung* (pp. 282–297). Frankfurt a.M., Germany: Campus.

Meier, C. (2000). Neue Medien—neue Kommunikationsformen? Strukturmerkmale von Videokonferenzen [New media—new communicative forms? Structural features of videoconferences]. In W. Kallmeyer (Ed.), *Sprache und neue Medien, Jahrbuch 1999* (pp. 195–221). Berlin, Germany: Walter de Gruyter.

Olson, G. M., & Olson, J. S. (1997). Making sense of the findings: Common vocabulary leads to the synthesis necessary for theory building. In K. A. Finn, A. J. Sellen, & S. B. Wilbur (Eds.), *Video-mediated communication* (pp. 75–91). Mahwah, NJ: Lawrence Erlbaum Associates.

Olson, J. S., Olson, G. M., & Meader, D. K. (1995). What mix of video and audio is useful for small groups doing remote real-time design work? *Proceedings of the 1995 Conference on Human Factors in Computing Systems* (pp. 362–368). New York: ACM Press.

Parker, L. A., & Olgren, C. H. (Eds.). (1984). *The teleconferencing resource book: A guide to applications and planning.* Amsterdam: North Holland.

Putnam, L. L., & Stohl, C. (1996). Bona fide groups. An alternative perspective for communication and small group decision making. In R. Y. Hirokawa & M. S. Poole (Eds.), *Communication and group decision making* (2nd ed., pp. 147–178). Thousand Oaks, CA: Sage.

Reuter, M. (1990). *Telekommunikation: Aus der Geschichte in die Zukunft* [Telecommunication: From history to future]. Heidelberg, Germany: R.V. Decker's/ Schenk.

Sacks, H., Schegloff, E. A., & Jefferson, G. (1974). A simplest systematics for the organization of turn-taking for conversation. *Language, 50,* 696–735.

Schwartzman, H. B. (1989). *The meeting: Gatherings in organizations and communities.* New York: Plenum Press.

Scott, C. R. (1999). Communication technology and group communication. In L. R. Frey (Ed.), D. S. Gouran, & M. S. Poole (Assoc. Eds.), *The handbook of group communication theory & research* (pp. 432–472). Thousand Oaks, CA: Sage.

Sellen, A. (1992). Speech patterns in video-mediated conversations. In P. Bauersfeld, J. Bennet, & G. Lynch (Eds.), *Proceedings of the Computer-Human-Interaction '92 Conference* (pp. 49–59). New York: Association for Computing Machinery.

Seibold, D. R., & Krikorian, D. H. (1997). Planning and facilitating group meetings. In L. R. Frey & J. K. Barge (Eds.), *Managing group life: Communicating in decision-making groups* (pp. 270–305). Boston: Houghton Mifflin.

Short, J., Williams, E., & Christie, B. (1976). *The social psychology of telecommunications*. London: Wiley.

Stohl, C., & Putnam, L. L. (1994). Group communication in context: implications for the study of bona fide groups. In L. R. Frey (Ed.), *Group communication in context: Studies of natural groups* (pp. 285–292). Hillsdale, NJ: Lawrence Erlbaum Associates.

Storck, J., & Sproull, L. (1995). Through a glass darkly: What do people learn in videoconferences? *Human Communication Research, 22*, 197–219.

Weinig, K. (1997). *Wie Technik Kommunikation verändert. Das Beispiel Videokonferenz* [How technology changes communication: The case of videoconferencing]. Münster, Germany: LIT-Verlag.

Wittgenstein, L. (1977). *Philosophische untersuchungen* [Philosophical investigations]. Frankfurt A.M., Germany: Suhrkamp.

COMMUNICATION IN BONA FIDE GROUPS:

A RETROSPECTIVE AND PROSPECTIVE ACCOUNT

Cynthia Stohl
University of California at Santa Barbara

Linda L. Putnam
Texas A&M University

In a special section of an issue of *Communication Studies* published in 1990, several scholars suggested that it was time for communication researchers to move away from the study of isolated, zero-history, laboratory groups and to strive for understanding the "real-world significance" of groups embedded in natural contexts. Crable (1990), then editor of the journal, wrote of our article (Putnam & Stohl, 1990), titled "Bona Fide Groups: A Reconceptualization of Groups in Context," "Having explained the nature of this category of group, they [Putnam and Stohl] proceed to explain how it might become a guide for future research—a guide, as it were, to research in this decade" (p. 199). After a comparison of conclusions drawn from studies of naturalistic groups that embraced a container metaphor of groups, we suggested that researchers expand their horizons to view the dynamic and interdependent boundaries of groups differently than they had in the past. We cautioned in this essay that:

there is a danger, however, in moving away from the laboratory to the field without careful consideration of how we study group communication. In effect, simply changing context or altering the population sample from which we draw group members may not reap the dividends of real-world significance. (Putnam & Stohl, 1990, p. 248)

By urging researchers to incorporate two important criteria of bona fide groups—*stable yet permeable boundaries* and *interdependence with immediate context*—we argued that communication researchers could detect associations among contexts, group deliberations, and message systems that remained obscured in traditional laboratory and field research. Consequently, we made the plea "to shift both the design and theory of small group studies to focus on bona fide groups" (p. 257).

The publication of this outstanding volume gives us the opportunity to assess changes in the study of groups over the past decade and to explore what contributions, if any, a bona fide group perspective has made to our understanding of group communication. Over the past several years, scholars have echoed the plea for this type of approach (e.g., Frey, 1994b; Putnam, 1994; Seibold, 1994; Waldeck, Shepard, Teitelbaum, Farrar, & Seibold, 2002) and conducted some studies informed by a bona fide perspective (e.g., Barge & Keyton, 1994; Berteotti & Seibold, 1994; Lammers & Krikorian, 1997), but this is the first entire volume that centers on the bona fide group perspective.

Before we begin our analysis, however, it is important to note that we are extremely gratified and humbled by the fact that such outstanding and, in many cases, established scholars have incorporated a bona fide group perspective into their own research agendas. The intellectual synergy, excitement, and value created when scholars go beyond their own perspectives to embrace new ideas is not only critical for the progress of a field of study but also provides the groundwork for future advancements. These communication scholars are leading the way for social scientists across a wide range of disciplines to expand their understandings of group phenomena. Moreover, we appreciate Larry Frey's efforts in envisioning and assembling this volume. He has played a major role in shaping the field of group communication during the past decade.

WHAT IS (AND IS NOT) A BONA FIDE GROUP PERSPECTIVE?

Over the years, we have come to realize that we need to provide additional clarity in explicating a bona fide group perspective. This epilogue provides us with an opportunity to clarify our ideas in light of these original studies and to ascertain ways that this book can advance group communication scholarship. We first identify the central tenets of this perspective through reviewing what a bona fide group perspective is and what it is not (see also Frey's introduction, this volume). We then use the structure from our original 1990 article as a framework to examine the contributions made by individual chapters and the book as a whole to a bona fide group perspective.

Overall, the bona fide group perspective captures "the emotional intensity, temporal fluctuations, and historical influences of group processes" as well as enables researchers to view any particular group phenomenon as "a process that shapes and is shaped by dynamic group boundaries and multiple contexts" (Putnam & Stohl, 1996, p.148). The challenge in embracing this perspective is incorporating the criteria of bona fide groups in ways that truly imbue the study of "real" groups. A bona fide group perspective makes several demands on researchers. Specifically, it requires new ways of studying group boundaries, attending to the complex network of communication processes that influence group action, and focusing on connectedness in ways that do not easily split into internal and external factors. From the very conceptualization of what a group is to the methods used, choice of concepts, and ways variables are operationally defined, a bona fide group perspective requires researchers to explore the production and reproduction of social contexts, social boundaries, and personal and collective identities.

Three assumptions underlie the bona fide group perspective. First, it is not methodologically determinant; that is, it can be incorporated into studies from a diverse set of methodological positions. Ethnographic studies, textual analysis, survey research, and field and laboratory experiments have the potential to incorporate and be congruent with the bona fide group criteria. Second, this perspective depicts a set of suppositions regarding communication and the social world. In particular, all groups, whether found in the laboratory or in the field, manifest the characteristics of bona fide groups; it is the researcher who chooses whether to incorporate those characteristics into a research design. Third, a bona fide group perspective does not privilege either external or internal relations; it enters into the study of group processes through a reciprocal focus on group boundaries and contextual interdependence, both of which are enacted through group communication. Unlike other theories of embeddedness and intergroup relations, such as Alderfer and Smith (1982; for a detailed comparison, see Putnam & Stohl, 1996), we argue that researchers should focus on the social constructions of group boundaries and the enactment of interconnected contexts; these interactions form the nexus for understanding group processes.

Within a bona fide group perspective, boundaries should not be conceived or studied as reified structures that separate groups from their environments but, rather, as structures that are created through interactions that shape group identity, establish connections between internal and external environments, and reflexively define group processes. Our perspective suggests that group boundaries shift as a result of interactions that take place in groups as influenced by and enacted through multiple and fluctuating memberships, conflicting role identities, varying senses of belonging, and group identity formation (see Putnam & Stohl, 1990, 1996; Stohl & Putnam, 1994).

Just as group boundaries are made permeable through interaction, interdependence of a group with its contexts captures the reciprocal relationship between a group and its relevant environments; such interdependence is a dynamic feature that is negotiated across time and other contexts. Contexts are socially constructed through intergroup and intragroup communication, coordinated actions among groups, negotiations of jurisdiction or autonomy, and ongoing interpretations in which individuals make sense of current and past intergroup relationships (see Putnam & Stohl, 1990, 1996; Stohl & Putnam, 1994).

WHERE ARE WE NOW?

As just discussed, when we first formulated this perspective, we included a detailed critique of group communication research conducted prior to 1990. Each of the critiques from our original article is italicized below. As we review the chapters in this book in light of those concerns, several conclusions are immediately obvious. First, group communication research has experienced enormous changes and progress in the last few years. The conceptual scope of research has been significantly expanded, the range of methods has become far less parochial, and the domain of inquiry is far more interesting and reflective of the complex issues evident in contemporary society. Second, attention to the dynamic nature of group boundaries and contexts has captured a broad range of issues, including the formation and reformation of group identity, task definition and redefinition, cyclical development and decision making, and the fragmented formulations of community and support that are endemic to modern society. The scholars featured in this volume are no longer confined to the boundaries of the past; their studies incorporate the rich and transforming contexts in which contemporary groups are embedded.

Critique 1 (1990):   Although group communication research is stronger theoretically and methodologically than in the past, it is still centered on narrow ranges of task-oriented interactions in primarily self-contained groups.

A close reading of this book indicates that not only do these studies expand the field of group communication by looking at diverse groups embedded in a wide range of social contexts but they also focus on group processes and practices that transcend traditional group phenomena such as decision making, problem solving, task completion, and performance effectiveness. These researchers ask bona fide questions, such as how groups "do groupness" (Meier), create and sustain communities (Howell, Brock, & Hauder), self-organize (Krikorian & Kiyomiya), manage privacy dilemmas (Petronio, Jones, & Morr), and negotiate borders (Buchalter). In other words, these studies address fundamental aspects of group development that were ignored in the past—specifically, ways members maintain their "groupness" while negotiating their internal and external worlds across time and space.

Although some of these studies seem, at first blush, to focus on traditional contained groups—such as a school board selecting a superintendent (Tracy & Standerfer), work teams in a participative environment (Oetzel & Robbins), or groups providing social support (Alexander, Peterson, & Hollingshead; Yep, Reece, & Negrón)—these studies exhibit new ways of conceptualizing "groups" and new ways of focusing on the recursive relationships between boundaries, contexts, and group processes. For example, Alexander et al. examine social support groups on the Internet communicating asynchronously, non-face-to-face, with thousands of members who vary in commitment, motivation, and online experience. The crux of the study is not that support groups are utilizing new communication technologies but, rather, that anyone can gain access to these groups, making the boundaries permeable and membership open to all. Unlike previous research on social support groups, people can gain entry into these Internet support groups even if they do not have the defining experience of the group's support focus (e.g., breast cancer or depression). By focusing on heterogeneous membership and permeable boundaries, these authors explore the implications of fluctuating membership on group interactions, a focus that reveals a different pattern of communication than typically emerges without attention to boundary issues. As an interesting complement, Yep et al.'s study of a social support group of "Asian Americans" living with HIV focuses on groups with traditional membership requirements, but by exploring how external culture affects internal group dynamics, this research transcends the treatment of groups as containers.

Tracey and Standerfer's study of a school board's hiring decision also positions research on group communication in a new way. Their reconceptualization of decision making as deliberation is consistent with previous work from a bona fide group perspective (see, e.g., Stohl & Holmes, 1993) and their results are illuminating. By focusing on group talk and exploring what has heretofore remained invisible—a group's dependency on prior decisions and members' awareness of the necessity of future interactions across contexts—Tracy and Standerfer provide unique insights regarding group members' participation and deliberation. Their attention to the ongoing enactment of group history, embedded influence of prior actions, relational development across contexts, and fluctuations in group boundaries and group identities provides an exemplar for future group communication research.

Critique 2 (1990):   *Traditional settings, methods, and variables seriously limit the ways in which we think about groups and our definitions of what constitute legitimate group research.*

The studies published in this text demonstrate that the domain of group communication research has expanded considerably in the last several years. This extension has led to several important changes— most notably, the presence in this volume and other recently edited collections of scholars heretofore not identified with group communication research. Blurring the boundaries among interpersonal communication, discourse and language, organizational communication, rhetoric, new media, and group communication will enrich and enliven the study of groups.

One apparent result of bridging these scholarly domains beyond the traditional social–scientific/sociopsychological approaches to groups is the presence of a wide variety of methods used to examine group processes and the influence of external linkages. Oetzel and Robbins, for example, interviewed group members and other employees across different levels of the cooperative supermarket they studied and they surveyed the entire organization using a well-established quantitative measure that assesses organizational identification. Krikorian and Kiyomiya combined large-scale longitudinal network analysis across online newsgroups with a content analysis of messages produced within those newsgroups. Tracey and Standerfer relied on discourse analysis to establish the past, immediate, and anticipated contexts that influenced school board deliberations. Sherblom used focus groups and survey questionnaires to examine international business teams and Houston depended on archival accounts of the Mt. Everest expedition she analyzed. Howell and Brock were participant observers in the Detroit youth group they studied. Keyton and Stallworth's exhaustive study of the collaboration that formed the Drug Dealer Eviction Program in Memphis, Tennessee, combined observations of formal and informal meetings, analyses of documents, and in-depth interviews. Meier's detailed micro-analytic discourse and visual analyses of the ways in which participants sought to allocate a group task (taking minutes) in the process of "doing groupness" illustrated the way new communication technologies call for new methodological approaches. Overall, group communication research is much more diverse topically and methodologically than it was in the past. We hope that this acceptance of multiple methodologies, however, does not result in the inadvertent dismissal of laboratory and field experimental designs, none of which were employed in these studies. As our 1990 article suggested, there is still a place for experimental methods within the study of bona fide groups.

Critique 3 (1990): Models of group interactions tend to focus only on the internal dynamics of the group; there is a need to incorporate models of intergroup system that reflect tacit and explicit interfaces between groups and their environments.

Perhaps no study in this volume better illustrates the new and broader interface between a group and its embeddedness in an intergroup system than does Parrish-Sprowl's case study of Eco-S, a strategic planning committee for a newly-formed recycling company in post-Communist Poland. In Parrish-Sprowl's words, this group represents "a moment in a larger cultural conversation." He shows how interaction in the group, although designed to pave the way for a new model of corporate action, reproduced past ideological conceptions of productivity, economic structure, culture, and appropriate ways of being a group. The study, thus, illustrates how a group may create and maintain groupness by communicatively clinging to its past while simultaneously embracing and enacting a new future.

Other studies in this volume incorporate intergroup interaction in very different ways than has previously been done. For example, Alexander et al.'s study focuses directly on communication across and within group boundaries. They found that crosspostings (sending the same message to multiple online groups and, thereby, engaging in intergroup communication) were a significant aspect of most online support groups and that groups with the most external communication offered different types of social support than did those with less intergroup communication. A significant and somewhat ironic finding was that members of the depression support groups were more satisfied and had the least number of crosspostings in comparison to the other groups studied. This result points to new directions for future research on the effects of group homogeneity and homophilly on members' attitudes and intergroup communication.

Krikorian and Kiyomiya's study also addresses intergroup communication without privileging external over internal processes. They explored the decline of online newsgroups by developing a "Bonafide Newsgroup Model" that treats groups as self-organizing systems. They then examined communication patterns and "member interdependence" by focusing on the network-tie intersection that occurs between members of newsgroups through message exchange. This use of network theory and methodology to understand a group's interdependence with its contexts provides a useful way for researchers to conceptualize this complex and critical feature.

This study shows how network analyses enable researchers to explore structural boundaries, in situ, as they are created, sustained, altered, and discontinued over time.

In Sherblom's study of international teams, the groups' projects and specific tasks are conceptualized in terms of boundaries, immediate context (in-country management), and long-term expectations arising from the teams being embedded in an organizational hierarchy (corporate headquarters). Only through focusing on the nexus of internal and external deliberations, the interdependence of groups with their relevant contexts, and the multiple identities that group members enact could scholars understand a business team's "rationale decision to write two reports instead of one." In this case, a bona fide group perspective highlights the point that decision quality is not an objective characteristic of group deliberations nor is it necessarily apparent at the time of making a decision (for a discussion of functional group theory and a comparison with a bona fide group perspective, see Stohl & Holmes, 1993).

Critique 4 (1990): Boundaries of groups are taken for granted and viewed as static and unchanging; we do not have constructs that embody boundary permeability.

A brief perusal of the table of contents of this volume indicates that, during the 1990s, scholars have begun to address boundary issues as a "problematic" in group communication research. Petronio et al.'s work, for example, is part of a larger research agenda, which, using boundary as a central metaphor, develops a practical theory of privacy management. Their approach captures the communication exigencies that develop when families are forced to change who is and who is not included in the privacy boundary, an issue that is fundamental to all group life. Highlighting boundary turbulence, their work uncovers the dynamic and, at times, paradoxical processes that alter family systems and influence who can and cannot receive certain kinds of information. What is particularly exciting about this approach is the ways in which internal boundaries are formed and maintained by establishing different networks among individuals and groups, ones that were not necessarily part of the original group's system or the "defined" family.

A radical change in conceptions of group boundaries surfaces as these studies incorporate concepts such as constituencies, collaboration, and community. Buchalter's account of the struggles for neighborhood in Queen Village, conceived as a continuously negotiated social agreement, has implications far beyond that locale. Her case study vividly demonstrates how shifting group borders, defense of traditional boundaries, negotiation at the edges, and interpenetration of surrounding systems profoundly influence people's collective and individual experiences.

Lange's study of a large-scale environmental collaboration and Keyton and Stallworth's study of a city-wide collaboration are rooted in the complex relationship/boundary structure that characterizes all such partnerships. Lange sees collaborations as comprised of "multiple linkages among many constituency groups and stakeholders"; consequently, discussions of fairness, political viability, relations with the press, and definitions of local and global as "second table" constituencies are issues that embody the collaboration's interdependence with its contexts. Lange highlights the multiple paradoxes that arise from constituents' differing senses of appropriate boundary management, views of representation and representativeness, and notions of self- and group interest. Both Lange and Keyton, as well as Stallworth, conclude that in collective action groups, the issue of representation (who is "in" and who is "out") can never be fully resolved. Despite community-building and transformation efforts, group boundaries, however amorphous they may be, are situated within contested constituent communication.

Critique 5 (1990): To reinvigorate the study of group communication, category systems that capture the complexity and exciting qualities of the group situations we experience everyday are necessary. For example, traditional coding systems need to be redesigned to show how communication within a group is constrained by and constrains the group's environments. It is critical that we develop categories that reflect multilevel relationships within and outside a group as well as track internal dependence on external authorities.

The development of group communication coding schemes is always a difficult and time-consuming process and to integrate the tenets of a bona fide group perspective into coding schemes makes this process even more difficult. To study the emergence of group roles, for instance, a researcher should incorporate external role relations and role episodes from the intergroup contexts into an analysis of internal functions that members serve. Among these chapters, at least three different projects develop coding schemes informed by a bona fide group perspective. The work of Alexander et al. on Internet social support groups provides an excellent example. They coded messages exchanged by group members based on the multiplicity of roles members could occupy within and outside the group and also coded references made to other Internet support groups and organizations through analyzing crosspostings. They, thus, sought to capture the interconnectedness of these groups in terms of actual message behavior. They also explored the effects of other group memberships by asking members to evaluate their own individual embeddedness and found that memberships in multiple groups exerted significant influence on internal group communication.

Meier's integration of Goffman's (1981) participation frameworks and his unsuccessful attempts to construct a coding scheme that embedded issues of identity and boundary in the use of pronouns (e.g., "you vs. we") during a videoconference group session raises an important point about employing coding schemes to study bona fide groups. As the law of requisite variety indicates, coding schemes should be as complex as the phenomena being studied. A bona fide group perspective complicates what needs to be included in a coding scheme because researchers must attend to several levels, modalities, and spheres of influence simultaneously. In Meier's study, participants' verbal messages, as well their nonverbal variations in orientations toward the camera, laughter, and paralinguistic cues (e.g., soft vocalizations), shaped group members' boundaries and sense of location. Shared laughter and other group nonverbal behaviors did not carry across sites, instantiating site-specific boundaries in ways that were potentially counterproductive to later group deliberations. This research demonstrates that when creating coding schemes in studies of bona fide groups, researchers need to develop systems that reflect the dynamic interplay of boundaries and contexts.

Besides coding messages exchanged within and between groups, Krikorian and Kiyomiya set forth a newsgroup extinction model comprised of four propositions: two constitute processes internal to the groups through exploring message participation and threads; two focus on permeable group boundaries through addressing spamming and crossposting. Overall, the development of schemes for coding communication in groups is still in its infancy, but these studies have made an excellent start.

Critique 6 (1990): Studies need to assess interactions and perceptions of group interactions with external stakeholders.

Our final concern with the literature published during the 1980s was the lack of attention to constituents "outside" a group who were clearly central to the internal dynamics of the group. We urged scholars to employ descriptive methods to capture the internal dynamics of a group and the reflections of individuals and groups external to but influential in the group's internal processes. The studies in this volume have certainly taken this recommendation to heart. Several of these chapters analyze the reactions of external stakeholders and how the group interprets and employs these reactions. Howell et al., for example, not only address ways in which multiple memberships in other community groups foster representations of defined constituents but they also explore ways in which other stakeholder groups (such as the Detroit youth) were brought into the community group's deliberations. Lange's study also clearly exemplifies ways in which the embedded nature of group life is a fundamental feature of group processes.

WHERE SHOULD WE GO FROM HERE?

The bona fide group perspective is founded on the notion that boundaries are not objective, nor are they defined by goals, tasks, physical locations, or presence of group members. Group boundaries, instead, are enacted as members connect with their social contexts, construct their multiple roles, and live out their histories. The chapters in this volume reveal that both internal and external group processes shape the negotiation of boundaries, particularly on issues such as representations, fluctuating and variable memberships, networks of relationships, and roles in the intergroup system. However, if boundaries are blurred and overlapping at the edges, how can we improve our research designs to grasp the issues most critical to group processes, the intergroup system, and the nature of connectedness?

Two concepts that seem salient for future research on bona fide group are "liminality" and "nexus" (Martin, 2002). *Liminality* centers on those moments of transition in which a group exists in a suspended state, such as not belonging to the past or to the future or not being disconnected or tightly connected. In effect, a liminal state is the moment of transition when a group is in-between states of development and holding different interpretations about those states. It becomes a pivotal point for understanding blurred, permeable, and fluctuating boundaries because it centers on the process of redefining or shaping boundaries and the ways participants make sense of this process. As Martin (2002) pointed out about organizational culture, it is easier to understand permeable boundaries by focusing on the workings of groups at the edges where old boundaries are being rejected and new ones are being formed.

An example of liminality might be when someone challenges a group member's representative roles and identities that result from membership in multiple groups. This pattern occurred in Lange's research on The Applegate Partnership Board, in which each of the group members represented constituency groups and the legitimacy of particular stakeholders was called into question. When representative roles are contested, the intergroup and intragroup identities of members are tested, directing communication to the blurred and fluctuating group boundaries. Thus, the discourse or interaction about representative roles within and outside the board was central to capturing the moment of transition in which group members saw their boundaries as fluctuating. This type of boundary negotiation is similar to the Bona Fide Group Collaboration Model, in which the members of a particular group act as partners for their constituent groups and negotiate a system of collaboration among the partners for work on a particular project (Stohl & Walker, 2002). Formal and informal interactions within the collaborative group and between their constituents and the partnership become a fluid and permeable system in which boundaries are in states of negotiation.

In a similar manner, Tracey and Standerfer's study of a school board's hiring decision centers on liminality when it highlights those moments of transition as the group is caught in limbo between its history and its future interactions. In effect, the communication among school board members and outside the group about the board's deliberations creates moments of transition in which members must renegotiate their interdependence with the past, present, and future of the board. Similarly, Parrish-Sprowl's study of Eco-S illustrates liminality through focusing on the transition between clinging to the past while embracing a new future within a larger cultural/societal conversation rooted in economic and ideological changes.

In these examples, group members enact and respond to moments of transition in their discourse, not just within the group but also within the larger systems or contexts in which the group functions. Moreover, the focal point of this analysis is on the transition moments or the times in which seemingly stable boundaries and memberships become problematic. Another point that seems critical to studying liminality is centering on the communication/discourse/interaction that captures both the social construction and the fluidity of negotiating boundaries. Many of the studies in this volume focus on the structures, functions, and complexities of bona fide groups, but only some of them really capture ways in which communication enacts permeable boundaries and how members make sense of these enactments.

A second critical concept for future research on bona fide groups is *nexus*, which centers on the points of connection or overlapping group links. As a construct, nexus serves as a focal point for studying the bona fide characteristic of "interdependence with immediate contexts." Groups that are nested in other groups (e.g., in organizations and national/multinational cultures) represent microcosms within complex, overlapping contexts. This complexity includes multiple connections to local, regional, and national groups. Nexus provides a way to isolate the linkages and to focus on how interdependence is or is not negotiated through group interaction. A graphic view of nexus would be to treat it as the shifting residue or the intersection points among a set of concentric circles. Unlike pictorial diagrams, however, the circles and intersections are moving and shifting as boundaries change, members come and go, and linkages become tighter or more loosely coupled. Nexus can be captured by studying interactions that reference issues of jurisdiction, interdependencies, linkages and connections, and coordination across groups and their social/organizational contexts.

The studies in this volume that examine intergroup processes address issues related to nexus. In particular, Alexander et al.'s focus on crosspostings in social support networks, Krikorian and Kiyomiya's study of network ties and intersections in online newsgroups, and Sherblom's examination of international business teams each illustrate some aspect of nexus. Although some of these studies examine the nature of tight and loose couplings, others presume that connections and network ties exist if the linkages are present; others presume interdependency rather than making it a variable or a focal point for examination. The key questions are to what extent interactions across groups create patterns that define the nature of interdependence, what are these patterns, and how can the nexus of connections help us to understand the ways these patterns are communicatively constructed. Coding group interaction to capture internal and external links to other groups, tracking the formation of networks about particular dependency issues, and investigating the paradoxes and dilemmas inherent in multiple group linkages are good examples of efforts to capture the nexus of intersecting groups and contexts.

In addition to identifying constructs that embrace the characteristics of bona fide groups, new methodologies for studying bona fide groups are important, as Frey (1994a, 1994b) pointed out in his discussions of research in natural group settings. As noted earlier, we commend the breadth and richness of methods used by contributors to this volume. Our concern for methods, however, centers more narrowly on the best ways to capture liminality and nexus as communication concepts for studying bona fide groups—that is, on how we can isolate moments of transition and the intersections of multiple, overlapping group communication in patterns of talk. Clearly, studies that code group interaction, track actual communication between members and constituents, analyze networks, and center on discourse within and between groups provide options for scholars to focus on moments of transition and the intersection of negotiated boundaries. One of these approaches, discourse analysis, however, seems underutilized as a method for investigating bona fide groups (for a detailed discussion of approaches to discourse analysis in studying collectivities, see Putnam & Fairhurst, 2001).

In this volume, Meier's research and Tracey and Standerfer's study rely on language analysis to examine the nuances of boundary fluctuation in, respectively, groups meeting via videoconferencing technology and interconnectedness among the past, present, and future deliberations of a school board and its constituents. In particular, references to linguistic elements, such as pronoun use, verb tense, speech acts, and topic shifts, provide strong indicators of liminality and negotiation of the nexus of group boundaries. Researchers might also examine liminality by focusing on paradoxes, inconsistencies, and ironies that surface in moments of transition. The chapter by Lange on collaborative partnerships of environmental groups and the one by Keyton and Stallworth on a city-wide collaboration acknowledge the paradoxes inherent in bona fide groups. Researchers now need to analyze interactions that enact, maintain, and manage these paradoxes through ironies and contradictions that surface in the discourse of representations, multiple memberships, and levels of commitment.

Other discourse perspectives that can aid in studying the multiple layers and features of bona fide groups include cultural symbols, such as metaphors, narratives, rituals, and rites. These rhetorical features of language reveal symbolic connections between groups and their relevant contexts through the discourse of comparison and contrast, the coconstruction of stories, the use of jargon and terms that demonstrate multiple memberships, and the enactment of rites and ceremonies that signal belongingness and commitment. These features of life in bona fide groups are critical for deciphering how group members interpret their natural contexts.

Studies of conversation and other texts have the potential to situate group discourse at one level of analysis and examine contexts, intergroup connectedness, and layers of interdependence at another level of analysis (Cooren & Taylor, 1998; Taylor & Cooren, 1997). Texts not only refer to the residues of conversations but also to other features of the immediate contexts that impinge on and are affected by group deliberations, such as time constraints, architectural space, and technologies. The interplay of conversation among group members with societal, intergroup, or organizational texts provides a way to capture the nexus of these features of bona fide groups by locating their enactments in discourse. Discourse analysis, thus, offers great potential for future work on bona fide groups.

In summary, this volume demonstrates how much group communication research has changed in the past decade and how the six critiques we posed in 1990 no longer are salient—particularly with respect to examining only self-contained groups, employing traditional methodology, centering analyses solely on internal group processes, and not assessing perceptions of external stakeholders. This volume also illustrates that a bona fide group perspective fosters but moves beyond studying groups in natural settings by centering on two critical characteristics: stable, yet permeable, group boundaries and interdependence of a group with its relevant contexts. The studies reported in this text stand in sharp contrast to the traditional container model of groups by exploring the links between internal and external environments, examining representative roles and fluctuations in group memberships, and investigating the intergroup systems that impinge on the internal dynamics of a group. These characteristics, however, are not limited to naturalistic research methods; laboratory experiments are also needed to test these models and characteristics of bona fide groups.

The studies reported in this volume also point to the need for additional theory development of the bona fide group perspective. In particular, this approach needs constructs that lead to particular arenas for investigation—ones that can capture the fluidity and complexity of bona fide groups. In this epilogue, we presented two such constructs that focus attention on particular features of bona fide groups: liminality and nexus. By centering on the moments of transition when a group's boundaries are forming or being changed, researchers can orient their investigations to the dynamic and evolving nature of permeable boundaries; through focusing on nexus as the points of connection and foci of overlapping group links, researchers can capture the intersections among nested groups and focus on interactions aimed at negotiating jurisdiction, coordination, and interdependence. Clearly, this volume demonstrates both the viability and the potential for a bona fide group perspective. It is an exciting addition to the field and a major contribution to developing this alternative perspective of group communication.

REFERENCES

Alderfer, C., & Smith, K. (1982). Studying intergroup relations embedded in organizations. *Administrative Science Quarterly, 27*, 35–65.

Barge, J. K., & Keyton, J. (1994). Contextualizing power and social influence in groups. In L. R. Frey (Ed.), *Group communication in context: Studies of natural groups* (pp. 85–105). Hillsdale, NJ: Lawrence Erlbaum Associates.

Berteotti, C. R., & Seibold, D. R. (1994). Coordination and role-definition problems in health-care teams: A hospice case study. In L. R. Frey (Ed.), *Group communication in context: Studies of natural groups* (pp. 107–131). Hillsdale, NJ: Lawrence Erlbaum Associates.

Cooren, F., & Taylor, J. R. (1998). The procedural and rhetorical modes of the organizing dimension of communication: Discursive analysis of a parliamentary commission. *Communication Review, 3*(1/2), 65–101.

Crable, R. E. (1990). Special section: Editor's introduction. *Communication Studies, 41*, 199.

Frey, L. R. (1994a). Call and response: The challenge of conducting research on communication in natural groups. In L. R. Frey (Ed.), *Group communication in context: Studies of natural groups* (pp. 293–304). Hillsdale, NJ: Lawrence Erlbaum Associates.

Frey, L. R. (1994b). The naturalistic paradigm: Studying small groups in the postmodern era. *Small Group Research, 25*, 551–577.

Goffman, E. (1981). *Forms of talk*. Philadelphia: University of Pennsylvania Press.

Lammers, J. C., & Krikorian, D. H. (1997). Theoretical extension and operationalization of the bona fide group construct with an application to surgical teams. *Journal of Applied Communication Research, 25*, 17–38.

Martin, J. (2002). *Organizational culture: Mapping the terrain*. Thousand Oaks, CA: Sage.

Putnam, L. L. (1994). Revitalizing small group communication: Lessons learned from a bona fide group perspective. *Communication Studies, 45*, 97–102.

Putnam, L. L., & Fairhurst, G. T. (2001). Discourse analysis in organizations: Issues and concerns. In F. M. Jablin & L. L. Putnam (Eds.), *The new handbook of organizational communication: Advances in theory, research, and methods* (pp. 78–136). Thousand Oaks, CA: Sage.

Putnam, L. L., & Stohl, C. (1990). Bona fide groups: A reconceptualization of groups in context. *Communication Studies, 41*, 248–265.

Putnam, L. L., & Stohl, C. (1996). Bona fide groups: An alternative perspective for communication and small group decision making. In R. Y. Hirokawa & M. S. Poole (Eds.) *Communication and group decision making* (pp. 147–178). Thousand Oaks, CA: Sage.

Seibold, D. R. (1994). More reflection or more research? To (re)vitalize small group communication research, let's "just do it." *Communication Studies, 45*, 103–110.

Stohl, C., & Holmes, M. (1993) A functional perspective for bona fide groups. In S. A. Deetz (Ed.) *Communication yearbook* (Vol. 16, pp. 601–614). Newbury Park, CA: Sage.

Stohl, C., & Putnam, L. L. (1994). Group communication in context: Implications for the study of bona fide groups. In L. R. Frey (Ed.), *Group communication in context: Studies of natural groups* (pp. 284–292). Hillsdale, NJ: Lawrence Erlbaum Associates.

Stohl, C., & Walker, K. (2002). A bona fide perspective for the future of groups: Understanding collaborating groups. In L. R. Frey (Ed.), *New directions in group communication* (pp. 237–252). Thousand Oaks, CA: Sage.

Taylor, J. R., & Cooren, F. (1997). What makes communication "organizational"? How the many voices of a collectivity become the one voice of an organization. *Journal of Pragmatics, 27*, 409–438.

Waldeck, J. H., Shepard, C. A., Teitelbaum, J., Farrar, W. J., & Seibold, D. R. (2002). New directions for functional, symbolic convergence, structuration, and bona fide group perspectives of group communication. In L. R. Frey (Ed.), *New directions in group communication* (pp. 3–24). Thousand Oaks, CA: Sage.

ABOUT THE EDITOR

Lawrence R. Frey (PhD, University of Kansas, 1979) is Professor and Associate Chair of the Department of Communication at the University of Colorado at Boulder. He is the author or editor of 10 books, 3 special journal issues, and more than 50 published book chapters and journal articles. He is the recipient of nine distinguished scholarship awards, including the 2000 Gerald M. Phillips Award for Distinguished Applied Communication Scholarship from the National Communication Association (NCA); the 2000 Ernest Bormann Research Award from NCA's Group Communication Division, for his coedited text (with Dennis S. Gouran and Marshall Scott Poole) *The Handbook of Group Communication Theory & Research*; a 1999 Special Recognition Award from NCA's Applied Communication Division for an edited special issue of the *Journal of Applied Communication Research* on "Communication and Social Justice Research"; the 1998 National Jesuit Book Award (Professional Studies Category) and the 1988 Distinguished Book Award from NCA's Applied Communication Division for his coauthored text (with Mara B. Adelman) *The Fragile Community: Living Together With AIDS*; and the 1995 Gerald R. Miller Award from NCA's Interpersonal and Small Group Interaction Division and the 1994 Distinguished Book Award from NCA's Applied Communication Division for the first edition of this volume. He is a past president of the Central States Communication Association and a recipient of the Outstanding Young Teacher Award from that organization.

ABOUT THE AUTHORS

Stewart C. Alexander (PhD, University of Illinois at Urbana–Champaign, 2002) is a fellow at the Veterans Affairs Center for Primary Health Services Research in Durham, NC. His primary research interests concern how particular features of support-seeking messages are related to the type and quality of support individuals receive in Internet support groups.

Bernard L. Brock (PhD, Northwestern University, 1965) is Professor Emeritus of Communication and Codirector of the Center for Arts and Public Policy at Wayne State University. He teaches contemporary rhetorical theory and criticism with applications to political campaigns and social movements. He has published over 40 professional articles and book chapters and is the author of the texts *Kenneth Burke in the 21st Century* and *Kenneth Burke and Contemporary European Thought: A Rhetoric in Transition* and a coauthor of the texts *Methods of Rhetorical Criticism: A Twentieth-Century Perspective* (3 editions) and *Public Policy Decision-Making: Systems and Comparative Advantages Debate*. He has been active in political campaigns throughout the Detroit metropolitan area.

Rona Buchalter (PhD, University of Pennsylvania, 1998) teaches at the Annenberg School for Communication at the University of Pennsylvania. Her research interests focus on the boundary-defining practices of groups, the significance of identifying group members, and the political and communicative utilization of public spaces, particularly urban spaces. Previous research on the narrative uses of public, urban space has been presented at the International Communication Association and Social Science History Association conventions, among others. She also manages real estate in Philadelphia.

Eric Hauser (PhD, Wayne State University, 1988) is Assistant Professor of Communication at the University of South Carolina at Sumter. He studies the development of community, especially through Internet technologies.

Andrea B. Hollingshead (PhD, University of Illinois at Urbana-Champaign, 1993) is Associate Professor of Speech Communication and Psychology at the University of Illinois at Urbana-Champaign. Her research investigates transactive memory, knowledge management, and information processing in groups and organizations. She also studies the effects of technology and the Internet on the ways that groups communicate, collaborate, and create community. She is a coauthor (with Joseph McGrath) of the book *Groups Interacting with Technology* and her work has appeared in journals such as *Human Communication Research*, *Communication Yearbook*, *Journal of Communication*, *Communication Education*, and *Journal of Personality and Social Psychology*.

Renée Houston (PhD, Florida State University, 1996) is Assistant Professor in the Department of Communication and Theatre Arts at the University of Puget Sound. Her research interests include organizational communication, collaboration, computer-supported cooperative work, technology and gender, and technology in international development. She has consulted with organizations in a variety of capacities and industries, including public transit, hospitals, the United States Air Force, and libraries. For her work with the Utah Transit Authority, she won top honors from the International Association of Business Communicators. Her work has appeared in journals such as *Communication Theory, Management Communication Quarterly,* and *World Futures*.

Sharon L. Howell (PhD, Wayne State University, 1983) is Professor of Communication at Oakland University, where she teaches public argument, multicultural communication, and social movements. She is the author of the text *Reflections of Ourselves: Mass Media and the Evolution of Female Identity*, has published numerous articles on social movements, and contributes articles regularly to Detroit-area newspapers. She has been a community organizer for over three decades and currently cochairs Detroit Summer.

Susanne Jones (PhD, Arizona State University, 2000) is Assistant Professor in the Department of Communication at the University of Wisconsin-Milwaukee. Her areas of research include comforting message perception and production processes as well as the study of communication and emotion. Her work has appeared in *Communication Monographs, Human Communication Research*, and *Communication Research*.

Joann Keyton (PhD, The Ohio State University, 1987) is Professor in the Communication Studies Department at The University of Kansas. Her primary teaching responsibilities are organizational communication, group communication, and communication research methods. Her research has appeared in *Communication Studies, Management Communication*

Quarterly, Journal of Applied Communication Research, Small Group Research, Southern Communication Journal, and *The Handbook of Group Communication Theory & Research.* She is the author or editor of 3 books, 2 special journal issues, and more than 30 book chapters and journal articles. She has served as an associate editor of five editorial boards and is the editor of the *Journal of Applied Communication Research.*

Toru Kiyomiya (PhD, Michigan State University, 2000) is Assistant Professor on the Faculty of Business Communication and English at Seinan Gakuin University, Japan. His MA was in Labor Relations and Human Resources (Michigan State University) and he previously taught at the University of Tulsa and the University of Texas at San Antonio. His concentration of study is in the fields of organizational communication and cross-cultural management. Current research interests include organizational conflicts and negotiation, industrial and organizational democracy, diffusion of innovation, social network analysis, and theories of change and communication.

Dean Krikorian (PhD, University of California, Santa Barbara, 1997) is Assistant Professor in the Department of Communication and the Director of the Communication Network Analysis Laboratory at Cornell University. Prior to this appointment, he served as Visiting Instructor in the Department of Communication at Michigan State University and Post-Doctoral Researcher in the Department of Telecommunication at Michigan State University (1996–1998). His research specialties are in group and organizational communication networks, self-organizing systems, and Internet communication processes. Recent publications include the examination of the role of communication theory and proxemics in graphical chat rooms, bona fide groups as surgical teams, and emergent networks in organizational process reengineering efforts.

Jonathan I. Lange (PhD, University of Washington, 1981) is Professor of Communication and Director of Training and Organization Development at Southern Oregon University, where he teaches courses in dispute resolution and organizational communication and provides training and development services to organizations in the region. He has conducted research on radical environmentalism, environmental information campaigns, and, more recently, collaborative conservation. He has acted as a facilitator for a number of national environmental collaborations.

Christoph Meier (Dr. rer.soc., University of Giessen, 1996) is Senior Researcher at the Fraunhofer Institut für Arbeitswirtschaft und Organisation (FhG-IAO) in Germany. He has been engaged in extended ethnographic research on the Nuba in the Republic of Sudan and has been working for several years on the analysis of (technically mediated) communication, focusing on the interactional dynamics in multiperson gatherings such as business meetings. He has taught and published work on qualitative research methods (including ethnography and conversation analysis) and their potential for both the field of computer-supported cooperative work and team supervision. More recently, his research interests have shifted toward telecooperation, team development, and knowledge management in distributed teams and virtual organizations.

Mary Claire Morr (PhD, Arizona State University, 2002) is Assistant Professor in the Department of Human Communication at the University of Denver. Her research interests include family membership, privacy management in families, and initiation of romantic relationships. Her work has been published in *Group Facilitation* and *Communication Reports*.

Emma L. Negrón (PhD, University of Southern California, 1993) is a psychotherapist who has worked in the mental health field for the last 18 years. Her research has been presented at the Western States Communication Association and National Communication Association conventions. She is currently a supervising Licensed Clinical Social Worker at Enki (East Los Angeles Mental Health Service) and a psychotherapist in private practice in Los Angeles.

John G. Oetzel (PhD, University of Iowa, 1995) is Associate Professor in the Department of Communication at the University of New Mexico. His research interests focus on the impact of diversity on communication in groups and organizations.

John Parrish-Sprowl (PhD, Bowling Green State University, 1983) is Professor and Chair of Communication Studies at Indiana University Purdue University Indianapolis. He has written numerous articles and book chapters based on research that explores the communication processes leading to change and transformation in organizations and societies. During the 1990s, much of his work has been in Poland, Russia, and Africa. He has extensive involvement in research, teaching, and consulting in both Eastern Europe and Africa. In addition, he has assisted in the development of communication studies in both Poland and Russia. Along with his international work, within the United States, he is active in research, teaching, and consulting related to organizational change and transformation.

Jennifer L. Peterson (PhD, University of Illinois at Urbana–Champaign, 2002) is Assistant Professor in the Department of Communication at the University of Wisconsin-Milwaukee. Her primary research interests include the use of Internet support groups and the general social support systems of people with rare or stigmatized illnesses.

Sandra Petronio (PhD, University of Michigan, 1979) is Professor in the Department of Communication and has an appointment in the School of Medicine at Wayne State University, Detroit, MI. Her primary area of research is in privacy and disclosure, and she has expertise in family communication, interpersonal relations, and health communication issues. She has published 5 books and over 40 articles, served as editor of the *Western Journal of Communication*, as well as the editor of several special issues of *Communication Research* and the *Journal of Applied Communication Research*, and has presented numerous scholarly papers at international, national, and regional conventions. Over the last 20 years, she has developed the communication privacy management theory, recently completing a book about this theory to be published by SUNY Press. She is currently the president of the Western States Communication Association.

Linda L. Putnam (PhD, University of Minnesota, 1977) is Professor in the Department of Speech Communication and Director of the Program on Conflict and Dispute Resolution in the George Bush School of Government and Public Service at Texas A&M University. Her current research interests include negotiation and organizational conflict, groups in organizations, and language analysis in organizations. She is the coeditor of 4 books and has published 90 journal articles and book chapters in the areas of organizational communication, conflict management, and group communication. She is the 1993 recipient of the Charles H. Woolbert Research Award for innovative research in communication, the 1999 recipient of the Distinguished Scholar Award from the National Communication Association, past president of the International Association for Conflict Management, and is a Fellow and past president of the International Communication Association.

Sachiko T. Reece (MA, Pepperdine University, 1975) is a doctoral candidate at Kyoto University in Japan. She is a faculty member of the C. G. Jung Institute of Los Angeles, training consultant at the Kedren Community Mental Health Center in South Central Los Angeles, and field instructor for psychiatric residents at the University of Southern California. She has published research papers, in Japanese and in English, on Jungian psychotherapy and Sandplay therapy for clients living with HIV and/or AIDS and children with severe emotional and behavioral disturbances. She has a private practice in Los Angeles.

Jean Robbins (MA, University of New Mexico, 1998) is an independent contract mediator in Albuquerque, NM, for workplace disputes. She also works in the visual arts.

John C. Sherblom (PhD, University of Maine, 1986) is Professor of Communication in the Department of Communication and Journalism at the

University of Maine. His research interests include the study of organizational groups and teams and the often unrecognized influences on the relational processes and outcomes of interpersonal, group, and organizational communication systems. He has coauthored two texts, including *Small Group and Team Communication* (two editions); published articles in a number of journals, including *Communication Quarterly*, *Human Communication Research*, *Journal of Applied Communication Research*, and *Journal of Business Communication*; and is the current editor of *Communication Research Reports*.

Virginia Stallworth (MA, The University of Memphis, 1998) is Development and Community Relations Director for the Child Advocacy Center in Memphis, TN. During the time she completed her MA degree, Ms. Stallworth was also a member of the board of directors of the National Organization for Women and the president of the Memphis Chapter of that organization.

Christina Standerfer (MA, University of Arkansas, Little Rock, 1988) is a doctoral candidate in the Communication Department and Director of Service Learning at the University of Colorado at Boulder. Besides her interests in reconceptualizing group communication scholarship, she currently is working on a rhetorical model for civil society based on the discursive practices of people engaged in national service initiatives.

Cynthia Stohl (PhD, Purdue University, 1982) is Professor of Communication at the University of California at Santa Barbara. She teaches a variety of courses at both the graduate and undergraduate levels in organizational, global, and group communication, and has published widely in these areas. She is the author of more than 50 articles in management, communication, and sociology journals and handbooks. Her book *Organizational Communication: Connectedness in Action* received the 1995 National Communication Association (NCA) Award for the "best book" in organizational communication and she has twice received NCA's Award for Outstanding Research, "Best Article" in organizational communication, in 2001 and 1998.

Karen Tracy (PhD, University of Wisconsin, 1981) is Professor of Communication at the University of Colorado at Boulder and is the current editor of the journal *Research on Language and Social Interaction*. She is the author of *Colloquium: Dilemmas of Academic Discourse* and a set of journal articles examining different facets of interactional trouble in citizen calls to the police and to 911. She is presently at work on a book about the Boulder Valley School Board case, tentatively titled *School Board: Argument and Emotion in Public Talk*.

Gust A. Yep (PhD, University of Southern California, 1990) is Professor of Speech and Communication Studies and Human Sexuality Studies at San Francisco State University. He is the editor of a forthcoming special double issue of the *Journal of Homosexuality* that focuses on "Queer Theory and Communication" and coauthor of the text *Disclosure of HIV/AIDS in Interpersonal Relationships: A Handbook for Practitioners and Researchers* (Lawrence Erlbaum Associates). In addition to being published in numerous anthologies, his work has appeared in scholarly publications, including *AIDS Education and Prevention, CATESOL Journal, Hispanic Journal of Behavioral Sciences, International and Intercultural Communication Annual, International Quarterly of Community Health Education, Journal of American College Health, Journal of Gay, Lesbian and Bisexual Identity, Journal of Homosexuality, Journal of Lesbian Studies,* and *Journal of Social Behavior and Personality.* He is recipient of more than a dozen research grants and several teaching and community service awards. In 1999, Dr. Yep was the university-wide nominee for the Carnegie Foundation "U.S. Professors of the Year" Award.

AUTHOR INDEX

SUBJECT INDEX

A

Accidental privacy dilemmas
  boundary management and
    consequences, 45–49
  defined, 38
  with multiple discoveries, 47–49
  preparedness in, 46–47
Accommodative dilemmas, 30
Adventure Consultants expedition
  (IFEE), 139, 142, 147–148. *See also*
  Mt. Everest expeditions
AIDS
  AIDS-related stigma, 166–169, 174
  AIDS risk reduction model, 158–159
  AIDS support groups. *See* HIV/AIDS
    support groups
Alcoholics Anonymous (AA), 311
  support groups
    emotional support, 322
    esteem support, 314, 322
    general characteristics of, 311
    informational support, 318–320
    intergroup communication, 323
    membership and group
      boundaries, 317–318, 327
    primary function of, 328
    satisfaction with forms of support,
      324
    tangible support, 314, 323
Alternative dispute resolution (ADR)
  methods, 209–210, 218
Alternative newsgroups
  (alt. newsgroups), 340–341. *See also*
  Newsgroups
American Association of Science, 344
Applegate Partnership
  context and background of, 213–214
  critiques of environmental
    collaborations and, 227–228

history of, 214–216
intraconstituency communication,
  223–227
problem of "unequal access," 228
representative-constituency
  communication, 216–223, 227
research methodology for studying,
  212–213
transformative dispute resolution,
  228–231
"Asian Americans"
  AIDS risk reduction model and,
    158–159
  cultural characteristics of, 163–164
  prevalence of HIV/AIDS among, 158
  See also HIV/AIDS support groups,
    "Asian American"
Association of Internet Researchers, 344
Asynchronous groups, 310, 339
Attention-deficit disorder (ADD), 311.
  support groups
    emotional support, 322–323
    esteem support, 322
    general characteristics of, 311
    informational support, 320–321
    intergroup communication,
      323–324
    membership and group
      boundaries, 318, 327
    primary function of, 328
    satisfaction with forms of support,
      324–326
    tangible support, 323
Autocatalysis, 354

B

Babbitt, Bruce, 215
Balcerowicz Plan, 294

435